The

AUTOBIOGRAPHY

of

CARL SCHURZ

The
AUTOBIOGRAPHY
of
CARL SCHURZ

An abridgment in one volume by
WAYNE ANDREWS

With an introduction by
ALLAN NEVINS

CHARLES SCRIBNER'S SONS · New York

INTRODUCTION

A Fighting Idealist

IF CARL SCHURZ's autobiography, the most vital parts of which are
again made available to readers in this volume, were merely the story
of his richly adventurous career, we might term it an enthralling but
not a great book. Yet that it is a great autobiography none can deny,
for it is the reflection of a leader who united to high abilities the
loftiest qualities of character, and who dedicated them to justice and
freedom with a kindling ardor. An important figure in both German
and American life, Schurz was revolutionist, patriot, orator, and
journalist; he was general, statesman, and reformer. Early in life he
thought out a set of noble political and social concepts, and through
stormy years he clung to them with unshakable purpose. We have
here both a fascinating story, and the fervent testament of a fighting
idealist. The first element is magnified in value by the second.

Simply as a recital of events, this is one of the most romantic narratives of the 19th century. Its pages present hairbreadth feats of daring,
vicissitudes of fortune from prison cell to Presidential cabinet-room,
and battles in the field and the Senate. They offer graphic sketches of
memorable personages from Kossuth and Lincoln to Bismarck. They
contain humorous bits, quick insights, and illuminating anecdotes related to the whole American and European scene. Nowhere does the
suspense of the tale flag and seldom do its colors pale. But the real distinction of the book lies in its pervasive ardor; the ardor of a heart afire
for liberty and equity, of a battler whose nerve never flinched. Courage is not a rare virtue; but the resolutely independent and discriminating courage of Schurz, which made him ready in the name of principle
to face any public clamor, and to turn against an old friend almost as
quickly as against an old foe, is rare indeed.

How well the character of the man emerges even in the first of
the three well-defined sections into which his career falls—the years

as a German rebel! Studying philosophy and history at Bonn, the dreamy, generous-hearted youth fell, like others, under the spell of his poet-teacher Johann Gottfried Kinkel, and became one of the insurgents of 1849, an adjutant to the commander of the fortress of Rastatt. He was all enthusiasm. At a meeting in the university hall, hearing a speaker utter some repugnant sentiment, he had found himself on his feet pouring out his vehement sentiments with rapt eloquence, until he was awakened by the final applause as from a trance. "How old are you?" demanded a professor. And when he replied that he was nineteen, the professor commented: "Too bad; still too young for our new German parliament." He had caught up his musket with a last glance from his study window at the Rhine and the lovely Seven Mountains; how often, gazing at this scene, he had thought "of a quiet and beautiful life." But he gladly risked his life. When Rastatt was about to surrender he was intrepid: "I am a Prussian, and us Prussians they will probably shoot dead. I will therefore try to escape"— and an almost incredible escape he made through the sewer running down to the Rhine.

This was an impressive beginning; but he carried romantic daring to a new height when the next year he ventured back to Berlin in disguise to try to liberate Kinkel, who after a trial for treason had been thrown into prison for life. When, with the help of devoted sympathizers, he executed this plucky feat, his name and Kinkel's rang through Europe. Only a young man whose chivalry equalled his bravery would thus have risked death for his friend; and with a well-earned aura about his head he reached Leith in a German vessel and made his way to the free air of London.

It is the record of the second part of Schurz's career, however, his share in the American struggle between slavery and freedom, which is charged with the most drama, charm, and instruction. Here we have a graphic personal delineation of the country in the throes of sectional strife and civil war. His picture of the Middle West as, full of vigor and determination, it emerged from its first pioneer stage, is especially appealing. He came to Wisconsin with two years experience in London and Paris, where he had taught music and written for German papers, and with three years more in Philadelphia, where he had perfected his English. He came also with a beautiful young wife, Margaret Meyer, of a mercantile family in Hamburg. But above all he came with a characteristic enthusiasm for the pristine morning sparkle of the West, and the heartiness, cheerfulness, and sincerity of its democratic population. He saw realistically the ruder aspects of

life. His account of political campaigning in the upper Mississippi
Valley brings clearly before us the bad roads, rancid meals, dirty beds,
vulgar manners, and abusive newspapers of the region. But his faith in
the American people and their political and social system was undisturbed by hardship. He perceived that the mixture of crudity and
progress, or virtue and vice, of generosity and greed, was a natural
outgrowth of freedom, and was the essence of democracy. The slow
victories of enlightenment were achieved not by some agency outside
the people, but by the people themselves, and hence were all the more
durable.

This ardor for democracy and freedom, combined with his intellectual grasp and his eloquence, quickly made him a political power in
the Northwest. His speeches in 1856 helped carry Wisconsin for
Frémont by more than 13,000 votes; a discourse on "The Irrepressible
Conflict" in the year of the Lincoln-Douglas debates won national
attention. When the Republican national convention met in the
Chicago Wigwam in 1860, his initiative placed in the platform a firm
guarantee of the political rights of immigrants. As head of the Wisconsin delegation he steadily cast its vote for Seward—a loyalty which
Seward requited by covert hostility; but his high standing in the party
was recognized by his appointment to the committee which went to
Springfield to notify Lincoln of his nomination, and by his inclusion
in the executive committee of seven men which directed the campaign.
So modest is his account of himself that a reader might not realize that
his unwearied stump-speaking for Lincoln, both in German and English, had much to do with the decisiveness of the Republican victory
in the Northwest; and that Lincoln's appointment of him as minister
to Spain was but a just reward for his brilliant forensic labors.

Because of his fervent interest in both people and causes, his charm
of manner, and his wit, he had a rare talent for making acquaintances
among prominent men. No other single book of American memoirs,
not even J. Q. Adams' long diary, contains so many striking portraits
of political and military leaders. He had hardly landed in America
before he was a fast friend of Jay Cooke, whom he admired. Though
he had a keen eye for the shoddy and false, and his sketches of a few
men, like Stephen A. Douglas, Caleb Cushing, and General O. O.
Howard, are caustic, he in general shows a discriminating appreciation
of the leading personages of the time. His best portraits are really character studies, depicting both the inward and outward man. This is true
of his picture of Seward, so able, so devious, at times so clearheaded,
and at other times so befogged by misconceptions that were "almost

hallucinations"; his picture of Sumner, the "enlightened doctrinaire"; and his picture of McClellan, who knew how to organize a superb army, but whose inability to use it was "actually inexplicable." And in presenting character, Schurz knows how to use the revealing incident or telling speech. It is he who records William D. Kelley's remark as the Republican deputation in 1860 left Lincoln's house: "Well, we might have done a more brilliant thing, but we could hardly have done a better thing." And what could be more eloquent of Seward's inner littleness than the outburst of 1861 which Schurz reports: a peevish explosion in which Seward asserted that although he had been entitled to the Republican nomination, "I had to stand aside and see it given to a little Illinois lawyer!"

In later years Schurz was to write a brief biography of Lincoln which will always remain a classic, and which proves how fully he understood the greatness of the man. These memoirs show by what steps he reached this comprehension. Whenever Lincoln appears, Schurz's intense interest in him gives us a memorable scene. What reader of the description of their first meeting, on a train rattling across the prairies of western Illinois to the Lincoln-Douglas debate in Quincy in 1858, can ever forget it? Lincoln approved Schurz's draft of a speech to be delivered in Cooper Union on March 6, 1862, adding: "Maybe you will hear something from me on that same day"— and sure enough, on that day the President sent Congress his proposal for compensated emancipation.

It must in all candor be said that Schurz's narrative of his military services should be read with some critical reservations. He was not quite so preternaturally wise at Chancellorsville, for example, as he suggests. As Lincoln at one point frankly wrote him, some men thought as poorly of Schurz's generalship as other men thought of the President's statesmanship. But while the veteran of Rastatt, if veteran he can be called, describes his role in the field fully, he is not really immodest. He did play a valiant part at Second Manassas, at Gettysburg, at Chattanooga, and in Sherman's march to the sea. His statements on strategy are sound and incisive, and his unfavorable estimates of Meade and Hooker are as convincing as his briefly favorable references to Grant and Sherman. No students of the conflict can neglect Schurz's interesting chapters.

He had gone into the Civil War a Republican, and if Lincoln had lived, a Republican he would have remained. But the gross mismanagement of Reconstruction by Andrew Johnson, Thaddeus Stevens, Charles Sumner, and the other leaders of the nation 1865–1868, and the equally saddening display of incompetence and corruption by the Grant Administration later, converted him into an Independent. An honest idealist, he felt, could take no other stand. Johnson commissioned him in 1865 to travel through the South so as to prepare a report on the condition of both whites and blacks, and on the state of public feeling. He concluded that it would be wise to send a Congressional committee into the old Confederacy to study the situation in detail, and formulate proposals for constructive legislation. But his recommendations came to naught. He then turned to journalism, first in Detroit and later in St. Louis; and early in 1869 the Missouri legislature elected him to the Senate, of which he became the first German-born member, and one of the most distinguished luminaries.

Schurz did not live long enough to describe the great part he played as Senator, as Secretary of the Interior under Hayes, as an editor successively of the New York *Evening Post* and *Harper's Weekly*, and as perhaps the most consistent champion of liberal causes in the country. Before he left the Senate in 1875, he had broken with Republicanism and defied the Grant Administration. He had quarreled with Grant over the harsh treatment of the Southern States, the ill-advised attempt to annex Santo Domingo, and the flagrant corruption in half the government departments. He had helped organize the Liberal Republican movement of 1872, and had advocated the election of Horace Greeley to the Presidency. It was as one of the ablest and most courageous reformers in the country that Hayes in 1877 made him head of a branch of the government notoriously seamed with dishonesty and mismanagement. There he fought the powerful corporations stealing timber and mineral lands; the crooked Indian agents; the State governments anxious to lay hands on the public domain; and the army forces encroaching on Interior Department authority. His unswerving adherence to duty strengthened the nation's sense of the importance of civic rectitude.

Throughout his later career Schurz was one of the most eloquent champions of governmental reform and social justice in the nation. He fought steadily for tariff reform; for civil service reform; for currency reform; for reform in the treatment of the Negro, the Indian, and the immigrant; and for the reform of government in the cities, the States, and the nation. He fought Tammany, he fought Tom Platt, he fought Hanna. He was one of the first conservationists in our history. His support of Grover Cleveland in 1884 helped change the course of political events, for without it Cleveland would probably have been defeated. As he had begun his American career by powerful exertions in the struggle against slavery, so he closed it by playing an eloquent part in the struggle against imperialism; against the extension of American sovereignty over peoples alien in blood and tradition, and against the movement for a big navy and a truculent or jingoistic attitude toward other nations.

Like his friends James Russell Lowell, E. L. Godkin, and George William Curtis, he supported the best intellectual and cultural impulses of his time. He was greatly interested in literature, in music, and in the improvement of university education. History especially appealed to him, and he wrote a two-volume life of Henry Clay which may be termed a contribution to American letters. Indeed, as this book proves, his mastery of English was remarkable; one of his Columbia friends used to say that his achievement of a finished command of the English tongue was the most impressive intellectual feat he had ever known. Though he was an internationalist in the best sense of the word, his American patriotism was so pure and steadfast that he never allowed himself, like some others of the same origin, to be called or regarded as a German-American; he could not be a hyphenate. Sometimes his unbending independence irritated even his best contemporaries. Grover Cleveland, for example, once protested that he was "a hard master." But taken all in all he was one of the most admirable spirits of his era, and Americans should treasure this record of his life as the expression of a memorable and inspiring personality.

ALLAN NEVINS

CONTENTS

CONTENTS

The
AUTOBIOGRAPHY
of
CARL SCHURZ

CHAPTER I

Growing up in Germany

I was born in a castle. This, however, does not mean that I am of aristocratic ancestry. My father was, at the time of my birth, a schoolmaster in Liblar, a village of about eight hundred inhabitants, on the left bank of the Rhine, three hours' walk from Cologne. His native place was Duisdorf, near Bonn. Losing his parents in early childhood, he was adopted into the home of his grandfather, a man belonging to the peasant class, who possessed a small holding of land upon which he raised some grain, potatoes and a little wine. Thus my father grew up a true peasant boy.

Upon his discharge from military service my father entered, as a pupil, a teachers' seminary at Brühl, and was soon appointed schoolmaster at Liblar. He had received a little instruction in music at the seminary and had learned to play the flute. This enabled him to teach simple songs to the school children and to form a glee club, composed of the youths and maidens of the village. In this glee club he made the acquaintance of my mother, Marianna Jüssen, whom he married in 1827. My mother was the daughter of a tenant-farmer, Heribert Jüssen, who occupied part of a seignorial castle called "Die Gracht," near Liblar. My father and mother lived, for several years after their marriage, with my grandparents; and so it happened that I, their firstborn, came into the world on March 2, 1829, in a castle. The estate as a whole was called by the people "Die Burg," and my grandfather was known in the village and surrounding country as "Der Burghalfen." "Halfen" was the name given originally to the farmer-tenants who went halves with the lord of the estate in the proceeds of the crops.

My grandfather was a man of huge proportions: over six feet in height, with powerful chest and shoulders, and massive features to correspond; square chin; a firm mouth and full lips; large straight nose;

3

fiery dark eyes with bushy eyebrows; a broad forehead, shadowed with curly brown hair. His strength of muscle was astounding. Once, at a kirmess festival, when several other halfen were his guests, my grandfather accepted a challenge to lift in his arms the great anvil which stood in the blacksmith's forge on the other side of the moat, and to carry it over the drawbridge, through the gate, into the house, up the stairs to the loft, and back again to the forge. I can see him now, striding along, up and down the creaking stairs, with the heavy block of iron in his arms, as though he were carrying a little child.

I must have been a little over four years old when my parents left the castle to establish a home of their own in the village of Liblar. The village consisted of one street. Midway on an elevation stood the parish church with its pointed steeple and cross. The houses, mostly one-storied and very small, were of whitewashed plaster, with frames and beams exposed, and tiled roofs. There were perhaps half a dozen brick buildings in the village, belonging to the count. The inhabitants of Liblar, small farmers, laborers, mechanics and a few inn- or shop-keepers, took an especial pride in their village because its street was paved with cobblestones. Notwithstanding our house had two stories, it was very small, with ceilings so low in the upper story that my grandfather when standing upright almost touched them with his head.

Before I was six years old my father took me into the village school of which he was the teacher. I remember that I could read and write very early, but not how I acquired those arts. Much I owed to the instruction which my father gave me at home. I had frequented the village school hardly a year when my father resigned his position as schoolmaster. The salary, about $90 a year, was too pitiably small to support the family, to which in the meantime two little girls had been added.

My father, like all who feel within themselves a yearning for knowledge with few opportunities for satisfying it, had the earnest ambition to give to his children the education that fate had denied to him. With this object in view he made a start in a new direction, and opened a hardware-shop, for which he appropriated a part of the house which had once been a cow-stable, hoping that the business would gradually yield an income sufficient for the family needs. In me he believed that he had discovered an aptitude for study. He therefore decided that at the proper age I should go to the "gymnasium" and later to the university, to be fitted for one of the learned professions. For the time being I continued to attend the village school, but the instruction I received there was early supplemented in various directions. It was my

father's especial wish that all his children should study music. To this
end, when I was about six years old, a queer little piano was procured
which had neither pedals nor damper, and possessed several peculiarities incident to old age. But it served well for my first finger exercises,
and to me the instrument was very beautiful.

When I was in my ninth year my father thought I had outgrown
the village school in Liblar. He therefore sent me to a school of a
somewhat higher order in Brühl, which was connected with the
teacher's seminary there, and was regarded as a model institution. The
schoolrooms were in an old Franciscan monastery, and I remember
with a shudder the tortures to my sensitive musical ear when my
father, in order to present me to the principal, led me through a long
corridor, in each window-recess of which stood a young man prac-
tising finger-exercises on the violin, so that at least a dozen instruments
giving out discordant sounds were to be heard at the same time. The
instruction I received from the well-equipped master was excellent,
and at the same time I continued my lessons in Latin and my musical
studies. I also began to live among strangers, boarding during the winter in the modest home of a butcher's widow. In the summer I walked
to school from Liblar to Brühl and back every day of the week—a
walk of about eight miles.

I was ten years old when my father took me to the gymnasium at
Cologne, usually called the "Jesuit Gymnasium," although it had no
connection with that religious order. In those days Cologne had about
ninety thousand inhabitants, and was, as I supposed, one of the finest
cities in the world. My grandfather had taken me there several years
before on a visit, and well do I remember the two things that then
interested me most: the cathedral tower with the huge crane on top,
and the convict chain-gangs sweeping the streets—sinister-visaged fellows in clothes striped dark gray and yellow, with heavy iron chains
on their feet that rattled and clanked dismally on the pavement stones,
one or more soldiers standing guard close by, gun in hand. I remember
also how my grandfather reproved me for taking off my cap to everybody whom we met in the streets, as was the custom in our little village
at home; for he said there were so many people in Cologne that were
one to attempt to bow to them all there would be no time left for anything else; that one could never become acquainted with all those persons, and many of them were not worth knowing; and finally, that
such deference on my part would mark me at once as a country boy
and make me appear ridiculous.

My scale of living at Cologne was, of necessity, extremely modest.

Board and lodging had been provided for me by my parents at the house of a locksmith. I slept in the same bed with the locksmith's son, who was also a mechanic, and took my meals at the family table with the journeymen and apprentices. Severe decorum was exacted of all; the master led the conversation, and only the foreman occasionally took part in it. I had no social intercourse whatever with persons of good education outside of school; but within school many helpful influences surrounded me.

I was in the Upper Secunda (or third year of high school) when our professor of German gave us, as the subject of a composition, a memorial oration on the battle of Leipzig. Believing it to be my duty to write exactly what I thought about that event, I expressed with entire frankness my feelings about the ill-treatment the German people had suffered after their heroic efforts on that battlefield, and my hope of a complete regeneration of the German fatherland. I was profoundly in earnest. I wrote that memorial oration, so to speak, with my heart's blood. When the professor, at one of the next lessons, returned the papers to us in the class room, with critical remarks, he handed mine to me in silence. It bore this footnote: "Style good; but views expressed nebulous and dangerous." After the adjournment of the class he called me to his side, put his hand upon my shoulder and said, "What you wrote has a fine sound; but how can such things be allowed at a royal Prussian gymnasium? Take care that it does not happen again." From that time on he refrained from giving subjects to the class which might tempt us to political discussion.

In the meantime dark clouds were gathering over our home. My grandfather's retirement from the Burg had been followed by evil consequences; it was as if the firm ground had been taken from under our feet. The proceeds of the sale of the inventory had been entrusted to my youngest uncle for investment. He groped about for a considerable time and finally hit at the idea of trading in grain. In connection with this plan my father, who was in need of a larger income than his little hardware business yielded, decided to erect a building of which the ground floor was to be a large amusement hall and the upper story a granary. In one of his many books he had read the description of some new method of construction which caught his fancy and which had the charm of novelty. The building was successfully erected, but it cost far more than had been anticipated. It appeared also that the festive occasions proved too few to make the letting of the amusement hall profitable, and the granary yielded even less. My uncle's grain business soon became highly speculative and he promised himself mountains of gold from it. When he drifted into embarrassment, of course his brothers and brothers-in-law came to the rescue, thus involving themselves also in affairs of which not one of them had any knowledge.

Suddenly my parents were cheered by apparently more hopeful prospects. My father found an opportunity for selling his property in Liblar at a price which would enable him to discharge his obligations and furnish the means for a new livelihood. As soon as the sale was concluded he removed with the family to Bonn, where I was to go to the university after having absolved the gymnasium. In Bonn my father made arrangements with an old friend which put him in possession of a spacious house, the lower part of which was used as a restaurant for students, while in the upper stories were several rooms to be let.

But then a great misfortune fell upon us. The purchaser of the property in Liblar, with whom my father had made a very imperfect contract, declared that he had become dissatisfied with the arrangement and that he proposed to forfeit the little sum paid in advance, and not take the property. This was a hard blow. My father tried, unsuccessfully, to hold the purchaser to the bargain, and no other purchaser could be found. To return to Liblar was impossible, as my father was then bound to his new arrangements in Bonn. Now the bills of exchange became due, which in anticipation of the money coming to him from the sale in Liblar he had given to his creditors. He could not meet them; the bills were protested, and suddenly I received in Cologne the news that some of the creditors had thrown my father into the debtors' prison. This struck me like a clap of thunder. I ran to the prison house and saw my father behind an iron bar. It was a distressing meeting, but we endeavored to encourage one another as best we could. He explained to me his circumstances, and we considered what might best be done to extricate him from this humiliating situation.

I was then seventeen years old and on the point of passing into the highest class of the gymnasium, but evidently I could no longer remain in Cologne. I hurriedly took leave of my teachers and friends, and devoted myself entirely to the affairs of the family. My uncles would have been glad to assist us, but they themselves were involved in grievous embarrassments. Business matters were entirely foreign and repugnant to me; but necessity is a wonderful schoolmaster, and I felt as if in a day I had grown many years older. After much traveling to and fro I succeeded in making arrangements sufficiently satisfactory to the creditors to induce them to release my father. Those were very dark days.

When my father was thus enabled again to take our affairs into his own hands, the question arose, what was to become of me. Was I to abandon my studies and enter upon a new course of life? This idea was rejected at once; but circumstances did not permit my return to Cologne. I had to remain with my family. We therefore formed the bold plan that I should begin at once as an irregular student to attend lectures at the university, and at the same time to pursue those studies which would make it possible for me to pass the graduation examination in Cologne the next year. This plan was bold in so far as it was generally understood that when a young man left the gymnasium without having completed the course and then came back to pass the examination required for regular standing at the university, that examination was often made exceptionally severe in order to discourage the practice. But there was no hesitation in attempting the difficult task. Meanwhile, my mind had also settled upon a calling. I was fond of historic and linguistic studies, and believed I possessed some literary capacity. I therefore resolved to prepare myself for a professorship of history, and so began to attend philological and historical lectures.

Although not yet regularly immatriculated at the university at Bonn, I received a warm welcome from a group of fine young men, the Burschenschaft Franconia—one of that class students' associations which after the wars of liberation of 1813, '14 and '15 had been organized at various German universities, in obedience to a patriotic impulse. My admission to this fellowship I owed to my Cologne friends, Petrasch and von Weise, who had preceded me at the university and had spoken a good word for me to their brethren of the Franconia society, probably with an exaggerated account of my literary capabilities. This I discovered upon the occasion of my first appearance at the Franconia "Kneipe," when it was the evident intention of both my friends to make a show of my talents. But I was at that time an extremely bashful youth, always silent and awkward in the presence of strangers. I shall never forget the feeling of utter helplessness that came over me when Petrasch introduced me to the presiding officer of the society, Johannes Overbeck, a self-poised young man several years my senior, and a brilliant student who had already published a volume of original poems. All this I knew and it had impressed me greatly. In answer to the friendly greeting he gave me I blushed and stammered and only managed to articulate an occasional yes or no. I was quite conscious of the sorry figure I was cutting, and what was worse, aware that Petrasch and Weise were disappointed and ashamed of me. It was the first occasion in life when I was brought in contact with men from other parts of Germany; and they, especially the

North-Germans, had something superior and deliberate in their ways that greatly impressed me.

My irregular standing at the university did not permit me to be received as a full member into the Franconia, but I was admitted as a guest to their convivial meetings. For a long time I sat a mute spectator at the jovial gatherings of my friends, but finally my hour came. One of the principal events of the convivial evenings was the reading aloud of the *Kneipzeitung*, a humorous paper, written and read in turn by different members. To write a good *Kneipzeitung* was the object of general ambition, and those papers not seldom possessed decided literary merit. As I sat or moved, a quiet observer among my friends, abundant opportunity was afforded me to study the peculiarities of my new companions. My observation finally took form in a parody of the "Auerbach cellar scene" in "Faust," in which I made the leading members of the Franconia the *dramatis personæ*. The satire was pointed, though of course not ill-natured. When I had finished the composition I showed it in confidence to Petrasch. He shouted with delight, and was certain that nothing better had ever been written by any member of the society. This of course I refused to believe, but yielded to his entreaties that I turn it into a *Kneipzeitung* and that he should be the one to read it aloud at the next reunion. I insisted that he keep its authorship strictly secret, which he promised. When finally the evening came for its presentation my heart was in my throat, and my face red with blushes, as the assembled company burst into repeated laughter and applause. The success of the paper was complete. Petrasch declared that the writer wished to remain unknown, but with this the audience would not rest content. Of course nobody suspected me. My friend, as proud of the achievement as if it had been his own, winked at me across the table and whispered audibly, "May I not tell?" This alone would have been sufficient to betray me, but another member sitting near recognized my handwriting. And now there was a great hurrah. From all sides they rushed upon me; there was no end of congratulation and handshaking; and Petrasch, looking around at the assembled company, called out: "There, now, what did I tell you?"

Much time I could indeed not give to my friends during my first university year at Bonn, for the graduation examinations at the Cologne gymnasium, upon which my whole future depended, were still ahead, and they ever stood before me like a threatening specter. Aside from the historical and philological lectures which I attended, I had to acquire all that was taught in the upper class of the gymnasium by way of self-instruction, and with the exception of higher mathematics and of natural science I succeeded in doing this, but, of course, not without much labor. At last, in September, 1847, the crisis came, and I journeyed to Cologne, accompanied by the prayers of my family and the cordial wishes of all good friends. Fortune favored me again, and all went well. I knew the sixth canto of the Iliad by heart, and it so happened that the examiner in Greek gave me a part of that canto to translate, which I could do without looking at the book. In addition to this, the result of my examination in history and my compositions in German and Latin were sufficiently satisfactory to move the examiners to overlook my weakness in other branches. Upon the conclusion of the ordeal the government commissioner, who had before seemed to me the personification of grim fate, handed me my graduation papers with an especially cordial handshake, and he gave me many good wishes for future success on my way. I returned to Bonn in triumph.

It was at the beginning of the winter semester of 1847–8, at Bonn that I made the acquaintance of Professor Gottfried Kinkel. As a lecturer he proved himself exceedingly attractive by his interesting personality as well as by the charm of his delivery. Kinkel was a very handsome man, of regular features and herculean stature, being over six feet in height and a picture of strength. He had a wonderful voice, both strong and soft, high and low, powerful and touching in its tone, gentle as a flute and thundering like a trombone—a voice which seemed to command all the registers of the church organ.

He delighted to put the professor aside and to let himself go when in the circle of his family and friends in unrestrained hilarity. He drank his glass of wine—with moderation, to be sure—laughed heartily at a good jest and even at a poor one, drew from all circumstances of life as much enjoyment as there was in them, and grumbled little when fate was unkind. Thus one soon felt at home in his company. He had indeed also his detractors, who accused him of being what they called "vain." But who is not vain, each one in his way?

Meanwhile, in the prosecution of my studies I had taken up with ardor the history of Europe at the period of the great Reformation. I expected to make this my specialty as a professor of history. The great characters of that period strongly attracted me and I could not resist the temptation to clothe some of them in dramatic form. So I planned a tragedy, the main figure of which was to be Ulrich von Hutten, and I began to elaborate some scenes in detail.

CHAPTER II

The Revolution of 1848

O NE morning, toward the end of February, 1848, I sat quietly in my attic-chamber, working hard at my tragedy of "Ulrich von Hutten," when suddenly a friend rushed breathlessly into the room, exclaiming: "What, you sitting here! Do you not know what has happened?"

"No; what?"

"The French have driven away Louis Philippe and proclaimed the republic."

I threw down my pen—and that was the end of "Ulrich von Hutten." I never touched the manuscript again. We tore down the stairs, into the street, to the market-square, the accustomed meeting-place for all the student societies after their midday dinner. Although it was still forenoon, the market was already crowded with young men talking excitedly. There was no shouting, no noise, only agitated conversation. What did we want there? This probably no one knew. But since the French had driven away Louis Philippe and proclaimed the republic, something of course must happen here, too. Some of the students had brought their rapiers along, as if were necessary at once to make an attack or to defend ourselves. We were dominated by a vague feeling as if a great outbreak of elemental forces had begun, as if an earthquake was impending of which we had felt the first shock, and we instinctively crowded together.

The next morning there were the usual lectures to be attended. But how profitless! The voice of the professor sounded like a monotonous drone coming from far away. What he had to say did not seem to concern us. The pen that should have taken notes remained idle. At last we closed the notebook with a sigh and went away, impelled by a feeling that now we had something more important to do—to devote ourselves to the affairs of the fatherland. And this we did by seeking as quickly as possible again the company of our friends, in order to discuss what had happened and what was to come. In these conversations, excited as they were, certain ideas and catchwords worked themselves to the surface, which expressed more or less the feelings of the people. Now had arrived in Germany the day for the establishment of "German Unity," and the founding of a great, powerful national German Empire. In the first line the convocation of a national parliament. Then the demands for civil rights and liberties, free speech, free press, the right of free assembly, equality before the law, a freely elected representation of the people with legislative power, responsibility of ministers, self-government of the communes, the right of the people to carry arms, the formation of a civic guard with elective officers, and so on—in short, that which was called a "constitutional form of government on a broad democratic basis." Republican ideas were at first only sparingly expressed. But the word democracy was soon on all tongues, and many, too, thought it a matter of course that if the princes should try to withhold from the people the rights and liberties demanded, force would take the place of mere petition. Of course the regeneration of the fatherland must, if possible, be accomplished by peaceable means. A few days after the outbreak of this commotion I reached my nineteenth birthday. I remember to have been so entirely absorbed by what was happening that I could hardly turn my thoughts to anything else. Like many of my friends, I was dominated by the feeling that at last the great opportunity had arrived for giving to the German people the liberty which was their birthright and to the German fatherland its unity and greatness, and that it was now the first duty of every German to do and to sacrifice everything for this sacred object. We were profoundly, solemnly in earnest.

Exciting news came from all sides. In Cologne a threatening ferment prevailed. In the taverns and on the streets resounded the "Marseillaise," which at that time still passed in all Europe as the "hymn of liberty." On the public places great meetings were held to consult about the demands to be made by the people. A large deputation forced its way into the hall of the city council, vehemently insisting that the municipality present as its own the demands of the people of Cologne to the king. The streets resounded with the military drumbeat; the soldiery marched upon the popular gatherings, and Willich, as well as another ex-artillery officer, Fritz Anneke, were arrested; whereupon increasing excitement.

The Rhenish members of the prorogued United Diet implored the

president of the province to urge upon the king an immediate acceptance of the demands of the people as the only thing that could prevent
bloody conflicts. In Coblenz, Düsseldorf, Aachen, Crefeld, Cleves and
other cities on the Rhine similar demonstrations took place. In South
Germany—in Baden, Hessen-on-the-Rhine, Nassau, Würtemberg,
Bavaria—the same revolutionary spirit burst forth like a prairie-fire.
In Baden the Grand Duke acceded almost at once to what was asked
of him, and so did the rulers of Würtemberg, Nassau, and Hessen-
Darmstadt. In Bavaria, where even before the outbreak of the French
revolution in February the notorious Lola Montez, favorite of King
Ludwig I., had had to yield her place near the throne to the wrath of
the people, uproar followed uproar to drive the king to liberal concessions. In Hessen-Cassel the "Elector" also succumbed to the pressure when the people had armed themselves for an uprising. The
students of the university of Giessen sent word to the insurgent
Hessians that they stood ready to help them. In Saxony the defiant
attitude of the citizens of Leipzig, under the leadership of Robert
Blum, quickly brought the king to terms.

Great news came from Vienna. There the students of the university
were the first to assail the Emperor of Austria with the cry for liberty
and citizens' rights. Blood flowed in the streets, and the downfall
of Prince Metternich was the result. The students organized themselves as the armed guard of liberty. In the great cities of Prussia
there was a mighty commotion. Not only Cologne, Coblenz and Trier,
but also Breslau, Königsberg and Frankfurt-on-the-Oder, sent depu-
tations to Berlin to entreat the king. In the Prussian capital the masses
surged upon the streets, and everybody looked for events of great
import.

While such tidings rushed in upon us from all sides like a roaring
hurricane, we in the little university town of Bonn were also busy
preparing addresses to the sovereign, to circulate them for signature
and to send them to Berlin. On the 18th of March we too had our
mass demonstration. A great multitude gathered for a solemn procession through the streets of the town. The most respectable citizens,
not a few professors and a great number of students and people of
all grades marched in close ranks. At the head of the procession Professor Kinkel bore the tricolor, black, red and gold, which so long
had been prohibited as the revolutionary flag. Arrived on the market-
square he mounted the steps of the city hall and spoke to the assembled
throng. He spoke with wonderful eloquence, his voice ringing out
in its most powerful tones as he depicted a resurrection of German

unity and greatness and of the liberties and rights of the German people, which now must be conceded by the princes or won by force by the people. And when at last he waved the black, red and gold banner, and predicted to a free German nation a magnificent future, enthusiasm without bounds broke forth. People clapped their hands, they shouted, they embraced one another, they shed tears. In a moment the city was covered with black, red and gold flags, and not only the Burschenschaft, but almost everybody wore a black-red-gold cockade on his hat. While on that 18th of March we were parading through the streets suddenly sinister rumors flew from mouth to mouth. It had been reported that the king of Prussia, after long hesitation, had finally concluded, like the other German princes, to concede the demands that were pouring upon him from all sides. But now a whispered report flew around that the soldiery had suddenly fired upon the people and that a bloody struggle was raging in the streets of Berlin.

The king seemed at first sternly determined to put down the insurrection at any cost; but as the street battle proceeded he became painfully conscious of its terrible character. Reports arrived in rapid succession. He would now give an order to stop the fight and then an order to go on. Shortly after midnight he wrote with his own hand an address to "My dear Berliners." He began by saying that the firing of the two shots which had caused the excitement had been a mere accident, that a band of miscreants, mostly foreigners, had taken advantage of this misunderstanding to goad many of his good subjects into this fratricidal fight. Then he promised to withdraw the troops as soon as the insurgents would remove the barricades, and he implored them "to listen to the fatherly voice of their king, to which the grievously suffering queen joined her affectionate and tearful prayers." But the address failed to produce the desired effect. It was accompanied with the roar of cannon and the rattle of musketry, and the fighting citizens rather resented being called "a band of miscreants."

At last, on the afternoon of Sunday, the 19th of March, when one of the high commanders of the troops, General Möllendorf, had been captured by the citizens, the withdrawal of the troops was resolved upon. Peace was concluded on the understanding that the army should leave Berlin, that there should be freedom of the press, and that Prussia should have a constitution on a broad democratic basis. When the soldiery had marched off something happened that in dramatic force and significance has never been surpassed in the history of revolutions. From all parts of the city solemn and silent processions moved toward the royal palace.They escorted the bodies of those of the people who had been killed in the battle; the corpses of the slain were carried aloft on litters, their gaping wounds uncovered, their heads wreathed with laurel branches and immortelles. So the processions marched into the inner palace court, where the litters were placed in rows in ghastly parade, and around them the multitude of men with pallid faces, begrimed with blood and powder smoke, many of them still carrying the weapons with which they had fought during the night; and among them women and children bewailing their dead. Then the king was loudly called for. He appeared in an open gallery, pale and dejected, by his side the weeping queen. "Hat off!" the multitude shouted, and the king took off his hat to the dead below. Then a deep voice among the crowd intoned the old hymn, "Jesus, meine Zuversicht"—"Jesus, my Refuge," in which all present joined. The chorus finished, the king silently withdrew and the procession moved away in grim solemnity.

The "Prince of Prussia," the oldest brother of the childless king and presumptive heir to the throne—the same prince who as Kaiser William I. was in the course of events to become the most popular monarch of his time—was reported to have given the order to fire on the people, and the popular wrath turned upon him. By order of the king the prince left Berlin under cover of night and hurried to England. Excited crowds gathered in front of his palace on the street "Unter den Linden." There was no military guard to protect the building. A university student put upon its front the inscription "National property," and it was not touched. Immediately after the street battle had ceased the shops were opened again as in ordinary times.

Arms were distributed among the people from the government armories. The king declared, "I have become convinced that the peace and the safety of the city cannot be better maintained than by the citizens themselves." On the 21st of March Frederick William IV. appeared again among the people, on horseback, a black-red-gold scarf around his arm, a black-red-gold flag at his request carried before him, a huge tricolor hoisted at the same moment on the royal palace. The king spoke freely to the citizens. He would "place himself at the head of the movement for a united Germany; in that united Germany Prussia would be merged." He swore that he wanted nothing but a "constitutional and united Germany." At the university building he turned to the assembled students, saying, "I thank you for the glorious spirit you have shown in these days. I am proud that Germany possesses such sons." It was understood that a new and responsible ministry had been appointed, composed of members of the liberal opposition; that a constituent assembly to be elected by the Prussian people should be convoked to frame a constitution for the kingdom of Prussia; and a national parliament to be elected by the people of all the German states, to meet at Frankfurt for the purpose of uniting all Germany under a new constitutional government. The people of Berlin were in ecstasy.

"The heroes fallen in the glorious struggle for social and political liberty," as the proclamation of the municipal assembly called them, were carried for burial to the Friedrichshain cemetery, accompanied by two hundred thousand citizens, who took the coffins past the royal palace, where the king again stood with uncovered head.

Such were the great tidings the country received from Berlin. Thus the cause of liberty and national union seemed to have achieved a decisive and irreversible victory. The kings and princes themselves, foremost the King of Prussia, had solemnly promised to serve it. The jubilation of the people was without bounds.

About this time, upon the occasion of a crowded public meeting of university men in the "Aula," the great university hall at Bonn, I found myself, quite unintentionally, thrust into a conspicuous position among my fellow-students. I do not remember the special purpose for which the meeting was held. Profesor Ritschl, our foremost philologist and, if I recollect rightly, at that time dean of the philosophical faculty, a very highly esteemed and popular man, was in the chair. I stood among the crowd. I had thought much and formed a decided opinion of the subject which was under discussion, but did not attend the meeting with the intention of taking part in the debate. Suddenly I heard some of the speakers say something very repugnant to my feelings, and following a sudden impulse, I found myself the next moment speaking to the assembly. I have never been able to recollect what I said. I only remember that I was in a nervous condition until then entirely unknown to me; that thoughts and words came to me in an uninterrupted flow; that I spoke with vehement rapidity, and that the applause following my speech wakened me out of something like a dream. This was my first public speech. When the meeting had adjourned I met at the exit of the hall Professor Ritschl. As I attended some of his lectures he knew me. He put his hand upon my shoulder and asked:

"How old are you?"

"Nineteen years."

"Too bad; still too young for our new German parliament."

I blushed all over; that I should become a member of any parliament—that was a thought to which my ambition had never soared. I feared the good professor had permitted himself to joke with me.

The political horizon which after the revolution in March looked so glorious soon began to darken. The national parliament at Frankfurt elected in the spring, which represented the sovereignty of the German people in the large sense and was to give to the united German nation a national government, counted among its members a great many men illustrious in the fields, not of politics, but of science and literature. But it soon showed a dangerous tendency of squandering in brilliant, but more or less fruitless, debates much of the time which was sorely needed for prompt and decisive action to secure the legitimate results of the revolution against hostile forces.

Our eyes were turned still more anxiously upon Berlin. While the jubilation over the "Märzerrungenschaften"—the results of the revolutionary movements in March—at first seemed to be general, and even the adherents of absolutism put a good face on a bad business, soon a separation into different party-groups began between those whose principal aim was the restoration of order and authority—the conservatives; those who wished slow and moderate progress—the constitutionalists; and those who aimed at securing the fruits of the revolution in "a constitutional government on the broadest democratic basis"—the democrats. Instinctive impulse as well as logical reasoning led me to the democratic side. There I met Kinkel again, and our friendship soon became very intimate. In the course of our common activity the formal relations between teacher and pupil yielded to a tone of thorough comradeship.

In the beginning the zealous work of agitation absorbed almost all our time and strength. Kinkel, indeed, still delivered his lectures, and I also attended mine with tolerable regularity; but my heart was not in them as before. All the more eagerly I studied modern history, especially the history of the French Revolution, and read a large number of politico-philosophical works and of pamphlets and periodicals of recent date, which treated of the problems of the time. In this way I endeavored to clear my political conceptions and to fill the large gaps in my historical knowledge—a want which I felt all the more seriously as my task as an agitator was to me a sacred duty.

First we organized a democratic club consisting of citizens and students. Then we founded a local organ for the democratic party, the *Bonner Zeitung,* a daily paper, the editorship of which was undertaken by Kinkel, while I, as a regular contributor, had to furnish every day one or more articles. And finally, once or twice a week, in fact as often as we could, we marched out to the neighboring villages to preach to the country people the political gospel of the new time, and also to organize them into democratic clubs.

For a while Frederick William IV. seemed to be pleased with the rôle of a leader in the national movement which the revolution had made him assume. His volatile nature seemed to be warmed by a new enthusiasm. He took walks on the streets and talked freely with the people. He spoke of constitutional principles of government to be introduced as a matter of course. He loudly praised the noble generosity which the people of Berlin had manifested toward him in the hours of stress. He ordered the army to wear the black-red-gold cockade together with the Prussian. On the parade ground at Potsdam he declared to the sulking officers of the guards "that he felt himself perfectly safe, free and happy among the citizens of Berlin; that all the concessions made by him had been made of his own free will and according to his own convictions, and that nobody should dare to question this." But when the Prussian constituent assembly had met in Berlin and began to pass laws, and to design constitutional provisions, and to interfere with the conduct of the government in the spirit of the revolution, the king's mind gradually opened itself to other influences, and those influences gained access to him and surrounded him all the more readily since he removed his residence from Berlin to his palace at Potsdam, a little town preponderantly inhabited by courtiers and soldiers and other dependents of the government. Thus the king's immediate contact with the people ceased, his conferences with the newly appointed liberal ministers were confined to short formal "audiences," and voices appealing to old sympathies, prepossessions and partialities were constantly nearest to his ear.

There was the army, traditionally the pet of the Hohenzollerns, smarting under the "disgrace" of its withdrawal from Berlin after the street battle, and pining for revenge and restoration of its prestige. There was the court nobility, whose business it always had been to exalt and flatter the royal person. There was the landed aristocracy, the "Junker" element, whose feudal privileges were theoretically denied by the revolutionary spirit and practically invaded by the legislative action of the representatives of the people, and who artfully goaded the king's pride. There was the old bureaucracy, the power of which had been broken by the revolution, although its personnel had but little been changed, and which sought to recover its former sway. There was the "old Prussian" spirit which resented any national aspirations that might encroach upon the importance and self-appreciation of specific Prussiandom, and which still had strength in the country immediately surrounding Berlin and in some of the eastern provinces. All these forces, which in a general term were popularly called "the reaction," worked together to divert the king from the course he had ostensibly taken immediately after the revolution of March, with the hope of using him for the largest possible restoration of the old order of things—well knowing that if they controlled him, they would, through him, control the army, and then with it a tremendous, perhaps decisive, force in the conflicts to come. And this "reaction" was greatly strengthened by the cunning exploitation of some street excesses that happened in Berlin—excesses which in a free country like England might, indeed, have brought forth some vigorous measures of repression by the police, but would certainly not have induced anybody to call the practicability of civil freedom or of the constitutional principles of government in question. But these occurrences were used in Prussia with considerable effect to frighten the timid men of the bourgeoisie with the specter of general anarchy, and to persuade the king that after all the restoration of unrestrained royal power was necessary for the maintenance of law and order.

On the other hand, the visible development of the reaction had the effect of producing among many of those who stood earnestly for national unity and constitutional government, a state of mind more open to radical tendencies. The rapid progress of these developments was clearly perceptible in my own surroundings. Our democratic club was composed in almost equal parts of students and citizens, among whom there were many of excellent character, of fortune and good standing, and of moderate views, while a few others had worked themselves into a state of mind resembling that of the terrorists in the French Revolution. Kinkel was the recognized leader of the club, and I soon became a member of the executive committee. At first the establishment of a constitutional monarchy with universal suffrage and well-secured civil rights would have been quite satisfactory to us. But the reaction, the threatened rise of which we were observing, gradually made many of us believe that there was no safety for popular liberty except in a republic. From this belief there was only one step to the further conclusion, that in a republic, and only in a republic, all evils of the social body could be cured, and the solution of all the political problems would be possible. The idealism which saw in the republican citizen the highest embodiment of human dignity we had imbibed from the study of classic antiquity; and the history of the French Revolution satisfied us that a republic could be created in Germany and could maintain its existence in the European system of states. In that history we found striking examples of the possibility of accomplishing the seemingly impossible, if only the whole energy resting in a great nation were awakened and directed with unflinching boldness. Most of us indeed recoiled from the wild excesses which had stained with streams of innocent blood the national uprising in France during the Reign of Terror. But we hoped to stir up the national energies without such terrorism. At any rate the history of the French Revolution furnished to us models in plenty that mightily excited our imagination. How dangerously seductive such a play of the imagination is, we were of course then unaware.

In the course of the summer Kinkel and I were invited to represent the club at a congress of democratic associations in Cologne. This assembly, in which I remained a shy and silent observer, became remarkable to me in bringing me into personal contact with some of the prominent men of that period, among others, the leader of the communists, Karl Marx. He could not have been much more than thirty years old at that time, but he already was the recognized head of the advanced socialistic school. The somewhat thick-set man, with his broad forehead, his very black hair and beard and his dark sparkling eyes, at once attracted general attention. He enjoyed the reputation of having acquired great learning, and as I knew very little of his discoveries and theories, I was all the more eager to gather words of wisdom from the lips of that famous man. This expectation was disappointed in a peculiar way. Marx's utterances were indeed full of meaning, logical and clear, but I have never seen a man whose bearing was so provoking and intolerable. To no opinion, which differed from his, he accorded the honor of even a condescending consideration. Everyone who contradicted him he treated with abject contempt; every argument that he did not like he answered either with biting scorn at the unfathomable ignorance that had prompted it, or with opprobrious aspersions upon the motives of him who had advanced it. I remember most distinctly the cutting disdain with which he pronounced the word "bourgeois"; and as a "bourgeois," that is as a detestable example of the deepest mental and moral degeneracy he denounced everyone that dared to oppose his opinion. Of course the propositions advanced or

advocated by Marx in that meeting were voted down, because everyone whose feelings had been hurt by his conduct was inclined to support everything that Marx did not favor. It was very evident that not
only had he not won any adherents, but had repelled many who otherwise might have become his followers.

From this meeting I took home with me a very important lesson:
that he who would be a leader and teacher of men must treat the
opinions of his hearers with respect; that even the most superior mind
will lose influence upon others if he seeks to humiliate those others by
constant demonstrations of his superiority. That public man will be
most successful in enlightening and winning the ignorant who puts
himself upon their standpoint, not with condescension, but with sympathy.

The most interesting event of those days which I have cherished in
my memory was the student-congress in Eisenach, which occurred in
September, 1848, and which I attended as one of the chosen representatives of the university men of Bonn. This was the first long journey
of my life.

The pleasant little town of Eisenach, at the foot of the Wartburg,
where Luther translated the Bible into good German and threw his
inkstand at the head of the devil, had repeatedly been selected by the
old Burschenschaft as the theater of its great demonstrations. We organized ourselves according to parliamentary rules so that our oratorical performances might begin at once. All the German universities,
including those of Austria, having sent delegations to this congress, the
meeting was large in numbers and contained many young men of uncommon gifts. Those who attracted the most attention both within
and without our assembly were the Viennese, of whom nine or ten
had reported themselves. They wore the handsome uniform of the
famous "academic legion"—black felt hats with ostrich plumes, blue
coats with black shining buttons, tri-colored, black-red-gold sashes,
bright steel-handled swords, light gray trousers, and silver-gray cloaks
lined with scarlet. They looked like a troop of knights of old. When
the citizens of Eisenach, who had received us with most cordial kindness, gave a ball in our honor, all competition with the Viennese for the
favors of the fair sex was in vain. But it was not their outward appearance alone that distinguished them.

Nowhere had the university students played so important and
prominent a part in the revolutionary movement as in Vienna. To
them was largely owing the uprising that drove Prince Metternich
from power. It was, therefore, not astonishing that the Viennese legion-

aries, who had already made so much history, were among us regarded as the heroes of the day, and that with eager attention we listened to their reports about the condition of things in their country. Those reports, however, opened a prospect of further serious troubles if not of a tragical end, and of this our Viennese friends were sadly conscious.

While we were still planning various excursions from Eisenach into the surrounding country, our Viennese friends informed us that they had received letters about the threatening situation of things, which obliged them to return to Vienna without delay. They parted from us with a real "morituri salutamus." "In a few days," they said, "we shall have to fight a battle in Vienna, and then you may look for our names on the list of the dead."

Momentous news soon confirmed the predictions of our Viennese friends in Eisenach. Hungary had in the days of March asserted a high degree of political autonomy under a "personal union" with Austria. It had its own ministry residing in Pesth, without whose counter-signature no order of the Austrian emperor concerning Hungary should be valid. The to a large extent independent Hungarian government was an object of detestation to the Austrian court-party. That party resorted to various intrigues, which resulted in a direct breach between the Austrian and Hungarian governments, in the killing of an imperial emissary by an excited multitude in Pesth, and in the creation by the Hungarians of a national government-commission in Hungary, followed by a proclamation from the Austrian emperor which virtually amounted to a declaration of war. The Hungarians prepared for the struggle, and when in October Austrian troops were dispatched from Vienna for the subjugation of Hungary, the people of Vienna, the students at their head, rose in revolt against their own government, with the feeling that the attempt to destroy the constitutional rights of the Hungarians was at the same time directed against the rights of the German Austrians, and against all the fruits of the revolution. The minister of war, Count Latour, was hanged to a lamp-post by an infuriated crowd. After a bloody fight the insurrectionists controlled the city. The commander of the garrison, Count Auersperg, found himself obliged to evacuate the town, but he entrenched himself in a strong position outside, and was soon reinforced by large bodies of troops under Prince Windischgrätz. Windischgrätz took command of the army, attacked the city of Vienna on October 23, and after long and bloody struggles he put down the last resistance on the 31st. Vienna was then subjected to the unlimited arbitrariness of military rule, and the revolutionary movement in German Austria had an end.

With this catastrophe coincided a marked turn of affairs in Prussia. Since March the Prussian government had moved in constitutional forms. But the king and his immediate surroundings had on various occasions manifested a disposition which hardly harmonized with those pledges and called forth grave apprehensions. On October 31 the Prussian Constituent Assembly gave voice to the general sympathy with the struggling people of Vienna and resolved to request his Majesty's government "to take speedy and energetic steps to induce the German central power in Frankfurt to effectually protect the imperiled liberties of the people in the German districts of Austria, and to restore peace." The president of the ministry, General von Pfuel, supported this resolution. The next day he found himself compelled to resign, and the king then appointed a ministry of decidedly reactionary character, at the head of which he put Count Brandenburg, and the leading spirit of which was Herr von Manteuffel. The Constituent Assembly solemnly protested, but in vain. On November 9 the Brandenburg ministry presented itself to the Assembly with a royal message which transferred the meetings of that body to another place and prorogued its sessions until November 27. By a large majority the Assembly denied the right of the royal government to do these things, but the next day the house was surrounded by large bodies of troops under General Wrangel, who gave the order that nobody should be permitted to enter, but anybody might leave the building. On November 11 the civil guard of Berlin was dissolved and in a few days disarmed. The Assembly moved from one place to another, constantly followed by the soldiery, until finally on November 15, at its last meeting, it refused to vote the supplies, and declared "that this ministry had no right to dispose of the moneys of the state or to levy taxes, so long as the Constituent Assembly could not undisturbed continue its deliberations in Berlin." These events called forth immense excitement all over the country. They seemed to prove that the reactionary court-parties were determined to sweep away by force all the fruits of the revolution.

The democrats in Bonn, among whom we students played a prominent part, were zealous in demonstrating their determination to support the Constituent Assembly. The declaration that we would refuse the payment of taxes coming from the students looked somewhat like a huge joke, because we had none to pay. The problem we had to solve, therefore, consisted in persuading other people to refuse to pay their taxes. We believed we could strike a demonstrative blow by stopping the levying of octroi duties which were levied at the gates of the

city on the food-stuffs brought to the town. We did this in driving
the revenue officers from their posts, which pleased the peasants, who
were at once ready to bring their products free of duty into the city.
This led to conflicts with the police in which, however, we easily had
the upper hand.

Now it appeared to us necessary to seize upon the general machinery
of the tax-department. The next day a committee, of which I was a
member, appeared at the city hall to take possession of it. The Burgomaster received us with great politeness and listened quietly to what
we had to say to him about the authority of the Constituent Assembly
and its power to stop the payment of taxes; but he tried to amuse us
with all sorts of evasive talk. At last we became impatient and demanded an immediate and definite answer according to which we
would resolve upon further measures. Suddenly we noticed a change
in the expression of the Burgomaster's face. He seemed to hearken to
something going on outside and then, still politely but with a sort of
triumphant smile on his lips, he said: "Gentlemen, your answer you
will have to receive from somebody else. Do you hear that?" Now we
hearkened too, and heard a still distant, but approaching, sound of a
military band playing the Prussian national air. The music sounded
nearer and nearer in the street leading up from the Rhine. In a few
minutes it reached the market-place and behind it came the heavy
tramp of an infantry column which presently filled a large part of the
square in front of the city hall. Our conversation with the Burgomaster of course came to a sudden end and we thought it very decent on
his part that he permitted us to leave the building undisturbed.

In the evening we had a meeting of our democratic committee to
consider what was next to be done. The first impulse was to attack
the soldiers and if possible to drive them out of the town. This would
have been a desperate enterprise, but it was taken seriously in view.
After mature consideration, however, we all recognized that a fight
in Bonn, even a successful one, could have real importance only as a
part of a more general uprising. Cologne was naturally regarded as the
capital of the Rhineland and as the central focus for all political movements. It was there we had to seek our support, and from there to get
our orders. We had already received from Cologne a report that
feverish excitement prevailed in that city, and that the signal for a
general uprising was to be expected from the democratic leaders. For
this we were to prepare quietly and quickly, but we were to avoid
everything like an isolated attempt. We sent a messenger to Cologne
to inform our friends of what had occurred in Bonn and to get further

instructions. In the meantime we made arrangements to collect as many as possible of the muskets of our civic-guard and to make cartridges, which was done with great zeal.

But now disquieting news came about what happened in the vicinity of the gates of the city. Large crowds of peasants from the neighboring villages had assembled outside. They had received information about the coming of the soldiers to Bonn and thought that the democrats and the students must be in great danger. They had now come to help us. Many of them probably imagined the expulsion of the troops from the city to be as easy as had been the driving away of the tax officers from the gates. Some of them were spoiling for a fight. We had indeed reason for apprehending that they would press into the city and involve us in a street-battle with the soldiers under very unfavorable circumstances. It was not an easy task to persuade those impatient people to go home and to keep themselves ready to aid us as soon as the signal for action should come from Cologne. The whole night our committee waited for the return of the messenger we had sent there. About daybreak we separated, but only to meet again after a short rest. The preparations for war continued in the meantime. Not one of us slept in his own quarters, so as not to be easily found in case the authorities should try to arrest us. I took refuge in a friend's room that was filled with muskets and cases of cartridges which were stored there ready for distribution.

Our messenger did not return from Cologne before evening of the next day. He reported that our friends did not feel themselves able to attempt a blow with any prospect of success against the large masses of troops gathered there; that they would confine themselves to the continuation of the "passive resistance," and that they urgently recommended to us to abstain from all violent steps until further orders. Nothing remained to us therefore but to swallow our wrath and to keep our friends in the open country quiet. What happened with us, happened all over the kingdom of Prussia. The Constituent Assembly had yielded to the government a bloodless victory and the resolution to refuse the payment of taxes soon became a dead letter.

But it looked as if the whole affair would come home to the democratic leaders among the students in a disagreeable way. There was a rumor that against three or four of us, against me among others, warrants had been issued, and that we had to expect our arrest any moment. Whether it was really so, I did not know, but it was so believed; and our friends went at once to work to protect us from harm. They spread the impression among the citizens of Bonn that if we were touched by the police, all the students would quit the city. Now, as the prosperity of Bonn depended in a great measure upon the presence of the students, this caused no little alarm among the good burghers. Many of them urgently asked the Burgomaster to use his whole influence to obtain from the higher authorities the promise that nothing should happen to us, and thus to avert the threatening calamity. In fact we were informed by our friends in the course of a few days that such a promise had indeed been given, and that for once we should escape unharmed. We therefore left our hiding places, and I continued to write for our newspaper, to address meetings and to attend lectures, so far as I could find time to do so.

About this time Frederick William IV., after having won his victory over the Constituent Assembly, felt himself strong enough to give to Prussia a constitution of his own exclusive making, without submitting it for assent to the representatives of the people. This constitution of his provided for a Diet consisting of two Chambers. The Chambers were convoked at once and Kinkel stepped forward in Bonn as a candidate for the lower House. He was elected by a large majority, and had to take his seat soon after.

Of the larger parliamentary bodies that had issued from the revolution of March, only the national parliament in Frankfurt was still in existence. It had at its immediate disposal no administrative machinery, no army, no treasury, only its moral authority; all the other things were in the hands of the different German state governments. The only power of the national parliament consisted in the will of the people.

But that parliament was laboring under an overabundance of learning and virtue and under a want of that political experience and sagacity which recognizes that the better is often the enemy of the good, and that the true statesman will be careful not to imperil that which is essential by excessive insistence upon things which are of comparatively little consequence. The world has probably never seen a political assembly that contained a larger number of noble, learned, conscientious and patriotic men, and it will be difficult to find a book of the same character richer in profound knowledge and in models of lofty eloquence than its stenographic reports. But it did not possess the genius that promptly discerns opportunity and with quick resolution takes fortune by the forelock; it was not mindful of the fact that in times of great commotion the history of the world does not wait for the theoretical thinker. And thus it failed.

The parliament indeed recognized soon after its opening that an executive organ was required; and thus it resolved upon the institution of a "provisional central power," with a sort of lieutenant-emperor at its head. To this office it elected the Archduke Johann of Austria, who enjoyed the reputation of being a liberal. He was authorized by the parliament to appoint an imperial ministry. But his minister of foreign affairs had no diplomatic machinery under him; his minister of war no soldiers except such as were lent to him by some of the several state governments; and his minister of finance no fiscal machinery, no tax-levies, and no money except what the several state governments contributed. All the things which together constitute the substantial force of a government remained after all in the control of the several German states. Under these circumstances the national parliament could indeed issue its ordinances and have them proclaimed through the national executive, but the governments of the several German states felt that they need not pay much more attention to them than they pleased.

And yet, the parliament had still its principal task before it: to complete the constitution of the German empire, to introduce it practically, and thereby to satisfy the great national want of the German people. It was still engaged in learned and arduous debates about the fundamental right, and liberties the German citizens should possess; it still had to solve doubts as to whether Germany should have a Reichstag to be elected by all the people and whether the head of the national government should be a hereditary or only an elective Kaiser, or a President, or instead of a single head, an executive committee. It had still to determine of what countries and parts of countries the German empire should consist; whether the German-Austrian districts should form a part of it, and which of the two German great powers, Austria or Prussia, should in this event have the hegemony. The parliamentary struggle on these questions lasted long, and only when the reactionary Austrian minister, Prince Felix Schwarzenberg, demanded that the whole of Austria, organized as a united state with its nearly thirty millions of non-German inhabitants, should form part of the German empire—a demand with which the creation of a really German national union seemed entirely incompatible—only then did the parliament come to a decision. The majority declared itself for a hereditary Kaiser, and on March 28, 1849, elected to that office the King of Prussia.

And now came the bitterest disappointment of all. Frederick William IV. refused the crown. He had indulged himself in all sorts of fantastic dreams about the manner in which Germany might be united, but found that the constitution now presented to him in all essential points diverged seriously from his own conceits. The national parliament he thought had no right to offer to him or anybody else a crown; such an offer could, in his opinion, legitimately be made only by a free resolution of the German princes. Neither would the acceptance of the German imperial crown be compatible with his feelings of friendly obligations to Austria. His refusal to accept the imperial crown and the constitution of the empire turned the general enthusiasm of the people throughout the country into general dismay and indignation. On April 11 the national parliament declared that it would stand by the constitution it had made. By the 14th the legislative bodies of the governments of twenty-three German states had signified their acceptance of that constitution and of the election of the king of Prussia as Kaiser. But Frederick William IV. persisted in his declination, and the kings of Bavaria, Hanover and Saxony also continued to signify their unwillingness to assent.

On May 4 the national parliament appealed to the "governments, the legislative bodies, the communities in the several states and to the whole German people to stand up for the recognition and the introduction of the national constitution." This appeal sounded very much like a summons to arms, and in various parts of Germany it had already been anticipated. In the Bavarian Palatinate, on the left bank of the Rhine, a detached province of the kingdom of Bavaria, the people had already on April 30 risen up with rare unanimity, and declared in immense mass-meetings that whatever the Bavarian government might do, they would stand and fall with the national constitution. They went even farther. They instituted a provisional government to replace the authorities acting under the king of Bavaria. The revolt rapidly spread to the neighboring grand duchy of Baden, where the whole army of that state, with the exception of a small body of cavalry, joined the revolt and surrendered to it the important fortress of Rastatt. The Grand Duke of Baden took to flight, and a provisional government composed of popular leaders assumed the place of his ministry. In the kingdom of Saxony the people of Dresden, the capital city, attempted to force the king to recognize the national constitution. There too the king found himself obliged to flee after a short struggle between the people and the military, and a provisional government was organized. The king of Saxony applied to the Prussian government for aid. This was willingly granted, and after a bloody fight in the streets of Dresden the revolt was suppressed and the authority of the Saxon king restored by Prussian bayonets.

What were the adherents of the national cause in Prussia to do while their king sent Prussian soldiers to overcome the national movement outside? Uprisings were attempted in Berlin and Breslau, but speedily overcome by force of arms. In the Rhenish provinces the excitement was tremendous. In Cologne a meeting was held of the representatives of the country communes, which almost unanimously demanded the recognition of the national constitution and threatened the defection of the Rhineland from the Prussian monarchy in case of non-compliance. But the Prussian government had long ceased to be frightened by mere mass-meetings or by high-sounding phrases, when there was not a strong revolutionary force behind them.

Clearly, to save the national constitution, quick action was absolutely needed. Again the Rhenish people turned their eyes upon their capital, Cologne; but such masses of troops had been concentrated there that a rising would not have had the slightest prospect of success. In the manufacturing districts on the right bank of the Rhine the revolt really broke out. The immediate occasion was an order issued by the Prussian government to mobilize the army-corps of the Rhine province for the purpose of sending it against the defenders of the national constitution in the Bavarian Palatinate and in Baden, where provisional governments had been set up by the revolutionists. To this end the "Landwehr" (military reserve) in the Rhineland and in Westphalia was called into active service. The members of the Landwehr were men between twenty-five and thirty-five, peasants, tradesmen, artisans, merchants or professional men, many of them fathers of young families. To interrupt their daily work and to leave their wives and children involved to most of them a heavy sacrifice. This sacrifice was all the heavier when they were called upon to help beat down those who in Baden and in the Palatinate had risen for the unity of the fatherland and the liberty of the people, and with whom many, if not a large majority, of the members of the Landwehr warmly sympathized. So it happened that numerous meetings of the Landwehr men were held for the purpose of declaring that they would not obey the summons to arms. In Düsseldorf, Iserlohn and Elberfeld, apparently formidable uprisings took place.

Such uprisings could clearly have had a possibility of success only had they become general throughout the country; and indeed it looked for a moment as if the disaffection of the members of the Landwehr in the Rhineland and Westphalia would spread and become the starting-point of a powerful general movement. But what was to be done had to be done quickly.

In this aspect the question of the moment confronted us in Bonn. Kinkel had returned from Berlin and was on the spot. The Chamber, of which he was a member, had once more urged the king to recognize the national constitution and to accept the imperial crown, and the king thereupon had dissolved it. Kinkel was then in Bonn the recognized democratic leader. Now he had to show his ability to act promptly or to relinquish the leadership to others in the decisive hour. He did not hesitate a moment. But what was to be done? That the Landwehr, at least the largest part hereof, did not wish to take up arms against the defenders of the national constitution was certain. But in order to maintain this refusal, the Landwehr had to take up arms against the Prussian government. To make this resistance effective, immediate organization on a large scale was necessary. If the members of the Landwehr were ready for that, they could do nothing simpler and better than to take possession of the arms which were stored in the different Landwehr armories, and then under their own leaders make front against the Prussian government. Such an armory was situated at Siegburg, a little town a short distance from Bonn on the right bank of the Rhine. It contained muskets and other equipment enough to arm a considerable body of fighters, who then, joined to the insurrectionists in the manufacturing districts, might have formed a respectable power and spread the rising in all directions. This was the thought which occurred with more or less clearness to the democrats in Bonn, and they found also a military head for the execution of the plan in the person of a late artillery lieutenant, Fritz Anneke, who came from Cologne. The Landwehr of the district had been summoned to Siegburg on May 11, to be mustered into service. Thus time was pressing.

On May 10 we had in Bonn a meeting of Landwehr men from the town and the immediate neighborhood. The citizen elected to preside admonished the men to refuse obedience to the call of the Prussian government; if arms were to be taken up at all, it must be against those who sought to rob the German people of their liberty and unity. The men received this admonition with many signs of warm assent. The meeting continued during the whole day. The number of Landwehr men coming in increased from hour to hour. Different speakers addressed them, all in the same sense, and, as it appeared, with the same effect. It was agreed that the blow against the armory at Siegburg should be struck the following night. To this end it was essential to hold the men together during the day, so that as large a number as possible might take part in the expedition.

To keep the men together during the whole day was not easy. Some money had been raised to provide for their meals. But that alone was not sufficient. Kinkel, after having delivered his last lecture at the university, spoke to the meeting at four o'clock of the afternoon. With glowing words he inflamed the patriotic sentiments of the audience, admonishing them urgently to stay together, as now the hour of decisive action had come, and promised them at the conclusion of his speech that he would soon be with them again, to share their fate at the moment of danger.

I had been instructed to see to it that the ferry across the Rhine should be at our disposal. It was dark when I went to my appointed place on the bank of the river. There I found a fellow-student, Ludwig Meyer, with whom I crossed the river in a rowboat. On the other side we met according to agreement a troop of companions. At once we took possession of the ferry, the so-called flying bridge, ordered the ferryman to swing it over to Bonn, and then to take it back to the right bank of the Rhine, loaded with a crowd of armed men. This was the force that was to march to Siegburg and seize the armory. Kinkel appeared well armed. Two of our friends were on horseback, the rest on foot, most of them provided with weapons of some kind, but not a great many with guns. To me was given a rifle, but without fitting ammunition.

Our commander, Anneke, mustered the crowd and divided it into sections. Our column being formed in order, Anneke made a short speech, in which he set forth the need of discipline and obedience, and then the march began. About half an hour after our start one of our horsemen, who had remained behind, came up at a gallop with the report that the dragoons, then garrisoned in Bonn, were at our heels, to attack us. Long before we approached the river, we heard not far behind us the trumpet-signal ordering the dragoons to trot their horses. Anneke, who evidently was not very confident of the ability of his men to face regular soldiers in a fight, halted our column and told us that we were evidently not in a condition to offer successful resistance to regular troops; we should therefore disperse, and if we wanted to make ourselves further useful to the cause of the fatherland, we might find our way to Elberfeld or to the Palatinate, where he was ready to go. This signal to disperse was at once obeyed. Most of the men scattered over the surrounding cornfields, while some of us, perhaps twenty, stood still by the side of the road. The dragoons quietly passed us at a trot on their way to Siegburg. There were only some thirty of them, not enough therefore to overcome us or even to force their way through on the road, if those of us who had firearms had offered an orderly resistance.

When the dragoons had passed by and only a handful of our people had again found themselves together, a feeling of profound shame overcame us. Our enterprise had not only come to an unfortunate, but a ridiculous and disgraceful end. Our column had taken to the fields before only a handful of soldiers, scarcely one-third of our number. And this after the big words with which many had pledged themselves to the cause of German liberty and unity.

CHAPTER III

I Escape from the Prussians

IN Mainz I learned from a member of the democratic club that Kinkel had already passed through on his way to the Palatinate. I marched on to Kaiserslautern and found Kinkel and Anneke both in the best of humor. They welcomed me heartily, quartered me in a tavern, and told me that soon they might give me something to do.

I was now and then sent to popular meetings which were held to warm the patriotic zeal of the masses; and once I received an order to effect the arrest of a priest who used his influence in his parish—a large village of about three thousand inhabitants—to keep the young men from enlisting in the military organizations then forming. This was regarded as a sort of high treason against the new order of things; and the priest being looked upon as a desperate person who might possibly offer resistance, a little body of fifty men was to accompany me in order to aid me in the execution of my orders. This armed force did, indeed, not look very formidable; the lieutenant who commanded it was in civilian dress, except that he wore a plume on his hat and a tricolored sash, and a sword. Among the men there was only one military uniform, that of a member of the national guard of Strasburg, whence he had come to enjoy with us the revolutionary frolic in the Palatinate. The rest of the men were in their daily garb. There were only about a dozen muskets among them, mostly with old flint locks. The rest of the armament consisted of spears and scythes fastened straight on poles. As a commissioner of the provisional government, I was distinguished by a tri-colored sash and a sword; I also carried a pistol in my belt, but without cartridges. Thus equipped we marched across the country to the village in which the treasonable priest carried on his mischievous activity. Within sight of the village we halted, and there being nobody among my men who was acquainted with the whereabouts, I sent three of them, without arms, ahead to reconnoiter the location of the parsonage. Two of them should remain there after having discovered it, and the third was to return to serve the expedition as a guide.

When I marched into the village at the head of my armament I found the streets a picture of profound peace. It was a beautiful summer afternoon; the male inhabitants, agriculturists, were working in the fields; only a few old people and little children were to be seen at the doors of the houses or at the windows, looking at the strange procession with stolid astonishment. I must confess that I appeared to myself for the moment somewhat comical, but my official duty left me no choice. The parsonage was promptly surrounded by part of my force, so that my culprit should not slip away through a back door; the main body was drawn up in front of the house on the street. I knocked at the door and found myself soon in a plain but very comfortably furnished room with the priest before me. He was a young man, perhaps thirty-five years old; a robust figure and a well-formed head, with lively penetrating eyes. I tried to assume a severe martial attitude, and acquainted him at once, in short words, with my charge, put my hand upon his shoulder, as was customary in making an arrest, and called him my prisoner. To my astonishment he broke out in a merry laugh, which seemed quite genuine.

"You want to arrest me," he exclaimed; "that is nice. You are evidently a university student. I have been the same, and understand this sort of thing; the whole story is only a joke. Drink a bottle of wine with me." Thereupon he opened the door of the room and called to a servant to bring wine.

I did not like to be at once discovered as a university student, and resented that my mien of official authority should not impress him. So I said in as severe a tone as possible, "Reverend sir, this is not a joke. You have hindered in your parish the organization of the army; such treasonable conduct cannot be permitted by the provisional government. In the name of that provisional government I have arrested you. You must follow me; do not hesitate to obey. Your house is surrounded by soldiers; do not oblige me to use force!"

"Force! We will see about that!" he exclaimed, and in his eyes there gleamed something like anger and defiance, but he controlled himself, and continued in a serious but quiet tone: "There cannot be so much hurry about this that you may not listen to a word from me. Here is the girl with the wine, and if I must follow you, permit me at least to drink a glass with you, to your health. It is true I have warned my poor peasant boys not to enter the army and to expose themselves to be shot

for nothing. You yourself do not think that this insane revolt can succeed; in a few days the Prussians will chase your provisional government across the Rhine. Wherefore then this nonsense which may cost
many people their lives?" With this he pulled the cork out of the
bottle and filled two glasses. I had no time to consider whether, thirsty
as I was, I should drink with my prisoner, when I heard the bell on
the church steeple near by give a violent signal of alarm. This could
be nothing else than a tocsin; it seemed that the peasants had somehow
or other been informed of the danger threatening their priest, and as
if this church bell summoned them to his protection. The priest seemed
to understand the situation clearly; a sly smile flew across his face.

"How many men have you outside?" he asked.

"Enough," I answered.

I opened the window and saw crowds of peasants hurrying on from
all sides with flails and pitch-forks and bludgeons. My men were still
standing in line on the street; some of them seemed to look around
with anxiety at the villagers rushing upon the scene. I ordered the
lieutenant to post my men with their backs against the house and to let
nobody in; in case of an attack he should defend the door to the utmost of his ability. I directed him to give the same orders to the men
who watched the back door of the parsonage. The multitudes in front
of the house grew larger and larger. Threatening exclamations were
heard; evidently the situation was becoming complicated. Whether
the handful of my volunteers could resist that big crowd of fanatic
peasants appeared very questionable.

The priest still smiled. "My parishioners will defend me with their
lives. It looks to me as if your armed force were in their power."

Then a happy thought shot across my mind.

"In any case, you, Herr Pastor, are in my power," I answered,
drawing my pistol from my belt and cocking it. The priest would
have continued to smile if he had known that the pistol was not loaded.
He evidently thought it was a dangerous weapon, and his smile disappeared suddenly.

"What do you want?" he asked.

"I want you," I said with a show of coolness which, however, I did
not really feel; "I want you to step at once to this window and to ad-
monish your peasants to return to their homes without delay. You will
add that you have affairs with the provisional government in the interest of your parishioners; that you will go to the city in the company
of your friend here—that means me—to transact that business, and
that these armed volunteers have come to protect you on the way

against all danger and annoyance. While you make this speech to your peasants I stand with this pistol behind you. Do your business well, my friend; the provisional government will remember it." The priest looked at me for a moment with an expression of surprise, and smiled again, but it was an embarrassed smile; the pistol in my hand evidently did not please him. Then he rose, stepped to the window and was received by the peasants with loud exclamations. He commanded silence, and said exactly what I had prescribed to him. He did his business finely. The peasants obeyed without hesitation, and quiet reigned again in the streets. The priest and I then emptied our bottle of wine with all comfort. At dusk we left the house by the back door and wandered together toward the city like two old friends in merry conversation, my armed escort a hundred paces behind us. On the way I toyed with my pistol, throwing it into the air and catching it again with my hand.

"Take care," said the priest, "the pistol might go off."

"Impossible, Herr Pastor," I answered; "it is not loaded."

"What!" he exclaimed, "not loaded?"

We looked at one another and broke out into loud laughter.

I reported to the provisional government how the priest had helped me and my people out of a very precarious situation, and he was very kindly treated and allowed to return home forthwith. The provisional government had indeed much more important things to think of.

The attack which the merry Pfaelzers—at least many of them—had so long deemed improbable now really came. On the 12th of June a body of Prussian troops crossed the frontier. If the curses which those otherwise so good-natured people hurled against those Prussians had all been cannon balls, the Prussian troops could hardly have stood up against them; but the real fighting force at the disposal of the provisional government was so insignificant and so ill-equipped and undisciplined that an effective defense of the country was not possible. It was therefore necessary to avoid an encounter with the Prussians, and so it happened that the first military operation in which I participated consisted in a retreat. A few days before this my chief, Lieutenant Colonel Anneke, had instructed me to be ready to march at any moment, which I did not find difficult, because my baggage was extremely scant. I was given a horse, a fine bay, and as I had never learned to ride, my commander sent me to a riding school, where the master ordered me to mount the animal, explaining to me in a few words what I was to do with my legs and my hands to guide my mount; whereupon he struck him with a smart cut of his whip, and

I had to keep my seat as well as I could on my prancing steed. After this had gone on for an hour or so the master dismissed me, saying: "The next lesson you will get on the march." He was right; the constant exercise in active service gave me a pretty firm seat.

The sudden necessity of retreating considerably increased the general confusion. There was no end of orders and revocations of orders until we finally got started. I think it was in the night from the 13th to the 14th of June. With our artillery we had, indeed, no great difficulty, inasmuch as it consisted of very few pieces. At two o'clock in the night we mounted our horses and were off. A night march is almost always a miserable affair, especially a night march in retreat. Yet I must confess that the dull rumble of the wheels on the road, the rustle of the marching columns, the low snorting of the horses, and the rattling of the sabers and scabbards in the darkness, affected me as something especially romantic.

About sunrise after this first night's march we found ourselves in a deep gorge between precipitous ledges, near a place called Frankenstein, where we took a defensive position across the road to Neustadt. A cold morning brings, under such circumstances, a feeling of truly unromantic sober-mindedness with it, and I then learned that a hot cup of coffee, ever so thin, and a piece of dry bread, belong to the great benefactions of life. The Prussians, however, did not press us, and we remained undisturbed in our bivouac near Frankenstein during the entire day. On the 15th and 16th of June the troops of the Palatinate were drawn together near Neustadt-an-der-Hardt.

The spectacle of several well-armed battalions revived, to some extent, the courage of our troops, which had been somewhat dampened by the retreat, and here and there arose the cry that now the confounded Prussians might come on; but the retreat was continued and the Palatinate abandoned without the striking of a blow. About the 19th of June, 1849, some seven or eight thousand strong, we crossed the Rhine into Baden territory and marched toward Karlsruhe, the capital of the grand duchy.

Our entry into that neat little city created among the inhabitants a sensation which was by no means flattering to the troops of the Palatinate. The Karlsruhe burghers, who had been accustomed to the trim appearance of the grand duke's soldiers, did not seem to relish the picturesque and romantic appearance of our Palatinate fighters for liberty, but were rather inclined to close their doors and shutters as though feeling the necessity of protecting themselves against the inroad of a band of robbers. On the same day a camp was assigned to us outside of the city, and on the 20th of June we marched north-ward to the aid of the revolutionary army of Baden, which in the meantime had got into a critical situation.

On the 23d of June we advanced to Ubstadt and there we received the report that the next morning we would have to meet the Prussian vanguard. The orders which I received from my chief kept me busy on horseback until night, and it was late when I reached my quarters in the tavern at Ubstadt. My chief had already gone to rest. Upon all sides I heard the snoring of sleepers. Only the daughter of our host, a buxom young maiden of resolute expression of face, seemed to be at work. I asked her for a bed and something to eat, and both requests were granted by her with a robust outbreak of her feelings against the "accursed Prussians," who had nothing to do in the Badish land, and whom we should send home on the morrow with a sound thrashing. Now I expected within myself the solemn "emotions on the eve of battle" of which here and there I had read. But no emotions came; I fell asleep as soon as I had stretched myself out.

The engagement at Ubstadt was a comparatively small affair, with no purpose on our side but to retard the advance of the enemy until the Badish army could have reformed in our rear, and then slowly to fall back upon its position. At Ubstadt this instruction was carried out in a comparatively orderly manner. That such things cannot be done as perfectly with hastily organized and indifferently disciplined volun-teers as with well-schooled regular troops is a matter of course. The next day we had a more considerable engagement with the Prussian vanguard near Bruchsal, which again ended in a retreat on our part.

On the line of the Murg River, the left wing leaning on the fortress of Rastatt, the united corps of the revolutionists of Baden and of the Palatinate fought their last defensive fight on the 28th, 29th and 30th of June, 1849, in part very gallantly, although without success. On the evening of June 30 Lieutenant Colonel Anneke sent me with an in-struction concerning artillery ammunition into the fortress of Rastatt, where I was to wait for him in a certain fortification from which we could observe a large part of the battlefield. There he would call for me, he said. I discharged my order and then went to the place indicated by my chief, tied my horse to a gun carriage and sat down on the ram-part, where after having watched the fight outside for a little while I fell asleep from sheer fatigue in spite of the roaring of the cannon. When I awoke the sun was about to set. I inquired among the artillery-men standing around for Colonel Anneke, but nobody had seen him. I became restless and mounted my horse to look for my chief outside of the town. When I arrived at the gate the officer on duty informed me that I could not get out; that our army was pressed back toward the south, and that the fortress was completely surrounded by the Prussians. I galloped to the headquarters of the commander of the fortress and received there the confirmation of what I had heard. The prospect of remaining in the city with Prussians all around, and this not in obedience to orders, but by mere accident, struck me as exceedingly undesirable. I could not resign myself to it, and inquired again and again whether there was no way out, until at last an officer standing near the gate said: "I feel just as you do. I do not belong here and have tried all possible points where I thought I might slip through, but all in vain. We have to submit and remain." Of Anneke I found no trace. He had either left the city or perhaps had not been in it all.

Having given up all hope of escape, I reported myself to the Governor of the fortress, Colonel Tiedemann.

The duties assigned to me by the governor were not onerous. I had to spend certain hours on the highest gallery of the tower of the castle, armed with a telescope, to observe the enemy and to make report of what I might see. Then I had, periodically, to visit certain bastions and gates, and to inspect certain watches, and in addition to do such other things as the governor might see proper to entrust to me. To fit me for that duty I donned the uniform of a regular infantry lieutenant of the Badish army, which transformed me into a respectable-looking officer and gave me a sort of military consciousness which until then I had not possessed.

Suddenly one day—it was in the third week of the siege—a Prussian officer, under a flag of truce, came into the fortress with a summons to surrender, bringing the news that the revolutionary army had crossed the Swiss frontier, and had therefore ceased to exist; that not a single armed insurgent remained on German soil, and that the Prussian commander would consent to permit any man whom the garrison of Rastatt would entrust with such a mission, to convince himself of these facts with his own eyes, and to this end they would give him safe conduct wherever he might wish to go. This caused tremendous excitement. At once the governor called a general council of war, which, if I remember rightly, consisted of all officers of the garrison from captain upward. The council met promptly in the great hall of the castle. After a stormy discussion it was resolved that the offer of the Prussian commander should be accepted, and Lieutenant Colonel Corvin received the commission to explore the condition of things outside; and in case he found it to be as the Prussian flag of truce had represented, to negotiate for a capitulation on conditions as favorable as could be obtained.

On the second morning after Corvin's departure, in the gray dawn I lay down upon the sofa for a short rest. Soon I was awakened by the noise of heavy steps, rattling sabers and a confusion of voices. From what I saw and heard I concluded that Corvin had returned from his mission and that the great council of war was reassembling. The governor entered, demanded silence and asked Corvin, who stood at his side, to make his report orally to the whole assembly. Corvin then told us that, accompanied by a Prussian officer, he had traveled down to the Swiss frontier and had convinced himself on the spot that no revolutionary force was left in Baden, the revolutionary army having crossed into Switzerland, surrendered its arms, and dissolved. He had also satisfied himself from the newspapers, that in the rest of Germany there was not the slightest vestige of a revolutionary movement. Everywhere submission and quiet. The Hungarians, too, had suffered decisive defeats in consequence of the Russian intervention and would undoubtedly soon succumb. In short, the garrison of Rastatt was entirely forsaken, and could not hope for any relief; and finally, Corvin added, he had been informed at Prussian headquarters that the commander of the besieging army would insist upon a surrender of the fortress at discretion, without conditions of any kind.

Deep silence followed this speech. Every one of the hearers felt that Corvin had told the truth. Finally, somebody—I do not remember who —asked to be allowed to put some questions. Then there was a confusion of voices in which some hotheads talked of "dying to the last man"; whereupon the governor gave the floor to a former Prussian soldier, who had become an officer in the forces of the Palatinate. This officer said that he was as ready as anyone to sacrifice to our cause his last drop of blood, and that those of us who were Prussians, when they fell into the hands of the besieging army, would have to die in any case. Nevertheless he advised the immediate surrender of the fortress. If we did not surrender to-day, we would be obliged to do it to-morrow. We ought not to expose the citizens of the town, with their wives and children, to famine, or to another bombardment, and all in vain. It was time to make an end, whatever might happen to us personally. A murmur swept through the hall approving this advice, and then it was resolved that Corvin should try once more to secure, at the Prussian headquarters, for the officers and men of our garrison as favorable conditions as possible. But if after a reasonable effort he saw the impossibility of obtaining such conditions, he should agree with the Prussian headquarters upon the necessary arrangements for a surrender at discretion. When we left the hall most of us undoubtedly felt that nothing else could be hoped for.

"We Prussians will probably have to die in any case." These words echoed in my ear, and I was convinced of their truth. To these Prussians I belonged.

Toward daybreak I stretched myself once more on my accustomed sofa, and after several hours of profound sleep woke up with the thought, "To-day you will be taken by the Prussians, to be shot dead." Then I went to headquarters, where I learned that Corvin had not succeeded in negotiating any conditions, and that the surrender at discretion was a certain thing. At twelve o'clock noon the troops were to march through the gates to lay down their arms between two lines of Prussians outside on the glacis of the fortress. The orders had already been issued. I went to my quarters to write a last letter to my parents. I thanked them for all the love and care they had devoted to me, and asked them to forgive me if I had disappointed their hopes. I told them that following my honest convictions I had taken up arms for a cause that I believed to be right, for the liberty and unity of the German people, and if it should be my lot to die for that cause, it would be an honorable death of which they would never have reason to be ashamed. This letter I put into the hands of good Mr. Nusser, my host, who, with tears in his eyes, promised to put it into the mail as soon as communications should be opened again. In the meanwhile the hour of noon approached. Already I heard the signals calling the troops on the ramparts and in the barracks to the rally, and I prepared myself to go up to headquarters. Then a new idea suddenly flashed through my head. I remembered that only a few days previously my attention had been attracted to a subterranean sewer for the waters of the street gutters which, near the Steinmauerner gate, led from the interior of the city, under the fortifications, into an open field outside. This sewer was probably a part of an uncompleted drainage system. The entrance to it in the interior of the city was situated in a trench near a garden hedge. Outside it emptied into a ditch overgrown with shrubbery, which bordered a corn field. When these circumstances had first come to my knowledge, it had occurred to me that if the opening as well as the exit of that sewer were not well watched, spies might easily pass through it from the outside into the town. I had reported the matter to the governor, but immediately afterwards came the negotiations with the enemy, the mission of Corvin, and the excitement about the impending capitulation, which drove the affair of the sewer out of my mind.

I called my servant, who had prepared my belongings for the surrender. "Adam," I said, "you are a Palatinate man, a volunteer. I believe if you surrender to the Prussians you will soon be sent home. I am a Prussian, and us Prussians they will probably shoot dead. I will therefore try to escape, and I know a way. Let us therefore say good-bye."

"No, Herr Lieutenant," Adam exclaimed, "I shall not leave you. Where you go, I go." The eyes of the good boy sparkled with pleasure.

"But," said I, "you have nothing to gain, and we shall probably have to incur great dangers."

"Danger or no danger," replied Adam, with decision, "I remain with you."

At this moment I saw an artillery officer of the name of Neustädter, whom I knew well, pass by my window. He, like myself, was born in Rhenish Prussia, and had formerly served in the Prussian artillery.

"Where are you going, Neustädter?" I called to him through the window.

"To join my battery," he answered. "We are to surrender in half an hour."

"The Prussians will shoot you dead," I replied; "go with me and let us try to escape."

He stopped, came into the house and listened to my plan, which I explained to him in a few words.

"Good," he said; "I will go with you."

There was now no time to be lost. Adam was sent out to purchase a loaf of bread, two bottles of wine and some sausages. Then we put our pistols under our clothes, and rolled up our cloaks. In mine, a large dark cape lined with scarlet, received recently from our stores, I wrapped up a short carbine which I possessed. The bottles and the eatables which Adam had bought were packed up as well as we knew how. In the meantime the garrison began to march in close columns across the market-place. We followed the last column a short distance, and then turning into a side lane soon reached the inner mouth of our sewer. Without hesitation we slipped into it. It was between one and two o'clock in the afternoon of the 23d of July.

The sewer was a tube of brick masonry, sufficiently high and wide for us to move through it with bent knees and curved backs, half walking, half crawling. The water running through the sewer covered our feet and ankles. As we penetrated into the interior we found, here and there, narrow manholes covered on top with iron gratings, through which air and, during the day, some light came down. At such places we rested a moment and stretched ourselves out so as to get our spines into shape again. According to our calculation we should have reached about the middle of the sewer, when I happened to strike my foot against a piece of board lying in the water, which was just long enough to be squeezed between the walls of the sewer so that it served us as a sort of bench to sit upon. Upon this bench, which made our condition a little more comfortable, we huddled together for a longer rest.

Until then the constant movement to which we had been compelled had hardly permitted us to survey our situation. Now, sitting on the bench, we had leisure enough to collect our thoughts and to hold council as to what was further to be done. During the siege I had had frequent opportunity to observe the immediate surroundings of the fortress, and I therefore pretty well knew the ground on which the sewer emptied outside. I proposed to my companions that we should remain on the bench until about midnight, then leave the sewer, and seek cover in a field planted with corn, which I knew to be in the neighborhood. From there we could, if the sky was tolerably clear, overlook a little part of the road to Steinmauern, a village distant about an hour's walk from Rastatt, on the bank of the Rhine, and assure ourselves whether we might leave the protection of the cornfield without danger. And so, seeking cover from time to time in order to reconnoiter the road ahead of us, we might hope before daybreak to reach Steinmauern and there to find a boat that might carry us to the French side of the river. This plan was approved by my companions.

While we were thus engaged in taking counsel, we heard above us a dull, rumbling noise as from the wheels of vehicles and the heavy tread of great masses of men, from which we concluded that the Prussians were now entering the fortress and occupying the gates and the ramparts. We also heard the striking of a church clock which gave the hour, our bench being near one of the manholes, so that the sounds of the upper world reached us without much difficulty. About nine o'clock in the evening it began to rain so heavily that we could clearly hear the splashing of the water as it poured down. At first it seemed to us that the bad weather would be favorable to our plan of escape. But before long the matter appeared in a different light. We felt that the water was rising in our sewer, and soon it began to shoot through it with great vehemence like a mountain stream. After a while it flooded the bench upon which we were sitting and reached up to our chests. We also perceived living creatures which suddenly, with great activity, rushed and crawled around us. They were undoubtedly rats. "We have to get out," I said to my companions, "or we shall be drowned." We left our bench and pushed forward. I had hardly advanced a few steps when in the darkness I ran my head against a hard object. I touched it with my hands and discovered that the obstacle was an iron railing. At once the thought came to me that this railing had been put there for the purpose of cutting off, in time of siege, communication through the sewer between the interior of the town and the outside. This thought, which I communicated at once to my companions, brought us almost to despair. But when I grasped the railing with both hands, as a prisoner may sometimes shake the iron rods of his dungeon window, I noticed that it could be moved a little, and a further examination proved that it did not reach quite down to the bottom, but left a free space of about two feet. It was probably so arranged that it could be pulled up or let down, so that the sewer might be opened for purposes of cleaning and then shut again. Fortunately, nobody had, during the seige, known anything of this railing, and thus the possibility of escape still remained open to us.

Now, in order to slip through the low aperture under it we were obliged to crawl with our whole bodies through the water; but that circumstance, although disagreeable, did not disturb us. We pushed vigorously on, and when we believed ourselves to be near the outward opening of the sewer, we stopped a minute to gather strength and presence of mind for the dangerous moment of our issuing forth from our concealment.

Then a terrible sound struck our ears. Close ahead of us, distant only a few paces, we heard a voice call, "Who goes there?" and at once another voice answered, "Good friend." We stood still as if struck by lightning. In a short time we heard the same calls repeat themselves at a somewhat greater distance, and again and again. It was clear that we were close to the opening of the sewer, that outside there was a dense chain of Prussian guard posts, and that just then a patrol or round had been passing along that chain. Softly I ventured a step or two further on. Really, there was the mouth of the sewer overgrown with brush so thick that I stood in darkness almost as dense as was that in the interior of the canal. But when I raised myself up a little I could distinctly perceive the dark figures of a Prussian double sentinel immediately before me, as well as some camp fires at a short distance. Had we been able to get into the open without being noticed, which seemed almost impossible, still the road to Steinmauern was evidently closed to us.

Softly as we had come we crawled back into our sewer and sought safety there, at least for the moment. Fortunately the rain had ceased. The water was, indeed, still high, but it did not rise any more. "Back to our bench," I whispered to my companions. We crawled again under the railing and found our bit of plank. There we sat close together. Our next council of war had a certain solemnity about it. There were few words, but a good deal of thinking. It was clear, we could not venture into the open. To remain a longer time in the sewer was not to be thought of, because there was the danger that if it rained again we might be drowned. There was therefore nothing to be done but to go back into the town. But how could we go back into the town without falling into the hands of the Prussians? After we had exchanged these thoughts in a whisper, a long pause followed. At last I interrupted the silence, saying, "Let us eat and drink a little; good counsel may come then." Adam unpacked our provisions, and as we had eaten nothing since breakfast time of the preceding day— midnight was now long past—hunger and thirst were keen. Our bread was, indeed, quite wet, but it tasted good; also the sausages. We remembered, in time, that we must not consume our whole store, for we did not know when and where we should get the next meal. Moreover, we were more troubled by thirst than by hunger, as is always the case under such circumstances. For nearly twelve hours our feet had been in the water, and were therefore as cold as ice. This had driven the blood to our heads. Adam now opened one of the two bottles which he had bought for us, and we discovered that they contained rum instead of wine. Although rum had always been repugnant to me, still I drank like my companions, in eager draughts, and my brain remained entirely clear in spite of it.

After we had finished our meal Adam took the floor. "I have a widowed cousin in the town," he said. "Her house is not far from the entrance to the sewer. To reach it we have only to go through a kitchen garden or two. We might hide ourselves there in the barn until we find something better."

This proposition had our approval, and we resolved to make the attempt. At the same moment something occurred to me that was depressing in the extreme. I remembered that during the siege our garrison had a sentinel close to the entrance of the sewer. If this post was occupied by the Prussians too, then we sat in the sewer between two Prussian guards. I communicated my apprehension to my companions. But what was to be done? Possibly the Prussians had not occupied that post. Perhaps we might slip by. In any case, nothing else remained to us than to make the attempt.

When we left our bench to begin our retreat, we heard the church clock outside strike three. I went ahead and soon reached the last manhole. I availed myself of the opportunity to stretch myself out a little, when something happened that at the first moment appeared very unfortunate. I had used my short carbine in moving through the canal in a bent position, as a sort of crutch. When I lifted myself up the carbine fell from my arm into the water and caused a loud splash. "Hello!" cried a voice just above me. "Hello! There is something in this hole; come here." At the same moment a bayonet descended like a probe through the grating which covered the manhole. I heard it strike against the iron rods in time to duck myself and thus avoid being touched by it. "Now out quickly!" I whispered to my companions, "or we are lost." With a few hasty paces we reached the end of the sewer. Without looking around we jumped over a hedge into the nearest kitchen garden, and gained, with a rapid run, a second hedge, which we cleared in the same way. Then we halted, breathless under cover of some shrubs, to listen whether anybody was following us. We heard nothing. It is probable that the falling of my carbine into the water attracted the attention of the guard post in the immediate vicinity, and diverted it from the mouth of the sewer. Thus our escape may have been facilitated by the accident, which at first seemed so unfortunate.

When Adam looked around from our halting place he found that we were close by the house of his cousin. We leaped another hedge which separated us from the kitchen garden belonging to that house, but there we were greeted by the loud barking of a dog. To pacify the animal we sacrificed the last remnant of our sausages. Finding the door of the barn open, we entered it, stretched ourselves out on a pile of hay, and soon fell into a profound sleep.

But this rest was not to last long. I awoke suddenly and heard the church clock strike six. Adam had already risen and said he would now go into the house to ask his cousin what she could do for us. After a few minutes he returned and the cousin with him. I still see her before me—a woman of about thirty years, with a pale face and wide-open, anxious eyes. "For God's sake," she said, "what are you doing here? You cannot remain. This morning some Prussian cavalrymen will be quartered here, and they will surely look in the barn for litter for their horses. Then they will find you and we shall all be lost."

"But be reasonable, cousin," said Adam; "where can we go now? You certainly will not deliver us up."

But the poor woman was beside herself with fear. "If you do not go," she replied, with decision, "I must tell the soldiers that you are here. You cannot expect me to sacrifice myself and my children for you."

There was more talk, but all in vain. We had no choice; we must leave the barn. But where to go? The woman showed us through the open door a ditch covered with high and thick shrubbery on the other side of the little yard, in which we might hide ourselves. Our situation became desperate. There we stood, all three in the military uniform of Baden, easily recognizable as the soldiers of the revolutionary army. Now we were to have no other refuge but some shrubbery covering a ditch in the midst of a town teeming with hostile troops! Of course, we hesitated to leave the barn, although it was a dangerous resting place for us, but at any rate it offered us a roof over our heads, and perhaps it might be possible to find in it some hiding corner. We still hoped that Adam's cousin would yield to our prayers. She went to the house, as she had to expect every moment the arrival of the cavalrymen. After about half an hour she came back and said the cavalrymen were there and were just sitting at their breakfast. Now was the moment for us to pass through the yard without being seen by them. She insisted on this with such determination that we had to submit. Then we ran across the yard to the ditch, which on the opposite side was separated from the street by a tall board fence. It again rained hard, and in the immediate vicinity nobody seemed to be stirring. Thus we could, with some assurance, explore our new refuge. We found that at the end of the ditch cord wood was heaped up in the form of a hollow square, open on the side toward us. We could slip through the brush into the square and were in that close space pretty well protected from the eyes of the passerby. There we sat down on blocks of wood.

But what was to become of us now? The discomfort of our miserable situation, as well as our sitting there wet to the skin, we might easily have borne had we had the slightest prospect of escape. My faithful Adam, otherwise so good-natured, was much wrought up over the conduct of his cousin. Neustädter regarded our situation as hopeless, and asked whether it was not better to put an end to our distress by a voluntary surrender to the soldiers in the house. I must confess that my sanguine temperament, too, was severely tested. Still I gathered up courage, and we then resolved to trust to luck. So we sat there hour after hour waiting for something to turn up, with the heavy rain mercilessly streaming down on us, pictures of misery. About noon we heard steps in the garden near our place of concealment. Cautiously I looked out from the open side of our cord wood square, and perceived coming from the house a man with a saw in his hand. According to his looks and the tool he carried I concluded he must be a laborer, and as the laboring men throughout were in favor of the revolutionary cause, I did not hesitate to confide myself to him. I threw a little chip of wood at the man, which hit him on the arm, and as he stood still I attracted his attention by a low cough. He saw me and came to us. With as few words as possible I explained to him our situation, and begged him to find us a place of safety, and also to procure for us something to eat, as our last morsel was gone. My confidence was not misplaced. He promised to do what was possible. Then he left, but returned in half an hour, and showed us near by a large open shed. At the end of that shed there was a little closed compartment in which the laborers probably deposited their tools, and on top of this, under the roof of the shed, a small loft enclosed in boards. "I will break loose one of these boards," said our man. "You can then climb over the cord wood and slip under the roof of the loft and lie down there. I will soon come back and bring you something to eat."

We followed his advice, and succeeded in slipping into the little loft without being observed. The space we occupied was just large enough to permit us to lie side by side on our backs. We lay in a white dust, inches thick, which was, in view of the wet condition of our clothing, extremely disagreeable. But at least we felt secure for the time being. It was about one o'clock of the afternoon when we crawled into our new asylum. We waited quietly for our friend to bring us the necessary food, and would then consult with him about a plan of escape. But we heard the church clock strike two, three, and four, and our man did not return. Shortly after four o'clock a lively noise arose in the shed below. From the talk and the shouting and the rumbling we heard we concluded that a troop of cavalrymen must have arrived, and that they were now occupied in putting the shed in order for their horses. The horses came soon, and on all sides soldiers swarmed around us. Through the chinks of the wooden wall of our loft we could easily see them. Our situation became extremely critical. If it had occurred to one of those soldiers to investigate the compartment and to look into the loft, it would have been all over with us. Any kind of noise, a cough or a sneeze, would have betrayed us. We took the utmost pains to breathe softly, and longed for the night. The night came and we were still undiscovered, but the man on whose assistance we had counted had not yet shown himself.

We began to be very hungry and thirsty, and had neither a bit of bread nor a drop of water. What was left of our rum had been lost on the hasty run from the sewer to the house. Now we lay still like corpses. Gradually it became more quiet in the shed; soon we heard heavy snoring, and from time to time somebody moving around, probably to look after the horses. We were afraid to sleep ourselves, although very much exhausted.

At last I had an idea. When, during the third night, we heard the soldiers below snoring vigorously, I whispered to my neighbor, Neustädter, holding my mouth close to his ear, "Did you not, as we clambered over the cord wood, notice a little house about fifty paces from here?"

"Yes," said Neustädter.

"There must be a poor man living there," I continued, "probably a laborer. One of us must go to him and see whether he cannot help us. I should be glad to go myself, but I would have to clamber over you [Neustädter lay nearest to the opening in the board wall], and that might make a noise. You are, anyhow, the lightest of us. Will you try?"

"Yes."

I had a little money, for immediately before the capitulation we had received our soldiers' pay.

"Take my purse," I whispered, "and give to the man who lives in the little house ten florins, or as much as he asks. Tell him to bring us some bread and wine, or water, and to inform himself as soon as possible whether or not the Prussian guard posts are still standing outside of the fortress. If those posts have been drawn in, we can try tomorrow night again to get through the sewer. Now go and bring us a piece of bread if you can."

"Good," said Neustädter.

In a minute, lightly and softly like a cat, he had slipped through the hole in the board wall. My heart beat fast while he was gone. A false step, an accidental noise, would betray him. But in less than half an hour he came back just as lightly and softly as before, and lay down by my side.

"It is all right," he whispered; "here is a piece of bread, all he had in the house, and also an apple that in passing by I picked from a tree, but I am afraid it is still green."

The bread and the apple were soon divided among us, and devoured with avidity; and then Neustädter reported with his mouth to my ear, that he found in the little house a man and his wife. The man, to whom he had given the ten gulden, had promised to bring us some food, and also the desired information about the condition of things outside of the fortress.

This refreshed our spirits, and, much relieved, we slept alternately until high morning. Now we expected with every moment our rescuer, but one hour after another passed and he did not come. Were we again to be disappointed? At last, about noon, we heard somebody in the compartment immediately below us noisily moving things from one place to another; then a low cough. The next moment a head appeared in the opening of our board wall, and a man climbed up to us. It was our new friend. He brought a basket apparently filled with tools, but out of the depth of which he took two bottles of wine, a couple of sausages and a large loaf of bread.

"This is something for hunger and thirst," our friend whispered. "I have been also all around the city. The Prussian guard posts are no longer outside. I shall be glad to help you; only tell me what I am to do."

I now asked him to go to Steinmauern and look for a boat which in the coming night might take us across the Rhine. Then, about midnight, to be in the cornfield near the Steinmauern gate, outside of the fortress, and wait for us. He would hear the signal of a whistle; this he should answer, and then join us in order to take us to the boat. He should ask his wife to have something for us to eat at about eleven o'clock of the night.

I gave him a little more money, and he promised to do all I had asked, and disappeared again as he had come. Now we held a royal feast, during which our good humor made it very difficult for us to preserve the necessary silence. All the longer appeared to us the ensuing hours that were so full of hope and at the same time of anxiety.

Now we counted the minutes as the decisive moment approached. When it struck eleven Neustädter slipped out of the opening in the plank wall, stepped upon the pile of wood, and jumped lightly to the ground. I followed him. My legs had become very stiff in conse-quence of my lying for days and nights immovable on my back, and as I put my foot upon the wood several sticks fell down with a great noise. A moment later I heard not far away the tread of a patrol. I only had time to whisper back to my faithful Adam that he should remain until the patrol should have passed, and then follow me. I succeeded in reaching the little house before the patrol turned the corner of the lane. Neustädter was already there, and Adam came a a few minutes later.

"The patrol passed quietly by," said he, "and they snored so loud in the shed that any other noise would hardly have been heard."

The wife of our friend in the little house had prepared a precious repast of beef broth, with rice, for us. After this and a dish of boiled meat and roast potatoes had refreshed our strength, we set out through the garden for the sewer. The moon was shining brightly, and we kept cautiously in the shadows of the hedges. But when we arrived at the ditch close by the mouth of the sewer a new fright awaited us. A sentinel was pacing to and fro just beyond the sewer, hardly thirty feet away from it. We halted and stooped under the hedge. There was but one thing to do. As the man turned his back upon us and walked to the other side, one of us was to slip cautiously into the sewer. The two others had to do the same. In a few minutes we were re-assembled in the darkness of our refuge. We crawled ahead and found our old bench again, where we rested a while. Then pursuing our way we found the railing in its old place, dipped under it, and soon perceived a gleam of light through a mass of dark leaves, which suggested that the opening was immediately before us. We stood still once more to make our pistols ready for action. Whether after having been so wet, they would have gone off is very questionable. After all we had suffered, we were now determined to do our utmost. But the field was clear, the chain of guards had disappeared. The corn-field lay immediately before us. A low whistle on our part was promptly answered, and our man joined us a moment later.

He reported that the road was free. We marched vigorously on and in less than an hour we reached the village of Steinmauern. Our friend conducted us to the bank of the Rhine and showed us a boat in which a man lay fast asleep. He was quickly roused, and our friend announced to him that we were the men he was to take across the Rhine. "That will cost five florins," growled the boatman, who, upon my question as to what countryman he was, told me he came from Coblenz. I gave him the reward asked for, and offered also some more money to our kind friend. "You have given me already enough," he said; "what you still have you will be very much in need of. My name is Augustin Loeffler. Perhaps we may meet again in this world. God protect you."

Then we shook hands most cordially and parted. We fugitives stepped into the boat, and our friend wandered back to Rastatt. Many years later, when I was Secretary of the Interior in the government of the United States, I received one day a letter from Augustin Loeffler. It was dated at a little place in Canada. He wrote me that he had left Germany a short time after the revolutionary period, and was doing very well in his new home. He had read in the newspapers that I was one of the three young men who in that July night, 1849, had been conducted by him from Rastatt to the Rhine. In answer I expressed my joy at the receipt of his letter, and requested him to write again, but I have heard nothing from him since.

In an unexpectedly short time the boatman put us ashore in a dense growth of willows. It was between two and three o'clock in the morning, and as the surroundings seemed to be rather uninviting, we resolved to sit down upon old stumps of trees and there to await the light of day. At daybreak we arose to look for the nearest Alsatian village; but soon we discovered that we were on an island. A little house which stood in the middle of the island seemed to be the abode of a frontier guard of the grand duchy of Baden. So it looked as if we were still in the enemy's country, and as if the boatman from Coblenz had deceived us. The shutters and the doors of the little house were closed. We listened, but heard no sounds inside. A rapid run over the island convinced us that, excepting us three, there was no human being on it. We went to the water's edge opposite Alsatia, and in the rising sunlight saw on the other side two men whom we soon recognized to be French customs officers. We called out to them across the water that we were fugitives and desired to be taken over. One of the men came over to us in a little skiff and took us across to Alsatian soil. We gave up our arms to him and assured him and his comrade, amid great laughter, that we had brought with us from Rastatt nothing else subject to tariff duty. When I felt myself now really in freedom and security, my first impulse was, after a silence of four days, to shout as loudly as I could. My companions had the same feeling, and so we burst forth to our hearts' content, watched with great astonishment by the French officers, who may have taken us for madmen. We had landed near a little village called Münchhausen. The officers told us that in the town of Selz, near by there were many German fugitives, and to Selz therefore we went. On the way we gazed at one another in the clear sunlight, and discovered that we looked like savages. For days and nights we had waded or squatted in wet clothes in water, mud and dust. Our hair was matted and our faces were streaked with dirt. A near rivulet furnished us the indescribable luxury of a washing, and thus restored to human shape, we soon reached the inn at Selz.

The refugees there from Baden, none of whom had been in Rastatt, welcomed us heartily, and asked us at once for the story of our adventures. But our first wish was for a hot bath, a breakfast, and a bed. All this we obtained. I slept twenty-four hours with slight interruptions. Then I acquainted the company of refugees in the inn with the circumstances of our escape from Rastatt. From them I learned also for the first time that Kinkel had been captured by the Prussians in a fight near the fortress, before the beginning of the siege. When we left the Palatinate and he could no longer make himself useful in the offices of the provisional government, he had joined a battalion of volunteers and shouldered his musket as a private soldier. Thus he would share the lot of the revolutionary army. In the fight on the line of the Murg River he was wounded in the head and fell into the hands of the attacking Prussians. He was then incarcerated in one of the casemates at Rastatt, together with the captured garrison, in order to have him tried by court-martial, which would, no doubt, order him to be shot. This news threw a black veil over my joy at my own recovered freedom.

On the day after our arrival in Selz a police officer appeared at the inn, by the authority of the mayor, to learn our names, and also whether we expected to remain, or, if not, where we intended to go. "We want to go to Strasburg," I answered haphazard. The mayor gave us thereupon a sort of passport, with the instruction that we should report ourselves at once in Strasburg to the prefect. The depressing seriousness came over me that I was now really a homeless man, a fugitive, and under police surveillance. After having written to my parents and described to them my escape, we started for Strasburg without further delay. The real goal, however, of my journey was Switzerland, where, as I learned, Anneke and many others of my friends might be found.

If I had remained only a few days longer in Selz I should have seen my father in the same inn in which I had slept my first night in freedom. The mischance happened in this wise: The letter I had written to my parents on the day of the surrender at Rastatt, in the expectation that I would be taken prisoner together with the rest of the garrison, struck them like a clap of thunder, and at once my father set out to look for his son. Arrived in Rastatt, he reported himself at the office of the Prussian commander, to learn something about my fate. The commander received him kindly, but on inquiry could not give him any further information than that my name was not on the list of the captives. This surprised my father very much, and he requested permission to visit the casemates in which the prisoners were kept. This permission he received, and an officer accompanied him on this anxious search. From casemate to casemate they went three days long, and of one man after another they inquired about me, but all in vain. Many of those they saw knew me, but nobody knew what had become of me. Nobody had seen me on the occasion of the surrender. My father found Kinkel among the crowd. "What," Kinkel cried, "is Carl here, too? Alas, I believed him to be secure in Switzerland!"

In speechless grief the two men pressed each other's hand.

When my father had thus many days looked for me in vain, a ray of hope dawned upon him that after all I might have escaped. From citizens in Rastatt he learned that there were several refugees from Baden on the other side of the Rhine in Selz. Possibly one of these might be able to give him tidings about me. A few hours later my father appeared at the inn in Selz, and there he inscribed his name. Then he learned the whole story of my flight, and how only a few days before I had been in Selz and was now gone to Strasburg, with the intention of traveling further, nobody knew where, probably to Switzerland. My father burst into tears of joy, and exclaimed again and again, "That boy! That boy! Now I must quickly go home to tell his mother." As he could hardly hope still to find me in Strasburg, and expected to hear from me before long, he returned without delay to Bonn. One of the refugees from Baden, who had seen my father in the inn at Selz, and who had given him the happy news about me, told me all this a month later in Switzerland, and he could hardly master his emotion when he described to me my father's joy.

CHAPTER IV

My Life as a Refugee

EVENTUALLY I reached the house of a baker's widow, in the Dorf Enge, a suburb of Zürich. My friend Strodtmann found quarters in a neighboring inn. My other friends lived in the house of the schoolmaster. All this was very convenient and comfortable, although extremely simple. While Strodtmann was with me my thoughts moved in the atmosphere of the old conditions and surroundings, and my sojourn in Zürich appeared almost like part of a student's jaunt. But ten days later my dear good friend returned to Bonn, and what now began for me was the life of a refugee in its true reality. I had not become quite conscious of it all when I developed a violent fever which kept me in bed two weeks. The village physician, as well as the baker's widow and her daughter, took care of me, and after a time I fully recovered. But when I rose from my bed I found myself in a strange world. It came over me that I had absolutely nothing to do. My first impulse was to look for a regular occupation. But soon I convinced myself that a young man like myself, who might have given lessons in Latin, Greek or music, had little to hope for in a population which, although it had hospitably received a great mass of fugitives, did, after all, not like them much. The other refugees were in the same condition, but many of them looked down upon such endeavors with a certain contempt, so long, at least, as their pecuniary resources were not exhausted. They firmly believed that a new upheaval would occur in the old Fatherland before long. Nobody cultivates the art of deceiving himself with the windiest illusions more cleverly, more systematically and more untiringly than the political refugee. We succeeded easily in finding in newspapers some news that clearly indicated to us the inevitable and fast-approaching outbreak of a new revolution. We were certain that we would soon return triumphantly to Germany, there to be the heroes of the day, the true champions of a victorious cause. Why should we therefore trouble ourselves with cares for the future? It appeared to us much more important and appropriate to discuss and determine the part each should play in the coming action. With the profoundest seriousness we debated the question who should be a member of the provisional government, or minister, or military leader.

When winter came my lodgings in the house of the good baker's widow became uncomfortable on account of the cold. Then I took, with a companion in the Palatinate revolution, an old Prussian head forester by the name of Emmermann, two cosy rooms in the house of a merchant on the Schanzengraben. My chum had the typical face of an old forester, weather-beaten, illumined by keen eyes, furrowed with a network of deep wrinkles, and ornamented with a gigantic gray mustache. He was an old bachelor, an amiable, benevolent soul, and we lived together in cheerful peace and friendship. He told me often that his forest-house had been situated in the neighborhood of a place called Tronegg, which had been in the immemorial past the seat of the gloomy hero of the Nibelungen Lied, Hagen von Tronje.

Thus I lived in agreeable domestic conditions and continued diligently my military and historical studies. Although I avoided the tavern as much as possible, I did not keep entirely aloof from intercourse with a larger circle of refugees. We had a political club that met once a week, and in the transactions of which I took an interested part. This club was in correspondence with democratic friends in the Fatherland, informed itself about the state of the public mind and about everything that could be considered symptomatic of the coming new revolution, and endeavored to put in its own work here and there—an activity of which I learned only some time later how utterly illusory it was. From time to time it occurred to me that the revolution might delay its coming much longer than we believed, and I began to make plans for my own future. There was a rumor that the federal government of Switzerland intended to found a great university at Zürich. I thought if the new German revolution kept us waiting all too long, I might establish myself at the university as a "Privat-Docent" of history, and then win for myself by-and-by a regular professorship. For the time being I gladly accepted the proposition of my friend, Dr. Hermann Becker, dubbed the "red Becker" at the university, to write articles for the newspaper edited by him in Cologne, the remuneration for which was sufficient to keep me above water until something better could be found. Thus

I believed to perceive some bright spots in the fogs of the future.

My most remarkable acquaintance of those days was Richard Wagner, who, in consequence of his participation in the revolutionary uprising in Dresden, had been obliged to leave Germany, and now lived as one of the refugees in Zürich. He had then already written some of his most important creations, but his greatness was appreciated only by a very small circle of friends. Among the refugees at Zürich he was by no means popular. He passed for an extremely arrogant, domineering character, with whom nobody could long associate, and who treated his wife, the first one—a stately, good-natured, but mentally not highly gifted woman—very neglectfully. If anyone among us had then prophesied his magnificent career he would have found little credence. As an insignificant and reticent young man, of course, I did not come close to him. Although I met him and spoke with him occasionally, he probably never noticed me sufficiently to remember me.

In the course of time I should probably have succeeded in obtaining some position as teacher, if not at the university, at least at some other minor institution, had not my life of quiet study been interrupted by an event that was destined to turn it into very different channels. The unhappy lot of my friend, Professor Kinkel, was constantly in my mind, all the more as it had taken an unexpected and particularly shocking turn. After having been wounded in the head and taken prisoner by the Prussians, Kinkel was carried first to Karlsruhe, and then after the surrender of Rastatt, to that fortress, where he was to be tried by a court-martial. On the 4th of August Kinkel appeared before that tribunal, which was composed of Prussian officers. Sentences of death were at that time the order of the day. And there is no doubt that, at army headquarters as well as at the seat of the Prussian government, Kinkel's condemnation was desired and expected. But Kinkel conducted his defense himself, and even the warriors composing the court-martial, men educated in the strictest allegiance to royal absolutism, could not resist the charm of his wonderful eloquence. Instead of condemning him to death, they sentenced him to confinement for life in a fortress.

To Kinkel's friends, to the admirers of the poet, I may say, to a large majority of the German people, this sentence appeared cruel enough. But the Prussian government at once manifested its dissatisfaction with it, for the reason that it was too mild. A rumor arose that the verdict would be set aside on account of some neglected formalities, and that Kinkel was to be put before a new court-martial.

For weeks the poor prisoner, with alternate hope and fear, looked forward to the confirmation or rejection of the sentence, until at last, on the 30th of September, the following public announcement appeared:

"Warning. The late professor and member of a free corps, Johann Gottfried Kinkel of Bonn, having fought among the insurgents in Baden with arms in his hands against Prussian troops, has been sentenced by the court-martial instituted at Rastatt to lose the Prussian cockade and instead of the penalty of death only to confinement for life in a fortress. For examination of the legality of this sentence, it was submitted by me to the royal auditor-general, and by him to his Majesty, the king, for rejection on account of illegality. His majesty has graciously deigned to affirm the sentence, with the qualification that Kinkel shall undergo imprisonment in a civil penitentiary. According to this most high order, I affirm the verdict of the court-martial, to the effect that Kinkel is to be punished on account of treason with the loss of the Prussian cockade and with imprisonment for life, and that in execution of this sentence he shall be taken to a house of penal servitude; all of which is herewith brought to public knowledge.

"Headquarters, Freiburg, 30 September, 1849.
"The Commanding General von Hirschfeld."

Kinkel was first taken to the prison at Bruchsal in Baden, and soon afterwards to the penitentiary at Naugard in Pomerania. It was evidently intended to remove him as far as possible from the Rhineland, where sympathy for him was warmest. With shorn head, clothed in a gray prison jacket, he spent his days in spinning wool. On Sundays he had to sweep his cell. He was denied, so far as possible, all mental activity. His diet was that of the criminal in the penitentiary. From the day of his arrival in Naugard, October 8, 1849, until April, 1850, he received altogether only one pound of meat. But he moved the heart of the director of the penitentiary, and his treatment assumed gradually a more considerate character, a few small favors being granted to him. He was permitted more frequent correspondence with his wife, his letters being opened and read, however, by the officers; and he was relieved of the task of cleaning his cell. A little gift of sweetmeats, which his family sent at Christmas-time, was delivered to him. But he was still obliged to spin wool; and when our good Strodtmann, at that time a student in Bonn, appealed to the popular heart in Kinkel's behalf, in a poem called the "Spinning Song," the young poet was promptly dismissed from the university.

In the meantime the preparations for the trial of those who had taken part in the attack upon the Siegburg armory in May, 1849, went on in Cologne, and early in the year 1850 there was a rumor that the government intended to transport Kinkel from Naugard to Cologne in the spring, for the purpose of having him also tried for that revolutionary attack.

In February, 1850, I received a letter from Kinkel's wife. In burning colors she described to me the terrible situation of her husband and the distress of the family. But this high-spirited and energetic woman did not speak to me in the tone of that impotent despair which pusillanimously submits to an overpowering fate. The thought that it must be possible to find ways and means for the liberation of her husband gave her no rest day and night. For months she had been corresponding with friends in whose character she had confidence and whose energy she hoped to excite. Some of them had discussed with her plans for the rescue of her husband, and others had put sums of money at her disposal. But, so she wrote, nobody had shown himself ready to undertake the dangerous enterprise himself. What was needed, she said, was a friend who had sufficient tenacity of purpose, and who would devote his whole strength to the work until it should have succeeded. She herself would make the attempt did she not fear that her appearance in the vicinity of her husband's prison would at once excite suspicion and stimulate the watchfulness of his keepers. But it was necessary to act promptly, before the gnawing tortures of prison life should have completely destroyed Kinkel's mental and bodily strength. Then she informed me that Kinkel, according to rumor, would be taken to Cologne for trial on account of the Siegburg affair, and that there might then possibly be a favorable opportunity for his deliverance. She asked now for my advice, as she confided in my friendship as well as in my knowledge of the situation.

The night after the arrival of this letter I slept but little. Between the lines I could read the question whether I would not be the one to undertake the venture. It was this question that kept me awake. The spectacle of Kinkel in his prison jacket at the spinning-wheel was constantly before my eyes, and I could hardly endure the sight. I loved Kinkel dearly. I believed also that with his great gifts, his enthusiasm and his rare eloquence, he might still do great service to the cause of the German people. The desire to restore him if I could to Germany and to his family became irresistible. I resolved that night to try and make the attempt.

The next morning I began to consider the matter in detail. I remember that morning very clearly. Two doubts troubled me much. The one was whether I would be capable of carrying so difficult an undertaking to a happy end. I said to myself that Frau Kinkel, who after all had most to win and most to lose, seemed to believe me capable, and that it was not becoming in me to put my ability in doubt in the face of her confidence. But would those whose coöperation in so dangerous a risk was necessary give their confidence to so young a man as I was? I might perhaps gain it by a bold attitude. I cheered myself with the thought that as a young, insignificant and little known person I might better succeed in remaining unnoticed than would an older and more widely known man, and that therefore I might trust myself with less danger in the jaws of the lion. Finally, would older, more experienced, and more careful men be willing to do and dare all that might be required for the purpose of the task? Perhaps not. In short, this was, all things considered, a piece of work for a young man, and my youth appeared to me at last rather in the light of an advantage than of a hindrance.

My second doubt touched my parents. Could I with regard to them take the responsibility, after having just escaped from a terrible catastrophe, to put my life and freedom again in such jeopardy? Would they approve? One thing was clear: I must not in this case ask my parents for their permission, for I would then have to correspond with them about my project, and such a correspondence, subject to all possible chances of detection, might thwart the whole plan. No; in order to succeed, the undertaking must remain a profound secret, of which only those engaged in it were to have knowledge, and even then, if possible, only in part. To my family I could not confide it, for a conversation among them, accidentally overheard by others, might betray it. Therefore the question as to the approval of my parents I must answer myself, and I answered it quickly. They were among Kinkel's warmest admirers and devoted to him in loyal friendship. They were also good patriots. My mother, I thought, would say: "Go and save our friend." And thus all my doubts were overcome.

On the same day I wrote to Frau Kinkel that in my opinion she would probably only aggravate the lot of her husband if she permitted an attempt to liberate him in Cologne on the occasion of the Seigburg trial, because then the authorities would doubtless take the most comprehensive precautions. She should hold her pecuniary means together without thinking of anything to be undertaken soon, and wait patiently and silently until she heard again from her friend.

My letter was so worded that she could understand it, while it would not betray my intentions if it fell into wrong hands. As she also was familiar with my handwriting, I signed with a different name and directed the address to a third person whom she had mentioned to me. I conceived at once the plan to get secretly to Bonn for the purpose of talking over with her further steps, instead of risking such communications to paper.

Without delay I began my preparations. I wrote to my cousin, Heribert Jüssen, in Lind, near Cologne, whose outward appearance corresponded in all essential points with mine, asking him to procure from the police a traveling passport in his name and to send it to me. A few days afterwards the passport was in my hands, and now I could like an ordinary unsuspected mortal travel without difficulty wherever I was not personally known. Then I gave the officers of our club to understand that I was ready as an emissary to visit various places in Germany for the purpose of organizing branch clubs and to put them into communication with our committee in Switzerland. This offer was received with great favor, and I obtained, together with minute instructions, a long list of persons in Germany who could be depended upon. Of course of my real plans I did not give the slightest intimation. All was ready for my departure, and as I went on a secret expedition as an emissary, my friends found it quite natural that about the middle of March I should suddenly and entirely unnoticed disappear from Zürich.

I traveled down the Moselle to Coblenz, where I passed a quiet day, intending to take the night mail coach to Bonn. In this I succeeded without trouble. As I approached my home, however, the journey became more precarious. At about two o'clock in the morning I arrived in Godesberg, where I decided to leave the coach. The remainder of the way to Bonn I did on foot. The house of my parents was outside of the city on the Coblenzer Strasse, and I reached it by three o'clock in the morning. By a fortunate accident I still possessed the latchkey which I had used as a student, and it opened the back door. In this way I got into the house and soon stood in the bedroom of my parents. Both were sleeping profoundly. After having sat for a while quietly on a chair until the light of dawn crept in through the windows I woke them up. Their surprise was indescribable.

Very fortunately it so happened that Frau Johanna Kinkel visited my parents that same morning, and I had opportunity for a confidential talk with her. I told her that I was ready to devote myself to the liberation of her husband if she would put the enterprise entirely into my hands, speak to nobody about it, and not ask me for more information than I might voluntarily give her. With touching enthusiasm she thanked me for my friendship and promised everything. After having agreed upon what was at the time to be done or to be left undone, I gave her a receipt for a magic ink which I had obtained in Zürich. It was simply a chemical solution, which, when used as ink, made no mark on the paper. A letter containing indifferent subject-matter was to be written over this in ordinary ink; the person receiving the letter then was to cover the paper, by means of a brush or sponge, with another chemical solution, which made what had been written in ordinary ink disappear. Thereupon the paper was to be warmed near a stove or a lamp to make the communication written with the magic ink become legible.

When I had seen Frau Kinkel my most important business in Bonn was finished and I could give myself for some days, or so long as I could hope to remain undiscovered, to the joy of living once more with my family. With some of my oldest student friends I came together in the rooms of one of them, and there I met also a young student of medicine, Abraham Jacobi. Jacobi was a zealous democrat who afterwards won in America a great name for himself as a physician and scientist—so great, indeed, that many years later, when he had become one of the most prominent physicians of America, this revolutionary exile was distinguished by the university of Berlin with a call to a professorship. His invaluable friendship I have enjoyed down to this moment, and hope to enjoy it to the last.

Before many days the number of my friends who had been informed of my presence was so large, and the danger that I might be betrayed by some accidental conversation between them became so great, that I thought it necessary to disappear. In response to my request my cousin, Heribert Jüssen, whose passport and name I bore, came to Bonn with his vehicle to take me during the night to Cologne. The parting from my parents and sisters was very sad, but after all they let me go in a comparatively cheerful state of mind. I left with them the same impression I had left with my friends in Switzerland —that I was exclusively engaged in business entrusted to me in Zürich. When I left Bonn nobody knew of my purpose except Frau Kinkel.

In Cologne I found quarters in the upper story of a restaurant which was kept by a zealous democrat. The secret of my presence in Cologne was communicated to my nearest friends and to many others with such unconcern that I thought it was time to leave. Therefore I took a night train by way of Brussels to Paris. My intentions with regard to Kinkel I had confided to nobody in Cologne. Becker knew no more than that I had gone to Paris for the purpose of putting myself into communication with the German refugees living there, to write some letters about the situation of things in the French capital for his newspaper, and that I perhaps would spend some time in historical studies. In fact, all I had in view was to sit still in a secure place until the trial of the Siegburg affair, with all its excitements, was over, and Kinkel had been transported back to Naugard or to some other penitentiary, so that I might find him fixed at a certain place, and there begin my venturesome work.

While I was in Paris the trial of the participants in the Siegburg affair took place in Cologne. At an early hour on the 10th day of April, Kinkel left the penitentiary at Naugard accompanied by three police officers and arrived in Cologne on the 13th. On the journey, which was made in great secrecy, he was permitted to wear an ordinary overcoat and a little black hat, but as soon as he arrived in the penitentiary in Cologne he had to don the penitentiary garb again. A few days later Frau Kinkel was permitted to see her husband in the prison, but only in the presence of the turnkeys. She took with her her six-year-old Gottfried, who did not recognize his father with his closely clipped hair, his drawn features, and his convict dress, until he heard his voice.

The public trial before a jury of burghers opened on the 29th of April. Ten persons were accused "of an attempt to upset the present constitution of the kingdom, to excite the citizens or inhabitants of the state to sedition, to arm themselves against the royal authority, and to bring about a civil war by arming the citizens or inhabitants of the state against one another, or by inciting them so to arm themselves." Of the defendants, four were present, six having fled the kingdom, of whom I was one.

The population of Cologne was in feverish excitement. The court house was surrounded by an immense multitude eager to see Kinkel and to manifest their sympathy for him, the captive defender of liberty, the poet condemned to the penitentiary. The authorities had taken the most extensive measures to prevent any possibility of his being liberated. The carriage in which Kinkel rode from the prison to the court house was surrounded by a strong force of cavalry with drawn sabers. The streets he passed through, as well as all the approaches to the court house, were bristling with bayonets. On the court house square stood two cannon with an ammunition wagon, and the artillerymen ready for action. When Kinkel appeared he was, in spite of all this, received by the assembled multitude with thundering cheers. He had again been put into ordinary citizen's dress. On the way he appeared stolid and impassive. The aspect and the acclaim of the people revived him. Boldly and proudly he lifted up his closely clipped head as he strode from the carriage between lines of soldiers into the hall of justice. There his wife had, early in the morning, secured a place which she continued to occupy every day throughout the trial. The public prosecutor moved in Kinkel's case the penalty of death. The testimony of the various witnesses brought out the facts of the case as they were generally known; the public prosecutor, as well as the attorneys of the defendants, pleaded their causes with coolness and skill. My friend and fellow-student, Ludwig Meyer, made a manly speech in his own defense, and at last, on the 2d of May, Kinkel himself asked to be heard.

"The sufferings I have to bear are so terrible," he declared, "that your verdict can have no added terrors for me. Beyond the measure of the punishment at first imposed upon me, the authorities have increased mine by the horrible solitude of the isolated cell, the desolate stillness, in which no trumpet call of the struggling outside world will penetrate, and no loving look of faithful friends. They have condemned a German poet and teacher who in more than one breast has lighted the flame of knowledge and beauty, they have condemned a heart full of sympathy slowly to die in soulless mechanical labor, in denial of all mental atmosphere. The murderer, the lowest, most hideous criminal, is permitted as soon as the word of grace and pardon has descended upon him to breathe the air of his Rhenish home, to drink the water of his beloved river. The fourteen days I have been here have taught me how much consolation there is in the air and light of the homeland. But I am kept in the far-away gloomy north, and not even behind the iron bars of my prison am I allowed to see the tears of my wife, to look into the bright eyes of my children. I do not ask for your commiseration, for however bloody this law may be you cannot make my lot more terrible than it is. The man whom the public prosecutor has insinuatingly dared to accuse of cowardice has in this last year looked death in its various forms into the eyes so often, so nearly, so calmly, that even the prospect of the guillotine can no longer shake him. I do not want your compassion, but I insist upon my right. My right I put upon your consciences, and because I know that you citizens, jurymen, will not deny this right to your Rhenish compatriot. Therefore I expect with quiet confidence from your lips the verdict of not guilty. I have spoken; now it is for you to judge!"

The impression produced by these words has been described to me by eyewitnesses. At first the audience listened in breathless silence, but before long the judges upon the bench, the jurors, the densely crowded citizens in the hall, the prosecuting attorney who had conducted the case, the police officers who watched the accused, the soldiers whose bayonets gleamed about the door, burst out in sobs and tears. It took several minutes after Kinkel concluded his speech before the presiding judge found his voice again. At last the case was given to the jury. The jury instantly returned a verdict of "Not guilty." Then a thundering cheer broke forth in the hall, which was taken up by the multitude outside and resounded in the streets far into the city. Frau Kinkel pressed through the crowd to her husband. A police officer ordered his subordinates who surrounded Kinkel to hold her back, but Kinkel, rising to his full height, cried out with a commanding voice, "Come, Johanna! Give your husband a kiss. Nobody shall forbid you." As if yielding to a higher power the police officers stepped back and made way for the wife, who threw herself into her husband's arms.

The other defendants were now free to go home; only Kinkel, still under the sentence imposed upon him by the court-martial in Baden, was again quickly surrounded by his guards, taken to the carriage amid the resounding acclamations of the people and the rolling of the drums of the soldiers, and carried back to the jail.

As was to be expected, the authorities had taken every possible measure to prevent an attempt to liberate Kinkel in Cologne. The government had meanwhile also resolved not to take him back to the penitentiary at Naugard, but to imprison him in Spandau, probably because in Naugard warm sympathies with the sufferer had manifested themselves. To mislead Kinkel's friends and to avoid all difficulties on the way, he was not, as generally expected by the public, transported by rail, but in a coach, accompanied by two police officers.

When the excitement caused by the trial in Cologne had subsided, and Kinkel, sitting quietly in the Spandau penitentiary, had temporarily ceased to occupy public attention in an extraordinary degree, I left Paris for Germany. At the beginning of August I returned to Cologne, where I had another meeting with Frau Kinkel. She reported that the sum collected for the liberation of her husband had grown considerably, and I rejoiced to hear that it was sufficient to justify the beginning of active work. We agreed that the money should be sent to a confidential person in Berlin from whom I might receive it according to my requirements. Frau Kinkel also told me that she had found a method to convey to Kinkel information in a manner not likely to excite suspicion, if anything were undertaken in his behalf. She had written to him about her musical studies and put into her letters long explanations about the word "fuge." Kinkel had made her understand by words which were unintelligible to the officers who reviewed his letters, that he appreciated the significance of the word "fuge," Latin, "fuga," English, "flight," and that he was anxious to correspond more with her upon that subject. Frau Kinkel promised me to be very circumspect with her letters and not to cause him any unnecessary excitement, also not to become impatient herself if she should hear from me but seldom. So we parted and I started for the field of my operations.

At the railroad station I found my friend Jacobi, who was on his way to Schleswig-Holstein, to offer his services as a physician to our struggling brethren. A part of the way we could journey together. This was an agreeable surprise, but a much less agreeable surprise was it when in the coupé in which we took seats we found ourselves directly opposite to Professor Lassen of the University of Bonn, who knew me. We were greatly startled. Professor Lassen looked at me with evident astonishment, but as Jacobi and I began to chat and laugh as other young men would have done with apparent unconcern, the good orientalist probably thought that he was mistaken and that I could not possibly be the malefactor whom I resembled in appearance. On the 11th of August I arrived at Berlin. My passport, bearing the name of my cousin, Heribert Jüssen, and fitting me admirably in the personal description, was in excellent order, as the passports of political offenders venturing upon dangerous ground usually are, and thus I had no difficulty in entering Berlin, the gates and railroad stations of which were supposed to be closely watched by an omniscient police bent upon arresting or turning away all suspicious characters. Without delay I looked up some student friends who had been with me members of the Burschenschaft Franconia at the University of Bonn, and they gave me a hearty welcome, although they were not a little astonished to see me suddenly turn up in Berlin. They were discreet enough not to ask me for what purpose I had come, and thus made it easy for me to keep my own secret. Two of them, who occupied a small apartment on the Markgrafen Strasse, invited me to share their quarters; and as I went out and in with my friends the police officers on that beat no doubt regarded me as one of the university students, a good many of whom lived in that neighborhood.

CHAPTER V

I Rescue Kinkel

IMMEDIATELY after my arrival in Berlin I put myself in communication with several persons, who had been designated to me as trustworthy by Frau Kinkel, and by my democratic friends. I spent some time in studying them carefully, as I could not confide the purpose of my presence in Berlin to anyone of whom I might not be convinced that he would be useful in its accomplishment. After this review I told my secret to one of them only, Dr. Falkenthal, a physician who practiced and lived the life of an old bachelor in the suburb of Moabit. Falkenthal had already been in correspondence with Frau Kinkel. He had an extended acquaintance in Spandau and conducted me there to an innkeeper by the name of Krüger, for whom he vouched as a thoroughly reliable and energetic man. Mr. Krüger occupied in Spandau a highly respected position. He had for several years served his town as a member of the common council; he conducted the best hotel; he was a man of some property, and was also generally liked on account of his honorable character and his amiable disposition. Although much older than myself, we gradually became true friends. I found in him not only qualities of heart and soul thoroughly sympathetic to me, but also clear judgment, great discretion, unflinching courage, and a noble, self-sacrificing devotion. He offered me his hotel as headquarters for my enterprise.

I preferred, however, not to live in Spandau, as the presence of a stranger in so small a town could not well remain a secret. To dwell in the great city of Berlin appeared to me much less dangerous, at least during the long time of preparation which my undertaking would probably require.

The first point to be considered was whether it would be feasible to liberate Kinkel by force. I soon convinced myself that there was no such possibility. The armed guard of the penitentiary itself consisted only of a handful of soldiers and the turnkeys on duty. It would therefore have been possible for a number of resolute men to storm the building. But it was situated in the center of a fortified town filled with soldiers, and the first signal of alarm would have attracted an overpowering force. Such a venture would therefore have been hopeless. On the other hand, we knew of cases in which prisoners, even more closely watched than Kinkel was, had escaped by breaking through barred windows and tunneling walls, and then being helped to a safe place by their friends. But this, too, seemed hardly possible in our case for several reasons, among which Kinkel's lack of skill in the use of his hands was not the least serious. In any event, it seemed prudent to try first whether or not one or the other of the officers of the penitentiary could be induced to help us. This sort of business was extremely repugnant to me. But what would I not do to save a dear friend, who had been so badly and cruelly treated, and a champion of liberty who might still be so useful to a great cause?

Krüger selected two young men, well known to him, who were in friendly intercourse with some of the officers to be taken into our confidence. Their names were Poritz and Leddihn, vigorous, strong, and true men. They agreed to bring to me the one of the penitentiary guards who, they believed, might be most easily persuaded. Thus they introduced to me in a little beerhouse, in which I had a room to myself, a turnkey who had been, like most of his colleagues, a non-commissioned officer in the army and was now supporting a large family upon a very small salary. Poritz and Leddihn had vouched to him for my good faith, and he listened quietly to what I had to say. I presented myself as a traveler for a business house, who was closely related to the Kinkel family. I described to him the misery of the wife and the children, and how anxious they were, lest with the poor convict fare he would gradually waste away in body and mind. Would it not be possible to smuggle into Kinkel's cell from time to time a bit of meat or a glass of wine to keep up in a measure his strength, until the king's grace would take pity on him?

The turnkey thought Kinkel's lot indeed very deplorable. It would be a good work to alleviate it a little—perhaps not impossible, but perilous. He would consider what might be done. At the close of our conversation I slipped a ten-thaler note into his hand with the request that he buy with it some nourishing food for Kinkel if he could transmit it to him without danger. I intimated that business affairs required me to leave Spandau, but that I would return in a few days, to hear what report he could give about the condition of the prisoner. He could be certain of my gratitude.

Thus we parted. Three days later I went again to Spandau and met the turnkey in the same way as before. He told me he had succeeded in handing to Kinkel a sausage and a little loaf of bread, and that he had found the prisoner in comparatively good condition. He was also willing to do still more. Of course I did not wish him to do so at his own expense, and therefore gave him a second ten-thaler note which I accompanied with the request that he deliver into Kinkel's hands a few words written on a slip of paper, and bring back to me from Kinkel a word in reply. This too he promised to do. I wrote down a few words without a signature, containing about the following: "Your friends are true to you. Keep up your courage." It was less important to me to inform Kinkel of my presence than to satisfy myself that the turnkey had really carried out my instructions, and whether I could go farther with him.

Again I left to return in a few days. In the same manner as before my man turned up and brought me my slip of paper, which bore a word of thanks in Kinkel's hand. The turnkey had evidently kept his promise, and had thereby taken a step which compromised him greatly. Now it appeared to me time to come to the point. Thus I told him that the thought had crossed my brain what a splendid deed it would be to deliver Kinkel entirely from his dreadful situation, and, that before returning to my home on the Rhine, I thought it my duty to ask him whether this thing could not be accomplished through his aid. The man started and at once exclaimed this would be impossible; with such an attempt he could and would have nothing to do.

The mere suggestion had evidently terrified him, and I saw clearly that he was not the man whom I needed. Now I had to get rid of him and assure myself at the same time of his silence. I expressed to him my regret at his unwillingness, and added, that if he, who had been represented to me as a compassionate and at the same time courageous man, thought such an attempt hopeless, I had to accept his opinion and abandon the idea. I would therefore without delay depart for my home and not return. Then I hinted to him something about a secret and mysterious power which, if it could not liberate Kinkel, might become very dangerous to those who betrayed him. I succeeded indeed in intimidating him to such a degree that he begged me most earnestly not to bear any ill-will against him. I assured him that if he would bury in silence all that had happened, he might expect me to remain his friend. He might count even upon my further gratitude if, also, after my departure he would continue to furnish Kinkel from time to time with some nourishment. This he promised to do with demonstrative earnestness. Then I handed him another ten-thaler note and took leave of him forever.

So my first attempt had failed. I remained quiet for some days until Krüger, Leddihn and Poritz, who in the meantime had been watching the penitentiary people very carefully, communicated to me their conviction that my man had not disclosed anything. Thereupon my Spandau friends brought to me another turnkey. I began with him in the same manner as with the first, and everything seemed to progress favorably until I put the question whether or not he was willing to lend his hand in an attempt to set Kinkel free. The second man showed no more courage than the first, whereupon I dismissed him. A third man was brought, but he seemed so frightened by the first word that I did not put the decisive question to him at all.

Now it appeared to me prudent to let the affair rest for a while, at least until we could be perfectly assured that the three disquieted souls in the penitentiary had preserved silence. My sojourn in Berlin, too, began to become uncomfortable to me. The number of friends who knew of my presence in the Prussian capital had grown a little too large, and I was confronted too often by the question why I was there and what were my intentions. I therefore requested one of my friends to bid good-bye to the others in my behalf. I had departed not to return. Where I went, nobody knew. In fact, I went for a week or two to Hamburg. There I met my friend Strodtmann and got into communication with some people of our way of thinking. But the most agreeable society could not hold me long. By the end of September I returned to my work, but I did not go back to Berlin, thinking it safer to live with my friend, Dr. Falkenthal, in the suburb of Moabit.

At Spandau I received the report that everything had remained quiet. In general my secret had been well kept. To my friends in Berlin I had disappeared into regions unknown. Only one of them, a law student, by the name of Dreyer, once accidentally ran against me in Moabit. He may have had a suspicion as to what my business was, but I could firmly count upon his discretion. At a later period many persons who were entire strangers to me have stated that they were at that time in confidential relations with me, but such statements were unfounded. Even Dr. Falkenthal and Krüger did not at that time know my true name. To them I was, as my passport indicated, Heribert Jüssen, and among Dr. Falkenthal's neighbors, who sometimes saw me,

I passed for a young physician assisting the doctor in his studies. To strengthen this impression I always carried a little kit of surgical instruments with me. From Moabit I made my nightly excursions as before.

After my return from Hamburg I did not at once succeed in finding among the penitentiary officials the man I wanted. A fourth was introduced to me, but he too would undertake nothing more than to smuggle into Kinkel's cell some eatables and perhaps a written communication. I began to entertain serious doubts as to whether the plan so far pursued could be successfully carried out, for the list of the turnkeys was nearly exhausted. Then suddenly and unexpectedly I found the helper whom I had so long looked for in vain. My Spandau friends made me acquainted with Officer Brune.

At the first moment of our meeting I received from him an impression very different from that which his colleagues had made upon me. He too had been a non-commissioned officer in the army; he too had wife and children and a miserable salary like the others. But in his bearing there was nothing of the servile humility so frequently found among subalterns. When I talked to him of Kinkel and of my desire to alleviate his misery at least a little by conveying to him additional fare, Brune's face expressed none of the pitiable embarrassment of the man who is vacillating between his sense of duty and a ten-thaler note. Brune stood firmly upright like a man who is not ashamed of what he is willing to do. He talked with astonishing frankness without waiting for the gradual advance of my suggestions.

"Certainly," he said, "I will help as much as I can. It is a shame and a disgrace that so learned and worthy a gentleman should sit here among common rogues in this penitentiary. I would gladly help him out myself, if I had not to take care of my wife and children."

His indignation at the treatment Kinkel had received appeared so honest, and the whole manner of the man expressed so much courage and self-respect that I thought I might come to the point with him without circumlocution. And thus I told him point-blank that if the support of his family was his greatest trouble, I would be able to overcome that difficulty. Assured of this, would he then, I asked, be willing to lend a hand to Kinkel's escape?

"If it can be done," he answered; "but you know it is a difficult and dangerous thing. I will consider whether and how it may be done. Give me three days' time to think it over."

"Good," I replied, "do think it over; to judge from your accent you are a Westphalian."

"Yes, born near Soest."

"Then we are near neighbors; I am a Rhinelander. In three days then."

Those were three long days which I passed in Dr. Falkenthal's quarters. I sought to soothe my impatience by reading Dumas' "Three Musketeers" and a large part of Lamartine's history of the Girondists. But the book would fall again and again into my lap and my thoughts roam abroad.

On the evening of the third day I went again to Spandau and a heavy burden fell from my heart at Brune's first word.

"I have thought it over," he said. "I think we can do it."

I had to restrain myself for joy. Brune explained how some night in the near future, when the watch in the upper story of the penitentiary would be his and a certain other officer would be in the lower story, he might possess himself of the necessary keys and conduct Kinkel to the gate of the building. The plan, as he laid it before me, the details of which I shall return to later, appeared feasible.

But not until the night from the 5th to the 6th of November would the night watches be as he would have them. This suited me, for I too wanted some time for necessary preparations.

Then I informed Brune what provision I would be able to make for his family. A sum of money was at my disposal which was contributed partly by German democrats, and partly by personal admirers of Kinkel. This enabled me to offer to Brune a decent compensation. Brune was content. The question whether it would be best to ship him and his family to America he rejected at once. Perhaps he hoped to remain undiscovered as a participant in our enterprise or he preferred, in case of discovery, to suffer his punishment and to keep his family in the Fatherland.

Thus we were agreed. Now the important preparations were taken in hand. Frau Kinkel had instructed me to call personally for the sum of money at my disposal at the residence of a lady in Berlin, a friend of hers who was a relative of the celebrated Felix Mendelssohn Bartholdy. It was in the dusk of evening that I arrived at this lady's house. I was received by a somewhat solemn footman to whom I gave my name Heribert Jüssen. He showed me into a large drawing-room, in which everything—furniture, pictures, books, musical instruments— breathed comfort and refinement. I had to wait a little while, and the contrast between my own wild business and these peaceable and elegant surroundings became very sensible to me. At last a lady clad in black entered, whose features I could just discern in the twilight. She was no longer young nor altogether beautiful. But her presence radiated a rare charm. In her hand she carried a large pocketbook.

"You bring me greetings from a Rhineland friend?" she said with one of those mellow voices that touch the soul like a benefaction.

"Yes, cordial greetings," I replied, "from a friend who asked me to beg you for a package of valuable papers which she had put into your hands for safe-keeping."

"I knew that you would come at about this time," the lady replied. "In this pocketbook you will find all. I do not know your plans, but they must be good. You have my warmest wishes; God protect and bless you." Then she reached out to me her slender hand with a warm pressure, and I felt, after having left her, that her blessing had already become a reality.

That money was a heavy care to me. Never had I borne any responsibility of this kind for the property of others. In order not to expose this precious treasure to any accident, I carried it constantly with me tightly sewed in the inside pocket of my waistcoat.

The difficult task which I had still to perform before the decisive hour consisted in arranging for means of transportation to a safe place of refuge. Where should we turn after the escape of the prisoner? The frontiers of Switzerland, Belgium and France were too far away. We could not venture upon so long a journey through a hostile country. Nothing remained, therefore, but to try to reach the seacoast somewhere in order to cross over to England. After due consideration I concluded that the government would certainly take all precautions to watch every outgoing vessel in the harbors of Bremen and Hamburg. It appeared therefore prudent to choose another seaport, and so I turned to Mecklenburg. We had an influential and true friend in Rostock in the eminent jurist and president of the house of delegates, Moritz Wiggers, with whom I had become personally acquainted at the democratic congress in Braunschweig. I might also hope to reach Rostock more quickly than any other port—for we could not trust ourselves to the railroads—and the journey to Rostock offered the advantage that if we left Spandau about midnight, we might hope to cross the Mecklenburg frontier and thus to be beyond the immediate pursuit by the Prussian police about daybreak. I had also on my list of reliable persons a very considerable number of Mecklenburgers to whom I could apply for assistance.

I now set out to travel along the road which I had resolved to take, in order to make the necessary arrangements as to relays of horses and carriages for the decisive night and the day following. Of course, we could use only private carriages with, if possible, the owners on the box. Until then I had succeeded in keeping my secret within a very narrow circle of participants. But now it was necessary to draw a larger number of persons into confidence, and thus the danger grew in proportion. What I feared most was not malicious treachery, but excessive and indiscreet zeal. Everywhere I was met with hearty cordiality, and this cordiality was not confined to persons of the same political belief.

Of this I had a surprising example. My democratic friends had designated as specially trustworthy and helpful a gentleman living in the interior of Mecklenburg who was not on my list. I visited him and was very kindly received. He also assured me without hesitation of his willing assistance in the arrangement for relays. Then our conversation turned upon politics, and to my indescribable astonishment, my new friend declared to me that he considered our democratic ideas as well meant but as vain phantasies. He became quite eloquent in setting forth his opinion that human society would appear most delightful and would also be most happy if it were as variegated and checkered as possible in its division into estates and classes and ranks and conditions and callings, with princes, knights, merchants, clergymen, tradesmen, peasants, each and all with different rights and duties. Even monasteries he would have preserved with their abbots and abbesses, monks and nuns. In short, of all phases of human civilization the Middle Ages seemed to him the most congenial. "You see," he added with a kindly smile, "I am what you would call a full-blooded reactionary, and I don't believe at all in your liberty and equality and that sort of thing. But that they have put Kinkel, a poet and a sage, into a penitentiary on account of his idealistic imaginings, that is a revolting scandal, and although I am a good conservative Mecklenburger, I am at all times ready to help Kinkel out."

So we parted in the warmest agreement. But after all I did not feel quite comfortable about my new friend, and I talked afterwards with my democratic associates in Mecklenburg of the curious speeches of this gentleman and of my anxiety about him. "Do not borrow any trouble on that score," was the answer. "He is indeed a very curious saint and talks amazing stuff. But when there is a good deed to be done, he is as true as gold." And so he proved to be.

After a journey of several days my relays were arranged, and I could hope that a drive of less than thirty hours would take us from Spandau to Rostock. There we might confide ourselves to our good friends until a vessel should be ready to take us across the sea. To carry us from Spandau to the first relay, Krüger applied to a well-to-do farmer in the neighborhood by the name of Hensel, who had fast horses and would be glad to put them and his carriage and himself as driver at our disposal.

On November 4 I took leave of Dr. Falkenthal. He was acquainted with my plans in general, but I had not thought it necessary to initiate him into all the details. So he did not know the exact night in which the attempt was to be made, and he was also discreet enough not to ask me about it. But in bidding me farewell, he gave me a brace of pistols, which might serve me in close quarters. When I arrived in Spandau on the evening of November 4, I had a conversation with Brune, in which we talked over the details of our scheme, in order to assure ourselves that nothing had been neglected. Everything seemed to be in order.

Our programme disposed of, Brune said: "There is one more thing of which I do not like to speak."

I listened with some surprise. "What is it?"

"You have my fullest confidence," Brune continued. "What you have promised to do for my family that you will honestly do—if you can."

"Certainly I can. I have the means in my possession."

"That is not what I mean," Brune objected. "If everything goes well to-morrow night, then I am as sure of the money as if I had it in my pocket. That I know. But maybe all will not go well. The thing is dangerous. Accident may have its play. Something can happen to you and to me too, in fact, to both of us. And what will then become of my family, my wife and my children?"

He was silent for a moment and so was I. "Now, what further?" I asked.

"Considering the matter calmly," Brune slowly answered, "you will see yourself that the money must be in the hands of my family before I risk my head."

"You tell me yourself that I must consider this thing," I said with some hesitation. "Let me do so and I shall give you my answer as soon as possible. In the meantime will you prepare everything according to our agreement?"

"You may depend upon it."

Then we wished each other good-night.

The hour I spent after this in the solitude of my room in Krüger's hotel, taking counsel with myself, I have never forgotten.

The money, according to my notions an enormous sum, had been confided to me for a specific purpose; should it be lost without having accomplished this purpose, then it was all over with Kinkel, for such a sum could hardly be raised for him a second time. My personal honor would also be lost, for I would then have upon me a suspicion of dishonesty or at least a reproach of guilty recklessness. And was it not really great recklessness to confide this trust fund, upon a mere promise, without further guarantee, to a man who after all was a stranger to me? What did I really know of Brune? Nothing but that his face and his utterances had made upon me a most favorable impression and that he was held in good repute by his acquaintances. And these acquaintances had told me that they would have brought Brune first to me had they not thought that a man like him would hardly consider such a proposition. Indeed, they had added, that if he did it, he might be absolutely trusted.

I reminded myself that the war in Schleswig-Holstein was still going on. In the Schleswig-Holstein army, I thought, I might enlist as a volunteer under an assumed name and seek my fate on the field of battle, should the enterprise in Spandau miscarry, and the money be lost, and I at the same time escape. My friends would then at least believe in my honesty. This was the reasoning that led me to the decision to hand over the money to Brune before the fulfillment of his promise. I had just formed this conclusion when Krüger knocked at my door and said that Poritz and Leddihn were below; was there still anything more they could do for me?

"Yes," I answered. "I would ask them to bring Brune to me once again in a quarter of an hour to the Heinrich Platz."

Brune came with my friends. I took him aside.

"Mr. Brune," I said, "I will not let you go to bed with a load of doubt on your heart. We have spoken about the money. That money is a treasure confided to me. My honor hangs on it. Everything I trust to you—money, honor, freedom, all. You are a brave man. I wish to say to you that to-morrow evening at five o'clock I shall bring the money to your quarters."

Brune was silent for a moment. At last he heaved a sigh and replied: "I would probably have done it without this. To-morrow at midnight your friend Kinkel will be a free man."

I passed the larger part of the following day with Krüger, Leddihn, and Poritz, in going over the chances of our enterprise, in order to make provision for all not yet foreseen accidents. At last the evening came. I put the money for Brune into a cigar box and went to his dwelling. I found him alone in his scantily furnished but neat living-room, and handed the cigar box to him with: "Here it is; count it."

"There you do not know me," he answered; "if between us a mere word were not sufficient, we should not have begun together. What comes from you, I don't count."

"Is there anything to change in our plan?"

"Nothing."

"To-night, then."

"To-night, and good luck!"

Indeed, we had good reason to be confident of the success of our plan, barring incalculable accidents. The penitentiary building was situated in the center of the town, a large, barrack-like edifice, the bare walls of which were pierced by one large gate and a multitude of narrow slits of windows. On all four sides it was surrounded by streets. The entrance was on the main street. It led into a large gateway. Inside of that gateway there was, on the right, a door opening into the official dwelling of the director of the institution, and on the left a door leading into the guardroom of the soldiers on duty in the prison. At the end of the passage a third door opened upon an inner court. A stone staircase leading up from the hall united the lower with the upper stories. High up on the second story was Kinkel's cell. It had a window towards the rear of the edifice. This window was guarded by a screen which opened upwards so that a little daylight fell in from above and only a small bit of sky could be seen, but nothing of the surroundings below. The window was also guarded by strong iron bars, wire lattice and a wooden shutter, which was closed at night—in short, by all the contrivances that are usually employed to shut off a prisoner from all communication with the outside world. Moreover, the cell was divided into two compartments by a strong wooden railing, which reached from the floor to the ceiling. One of the compartments contained Kinkel's bed; in the other, during the day, he did his work. The two compartments were united by a door in the wooden railing, which every evening was securely fastened. The entrance to the cell from the corridor was guarded by two heavy doors, with several locks. In the street, under Kinkel's cell, stood day and night a sentinel. Another sentinel watched during the daytime the door of the building on the main street, but he was transferred to the inner court during the night—a regulation which proved very important to us. Had it not been for this stupid arrangement we would never have attempted what we did. The cell, the doors, the locks on the railings, were all examined several times every twenty-four hours by the turn-keys on duty.

The keys to Kinkel's cell, as well as those to the door in the inside wooden railing, were during the night, after Kinkel had been locked up in his compartment, kept in a locker in the room of the inspector, the so-called Revier room. As Brune had no access to the Revier room during the night, and the key had been confided to another superior officer, he had availed himself of some opportunity to procure a wax impression of that key, from which a duplicate key was made, enabling Brune to enter the Revier room during the night. The key to the locker containing the keys to Kinkel's cell was, as Brune knew, in the evening negligently put on top of that locker, so that without difficulty he could possess himself of the keys to the cell. Thus Brune believed himself fully able to enter the cell during the night and to take the prisoner out. It had been agreed that Brune, who had the watch of the night of the 5th to the 6th of November on Kinkel's corridor, should bring Kinkel down the stairs into the gateway. He was sure that he could take him without danger past the turnkey watching the lower floor. Whether he intended to interest that man in our affair, or to divert his attention in some manner, Brune did not tell me. He only assured me I might depend upon there being no difficulty about this. As soon as Kinkel was conducted into the gateway below, I was to be there to receive him. In one of the wings of the great door that opened upon the main street there was a little postern gate to facilitate the daily passage in and out. Of the key of this postern gate we had also procured a wax impression, and from it a duplicate key. Now, it was to be my task, shortly after midnight, after the town night watchman—for in Spandau there was at that time still a night watchman with spear and rattle—had passed by the building on the street, to open the postern gate, to step into the interior of the gateway, there to await Brune and Kinkel, to wrap Kinkel up in a cloak, to take him through the postern gate into the street and to hurry with him to Krüger's hotel, where he was to put on a suit of clothes, and then step with me into Hensel's carriage—and away.

I had asked Brune to provide Kinkel with a plentiful supply of food, so that he might be in a good physical condition. But to avoid long excitement, Kinkel was to be informed only on the evening of the 5th of November, the night of the attempt, that something was being done for him, and that he should go to bed at the accustomed hour, rise immediately before midnight, dress himself and be ready for the venture.

On the same day Leddihn and Poritz had entrusted two good, able-bodied friends with the charge of guarding the street corners nearest to the penitentiary during the night and to come to our aid if necessary. About midnight all my people were at their posts, and after the night watchman had passed down the street I approached the door of the penitentiary. I had covered my feet with rubber shoes, so as to make my step inaudible. A second pair of rubber shoes I had with me for Kinkel. In my belt I carried the pistols given to me by Dr. Falkenthal; in one pocket a well-sharpened dirk and in another a slingshot, with which to arm Kinkel in case of stress. I had thrown across my shoulders a large cloak with sleeves, which should serve Kinkel as a first wrap. So equipped I softly opened the postern gate to step into the gateway of the prison. I left that little gate ajar and the key sticking in the lock. The gateway was dimly lighted by a lantern hanging from the ceiling. My first task was to prevent the opening from the inside of the director's door on the right, and of the guard-room door on the left, and I did so by tying the doorhandles to the iron fastening of the bell rope with stout strings. This was the most delicate piece of work I had to do. Nothing moved. My gaze was riveted on the end of the passage opposite where Brune was to appear with Kinkel.

So I waited. One minute elapsed after another, but all remained still. I waited a full quarter of an hour, but nothing stirred. What did this mean? According to all calculations they ought to have joined me some time ago. My situation began to appear to me very precarious. Was Brune after all faithless? I took one of my pistols out of my belt and held it in my left hand ready to fire, and my dirk in the right. But I resolved to remain at my post until I could say to myself that the last chance of success was gone. Half an hour had passed and still everything was quiet as the grave. Suddenly I heard a faint rustle, and at the other end of the gateway I saw a dark figure appear like a specter out of the wall. My hands closed more tightly on my weapons. The next moment I recognized in the dim light the form of Brune. There he was at last, but alone. He put his finger upon his lips and approached me. I awaited him ready for the worst.

"I am unfortunate," he whispered with his mouth at my ear. "I have tried everything, I have failed. The keys were not in the locker. Come to me to-morrow and get your money back."

I said nothing in reply, but quickly untied the strings from the door handles, right and left, and then stepped out through the postern gate, locked it, and put the key into my pocket. I was hardly on the street when Leddihn and Poritz hastened to join me. With a few words I told them what had happened. "We were afraid you had been trapped," said Leddihn. "You stayed so long inside that we were on the point of coming after you to fetch you out."

Soon we reached Krüger's hotel, where Hensel stood ready with his carriage to take Kinkel and me away. The disappointment that followed my report was terrible.

"But there is something more to do this night," said I, "for my relays stand on the road deep into Mecklenburg. We must order them off."

I stepped into the carriage, an open vehicle with a top over the back seat. Hensel took the reins, and so we drove away. It was a melancholy journey. We were on the road something over three hours when we observed sparks of fire sputtering from a black object that came toward us. We quickly recognized it to be a carriage. I had steel and flint at hand and also struck sparks. This was the signal of recognition that I had agreed upon with my Mecklenburg friends. The carriage coming toward us stopped and so did we.

"Is this the right one?" asked a voice. This was the concerted question.

"It is the right one," I replied, "but our enterprise has failed. Pray turn back and advise the next relay and request our friends there to pass on the word in this way. But for Heaven's sake keep silent about the rest, lest all may be lost."

"Of course, but what a confounded disappointment! How did the failure happen?"

"Another time. Good-night."

The two carriages turned. We drove back in the direction of Spandau, but very slowly, almost as if a part of a funeral procession, both sitting silent. I tormented myself with the gravest reproaches. Could not the unfortunate accident that had crossed our plan easily have been prevented? Could we not have duplicated the keys to the cell as well as those to the postern gate and the Revier room? Certainly. But why had this not been done? Why had Brune not thought of it? But as Brune had not done so, was it not my duty to see to it? I had neglected that duty. Mine, mine only, was the fault of this terrible miscarriage. Mine the responsibility that Kinkel was not now a free man hurrying to the seacoast behind fleet horses. The fruit of long and dangerous labor had recklessly been jeopardized by my negligence. Would I ever be able again to reknit the torn threads of the scheme? And, if so, was it not probable that through the improvidence of some one of the participants rumors of what had happened would get abroad and Kinkel would be surrounded with the severest measures of precaution and even carried into another and more secure dungeon? But if nothing of this did happen—where was the money entrusted to me? No longer in my possession—in the hands of another man who might keep it if he would, and I perfectly powerless to recover it. And thus Kinkel's horrible lot might be sealed forever through my guilt. Thus my conscience put itself to the rack in that terrible night.

At last Hensel interrupted the silence. "How would it be," he said, "if we stopped for a few hours in Oranienburg? We could there feed our horses, sleep a little, and then comfortably drive on."

I was content. I began to feel very much exhausted; and then, if of last night's happenings anything had got abroad in Spandau and thereby any danger threatened, the prudent and watchful Krüger, I felt sure, would send somebody to find us on the road and to give warning.

It was very dark when we arrived at a hotel in Oranienburg. After I had permitted my thoughts to torment me a little longer, I fell asleep at last. When I awoke light shone through the windows of my room, and with me awoke also the consciousness of the whole weight of our failure, with even greater clearness than during the past night. Such awakenings belong to the unhappiest moments of human life. We breakfasted late, and it was on this occasion that for the first time I saw my companion, Mr. Hensel, in clear daylight. I had met him at Krüger's and on our night drive only in the dark. The stately broad-shouldered figure and the long dark beard had then struck my attention; but I could now see the clear, shrewd, and at the same time bold, sparkle of his eyes, and the expression of his face, which betokened a strong will as well as sincerity and kindness of heart. Hensel observed that I was in low spirits and tried to put a pleasant face upon things. He thought that our friends in Spandau were not only faithful, but also discreet, that the officers of the penitentiary in their own interest would keep silent, and that a new attempt would soon be possible. I willingly agreed with him. In fact I was busily thinking of what was now to be done, and such a thought is always the most effective antidote for discouragements. I have frequently in life had the experience that when we are struck by an especially heavy blow, we can do nothing better than to present to our minds all, even the worst, possible features of trouble that may still be in store for us, and so in our imagination drink the cup of bitterness down to the last drop; but then to turn our thoughts to the future and to occupy them entirely with that which must be done to prevent further misfortune, to repair the damage done, and to replace what has been lost by something equally desirable. This is a sure and rapid cure; for the consequences of the misfortune hardly ever will be as disastrous as imagined. Of course, I do not apply this to the loss of one very dear.

In returning to Spandau we were in no hurry. We even thought that it would be more prudent to arrive there in the dark, and therefore started only after noon at a slow trot. Arrived in Spandau, I learned from Krüger that all had remained quiet. I forthwith went to Brune's rooms. I found him there, evidently expecting me. The little cigar box stood on the table.

"That was cursed ill-luck last night," he said, "but it was not my fault. Everything was in the best of order, but as I opened the locker in the Revier room I could not find the keys to the cell. I searched and searched for them, but they were not there. This morning I learned that Inspector Semmler had accidentally, instead of placing them in the locker, put them into his pocket and carried them with him to his home."

For a moment he was silent. "There is the money," he continued, pointing to the cigar box; "take it; count it first; no thaler is missing."

I could not refrain from shaking the man's hand and in my heart asking his pardon for my doubts.

"What comes from you," I answered, repeating his words of yesterday, "will not be counted. But what now? I do not give up. Must we wait until you have the night watch again?"

"We might wait," he replied, "and in the meantime duplicate all the keys that we need so that this difficulty may not arise again; but," he added, "I have thought over the matter to-day. It is a disgrace that that man should sit in the convict's cell a day longer— I will try to help him this very night, if he has courage enough for a break-neck feat."

"What, this night?"

"Yes, this night. Now listen." Then Brune told me that the officer who during the coming night should have the watch on the upper stories, had been taken ill, and he, Brune, had offered to take his place. Thereupon he had thought he might without much difficulty take Kinkel into the loft under the roof and let him down with a rope from out of one of the dormer windows on the street. To this end he would of course again require the keys to the cell, but after the accident of last night, when the inspector took them home with him through mere thoughtlessness, they would certainly be again in their accustomed place. I should only see to it that the street below was kept free, while Kinkel was let down from the roof, and that he then be promptly received and carried off. "It is a somewhat perilous undertaking," Brune added; "from the dormer window down to the street it may be sixty feet, but if the Herr Professor has courage, I think we may succeed."

"I vouch for Kinkel's courage," I said; "what does not a prisoner dare for liberty?"

The details were rapidly considered and determined upon. I undertook to procure the necessary rope for Brune. He was to wind it about his body under the overcoat and take it into the penitentiary building in that way. About midnight I was to be in the dark recess of the door of the house opposite the gate of the penitentiary, from which I could observe the dormer windows of the building; when in one of them I should see the light of a lantern move up and down perpendicularly, three times, that would be a sign that everything was in order for the descent. If standing in my sheltered place I then struck sparks with my steel and flint, Brune would understand from this signal that everything was in safe order on the street.

With a hearty handshake I took leave of Brune and hurried to Krüger's hotel. Poritz and Leddihn, whom I had quickly sent for, procured at once a rope of the necessary length and strength, and carried it to Brune's dwelling. But after freeing Kinkel how should we get him away from Spandau? I had no relays of horses and carriages on the road; the preceding night everything had fitted in so excellently, but now? Fortunately Hensel was still in Krüger's house. When I told him what was to happen in the next few hours, he broke out in loud jubilation.

"I will take you with my own horses as far as they can travel," he exclaimed.

"But our nearest friend is in Neu-Strelitz," I replied; "that is a good many miles from here. Will your horses hold out that distance?"

"The devil take them if they don't," said Hensel. We resolved then to risk it and to confide ourselves to benignant fate. A short conversation with Poritz and Leddihn followed about the measures necessary to keep the streets clear of unwelcome intruders, while Kinkel was swinging down on his rope. Those measures were simple. My friends were to occupy the street corners with their stalwart fellows whom they had already employed last night, and if some belated reveler should show himself, they were to simulate intoxication and use all sorts of means to divert the unwelcome person from our path. In case of necessity they were to use force. Poritz and Leddihn vouched for everything.

"Happy coincidence," chuckled Krüger. "This evening some of the officers of the penitentiary are to celebrate a birthday in this hotel. There will be a bowl of punch, and I will make that punch especially irresistible."

"And you will detain those officers long enough?"

"You may be sure of that. Not one of them will cross your way." This prospect put us into the best of humor, and we had a cosy little supper together. Our thoughts were, however, constantly directed to the accidents that might again play mischief with us, and fortunately an important possibility occurred to us.

At the time of Kinkel's descent from the dormer window hanging on his rope, the rubbing of the rope against the edge of the brick wall might easily loosen tiles and brick which then would fall down and produce a loud clatter. We therefore resolved that Hensel should take his carriage immediately after midnight slowly along the street so that the rattle of the vehicle on the rough cobblestone pavement might drown all other noises.

Shortly before midnight I stood, equipped as on the night before, well hidden in the dark recess of the house door opposite the penitentiary. The street corners right and left were, according to agreement, properly watched, but our friends kept themselves as much as possible concealed. A few minutes later the night watchman shuffled down the street and when immediately in front of me swung his rattle and called the hour of twelve. Then he slouched quietly on and disappeared. What would I have given for a roaring storm and a splashing rain! But the night was perfectly still. My eye was riveted to the roof of the penitentiary building, the dormer windows of which I could scarcely distinguish. The street lights flared dimly. Suddenly there appeared a light above by which I could observe the frame of one of the dormer windows; it moved three times up and down; that was the signal hoped for. With an eager glance I examined the street right and left. Nothing stirred. Then on my part I gave the signal agreed upon, striking sparks. A second later the light above disappeared and I perceived a dark object slowly moving across the edge of the wall. My heart beat violently and drops of perspiration stood upon my forehead. Then the thing I had apprehended actually happened: tiles and brick, loosened by the rubbing rope, rained down upon the pavement with a loud clatter. "Now, good Heaven, help us!" At the same moment Hensel's carriage came rumbling over the cobblestones. The noise of the falling tiles and brick was no longer audible. But would they not strike Kinkel's head and benumb him? Now the dark object had almost reached the ground. I jumped forward and touched him; it was indeed my friend, and there he stood alive and on his feet. "This is a bold deed," were the first words he said to me. "Thank God," I answered. "Now off with the rope and away." I labored in vain to untie the rope that was wound around his body.

"I cannot help you," Kinkel whispered, "for the rope has fearfully lacerated both my hands." I pulled out my dirk and with great effort I succeeded in cutting the rope, the long end of which, as soon as it was free, was quickly pulled up. While I threw a cloak around Kinkel's shoulders and helped him get into the rubber shoes he looked anxiously around. Hensel's carriage had turned and was coming slowly back.

"What carriage is that?" Kinkel asked.

"Our carriage."

Dark figures showed themselves at the street corners and approached us.

"For Heaven's sake, what people are those?"

"Our friends."

At a little distance we heard male voices sing, "Here we sit gayly together."

"What is that?" asked Kinkel, while we hurried through a side street toward Krüger's hotel.

"Your jailers around a bowl of punch."

"Capital!" said Kinkel. We entered the hotel through a back door and soon found ourselves in a room in which Kinkel was to put on the clothes that we had bought for him—a black cloth suit, a big bear-skin overcoat, and a cap like those worn by Prussian forest officers. From a room near by sounded the voices of the revelers. Krüger, who had stood a few minutes looking on while Kinkel was exchanging his convict's garb for an honest man's dress, suddenly went out with a peculiarly sly smile. When he returned carrying a few filled glasses, he said, "Herr Professor, in a room near by some of your jailers are sitting around a bowl of punch. I have just asked them whether they would not permit me to take some for a few friends of mine who have just arrived. They had no objection. Now, Herr Professor, let us drink your health first out of the bowl of your jailers." We found it difficult not to break out in loud laughter. Kinkel was now in his citizen's clothes, and his lacerated hands were washed and bandaged with handkerchiefs. He thanked his faithful friends with a few words which brought tears to their eyes. Then we jumped into Hensel's vehicle. The penitentiary officers were still singing and laughing around their punch bowl.

We had agreed that our carriage should leave Spandau through the Potsdam gate which opens upon the road to Hamburg, and then turn in a different direction in order to mislead the pursuit that was sure to follow. So we rattled at a fast trot through the gate, and this ruse succeeded so well that, as we learned later, we were really the next day, in accordance with the report of the guard at the gate, pursued in the direction of Hamburg. Before we reached the little town of Nauen we turned to the right on a field road and reached the Berlin Strelitz turnpike near the Sandkrug. Our bays made the best of their speed.

Only when the keen night air touched his face, Kinkel seemed to come to a clear consciousness of what had happened. "I would like to hold your hand in mine," he said, "but I cannot; my hands are too much torn."

He then put his arm around me and pressed me once and again. I would not let him express his gratitude in words, but told him how the night before everything had been so well arranged, and how our plan had been crossed by an unfortunate accident, and what a mournful ride I had had in the same carriage only twenty-four hours before.

"That was the most terrible night of my life," said Kinkel. "After Brune had instructed me to hold myself ready, I waited for the appointed hour with the most confident expectation. Before midnight I was up. I listened as only an ear practiced in long isolation can listen. Now and then I heard a distinct noise of steps in the corridors, but they would not approach. I heard the clocks outside strike the hours. When midnight was past the thought first rose in me: 'Is it possible that this should fail?' Minute after minute went by, and all remained quiet. Then I was seized by an anguish which I cannot describe. The perspiration dropped from my forehead. Until one o'clock I had still a little hope, but when even then Brune did not come I gave up everything for lost. The most gruesome pictures rose in my imagination. The whole design had surely been discovered. You were in the hands of the police and also imprisoned for many years. I saw myself a miserable wreck in convict's garb. My wife and my children perished in misery. I shook the rails in my cell like a madman. Then I dropped exhausted upon my straw bed. I believe I was nearly insane."

"Well, and this night?"

"Oh, this night," Kinkel exclaimed, "I could hardly trust my eyes and ears when Brune with a lantern in his hand came into my cell and whispered to me, 'Get up quickly, Herr Professor; now you shall get out.' That was an electric shock. In a moment I was on my feet, but do you know that to-night again everything was on the point of going wrong?"

I listened eagerly, and again and again a cold shiver ran down my back as Kinkel proceeded with his story. Half an hour before midnight Brune was in Kinkel's cell. This time he had found the keys in the locker and had opened with two of them the cell doors. After having called Kinkel up, he attempted to open, with a third key, the door in the wooden railing. He tried and tried, but in vain. The key did not fit. Afterwards it appeared that the key with which Brune tried to open the cell door belonged to the window shutters, but that one of the keys for the doors of the cell also opened the door of the wooden railing. Thus Brune had the true key in his hand without knowing it or without thinking of it in the excitement. So Kinkel stood on one and Brune on the other side of the wooden railing, baffled and for a moment utterly bewildered. Then Kinkel grasped with the strength of despair one of the wooden rails, trying to break it by throwing the whole weight of his body against it, but in vain. Brune worked hard with his sword to the same end, also in vain. Then he said: "Herr Professor, you shall get out to-night even if it costs me my life." He left the cell and in a minute returned with an ax in his hand. With a few vigorous blows two of the rails were cut loose. Using the ax as a lever he effected an opening which just permitted Kinkel's broad-shouldered body to pass through. But had not the blows of Brune's ax alarmed the whole house? The two listened with suspended breath. All remained quiet. In fact, Brune had been no less prudent than daring. Before he swung his ax he had carefully closed the two thick doors of the cell. The sound of the blows which filled the interior of the cell was, as to the outside, very much deadened by the thick walls and by the heavy doors. They not only had not wakened any of the sleepers, but had not reached those that were awake, or if they did make any impression, it was as if the noise had come from the outside of the building.

Now Brune left the cell with Kinkel, the doors of which he again locked. Then they had to walk through corridors, up and down various stairways, and even to pass a night watchman. By Brune's clever management they succeeded in doing this. At last they reached the loft under the roof and the dormer window, through which the dangerous ride through the air had to be undertaken. Kinkel confessed to me that he was seized with a dizzy horror when he looked down upon the street below and then upon the thin rope which was to bear him; but when he saw my sparkling signal, the meaning of which Brune explained to him in a whisper, he regained his composure and boldly swung out over the precipice. At once the tiles and bricks began to rain about his head, but none of them struck him, only the hands which at first had taken too high a hold on the rope and through which it had to glide, suffered grievously. That was, however, a slight wound for so hard a struggle and so great a victory.

When Kinkel finished his narrative, Hensel took out of the hamper one of the bottles of precious Rhine wine that Krüger had provided us with for our journey, and we drank to the health of the brave Brune, without whose resoluteness and fidelity all our plans and labors would have come to nothing. It was a happy, enthusiastic moment, which made us almost forget that so long as we were on German soil the danger was not over, and our success not yet complete.

At a sharp trot we sped on through the night. I still hear Hensel's commanding call, "Boom up! Boom up!" as often as on the turnpike we reached a toll gate. Through Oranienburg, Teschendorf, Löwenberg, we flew without stop, but when we approached the little town of Gransee, nearly thirty-five miles from Spandau, it became clear that our two good bays would soon break down unless we gave them rest and some refreshment. So we stopped at a wayside tavern, near Gransee, and fed them—then forward again.

As daylight appeared I could for the first time look at Kinkel with leisure. How he was changed! He whom a little more than a year ago I had known as a youthful man, the very picture of health and vigor! His closely clipped hair was now tinged with gray, the color of the face a dead yellow, the skin like parchment, the cheeks thin and flabby, the nose sharp, and the face deeply furrowed. If I had met him on the street unexpectedly I should scarcely have recognized him.

"They have dealt hard with you," I said.

"Yes, it was the highest time for me to breathe free air again. A year or two more of that kind of life and I should have been burned to ashes, devastated body and soul. Nobody who has not himself suffered it knows what solitary confinement means and the debasement of being treated like a common criminal. But now," he added gayly, "now life begins once more."

And then he described in his humorous way how at that very moment in the penitentiary in Spandau they would be discovering that Kinkel, like a bird, had escaped from his cell, and how one turnkey after another with a troubled face would run to the director and the whole gang of them would put their heads together and notify the higher authorities; and how they would then examine the guards of the city gates, and how they would hear of a carriage that between twelve and one o'clock had rattled through the Potsdam gate, and how then a troop of mounted constables would be hurried after us in the direction of Nauen and Hamburg, while we were paying a visit to our friends in Mecklenburg.

"I only wish," remarked Hensel anxiously, "that we could make that visit a little more quickly." The sun was up when we greeted the boundary pole of Mecklenburg. Even there we did not by any means feel quite safe, although a little safer than on Prussian territory. The trot of our horses became slower and slower. One of them appeared utterly exhausted. So we had to stop at the nearest Mecklenburg inn, in Dannenwalde. There Hensel washed the horses with warm water, which helped a little, but only for a short time. In the town of Fürstenberg we had to unharness them for a longer stop because they could go no farther, having put over fifty miles behind them. But at last we reached Strelitz safely, where in the person of Judge Petermann, a city magistrate, we had an enthusiastic friend and protector, who already on the preceding night had been on the road with one of the relay carriages.

Petermann received us with so demonstrative a joy that I feared he would not refrain from proclaiming the happy event from the windows of his house to the passersby. In fact, he could not deny himself the pleasure of bringing in some friends. Soon we sat down to a plentiful meal, and with merrily clinking glasses we waited for another carriage and fresh horses. There we took a cordial leave of our friend Hensel. His two fine bays had lain down as soon as they reached the stable, one of them, as I learned later, never to rise again. Honor to his memory!

Petermann accompanied us on the further drive, which now went on with uninterrupted rapidity. In Neubrandenburg, as well as in Teterow, we changed horses, and by seven o'clock the next morning, the 8th of November, we arrived at the "White Cross Inn," on the Neubrandenburg turnpike near the city of Rostock. Petermann went at once to fetch our friend Moritz Wiggers, whose turn it now was to take the management of affairs. Without delay he sent us in a wagon, accompanied by a Rostock merchant by the name of Blume, to Warnemünde, a seaside resort on a fine harbor, where we were cared for in Wöhlert's Hotel. Petermann, happy beyond measure, that his part of the adventure was so successfully accomplished, turned back to Strelitz. On our journey we had accustomed ourselves to call Kinkel by the name of Kaiser and me by the name of Hensel, and these names we inscribed upon the hotel register.

The next day Wiggers returned with the news that there was only one brig on the roads, but that she was not ready to sail. A friend of his, Mr. Brockelmann, a merchant and manufacturer, thought it safest to send us across the sea on one of his own ships and to shelter us in his own house until that ship could be started. Thus we left our hotel, and a Warnemünde pilotboat carried us up the Warnow River. We landed near a little village, where Brockelmann awaited us with his carriage.

On a frosty Sunday morning we sailed, in the company of an armed escort, which our friends had composed of reliable men in sufficient numbers, as they believed, to resist a possible attack by the police, in two boats across the bay to the anchorage of the "Little Anna." Arrived on board, Mr. Brockelmann gave the captain, who was not a little astonished at receiving a visit from so large a company, his instructions: "You take these two gentlemen," he said, pointing to Kinkel and myself, "with you to Newcastle. You pass Helsingoer without stopping, and pay the Sound dues on your return. In stress of weather you will beach the vessel on the Swedish shore rather than return to a German port. If the wind suits you better for another harbor than Newcastle on the English or Scottish coast, you will sail there. The important thing is that you reach England as quickly as possible. I shall remember you if you carry out my orders punctually." The captain, whose name was Niemann, may have received these instructions with some amazement, but he promised to do his best.

Some of our friends remained with us until the steam tug hitched to the "Little Anna" had carried us a short distance into the open sea. Then came the leave-taking. As Wiggers tells in an elaborate description of the scene in a German periodical, Kinkel threw himself sobbing into his arms and said: "I do not know whether I shall rejoice at my rescue, or shall mourn that like a criminal and an outcast I have to flee my dear fatherland!" Then our friends descended into the tug, and with grateful hearts we bade them farewell. They fired a salute with their pistols and steamed back to Warnemünde, where, according to Wiggers, they celebrated the accomplished rescue with a joyous feast.

Kinkel and I remained on the poop of our schooner and gazed after the little steamboat that carried our good friends away. Then our eyes rested upon the shore of the fatherland until the last vestige had disappeared in the dusk of the evening. In our halting conversation now and then the question would recur: "When shall we return?"

At first the sea voyage was agreeable enough. A gentle breeze filled the sails, and the ship glided along pleasantly. But as morning dawned, wind and sea became more lively and Kinkel reported himself seasick. The wind increased, the sea ran higher, and Kinkel grew more and more miserable as the day progressed. He gathered himself up to go on deck, but soon returned to his berth. I tried to lift him up, but in vain. After a few hours of acute suffering he became quite desperate in his torment and he felt that he was going to die. He had a mind to tell the captain to carry him to the nearest port. His agony seemed to him intolerable. Had he escaped from prison to die such a wretched death?

On the tenth day of our voyage the sky cleared at last, and the first actual observation showed that our calculations had not been so very wrong and that three or four days would bring us to the English coast. So we headed for the port of Newcastle. Kinkel had in the meantime recovered all his bright humor, and would not permit me to remind him of his outbreaks of seasick despair. We were of good cheer, but rejoiced with our whole hearts when we saw the first strip of land rising above the horizon. Then the wind turned toward the south and the captain declared that we would have to cruise a considerable time against it in order to reach the port of Newcastle. The navigation council therefore met once more and resolved to steer in a northerly direction toward Leith, the harbor of Edinburgh. This was done, and the next evening we saw the mighty rocks that guard the entrance of that port. Then the wind suddenly died away and our sails flapped. Kinkel and I quoted for our consolation various verses from Homer: how the angry gods prevented the glorious sufferer Odysseus, by the most malicious tricks, from reaching his beloved home, Ithaca, but how at last, while he was asleep, he was wafted by gentle breezes to the hospitable shores of his island. And so it happened to us. After we had gone to bed in a somewhat surly state of mind, a light wind arose that carried us with the most gentle movement toward the long-wished-for port, and when we awoke next morning the "Little Anna" lay at anchor.

Now the good captain, Niemann, learned for the first time what kind of passengers he had carried across the North Sea under the names of Kaiser and Hensel. He confessed to us that the matter had appeared to him from the beginning quite suspicious, but he expressed in the heartiest manner his joy that he had contributed his part to Kinkel's liberation. Kinkel and I were impatient to get to land. Fortunately Mr. Brockelmann had not only given us letters to his correspondent in Newcastle, but also to a merchant in Leith, by the name of McLaren. These letters we wished to present at once, but the captain reminded us that the day was Sunday, on which a Scottish merchant would certainly not be found in his counting-house, and he did not know how we could find his residence. This difficulty we recognized. However, we were heartily tired of the "Little Anna," with its narrow cabin and its many smells. We resolved, therefore, to make our toilet and to go ashore, in order at least to take a look at Edinburgh.

We called at the counting-house of Mr. McLaren, in whom we found a very pleasant and polite gentleman, speaking German fluently. Letters from Mr. Brockelmann had told him everything about Kinkel and myself; he therefore greeted us with much cordiality, insisted on having our luggage taken from the "Little Anna" to his residence, and upon devoting himself entirely to us so long as we might choose to remain in Edinburgh. In McLaren's counting house we took leave of the good Captain Niemann. I have never seen him again, but many years afterwards I learned that he had perished on the North Sea in a heavy winter gale.

After having bought some presentable clothing and decent hats, thus acquiring an appearance similar to that of other men, we accepted Mr. McLaren's invitation to see Holyrood and to dine at his house, whereupon we took the night train for London.

After a few days of overfatiguing pleasure we started for Paris. To witness the meeting of Kinkel and his wife, after so long and so painful a separation, was hardly less delightful to me than it was to them. But with this delight our arrival in Paris imposed upon me also a heavy burden, which consisted in sudden "fame." Although I had received in Rostock, in Edinburgh, and in London, in small circles of friends, praise of the warmest kind, I was not a little astonished and embarrassed when I learned in Paris of the sensation created by the liberation of Kinkel. While Kinkel and I had been crossing the North Sea in the cabin of the "Little Anna," it had become generally known that I, a student of the university of Bonn, had taken a somewhat important part in that affair. The details of it were of course still unknown to the general public, but that sort of mystery is notoriously favorable to the formation of legends, and the Liberal newspapers in Germany had vied with one another in romantic stories about the adventure. The favorite and most accredited of those fables represented me like Blondel before the dungeons of Richard Cœur de Lion, attracting the attention of the imprisoned friend, not indeed with the lute of a troubadour, but in my case with a barrel organ, and thus detecting the window of his cell, and then effecting his escape in a marvelous way. Another myth brought me in communication with a Prussian princess, who, in a mysterious, and to herself very perilous, manner, had advanced my undertaking. Several newspapers put before their readers my biography, which consisted in great part of fantastic inventions, inasmuch as there was but little to say of my young life. I even became the subject of poetic effusions, which celebrated me in all sorts of sentimental exaggeration. My parents, as they afterwards wrote me, were fairly flooded with congratulations, which in great part came from persons entirely unknown to them.

Of course, the praise I received from my parents and the gratitude expressed by Frau Kinkel and her children were a real and a great satisfaction to me, but the extravagances which I had to read in German papers and to hear in the constantly extending circle of our acquaintance in Paris, disquieted me seriously. What I had done had appeared to me as nothing so extraordinary as to merit all this ado. Then there was also constantly present to my mind the thought, that without the help of a group of faithful friends, and especially without Brune's bold resolution at the decisive moment, all my efforts would have been in vain. And of Brune, who in those days was subject to a sharp and dangerous investigation, I could not speak without seriously compromising him. Thus I felt in submitting to praise as one who accepts credit for some things, at least, done by others, and this feeling was in a high degree painful to me. Moreover, in every company in which I showed myself I was asked time and again: "How did you succeed in carrying out this bold stroke? Tell us." Inasmuch as I could not tell the whole truth, I preferred to tell nothing. New legends were invented which if possible were still more fantastic than the old ones. This was so oppressive to me that I became very much averse to going into society, and I fear that I sometimes repelled those who came to me and pressed me with questions.

CHAPTER VI

My Life in London and Paris

THE Kinkel family resolved to settle down in England. Kinkel occupied himself for a little while with the study of the most important architecture, picture galleries, and other art collections in Paris, and then left for London. I preferred to stay in Paris for a while, partly because I hoped there to find special facilities for continuing my favorite studies, partly for the reason that Paris was regarded as the great focus of liberal movements on the continent, and I believed it was the most convenient point for one wishing to work as a newspaper correspondent. Thus we parted.

Of course I could not indulge in expensive social enjoyments. Aside from an occasional visit to the salon of the Countess d'Agoult, the well-known friend of Franz Liszt, my intercourse remained mainly confined to German exiles, some student and young artists who pursued their studies in Paris, and also some young Frenchmen who attended lectures at the Sorbonne or other institutions of learning, and in this circle I found very agreeable companions. We had every week a "musical evening"; sometimes in my room, in which young musicians—among them Reinecke, who afterwards became the famous director of the well-known "Gewandhaus Concerts" in Leipzig—reviewed the most recent composers, and now and then produced their own compositions, while I and others served as an enthusiastic public. On such occasions we used to drink a punch which, for reasons of economy, left nothing to be desired in point of weakness.

On the whole the atmosphere of Paris was not congenial to me, and with sincere pleasure I accepted an invitation of the Kinkel family, urging me to visit them in London and to spend at least a week or two in their happy home. Kinkel had rented in the suburb of St. John's Wood a little house, where I was most heartily welcomed as a guest. He had already found a profitable field of work as a teacher, and Frau

Kinkel gave music lessons. I found the whole family in a very cheerful state of mind, and we spent some happy days together. In fact I felt myself so much at home that Kinkel could easily persuade me to give up Paris and to come over to London, where I, as it seemed to me, would be able to make a comfortable living as a teacher without great difficulty. I then returned to Paris, as I thought only for a few weeks, but my departure from the French capital was to be delayed by an unexpected and very disagreeable incident.

One afternoon I accompanied on a walk the wife of my friend Reinhold Solger, a fellow-German refugee, a man of great knowledge and acquirements, who later was to occupy a respected position in the service of the United States. We were in the neighborhood of the Palais Royal when an unknown man stopped me and asked to have a word with me aside, as he had something very confidential to communicate to me. As soon as we were out of the hearing of Mrs. Solger he told me that he was a police agent, ordered to arrest me and to take me at once to the "Préfecture de Police." I excused myself to Mrs. Solger as best I could and accompanied the unwelcome stranger.

He conducted me first to a police commissioner, who inquired after my name, my age, my native city, and so on. I was astonished that the police, who seemed to know my name, did not know where I lived. I declared to the commissioner that I had absolutely no reason for concealing anything, and acquainted him with the number of the house in which I lived, as well as with the place in my room where the keys to all my belongings could be found; but I wished to know for what reason I had been taken into custody. The commissioner mysteriously lifted his eyebrows, talked of higher orders, and thought I would learn of this soon enough. Another police agent then conducted me to the "Préfecture de Police." There I was turned over to a jailer, who after I had surrendered the money I had with me and my pocket-knife to a subordinate turnkey, took me into a cell and locked me in. To the question whether I would not soon be informed of the reason of my arrest I did not receive any answer. My cell was a little bare room, sparingly lighted by a narrow window with iron bars high up in the wall. There were two small, not very clean, beds, two wooden chairs and a little table.

I expected every moment to be called to a hearing, for I thought that in a republic, such as France was at that time, they would not incarcerate anybody without telling him the reason therefor at once; but I waited in vain. Evening came and the turnkey informed me that I might have a supper, consisting of various dishes which he enumerated, if I were able and willing to pay for it; otherwise I would have to be content with the ordinary prison fare, which he described to me in a manner not at all alluring. I ordered a modest meal.

During the still night I thought over my situation. Had I really done anything in Paris that might have been considered punishable? I examined all the corners of my memory and found nothing. Of course the reason for my arrest could only be a political one, but however my opinions and sentiments might displease the government of President Napoleon, I certainly had not taken part in any political movement in France. In Paris I had only been an observer and a student. I did not doubt that while I was in prison the police would search the papers in my room, but that could not disquiet me, as I knew that nothing could be found there except some historical notes, a few literary sketches and some letters from friends of an entirely harmless nature. All the papers which might in any way have been considered questionable, as well as the pistols which I had carried with me during the Kinkel affair, I had been cautious enough to entrust to one of my friends for safekeeping. Nothing remained but the suspicion that I had been taken into custody at the instance of the Prussian government. But would the French Republic be capable of surrendering me to Prussia? This I deemed impossible; and thus I looked the future calmly in the face. But I was stung by a feeling of the degradation inflicted upon me by shutting me up in the same room with a common thief. It revolted my self-respect. And this could happen in a republic!

My indignation rose the following morning when I still failed to receive information about the cause of my arrest. At an early hour the thief was taken out of the cell and I remained alone. I asked the turnkey for paper, pen and ink, and in my best French I wrote a letter to the prefect, in which, in the name of the laws of the country, I demanded that I be informed why I had been deprived of my liberty. The turnkey promised to transmit the letter, but the day passed without an answer, and so another day, and still another. Neither did I receive a word from my friends, and I hesitated to write to any of them, because the receipt of a letter from me might have embarrassed them. In those few days I learned to understand something of the emotions which may torment the soul of a prisoner—a feeling of bitter wrath against the brutal power that held me captive; the consciousness of complete impotency which rose in me like a mockery of myself; the feverish imagination that troubled me with an endless variety of ugly pictures; a restless impetus that compelled me to run up and down for hours in my cell like a wild animal in its cage; then a dreary emptiness in mind and heart which finally ended in dull brooding without any definite thought.

On the morning of the fourth day I addressed a second letter to the prefect still more vehement and pathetic than the first, and shortly afterwards the turnkey told me that I would be taken to the bureau of the chief. In a few minutes I found myself in a comfortably furnished office-room and in the presence of a stately gentleman, who kindly asked me to sit down. He then complimented me elaborately upon the correctness of the French of my letters, which he called quite remarkable, considering my German nationality; and he expressed in the politest phrases his regret that I had been incommoded by my arrest. There was really no charge against me. It was only desired by the government that I select a place of residence for myself outside of the boundaries of France, and to this end leave Paris and the country as soon as might be convenient to me. In vain I tried to move this polite gentleman to a statement of the reasons which might make my removal from France so desirable. With constantly increasing politeness he told me that it was so desired in higher places. At last I thought to appease his evident trouble about my lacerated feelings by the remark that in fact the desire of the government did not incommode me at all, inasmuch as I had intended to go to London, and that my arrest had only delayed me somewhat in my preparations for departure. The polite gentleman was enchanted at this happy coincidence of my intentions with the desire of his government, and he told me finally not to be in too great a hurry with my preparations for leaving. He would be delighted if I felt myself under his especial protection while in Paris, where I might still remain two, three, four, even six weeks, if that would amuse me. He would then put at my disposal a passport for any foreign country; but after my departure he hoped that I would not embarrass him by returning to Paris without his special permission. Then he bade me farewell with a friendliness bordering on actual affection, and I left him with the impression that I had made the acquaintance of the politest and most agreeable police tyrant in the world.

The reason of my arrest, however, soon became quite clear to me. Louis Napoleon had begun the preparations for his coup d'état which was to do away with the republican form of government and to put him in possession of monarchical power. While the republicans deceived themselves about the danger that was looming up, and tried to ridicule the pretender as an "inane ape" of his great uncle, this man set all means in motion to win the army and the masses of the people for himself and his schemes.

About the middle of June I arrived in London. Kinkel had already selected rooms for me on St. John's Wood Terrace, not far from his house, and he had also found pupils for me to whom I was to give lessons in the German language and in music, the proceeds of which would be more than sufficient to cover my modest wants. The well-known paradox that you can have more in London for a shilling and less for a pound, than anywhere else, that is to say, that you can live very cheaply and comparatively well in modest circumstances, while life on a grand scale is very expensive, was at that time as well founded as undoubtedly it still is. I could have found a great many more pupils if I had been able to speak English. But, strange as this appeared to myself in later life, my musical ear still rebelled against the sound of the English language, and could not conquer its repugnance. The peculiar charm of its cadence I began to appreciate only as I learned to speak it with fluency. In the social circles to which I was admitted German and French were sufficient.

At that time I was favored by what I considered a mark of great distinction. One day I received a letter from Mazzini, written in his own hand, in which he invited me to visit him. He gave me the address of one of his confidential friends who would guide me to him. His own address he kept secret, for the reason, as was generally believed, that he desired to baffle the espionage of monarchical governments. That the great Italian patriot should invite me, a young and insignificant person, and so take me into his confidence, I felt to be an extraordinary distinction. Mazzini was looked upon in revolutionary circles, especially by us young people, as the dictatorial head of numberless secret leagues, as a sort of mysterious power which not only in Italy, but in all Europe, was felt and feared. Wonderful stories were told of his secret journeys in countries in which there was a price on his head; of his sudden, almost miraculous, appearance among his faithful followers here and there; of his equally miraculous disappearance, as if the earth had swallowed him; and of the unequaled skill with which he possessed himself of the secrets of the governments, while he knew how to conceal his own plans and acts. By us young men he was regarded as the embodied genius of revolutionary action, and we looked up to his mysterious greatness with a sort of reverential awe. I therefore felt, when I was called into his presence, as if I were to enter the workshop of the master magician.

The confidential friend designated by Mazzini conducted me to the dwelling of the great leader, situated in an unfashionable street. In the vicinity of his house we met several black-eyed, bearded young men, manifestly Italians, who seemed to patrol the neighborhood. I found Mazzini in an extremely modest little apartment, which served at the same time as drawing room and office. In the middle of the room there was a writing table covered with an apparently confused heap of papers. Little models of guns and mortars served for paper weights; a few chairs, and, if I remember correctly, a hair-cloth sofa, completed the furniture. The room as a whole made the impression of extreme economy.

Mazzini was seated at the writing table when I entered, and, rising, he offered me his hand. He was a slender man of medium stature, clad in a black suit. His coat was buttoned up to the throat, around which he wore a black silk scarf, without any show of linen. His face was of regular, if not classic, cut, the lower part covered with a short, black beard, streaked with gray. The dark eyes glowed with restless fire; his domelike forehead topped with thin, smooth, dark hair. In speaking, the mouth showed a full, but somewhat dark row of teeth. His whole appearance was that of a serious and important man. Soon I felt myself under the charm of a personality of rare power of attraction.

Our conversation was carried on in French, which Mazzini spoke with perfect ease, although with some of the accent peculiar to the Italians. He was constantly smoking while he spoke. He developed even in this confidential conversation between two men an eloquence such as in my long life I have hardly ever heard again—warm, insinuating, at times vehement, enthusiastic, lofty, and always thoroughly natural. The three greatest conversationalists with whom it has been my good fortune to come into touch were Mazzini, Dr. Oliver Wendell Holmes and Bismarck. Of these Dr. Holmes was the most spirited in the "bel esprit" sense; Bismarck the most imposing and at the same time the most entertaining in point of wit, sarcasm, anecdote, and narratives of historical interest, brought out with rushing vivacity and with lightning-like illumination of conditions, facts and men. But in Mazzini's words there breathed such a warmth and depth of conviction, such enthusiasm of faith in the sacredness of the principles he professed, and of the aims he pursued, that it was difficult to resist such a power of fascination. While looking at him and hearing him speak I could well understand how he could hold and constantly augment the host of his faithful adherents, how he could lead them into the most dangerous enterprises and keep them under his influence even after the severest disappointments.

Mazzini had undoubtedly given up, if not formally, yet in fact, his membership in his church. But there was in him, and there spoke out of him, a deep religious feeling, an instinctive reliance upon a higher Power to which he could turn and which would aid him in the liberation and unification of his people. That was his form of the fatalism so often united with great ambitions. He had a trait of prophetic mysticism which sprung from the depths of his convictions and emotions, and was free of all charlatanism, and all affectation, all artificial solemnity. At least that was the impression made upon me. I never observed in him any suggestion of cynicism in his judgment of men and things—that cynicism in which many revolutionary characters pleased themselves. The petty and usually ridiculous rivalries among the leaders of the exiles did not seem to touch him; and discord and quarreling among those who should have stood and worked together, instead of eliciting sharp and offensive criticism on his part, only called from him expressions of sincere and painful regret. The revolution he aimed at was not merely the attainment of certain popular rights, not a mere change in the constitution of the state, not the mere liberation of his countrymen from foreign rule, not the mere reunion of all Italy in a national bond; it rather signified to him the elevation of the liberated people to higher moral aims of life. There vibrated a truthful and noble tone in his conception of human relations, in the modest self-denying simplicity of his character and his life, in the unbounded self-sacrifice and self-denial which he imposed upon himself and demanded of others. Since 1839 he had passed a large part of his life as an exile in London, and in the course of this time he had established relations of intimate friendship with some English families. It was undoubtedly owing to the genuineness of his sentiments, the noble simplicity of his nature, and his unselfish devotion to his cause, not less than to his brilliant personal qualities, that in some of those families a real Mazzini-cult had developed which sometimes showed itself capable of great sacrifices.

I was honored with another meeting that has remained to me hardly less memorable. In October, 1851, Louis Kossuth came to England. After the breakdown of the Hungarian revolution he had fled across the Turkish frontier. His remaining on Turkish soil was considered objectionable by the Austrian government, and unsafe by his friends. The Sultan, indeed, refused his extradition. But when the republic of the United States of America, in general sympathy with the unfortunate Hungarian patriots, offered them an American ship-of-war for their transportation to the United States that offer was unhesitatingly accepted. But Kossuth did not intend to emigrate to America for the purpose of establishing there his permanent residence. He was far from

considering his mission as ended and the defeat of his cause as irretriev-
able. He, too, with the sanguine temperament of the exile, dreamed of
the possibility of inducing the liberal part of the old and also of the new
world to take up arms against the oppressors of Hungary, or at least
to aid his country by diplomatic interference. And, indeed, could this
have been accomplished by a mere appeal to the emotions and the
imagination, Kossuth would have been the man to achieve it.

When now, delaying his journey to America, he arrived in London
the enthusiasm of the English people seemed to know no bounds. His
entry was like that of a national hero returning from a victorious campaign. The multitudes crowding the streets were immense. He appeared in his picturesque Hungarian garb, standing upright in his carriage, with his saber at his side, and surrounded by an equally picturesque retinue. But when he began to speak, and his voice, with its
resonant and at the same time mellow sound, poured forth its harmony
over the heads of the throngs in classic English, deriving a peculiar
charm from the soft tinge of foreign accent, then the enthusiasm of the
listeners mocked all description.

Kossuth had been offered the hospitality of the house of a private
citizen of London who took an especial interest in the Hungarian
cause; and there during his sojourn in the British capital he received his
admirers and friends. A kind of court surrounded him; his companions,
always in their Hungarian national dress, maintained in a ceremonious
way his pretension of his still being the rightful governor of Hungary.
He granted audiences like a prince, and when he entered the room he
was announced by an aide-de-camp as "the Governor." All persons
rose and Kossuth saluted them with grave solemnity. Among the exiles
of other nations these somewhat undemocratic formalities created no
little displeasure. But it was Kossuth's intention to produce certain
effects upon public opinion, not in his own, but in his people's behalf,
and as to that end it may have seemed to him necessary to impress upon
the imagination of the Englishmen the picture of Hungary under her
own Governor, and also to illustrate to them the firm faith of the Hungarians themselves in the justice of their cause, it was not improper that
he used such picturesque displays as means for the accomplishment of
his purpose.

Our organization of German refugees also sent a deputation to Kossuth to pay their respects, and of that deputation I was one. We were
ushered into the reception-room in the customary way and there saluted by aides-de-camp with much gold lace on their coats—handsome
fellows, with fine black mustaches and splendid white teeth. At last

Kossuth appeared. It was the first time that I came near to him. The speaker of our deputation introduced us each by name, and as mine was called Kossuth reached out his hand to me and said in German: "I know you. You have done a noble deed. I am rejoiced to take your hand." I was so embarrassed that I could not say anything in response. But it was, after all, a proud moment. A short conversation followed, in which I took but small part. A member of our deputation spoke of the socialistic tendencies of the new revolutionary agitation. I remember distinctly what Kossuth answered. It was to this effect: "I know nothing of socialism. I have never occupied myself with it. My aim is to secure for the Hungarian people national independence and free political institutions. When that is done my task will have been performed."

In the meantime, the reports which we had received from our friends in Paris made us believe that Louis Napoleon, the president of the French republic, was an object of general contempt, and that he played a really ridiculous figure with his manifest ambition to restore the empire in France and to mount the throne, and that every attempt to accomplish this by force would inevitably result in his downfall and in the institution of a strong and truly republican government. The tone of the opposition papers in Paris gave much color to this view. Suddenly, on the 2d of December, 1851, the news arrived in London that Louis Napoleon had actually undertaken the long-expected coup d'état. He had secured the support of the army, had occupied the meeting-place of the national assembly with troops, had arrested the leaders of the opposition, as well as General Changarnier, who had been intrusted by the national assembly with its protection, had laid his hand upon several other generals suspected of republican sentiments, had published a decree restoring universal suffrage, which had been restricted by the national assembly, and issued a proclamation to the French people. In this he accused the parliamentary parties of criminal selfishness and demanded the establishment of a consulate, the consul to hold office for ten years. Exciting reports arrived in rapid succession. Members of the national assembly had met in considerable numbers and tried to organize resistance to the coup d'état, but were soon dispersed by military force. At last the news came that the people, too, were beginning to "descend into the streets" and to build barricades. Now the decisive battle was to be fought.

It is impossible to describe the state of mind produced among the exiles by these reports. We Germans ran to the meeting-places of the French clubs, because we expected to receive there the clearest and most reliable tidings, perhaps from sources which might not be open to the general public. In these clubs we found a feverish excitement bordering upon madness. Our French friends shouted and shrieked and gesticulated and hurled opprobrious names at Louis Napoleon and cursed his helpers, and danced the Carmagnole and sang "Ça Ira." All were sure of a victory of the people. The most glorious bulletins of the progress of the street fight went from mouth to mouth. Some of them were proclaimed by wild-looking revolutionary exiles, who had jumped upon tables, and frantic screams of applause welcomed them. So it went on a night, a day and again a night. Sleep was out of the question. There was hardly time for the necessary meals. The reports of victory were followed by others that sounded less favorable. They could not and would not be believed. They were "the dispatches of the usurper and his slaves"; "they lied"; "they could not do otherwise than lie"; but the messages continued more and more gloomy. The barricades which the people had erected in the night of the 2d and 3d of December had been taken by the army without much trouble. On the 4th a serious battle occurred on the streets of the Faubourgs St. Martin and St. Denis, but there, too, the troops had remained masters of the field. Then the soldiery rushed into the houses and murdered without discrimination or compassion. At last there was the quiet of the graveyard in the great city. The popular rising had been comparatively insignificant and powerless. The usurper who had but recently been represented as a weak-minded adventurer, the mere "nephew of his uncle," had succeeded in subjugating Paris. The departments did not move; there was no doubt the Republic was at an end, and with its downfall vanished also the prospect of the new revolutionary upheaval, which, on the impulse coming from France, was expected to spread over the whole European continent.

Stunned by all these terrible reports, and mentally as well as physically exhausted, we quietly returned to our quarters. After I had recuperated from this consuming excitement by a long sleep I tried to become clear in my mind about the changed situation of things. It was a foggy day, and I went out because I found it impossible to sit still within my four walls. Absorbed in thought, I wandered on without any definite aim, and found myself at last in Hyde Park, where, in spite of the chilly air, I sat down on a bench. In whatever light I might consider the downfall of the republic and the advent of a new monarchy in France, one thing seemed to me certain. All the efforts connected with the revolution of 1848 were now hopeless; a period of decided and general reaction was bound to come, and whatever the future might bring of further developments in the direction of liberal movement must necessarily have a new starting-point.

With this conviction my own situation became equally clear to me. It would have been childish to give myself up to further illusory hopes of a speedy return to the Fatherland. To continue our plottings and thereby bring still more mischief upon others, appeared to me a reckless and wicked game. I had long recognized the exile's life to be empty and enervating. I felt an irresistible impulse not only to find for myself a well-regulated activity, but also to do something really and truly valuable for the general good. But where, and how? The fatherland was closed to me. England was to me a foreign country, and would always remain so. Where, then? "To America," I said to myself. "The ideals of which I have dreamed and for which I have fought I shall find there, if not fully realized, but hopefully struggling for full realization. In that struggle I shall perhaps be able to take some part. It is a new world, a free world, a world of great ideas and aims. In that world there is perhaps for me a new home. Ubi libertas ibi patria—I formed my resolution on the spot. I would remain only a short time longer in England to make some necessary preparations, and then—off to America!

I had sat perhaps half an hour on that bench in Hyde Park, immersed in my thoughts, when I noticed that on the other end of the bench a man was sitting who seemed likewise to be musingly staring at the ground. He was a little man, and as I observed him more closely I believed I recognized him. Indeed, I did. It was Louis Blanc, the French socialist leader, a former member of the provisional government of France. I had recently in some social gathering been introduced to him, and he had talked with me in a very amiable and animated way. Indeed, I had found him uncommonly attractive. When I was through with my own thoughts I arose to go away without intending to disturb him, but he lifted his head, looked at me with eyes that seemed not to have known sleep for several nights, and said, "Ah, c'est vous, mon jeune ami! c'est fini, n'est ce pas? C'est fini!" We pressed one another's hands. His head sank again upon his breast, and I went my way home to inform my parents at once, by letter, of the resolution I had taken on that bench in Hyde Park. Some of my fellow-exiles tried to dissuade me from it, picturing to me all sorts of wonderful things which would happen very soon on the European continent and in which we refugees must take an active part; but I had seen too thoroughly through the unreality of these fantastic imaginings to be shaken in my resolve.

Now something happened that infused into my apparently gloomy situation a radiance of sunshine and opened to my life unlooked-for prospects. A few weeks previous to Louis Napoleon's coup d'état I had some business to transact with another German exile, and visited him in his residence in Hampstead. I vividly remember how I went there on foot, through rows of hedges and avenues of trees, where now, probably, is a dense mass of houses, not anticipating that a meeting of far greater importance than that with him was in store for me. My business was soon disposed of and I rose to go, but my friend stopped me and called out into an adjacent room, "Margaretha, come in, if you please, here is a gentleman with whom I wish you to become acquainted. This is my sister-in-law," he added, turning to me, "just arrived from Hamburg on a visit." A girl of about eighteen years entered, of fine stature, a curly head, something childlike in her beautiful features and large, dark, truthful eyes. This was my introduction to my future wife.

On the 6th of July, 1852, we were married in the parish church of Marylebone in London. In August we sailed from Portsmouth, and landed in the harbor of New York on a bright September morning. With the buoyant hopefulness of young hearts, we saluted the new world.

CHAPTER VII

My First Impressions
of
the United States

Having determined to make the United States my permanent home, I was resolved to look at everything from the brightest side, and not to permit myself to be discouraged by any disappointment. I knew that my buoyant Rhenish blood would help me much. But I was not so sure as to whether my young wife, whose temperament was not so sanguine as mine and who had grown up in easier conditions and in constant contact with sympathetic people, would be able as readily and cheerfully as I to accept the vicissitudes of life in a new country and a strange social atmosphere. But we were young—I twenty-three years old, and my wife eighteen—and much might be hoped from the adaptability of youth.

It was not easy to find a place of rest for our first night in the New World. We had heard of the Astor House as the best hostelry in New York. But the Astor House was full to overflowing, and so our carriage had laboriously to work its way from hotel to hotel, through the confusion of omnibuses and drays and other vehicles, up the thundering Broadway. But in none of them did we find a vacant room until finally we reached Fourteenth Street, where the Union Square Hotel offered a very plainly furnished room, but sufficient for our needs.

The recollection of our first dinner at the Union Square Hotel is still vivid in my mind. It was a table d'hôte, if I remember rightly, at five o'clock in the afternoon. Dinner-time was announced by the fierce beating of a gong, an instrument which I heard for the first time on that occasion. The guests then filed into a large, bare dining-room with one long row of tables. Some fifteen or twenty Negroes, clad in white jackets, white aprons, and white cotton gloves, stood ready to conduct the guests to their seats, which they did with broad smiles and curiously elaborate bows and foot scrapings. A portly, colored head-waiter in a dress coat and white necktie, whose manners were strikingly grand and patronizing, directed their movements. When the guests were seated, the head-waiter struck a loud bell; then the Negroes rapidly filed out and soon reappeared carrying large soup tureens covered with bright silver covers. They planted themselves along the table at certain intervals, standing for a second motionless. At another clang of their commander's bell they lifted their tureens high up and then deposited them upon the table with a bump that made the chandeliers tremble and came near terrifying the ladies. But this was not the end of the ceremony. The Negroes held fast with their right hands to the handles of the silver covers until another stroke of the bell resounded. Then they jerked off the covers, swung them high over their heads, and thus marched off as if carrying away their booty in triumph. So the dinner went on, with several repetitions of such proceedings, the Negroes getting all the while more and more enthusiastic and bizarre in their performances. I was told that like customs existed at other hotels, but I have never seen them elsewhere executed with the same perfection as at our first dinner in America. It may well be believed that they then astonished us greatly.

I remember well our first walk to see the town:—the very noisy bustle on the principal streets; the men, old and young, mostly looking serious and preoccupied, and moving on with energetic rapidity; the women also appearing sober-minded and busy, although many of them were clothed in loud colors, red, green, yellow, or blue of a very pronounced glare; the people, although they must have belonged to very different stations in life, looking surprisingly alike in feature and expression as well as habit; no military sentinels at public buildings; no soldiers on the streets; no liveried coachmen or servants; no uniformed officials except the police. We observed huge banners stretched across the street, upon which were inscribed the names of Pierce and King as the Democratic, and Scott and Gorham as the Whig, candidates for the presidency and the vice-presidency—names which at that time had, to me, no meaning, except that they indicated the impending presidential election and the existence of competing political parties. As to the American politics of the day, I had received only some vague impressions through my conversations with various persons. My friend Kinkel, who had visited the United States in 1851 in the interest of the revolutionary movement in Europe, had been received by President

Fillmore and had described him to me as a "freundlicher und wohlwollender Greis" (an amiable and benevolent old gentleman). Of the political parties he could tell me only that they both seemed to be dominated by the slave-holders, or at least to be afraid of the slavery question, and that most of the Germans in the United States were on the side of the Democrats, because they were attracted by the name of democracy and because they believed that the Democratic party could be more surely depended upon to protect the rights of the foreign-born citizens.

My wife and I longed for the face of a friend; and as there was nothing to hold us in New York, we resolved to visit Philadelphia, not with any purpose of permanent settlement, but thinking that it might be a good place for a beginning of systematic study. This it proved to be. We soon found among the recently immigrated Germans, and also among Americans, a sympathetic social intercourse, and with it that cheerfulness of mind which encourages interest in one's surroundings.

My first task was to learn English in the shortest possible time. I have, of late years, frequently had to answer inquiries addressed to me by educators and others concerning the methods by which I acquired such knowledge of the language and such facility in using it as I possess. That method was very simple. I did not use an English grammar. I do not think I ever had one in my library. I resolutely began to read—first my daily newspaper, which happened to be the *Philadelphia Ledger*. Regularly every day I worked through editorial articles, the news letters and despatches, and even as many of the advertisements as my time would allow. Then I proceeded to read English novels. The first one I took up was "The Vicar of Wakefield." Then followed Walter Scott, Dickens, and Thackeray; then Macaulay's historical essays, and, as I thought of preparing myself for the legal profession, Blackstone's "Commentaries," the clear, terse and vigorous style of which I have always continued to regard as a very great model. Shakespeare's plays, the enormous vocabulary of which presented more difficulties than all the rest, came last. But I did my reading with the utmost conscientiousness. I never permitted myself to skip a word the meaning of which I did not clearly understand, and I never failed to consult the dictionary in every doubtful case.

In Philadelphia I made my first acquaintances. At that period the Quaker, with his broad-brimmed hat, his straight coat, and his standing collar, and the Quakeress, with her gray dress, her white kerchief covering her shoulders, and her poke-bonnet, were still very familiar

figures on the streets of that city. Foremost among them in public esti-
mation at the time stood Lucretia Mott, a woman, as I was told, renowned for her high character, her culture, and the zeal and ability
with which she advocated various progressive movements. To her I
had the good fortune to be introduced by a German friend. I thought
her the most beautiful old lady I had ever seen. Her features were of
exquisite fineness. Not one of the wrinkles with which age had marked
her face, would one have wished away. Her dark eyes beamed with
intelligence and benignity. She received me with gentle grace, and in
the course of our conversation, she expressed the hope that, as a citizen,
I would never be indifferent to the slavery question as, to her great
grief, many people at the time seemed to be.

Another acquaintance of interest we made was that of Mr. Jay
Cooke and his family. We met them at Cape May, where at the beginning of the summer of 1853 we went with our first baby to escape
from the oppressive heat of the city. Mr. Cooke was then not yet the
great banker and financier he became during the Civil War, but he was
easily recognized as a man of uncommon ability, energy, and public
spirit. The attention of the Cookes was mainly attracted by the beauty,
grace, and ingenuous conversation of my wife, in her naïve German-
English, and as they were evidently good-hearted people of frank and
simple manners, we soon became fast friends and remained so for many
years. They were the first family of very strict and active church
members we learned to know intimately. They had in their house their
regular morning and evening prayers in which not only all the members of the family but also the servants took part, and in which the
guests of the house were invited, and, I suppose, expected to join. But
there was prevalent in the family an atmosphere of kindly toleration
and of buoyant cheerfulness which made everybody feel comfortable
and at home. When some years later I was, with many others, Mr.
Cooke's guest at his country seat "Ogontz," I saw him one morning in
the large hall devoutly kneel down with his family and household to
lead in prayer, and then, as soon as the prayer was over, jump up, clap
his hands with boyish glee, and cry out in his most jovial tones: "Now
let's be jolly!" There was a sort of rustic heartiness in his looks and his
whole being which appeared quite genuine and endeared him much to
his friends. It is generally recognized that, as a financier, he rendered
very valuable service to the country during the Civil War, and I do
not think anybody grudged him the fortune he gathered at the same
time for himself. When, in 1873, he lost that fortune in consequence
of his altogether too sanguine ventures in the Northern Pacific enter-

prise, and many others lost their money with him, he had much sympathy, and there was a widespread confidence that he would faithfully pay all his honest debts, which he did.

Some excursions into the interior of Pennsylvania, and to Connecticut, where a distant relative of ours conducted a manufacturing establishment, enlarged the range of my observation. On these occasions I made the acquaintance of a few specimens of the old Pennsylvania Germans, and of the Connecticut Yankees—two distinct elements of the population—both native, for several generations of those Pennsylvania Germans had lived in this country, but so different in language, in habits of thought, and in social traditions, customs, and notions, that the mere fact of their having lived, worked, and exercised the same political rights together in the Republic was to me a most instructive and encouraging illustration of the elasticity and the harmonizing power of democratic government.

What an astonishing spectacle these Pennsylvania Germans presented! Honest, pious, hardworking, prosperous people; good, law-abiding, patriotic American citizens; great-great-grandchildren of my own old Fatherland, who had for several generations tilled these acres and lived in these modest but comfortable houses and built these majestic barns, and preserved the German speech of their forefathers, only mixing it with some words and phrases of English origin. They called all English-speaking people "the Irish," and kept alive many of their old German domestic customs and habits, though they had lost almost all memory of old Germany.

But far more was my political education furthered by a visit to the city of Washington in the early spring of 1854. The seeming apathy of the public conscience concerning the slavery question was at last broken by the introduction of Senator Douglas's Nebraska Bill, which was to overrule the Missouri Compromise and to open all the National Territories to the ingress of the "peculiar institution." A sudden tremor shook the political atmosphere. While I could not take any interest in the perfunctory Democratic or Whig politics of the day, the slavery question, with all its social, political, and economic bearings, stirred me at once, and deeply. I could not resist the desire to go to Washington and witness the struggle in Congress. A student of medicine from Mississippi, Mr. Vaughn, whose acquaintance I had made in the Philadelphia boarding-house, and whose intelligence and fine character had greatly attracted me, offered me a letter of introduction to a friend of his family, Mr. Jefferson Davis, who was then Secretary of War. I also obtained letters to Senator Brodhead of Pennsylvania, Senator Shields of Illinois, and Mr. Francis Grund, a journalist who furnished the Washington news to various newspapers.

My first impressions of the political capital of the great American Republic were rather dismal. Washington looked at that period like a big, sprawling village, consisting of scattered groups of houses which were overtopped by a few public buildings—the Capitol, only what is now the central part was occupied, as the two great wings in which the Senate and the House of Representatives now sit were still in process of construction; the Treasury, the two wings of which were still lacking; the White House; and the Patent Office, which also harbored the Department of the Interior. The departments of State, of War, and of the Navy were quartered in small, very insignificant-looking houses which might have been the dwelling of some well-to-do shopkeepers who did not care for show. There was not one solidly built-up street in the whole city—scarcely a block without gaps of dreary emptiness. The houses were not yet numbered. The way they were designated was by calling them "the first of the five" or the "fifth of the seven" on Pennsylvania Avenue, or on Seventh Street, as the case might be. Pennsylvania Avenue, not far from the Capitol, was crossed by a brook called Goosecreek, alias "the Tiber," which was spanned by a wooden bridge; and I was told—perhaps falsely—that congressmen in a fuddled state, going home in the dark after an animated night-session, would sometimes miss the bridge and fall into the water, to be fished out with difficulty by the sergeants-at-arms and their assistants.

The hotel at which I stopped, the "National," the same in which Henry Clay had died less than two years before, was dingy beyond description, and there were hardly half a dozen residences, if as many, in the whole town, that had the appearance of refined, elegant, and comfortable homes. The streets, ill-paved, if paved at all, were constantly covered with mud or dust. But very few of the members of Congress "kept house." Most of them took their meals in "messes," having clubbed together for that purpose. Washington was called "the city of magnificent distances." But there was nothing at the ends of those distances, and, excepting the few public buildings, very little that was in any way interesting or pleasing. In many of the streets, geese, chickens, pigs, and cows had still a scarcely disputed right of way. The city had throughout a slouchy, unenterprising, unprogressive appearance, giving extremely little promise of becoming the beautiful capital it now is.

The first call I made was at the War Department, to present my letter of introduction to the Secretary, Mr. Jefferson Davis. Being respectful, even reverential, by natural disposition, I had in my imagination formed a high idea of what a grand personage the War Minister of this great Republic must be. I was not disappointed. He received me graciously. His slender, tall, and erect figure, his spare face, keen eyes, and fine forehead, not broad, but high and well-shaped, presented the well-known strong American type. There was in his bearing a dignity which seemed entirely natural and unaffected— that kind of dignity which does not invite familiar approach, but will not render one uneasy by lofty assumption. His courtesy was without any condescending air. Our conversation confined itself to the conventional commonplace. A timid attempt on my part to elicit from him an opinion on the phase of the slavery question brought about by the introduction of the Nebraska Bill did not meet with the desired response. He simply hoped that everything would turn out for the best. Then he deftly resumed his polite inquiries about my experiences in America and my plans for the future, and expressed his good wishes. His conversation ran in easy, and, so far as I could judge, well-chosen and sometimes even elegant phrase, and the timbre of his voice had something peculiarly agreeable. A few years later I heard him deliver a speech in the Senate, and again I was struck by the dignity of his bearing, the grace of his diction, and the rare charm of his voice —things which greatly distinguished him from many of his colleagues.

In Senator Shields of Illinois I found a very different character—a jovial Irishman who had won his high position in politics mainly through the reputation achieved by him as a volunteer officer in the Mexican War. He lived in a modest boarding-house near the Capitol, and the only ornament of his room, in which he received me, consisted of a brace of pistols attached crosswise to the bare, whitewashed wall. He welcomed me with effusive cordiality as a sort of fellow revolutionist from Europe—he himself, as an enthusiastic Irish Nationalist, being in a state of perpetual belligerency against England, which, however, did not interfere with his sincerity, zeal, and self-sacrificing spirit as an American patriot.

In the Senate he was naturally overshadowed by his colleague from Illinois, Senator Douglas. He would have been so had he been a much abler man than he was. He seemed to be fully conscious of this, for when I tried to obtain information from him about the great question then pending, he could only repeat some things Douglas had said, and predict that Douglas, the great leader, would have the people behind him. He altogether preferred to talk with me about my adventures in Germany and about the prospects of the revolutionary movements in Europe.

The third letter of introduction I had was addressed to Senator Brodhead of Pennsylvania. As I came from Philadelphia he may have regarded me as a constituent who might, perhaps, in the course of time acquire some influence among his neighbors, and he granted me a quiet evening hour in his room. I may have formed a wrong estimate of this statesman, but I had to confess to myself that I found him rather dull. He sought to entertain me with a labored discourse on the greatness of this country, the magnificent resources of the State of Pennsylvania, the excellent character of the Pennsylvania Germans, the intelligence of the new immigrants who had been brought to this country by the revolutionary troubles in Europe, and the virtues of the Democratic party, to which he and, he was glad to know, all the adopted citizens belonged. When I asked him for his opinion as to the right and wrong involved in the slavery question in general and the repeal of the Missouri Compromise in particular, he answered with the impressive solemnity of one who knows a great deal more than he feels at liberty to divulge, that the slavery question was a very important one, very important indeed; that it was also a very complicated and difficult one —indeed so difficult and complicated, that one must take great care not to be carried away by mere sentiment in forming one's judgment about it; and that the Abolitionists were very reckless and dangerous men, to whom good citizens should never listen. This did not satisfy me, and I continued my inquiries; whereupon he assured me that every good citizen must follow his party, and that, as to the Nebraska Bill, he, as a good Democrat and as an Administration man, would faithfully follow his party's lead. And then he wound up with this sentence: "On the whole, I do not take as much interest in measures and policies as in the management of men." This sentence, every word of it, has stuck fast in my memory, for it puzzled me greatly to discover the meaning of it. I thought I noticed that the Senator did not wish to be pressed further, and so I took my leave with an unsolved riddle troubling my mind.

The next day I met Mr. Francis Grund, the "veteran journalist," whose acquaintance I had made in the meantime. I asked him what Senator Brodhead might have meant when he said that he did not take as much interest in measures and policies as in the management of men. "Bless your innocent soul!" exclaimed Mr. Grund with a hearty laugh, "he meant that he does not care whether his party leads him this way or that way, but that his main business is to get post-offices and government clerkships and consulates and Indian agencies for the party hacks and his personal hangers-on. And he must keep on good terms with the Administration to get those things."

I was astonished. "And there are statesmen in positions as high as that of a United States senator who consider that their principal business?" I asked. "Yes," said Mr. Grund, "lots of them." And he counted off by name a large number of senators and a much larger number of representatives, of whom he said that the distribution of the patronage, the "public plunder," was the principal, if not the only occupation in which they took any real interest.

This was a shocking revelation to me. It was my first look into the depths of that great "American institution of government" which I subsequently learned to call by the name of "the spoils system." That the Americans changed all the postmasters in the country with every change of party in power, I had already heard of before I came to this country, and it had struck me as something remarkably absurd. But that very nearly all the offices under the present government should be treated as "public plunder," and that statesmen who had been sent to Congress to make laws in the interest of the whole country, should spend all their time and working strength in procuring and distributing that public plunder, and that a free and intelligent people should permit this, fairly confounded my comprehension. My new friend, Mr. Francis Grund, helped me to understand it.

As to the slavery question, which interested me more than all else, Mr. Grund's moral nature did not seem to be as much wrought up as mine was. He had hoped that the Compromise of 1850 would keep that question in the background for a long period. But the introduction of the Nebraska Bill had disturbed him very seriously, and he now feared that a decisive crisis would ensue. I diligently visited the galleries of the Senate and of the House to listen to the debates. I cannot say that the appearance of either body struck me as very imposing. I had attended, as a spectator, a sitting of the German Parliament of 1848 at Frankfort, several sessions of the French National Assembly at Paris in 1850, and one of the British House of Commons in 1852. Of these parliamentary bodies the Frankfort Parliament seemed to me the most dignified and orderly, the French Assembly the most turbulent, the House of Commons the most businesslike, and the American Congress I saw in 1854—and in succeeding years—the most representative. It was representative of its constituencies in average ability, character, culture, and manners. There was an air of genuine naturalness about the looks, the bearing, and the conduct of the members as well as of the proceedings—no artificially put-on dignity; commotion enough, but little affected furor, except with some Southerners, the business being done without much restraint of logic or method. The congressman with bushy chin-whiskers, wearing a black dress coat and a satin vest all day, a big quid of tobacco in his mouth, as in these days we sometimes see him as a comic figure on the stage, was then still a well-known type on the floor of the Senate and the House. There was much tobacco chewing with its accompaniments, and much lounging with tilting of chairs and elevation of feet on desks—much more than there is now in the same places; but then these things seemed more natural, and less offensive than they do now. There were also more evidences of a liberal consumption of intoxicants. I do not mean to say that there were not men of refined presence and bearing in the two Houses. There were, indeed, not a few; but the majority struck me as rather easy-going and careless of appearances.

Listening to running debates and to set speeches, I was astonished at the facility of expression which almost everybody seemed to command. The language may not always have been elegant or even grammatically correct, it may sometimes have been blunt and rough; but it ordinarily flowed on without any painful effort, and there was no hemming and hawing. Of the set speeches I heard, not a few were remarkable as specimens of "beautiful speaking," of so-called "hi-falutin," so inflated with extravagant conceits and big, high-sounding words, that now they would only provoke laughter, while at that time they were taken quite seriously, or even admired as fine oratory. Now and then one would hear in the course of a speech an old-fashioned Latin quotation, usually coming from some Southern man or some New Englander. But I also heard several speeches which were not only rich in thought but in an eminent degree vigorous, sober, and elegant in language.

My most distinct recollections are of the Senate. The most conspicuous figure in that body was Douglas. He was a man of low stature, but broad-shouldered and big-chested. His head, sitting upon a stout, strong neck, was the very incarnation of forceful combativeness; a square jaw and broad chin; a rather large, firm-set mouth; the nose straight and somewhat broad; quick, piercing eyes with a deep, dark, scowling, menacing horizontal wrinkle between them; a broad forehead and an abundance of dark hair which at that period he wore rather long and which, when in excitement, he shook and tossed defiantly like a lion's mane. The whole figure was compact and strongly knit and muscular, as if made for constant fight. He was not inaptly called "the little giant" by his partisans. His manner of speech accorded exactly with his appearance. His sentences were clear-cut, direct, positive. They went straight to the mark like bullets, and sometimes like cannon-balls, tearing and crashing. There was nothing ornate, nothing imaginative in his language, no attempt at "beautiful speaking." But it would be difficult to surpass his clearness and force of statement when his position was right; or his skill in twisting logic or in darkening the subject with extraneous, unessential matter, when he was wrong; or his defiant tenacity when he was driven to defend himself, or his keen and crafty alertness to turn his defense into attack, so that, even when overwhelmed with adverse argument, he would issue from the fray with the air of the conqueror. He was utterly unsparing of the feelings of his opponents. He would nag and nettle them with disdainful words of challenge, and insult them with such names as "dastards" and "traitors." Nothing could equal the contemptuous scorn, the insolent curl of his lip with which, in the debates to which I listened, he denounced the anti-slavery men in Congress as "the Abolition confederates," and at a subsequent time, after the formation of the Republican party, as "Black Republicans." But worse than that: he would, with utter unscrupulousness, malign his opponents' motives, distort their sayings, and attribute to them all sorts of iniquitous deeds or purposes of which he must have known them to be guiltless. Indeed, Douglas's style of attack was sometimes so exasperatingly offensive, that it required, on the part of the anti-slavery men in the Senate, a very high degree of self-control to abstain from retaliating. But so far as I can remember, only Mr. Sumner yielded to the temptation to repay him in kind.

While for these reasons I should be very far from calling Douglas an ideal debater, it is certain that I have never seen a more formidable parliamentary pugilist. To call him so must not be thought unbecoming, since there was something in his manners which very strongly smacked of the bar-room. He was the idol of the rough element of his party, and his convivial association with that element left its unmistakable imprint upon his habits and his deportment. He would sometimes offend the dignity of the Senate by astonishing conduct. Once, at a night session of the Senate I saw him, after a boisterous speech, throw himself upon the lap of a brother senator and loll there, talking and laughing, for ten or fifteen minutes, with his arm around the neck of his friend, who seemed to be painfully embarrassed, but could or would not shake him off. It might be said in extenuation, however, that then the general tone of the Senate was not so sober and decorous as it is now. After he had married his second wife, a lady of beauty and culture, who not only presided over his household but also accompanied him on his electioneering journeys, he became more tidy and trim in his appearance, and more careful in his habits, although even then there were rumors of occasional excesses. The bullying notes in his speeches remained the same until after the election of 1860.

I must confess that when I first saw him and heard him speak, I conceived a very strong personal dislike for Senator Douglas. I could not understand how a man who represented in the Senate a Free State, and was not bound to the cause of slavery either by interest or tradition, but must, on the contrary, be presumed to be instinctively opposed to slavery and to wish for its ultimate extinction—how such a man could attempt to break down all legal barriers to the expansion of slavery by setting aside a solemn compromise—without any over-ruling necessity, and then be credited with pure and patriotic motives. And that, even in his own opinion, there was no such necessity ap-peared from the fact that only shortly before he had professedly recognized the validity and binding force of the Missouri Compromise as a matter of course; indeed he himself had offered a bill to organize the Territory of Nebraska under the Missouri Compromise excluding slavery, and, since that time, nothing had happened to change the situation. Although by no means inclined to attribute sinister motives to anyone differing from me in opinion or sentiment, I saw no way of escape from the conclusion that, when Senator Douglas was charged with seeking to wipe out the legal barriers to the extension of slavery over territories dedicated to freedom, not in obedience to any neces-sity, not for any purpose of public good, but to open to himself the road to the presidential chair by winning the favor of the slave power, thus wantonly jeopardizing the cause of freedom for personal am-bition, that charge was sustained by overwhelming circumstantial evidence. And when then I saw him on the floor of the Senate plead his cause with the most daring sophistries and in a tone of most over-bearing and almost ruffianly aggressiveness, and yet undeniably with very great force and consummate cunning, I thought I recognized in him the very embodiment of that unscrupulous, reckless demagogy which, as my study of history had told me, is so dangerous to republics. These impressions made me detest him profoundly. And when the time came for me to take an active part in anti-slavery campaigns, I thought that of all our opponents he was the one that could never be arraigned too severely.

No contrast could have been more striking than that between Douglas and the anti-slavery men in the Senate as I saw them and listened to them from the gallery. There was to me something myste-rious in the slim, wiry figure, the thin, sallow face, the overhanging eyebrows, and the muffled voice of Seward. I had read some of his speeches, and admired especially those he had delivered on the Compromise of 1850. The broad sweep of philosophical reasoning and the boldness of statement and prediction I found in them, as well as the fine flow of their language, had greatly captivated my imagination. Before seeing him I had pictured him to myself, as one is apt to picture one's heroes, as an imposing personage of overawing mien and commanding presence. I was much disappointed when I first saw that quiet little man who, as he moved about on the floor of the Senate chamber, seemed to be on hardly less friendly terms with the Southern senators than with the Northern—his speeches were always personally polite to everybody—and whose elocution was dull indeed, scarcely distinct, and never sounding a resonant note of challenge or defiance. But he made upon me, as well as upon many others, the impression of a man who controlled hidden, occult powers which he could bring into play if he would. Indeed, I heard him spoken of as a sort of political wizard who knew all secrets and who commanded political forces unknown to all the world except himself and his bosom friend, Thurlow Weed, the most astute, skillful, and indefatigable political manager ever known. It is quite probable that the flavor of weirdness in his personal appearance and voice and the oracular tone of many of his utterances did much to strengthen that impression. I have to confess that he exercised a strong fascination over me until I came into personal contact with him.

Salmon P. Chase, the anti-slavery Senator from Ohio, was one of the stateliest figures in the Senate. Tall, broad-shouldered, and proudly erect, his features strong and regular and his forehead broad, high and clear, he was a picture of intelligence, strength, courage and dignity. He looked as you would wish a statesman to look. His speech did not borrow any charm from rhetorical decoration, but was clear and strong in argument, vigorous and determined in tone, elevated in sentiment, and of that frank ingenuousness which commands respect and inspires confidence. He had drawn up an address to the country setting forth the true significance of the Nebraska Bill, which went forth signed by a few anti-slavery men in Congress, and, without being so intended, proved to be the first bugle call for the formation of a new party.

Douglas, who seemed instinctively to feel its importance, emptied all the vials of his wrath upon the author of the manifesto, and it was to me a most inspiring experience to see the majestic figure of Chase standing with serene tranquillity under the hail of the "Little Giant's" furious vituperation.

I missed at that time hearing Charles Sumner speak, except once when he made a very few remarks in a calm tone to correct some misapprehension. The impression he made was that of a gentleman of refinement and self-respect, reminding me of some Englishmen of distinction I had seen. He was tall and well-built, his handsome but strong face shadowed by a wealth of dark locks. He was justly called "good-looking." His smile had a peculiar charm. He was talked of as a man of great learning and culture, and of that kind of courage that is unconscious of difficulty or danger, and which was already then said to have made the Southern pro-slavery senators stare in angry wonder.

Of the Southern senators I observed from the gallery, I especially remember three who struck me as types. One was Senator Butler from South Carolina. His rubicund face, framed in long silver-white hair, the merry twinkle of his eye, and his mobile mouth marked him as a man of bubbling good-nature and a jovial companion. He was said to have had a liberal education and to be fond of quoting Horace. On the floor he frequently seemed to be engaged in gay and waggish conversation with his neighbors. But when slavery was attacked, he was apt to flare up fiercely, to assume the haughty air of the representative of a higher class, and, in fluent and high-sounding phrase, to make the Northern man feel the superiority of the Cavalier over the Roundhead. This was what subsequently brought on his altercation with Sumner which had such deplorable consequences.

Of the more aggressive—I might say belligerent—type was Senator Toombs of Georgia, a large, strong-featured head upon a massive figure, his face constantly alive with high spirits, as capable of a hearty, genial laugh as of a mien of anger or menace; his speech rather boisterous, always fluent and resonant with vigorous utterances. Nobody could be more certain of the sanctity of slave property and of the higher civilization of the South. He would bring the North to its knees; he would drive the anti-slavery men out of public life; the righteous victory of the South was to him above doubt, and it would be so overwhelming that he would live to call the roll of his slaves in the shadow of the Bunker Hill monument. He was, it seemed to me, the very picture, not of the Southern aristocrat, but of the overbearing and defiant Southern middle-class allied with the rich slave-holding aristocracy. With all this there was, to me, something sympathetic in the man.

Still another type was represented to me by Senator Mason of Virginia, a thick-set, heavily built man with a decided expression of dullness in his face. What he had to say appeared to me to come from a sluggish intellect spurred into activity by an overweening self-conceit. He, too, would constantly assert in manner, even more than in language, the superiority of the Southern slave-holder over the Northern people. But it was not the prancing pride of Senator Butler nor the cheery buoyancy of the fighting spirit of Toombs that animated him. It appeared rather to be the surly pretension of a naturally stupid person to be something better than other people, and the insistence that they must bow to his assumed aristocracy and all its claims. When I heard Senator Mason speak, I felt that if I were a member of the Senate, his supercilious attitude and his pompous utterances of dull commonplace, sometimes very offensive by their overbearing tone, would have been particularly exasperating to me.

After the Senate, on the morning of the 4th of March, 1854, had passed the Kansas-Nebraska bill, I returned from Washington to Philadelphia. I took with me some very powerful impressions. I had seen the slave power officially represented by some of its foremost champions—overbearing, defiant, dictatorial, vehemently demanding a chance for unlimited expansion, and, to secure its own existence, threatening the most vital principle of free institutions, the right of free inquiry and of free utterance—aye, threatening the Union, the National Republic itself. I had seen in alliance with the slave power, not only far-reaching material interests and a sincere but easily intimidated conservatism, but a selfish party spirit and an artful and unscrupulous demagogy making a tremendous effort to obfuscate the moral sense of the North. I had seen standing against this tremendous array of forces a small band of anti-slavery men faithfully fighting the battle of freedom and civilization. I saw the decisive contest rapidly approaching, and I felt an irresistible impulse to prepare myself for usefulness, however modest, in the impending crisis; and to that end I pursued with increased assiduity my studies of the political history and the social conditions of the Republic, and of the theory and practical workings of its institutions. To the same end I thought it necessary to see more of the country and to get a larger experience of the character of the people. Especially did I long to breathe the fresh air of that part of the Union which I imagined to be the "real America," the great West, where new States were growing up, and where I would have an opportunity for observing the formative process of new political communities working themselves out of the raw. I had some relatives and some German friends living in Illinois, Wisconsin, and Missouri, and I started out to visit them in the autumn of 1854.

CHAPTER VIII

Wisconsin—and Wagner

A JOURNEY to the West in 1854 was not the comfortable sleeping-car affair on fast through trains that it is now, and travelers did not seem to be so nervously anxious to make the quickest possible time. I leisurely visited Pittsburg, Cincinnati, Cleveland, Indianapolis, St. Louis, and Chicago. All these cities were then in that period of youthful development which is confidently anticipating a great future. Society still felt itself on a footing of substantial equality—not, indeed, equality in point of fortune, but equality in point of opportunity and expectation. There seemed to be a buoyant, joyous spirit animating all classes, and between those classes—if, indeed, classes they could be called—an easy, unrestrained intercourse and co-operation. Of all the places I visited I found this least, perhaps, in St. Louis, where slave-holders—"old families" with aristocratic pretensions of social and political superiority—lived. There the existence of slavery, with its subtle influence, cast its shadow over the industrial and commercial developments of the city, as well as over the relations between the different groups of citizens. But St. Louis had, after all, much more of the elasticity of Western life than any of the larger towns in the slave-holding States, and had among its population a strong anti-slavery element. The political leader of that element was Mr. Frank P. Blair, a man of much ability and an energetic spirit. But the constituency of the anti-slavery movement, in St. Louis and in Missouri generally, was furnished mainly by the population of German birth or descent.

The bulk of that German population consisted, of course, of agriculturists, small tradesmen, mechanics, and common laborers. But there were many persons of education and superior capacity among them, who vigorously leavened the whole body. Two different periods of political upheaval in Germany, that of 1830 and the years immediately following, and that of 1848 and 1849, had served to drive out of the old Fatherland hosts of men of ability and character, and of both of these two "immigrations" the German element in St. Louis and neighborhood had its full share. Some of the notable men of the early '30's, the Engelmanns, Hilgards, Tittmanns, Bunsens, Follenius, Körners, and Münchs, settled down in and around Belleville in Illinois, near the Mississippi, opposite St. Louis, or not far from St. Louis, on the Missouri, there to raise their corn and wine. Those who, although university men, devoted themselves to agriculture, were called among the Germans, half sportively, half respectfully, the "Latin farmers." One of them, Gustav Körner, who practiced law in Belleville, rose to eminence as a judge, as a lieutenant-governor of Illinois, and as a minister of the United States to Spain. Another, Friedrich Münch, the finest type of the "Latin farmer," lived to a venerable old age in Gasconade County, Missouri, and remained active almost to the day of his death, as a writer for newspapers and periodicals, under the name of "Far West." These men regarded St. Louis as their metropolis and in a large sense belonged to the "Germandom" of that city.

They were strongly reinforced by the German immigration of 1848, which settled down in that region in considerable number, bringing such men as Friedrich Hecker, the revolutionary leader in Southwest Germany, who bought a prairie farm in Illinois, opposite St. Louis; and Dr. Emil Preetorius, Dr. Boernstein, Dr. Dantzer, Mr. Bernays, Dr. Weigel, Dr. Hammer, Dr. Wm. Taussig and his brother James, the Sigels, Franz and Albert, and others, who made their abode in the city of St. Louis itself. The infusion of such ingredients gave to the German population of St. Louis and its vicinity a capacity for prompt, intelligent, and vigorous patriotic action which, when the great crisis of 1861 came, made the pro-slavery aristocrats, who had always contemptuously looked down upon the "Dutch" as semi-barbarians, stare with amazement and dismay at the sudden appearance of their hardly suspected power which struck such telling blows for Union and Liberty.

Before leaving the vicinity of St. Louis I visited the German revolutionary leader, Friedrich Hecker, on his prairie farm near Belleville in Illinois. I had never personally met him in Germany, but had heard much about his brilliant qualities and his fiery, impulsive nature. He had started a republican uprising in South Germany at an early stage of the revolutionary movement of 1848, which, although quickly overcome by a military force, had made him the hero of popular songs. His picture, representing him in a somewhat fantastic garb, was spread all over Germany, and as an exile he had become a sort of legendary hero. Being a man of much study and large acquirements, he was entitled to high rank among the "Latin farmers."

His new home was a log-house of very primitive appearance. Mrs. Hecker, a woman of beauty and refinement, clad in the simple attire of a farmer's wife, plain but very tidy and tasteful, welcomed me at the door. "The Tiedemanns announced your coming," she said, "and we have been expecting you for several days. Hecker is ill with chills and fever and in very bad humor. But he wants to see you very much. If he uses peculiar language, do not mind it. It is his way when he is out of sorts." Mrs. Tiedemann, Hecker's sister in Philadelphia, had already told me of his tantrums. Thus cautioned, I entered the log-house and found myself in a large room very scantily and roughly furnished. Hecker was sitting on a low couch covered with a buffalo skin.

"Hello," he shouted in a husky voice. "Here you are at last. What in the world brought you into this accursed country?"

"Do you really think this country is so very bad?" I asked.

"Well—well, no!" he said. "It is not a bad country. It is good enough. But the devil take the chills and fever! Only look at me!" Then he rose to his feet and continued denouncing the chills and fever in the most violent terms.

Indeed, as he stood there, a man little over forty, he presented a rather pitiable figure. As a young lawyer at Mannheim and deputy in the legislative chamber of Baden, he had been noted for the elegance of his apparel; now he wore a gray woolen shirt, baggy and shabby trousers, and a pair of old carpet slippers. Mrs. Hecker, who noticed my look of surprise, whispered to me with a sigh, "Since we have lived here I cannot get him to make himself look decent." I had always heard that Hecker was a handsome man. And he might have been, with his aquiline nose, his clear blue eyes, his finely chiseled features, and his blonde hair and beard. But now that face looked haggard, sallow, and weary, and his frame, once so elastic, was drooping and hardly able to bear its own weight.

"Ah," said he, "you see what will become of an old revolutionist when he has to live on quinine pills." Then again he opened the vast resources of his vituperative eloquence on the malarial fever, calling it no end of opprobrious names. Gradually he quieted down, and we began to discuss the political situation. His wrath kindled again when speaking of slavery and the iniquitous attempt of Douglas to permit slavery unlimited expansion over the Territories. With all the fine enthusiasm of his noble nature he greeted the anti-slavery movement, then rising all over the North, as the dawn of a new era, and we pledged ourselves mutually to meet on the field in a common endeavor if that great cause should ever call for our aid.

I was invited to stay for the midday dinner, which I did. It was a very plain but good farmer's meal. Mrs. Hecker, who had cooked it, also helped in serving it. Two rather rough-looking men in shirt-sleeves, the farm-hands, sat with us at the table. This, as Hecker informed me, was the rule of the house. "Liberty, Equality, Fraternity," said he. But this fraternity did not prevent him from giving one of the farm-hands, who had in some way displeased him, after dinner, in my presence, a "dressing down" with a fluency, vigor, and richness of language which I should hardly have thought possible, had I not heard it.

From Hecker's farm I went to Chicago, and I shall never forget the first night I passed in that city. I arrived there by a belated train about an hour after midnight. An omnibus took me to the Tremont Hotel, where I was informed that every room in the house was occupied. The clerk directed me to another house, and I started out, valise in hand. The omnibus was gone and no hack to be had, and I walked to two or three other hostelries with the same result. Trying to follow the directions I had last received, I somehow lost my way, and overcome with fatigue I sat down on a curbstone, hoping that a policeman or some other philanthropic person would come that way.

Chicago had at that time sidewalks made of wooden planks, under which, it appeared, rats in incalculable numbers had made their nests. Troops of them I saw moving about in the gaslight. As I was sitting still, they playfully scampered over my feet. Efforts to scare them away proved unavailing. I sought another curbstone, but the rats were there too. At last a policeman hove in sight. For a minute he seemed to be in doubt as to whether he should not take me to the stationhouse; but having heard my story he finally consented to show me an inn where he thought I would find shelter. But there, too, every guest-room was occupied. They had just one bed free, which I might have, if I wished, but it was in a room without a window, a sort of large closet. I was tired enough to take anything. But an inspection of the bed by candlelight utterly discouraged every thought of undressing. I spent the rest of the night on a chair and hailed daylight with great relief.

Chicago was then a city of about 65,000 inhabitants. The blockhouse of old Fort Dearborn was still standing and remained so for several years. Excepting the principal public edifices, hotels, and business houses, and a few private residences, the town was built of wood. The partly unpaved and partly ill-paved streets were extremely dusty in dry, and extremely muddy in wet weather. I noticed remarkably few attempts to give dwelling houses an attractive appearance. The city had, on the whole, what might be called an unhandsome look. During my short visit I heard many expressions of exceedingly sanguine anticipation as to the future of the place—anticipations which have since proved hardly sanguine enough. But at that time there were also doubters. "If you had been here a year ago," a friend said to me, "you might have invested money in real estate to great advantage. But it is too late now." Everybody seemed very busy—so busy, indeed, that I was almost afraid to claim anybody's time and attention.

From Chicago I went to Wisconsin, and there I found an atmosphere eminently congenial. Milwaukee, with a population much smaller than that of Chicago, had received rather more than its proportional share of the German immigration of 1848. The city had possessed a strong German element before,—good-natured, quiet, law-abiding, order-loving, and industrious citizens, with persons of marked ability among them, who contributed much to the growth of the community and enjoyed themselves in their simple and cheery way. But the "Forty-Eighters" brought something like a wave of spring sunshine into that life. They were mostly high-spirited young people, inspired by fresh ideals which they had failed to realize in the old world, but hoped to realize here; ready to enter upon any activity they might be capable of; and eager not only to make that activity profitable but also to render life merry and beautiful; and, withal, full of enthusiasm for the great American Republic which was to be their home and the home of their children. Some had brought money with them; others had not. Some had been educated at German universities for learned professions, some were artists, some literary men, some merchants. Others had grown up in more humble walks of life, but, a very few drones excepted, all went to work with a cheerful purpose to make the best of everything.

They at once proceeded to enliven society with artistic enterprises. One of their first and most important achievements was the organization of the "Musical Society" of Milwaukee, which, in an amazingly short time, was able to produce oratorios and light operas in a really creditable manner. The "German Turn Verein" not only cultivated the gymnastic arts for the benefit of its own members, but it produced "living pictures" and similar exhibitions of high artistic value. The Forty-Eighters thus awakened interests which a majority of the old population had hardly known, but which now attracted general favor and very largely bridged over the distance between the native American and the new-comer.

The establishment of a German theater was a matter of course, and its performances, which indeed deserved much praise, proved so attractive that it became a sort of social center.

It is true, similar things were done in other cities where the Forty-Eighters had congregated. But so far as I know, nowhere did their influence so quickly impress itself upon the whole social atmosphere as in the "German Athens of America," as Milwaukee was called at the time. It is also true that, in a few instances, the vivacity of this spirit ran into attempts to realize questionable or extravagant theories. But, on the whole, the inspiration proved itself exhilaratingly healthy, not only in social, but soon also in the political sense.

From Milwaukee I went to Watertown, a little city about 45 miles further west. One of my uncles, Jacob Jüssen, was settled there with his family, among whom were two married daughters. Thus I dropped there into a family circle which was all the more congenial to me as this was the one of my uncles I had always been most fond of. The population of Watertown was also preponderantly German—not indeed so much impregnated with the Forty-eight spirit as were the Milwaukeeans. There were some Irish people, too, and some native Americans from New England or New York State, who owned farms, or ran the bank and a manufacturing shop or two, and two or three law offices. But these different elements of the population were all on a footing of substantial equality—neither rich nor poor, ready to work and enjoy life together, and tolerant of one another's pecularities. Of culture and social refinement there was, of course, very little. Society was no longer in the pioneer stage, the backwoods condition. But it had the characteristic qualities of newness. There were churches, and schools, and hotels, all very simple, but decent in their appointments, and, on the whole, reasonably well conducted. There was a municipal organization, a city government, constructed according to law, officered by men elected by the people. And these people had but recently flocked together from different quarters of the globe. There were comparatively few persons among them who, having been born in this country, had grown up in the practical experience of the things to be done and of the methods usually followed for the purpose. A large majority were foreign to the tradition of this republic. The task of solving certain problems by the operation of unrestrained municipal self-government, and of taking part through the exercise of the suffrage in the government of a State, and even of a great republic, was new to them. In Wisconsin the immigrant became a voter after one year's residence, no matter whether he had acquired his citizenship of the United States, or not: it was only required that he should have regularly abjured his allegiance to any foreign state or prince, and declared his intention to become a citizen of the United States. And of such early voters there were a good many.

This seemed to be, therefore, an excellent point of observation from which to watch the growth and the behavior of the political community composed of what might have been thought rather crude and heterogenous elements, comparatively uninfluenced by the guidance of the experienced native mind; to follow the processes by which the foreign-born man, the newcomer, develops himself into a conscious American, and to discover what kind of an American will result as a product of those processes.

The stimulating atmosphere of the West, as I felt it, was so congenial to me that I resolved to establish my home in the Mississippi valley. What I had seen and heard of the State of Wisconsin and its people was so exceedingly pleasing that I preferred that State to any other; and, as several of my relatives were domiciled at Watertown, and my parents and sisters had in the meantime come over from Europe and would naturally be glad to live near other members of the family, I bought some property there with a view to permanent settlement.

Before that settlement was effected, however, I had, on account of my wife's health, to make a journey to Europe. We spent some time in London. What a weird change of scene it was between the two worlds! The old circle of political exiles which I had left three years before was dispersed.

Whether Mazzini was at the time in London, I do not know. If he was, he held himself in that mysterious seclusion characteristic of him —a seclusion in which he met only his most confidential political agents and those English families whose members, completely under his wonderful fascination, were devoted to him to the point of almost limitless self-sacrifice.

But Kossuth was in London, and I promptly went to pay my respects. I had seen him only once, four years before, when he first visited England as the spokesman of his unfortunate country, which, after a most gallant struggle, had been overpowered by superior brute force. He was then the hero of the day. I have already described his entrance into London and the enthusiastic homage he received from what seemed to be almost the whole English people; how it was considered a privilege to be admitted to his presence, and how at a public reception he spoke a word to me that made me very proud and happy. He had then, at the invitation of the government,—I might say of the people of the United States,—proceeded to America, where he was received almost like a superior being, all classes of society surging around him with measureless outbursts of enthusiastic admiration. But he could not move the government of this Republic to active interference in favor of the independence of Hungary, nor did he obtain from his American admirers that "substantial aid" for his cause which he had looked and worked for, and thus he returned from America a profoundly disappointed man.

His second appearance in England convinced him that the boiling enthusiasm of the English people had evaporated. His further appeals in behalf of his cause met only with that compassionate sympathy which had no longer any stirring impulse in it, and it must have become clear to him that, for the time being at least, his cause was lost. At first he had appeared in England, as well as in America, in the character of the legitimate, although the deposed, ruler of Hungary, and his countrymen in exile had surrounded their "governor" with a sort of court ceremonial which was to express their respect for him, which flattered his pride, and which was accepted by many others as appropriate to his dignity. This "style" had, in Hungarian circles in London, been kept up for a while even after the disappearance of the popular enthusiasm. But it fell naturally into disuse when many of the followers, who had formed his brilliant retinue in triumphal progresses, dispersed to seek for themselves the means of living; when poverty had compelled him to retire into seclusion and modest quarters, and when, appearing on the street, he was no longer surrounded by cheering crowds, but at best was greeted with silent respect by a few persons who recognized him.

This was the condition of his affairs when I called at the very unpretending cottage he inhabited in one of the suburbs of London. The door was opened by a man well advanced in years, of an honest, winning countenance typically Hungarian, with keen dark eyes, broad cheek-bones, and gleaming teeth. From his appearance I judged that he was rather a friend, a devoted companion, than a servant, and such I afterwards learned him to be. Without ceremony he took me into a very plainly furnished little parlor where, he said, the "governor" would receive me.

After a few moments Kossuth came in and greeted me with cordial kindness. He had aged much since I had last seen him. His hair and beard were streaked with gray. Yet his voice still retained the mellow

tones which, but a few years ago, had charmed such countless multitudes. He spoke much of his American tour, praised the hospitable
spirit of the American people, and with quiet dignity expressed his
disappointment at the fruitlessness of his efforts. He drew a gloomy
picture of existing conditions in Europe, but thought that such a state
of things could not endure and that the future was not without hope.
After a while, Madame Kossuth came into the room, and Kossuth introduced me to his wife with some kind remarks. She spoke to me with
great politeness, but I must confess that I was somewhat prejudiced
against her. In her prosperity she had borne the reputation of being
haughty and distant, and her presumptuous attitude is said to have been
occasionally dangerous to her husband's popularity. In the case of such
characters the fall from greatness is usually not regarded as a claim
to especial sympathy. But as I saw her then, she seemed to be full of
tender care for her husband's health.

I left Kossuth's presence with a heart full of sadness. In him, in that
idol of the popular imagination, now reduced to impotence, poverty,
and solitude, I had seen the very personification of the defeat suffered
by the revolutionary movement of 1848.

It was on the occasion of this sojourn in London that I made the
acquaintance of Alexander Herzen, a natural son of a Russian nobleman of high rank, himself a Russian patriot in the liberal sense, who
had been obliged to leave his native country as a "dangerous man," and
who now, by his writings, which were smuggled across the frontier,
worked to enlighten and stimulate and inspire the Russian mind.
Malwida von Meysenbug, who lived in his family superintending the
education of his daughters, which she did with all her peculiar enthusiasm, brought us together, and we soon became friends. Herzen, at
least ten years older than I, was an aristocrat by birth and instinct, but
a democrat by philosophy, a fine, noble nature, a man of culture, of a
warm heart and large sympathies. In his writings as well as in his conversation he poured forth his thoughts and feelings with an impulsive,
sometimes poetic eloquence, which, at times, was exceedingly fascinating. I would listen to him by the hour when in his rhapsodic way
he talked of Russia and the Russian people, that uncouth and only half
conscious giant, that would gradually exchange its surface civilization
borrowed from the West for one of national character; the awakening
of whose popular intelligence would then put an end to the stolid
autocracy, the deadening weight of which held down every free aspi-
ration; and which then would evolve from its mysterious depths new
ideas and forces which might solve many of the problems now perplex-

ing the Western world. But, in his fervid professions of faith in the greatness of that destiny, I thought I discovered an undertone of doubt, if not despondency, as to the possibilities of the near future, and I was strongly reminded of the impression made upon me by some of Turgueneff's novels describing Russian society as it entertained itself with vague musings and strivings of dreary aimlessness.

Other impressions I gathered through my contact with some of Herzen's Russian friends who from time to time met in his hospitable house and at his table. At dinner the conversation would sparkle with dramatic tales of Russian life, descriptions of weird social conditions and commotions, which opened mysterious prospects of great upheavings and transformations, and which were interspersed with witty sallies against the government and droll satires on the ruling classes. But when, after dinner, the bowl of strong punch was put on the table, the same persons, who, so far, at least had conducted themselves like gentlemen of culture and refinement, becoming gradually heated, would presently break out in ebullitions of a sort of savage wildness, the like of which I had never witnessed among Germans, or French, or English, or Americans. They strongly reminded me of the proverb: "You scratch a Russian, and you find a Tartar."

Herzen himself always remained self-contained; but as an indulgent host he did not restrain his guests. Probably he knew that he could not. Once or twice he would say to me in an undertone, witnessing my amazement: "So they are! So they are! But they are splendid fellows for all that." And so, I suppose, they are indeed, not only as individuals but as a nation—a huge, unshapely mass, with a glossy polish on the outer surface, but fierce forces within, kept in control by a tremendous pressure of power, or superstition, or stolid faith, but really untamed and full of savage vigor. If they once break loose, awful cataclysms must result, producing in their turn—what? It is difficult to imagine how the Russian empire as it now is, from Poland to eastern-most Siberia, could be kept together and governed by anything else than an autocratic centralization of power, a constantly self-asserting and directing central authority with a tremendous organization of force behind it. This rigid central despotism cannot fail to create oppressive abuses in the government of the various territories and diverse populations composing the empire. When this burden of oppression becomes too galling, efforts, raw, crude, more or less inarticulate and confused, will be made in quest of relief, with a slim chance of success. Discontent with the inexorable autocracy will spread and seize upon the superior intelligence of the country, which will be inspired with a restless ambition to have a share in the government.

Before my return to America I had a joyful experience which I cannot refrain from describing. It was of an artistic nature. Frau Kinkel took me to a concert—in which Jenny Lind, then retired from the stage, was to sing the great aria of Agathe in the "Freischütz," and in which also Richard Wagner's overture to "Tannhäuser" was to be produced, Wagner himself acting as conductor of the orchestra. Frau Kinkel was one of the most highly educated and most accomplished musicians I have ever known. Still her musical principles and taste were severely those of the "old school," and she detested Wagner as a reckless and almost criminal demoralizer of the musical conscience. On the way to the concert she did not fail to give me a thorough lecture on Wagner's vices, his contempt of the most sacred rules of harmony, his impossible transitions from one key to another, his excruciating dissonances, his intemperate straining after sensuous effects, and what not. "It is true," she added by way of precautionary warning, "there is something exciting, a certain fascination in his music, and many people are carried away by it—some musicians, even, of whom something better might have been expected. But I hope when you hear it, you will remain cool and not lose your critical sense."

As to the performance of Jenny Lind, Frau Kinkel and I were altogether of the same mind and feeling. Jenny Lind was then no longer young. Her voice might, perhaps, not have retained all its original birdsong-like lightness of warble. But there was still that half veiled tone, as if there were something mysterious behind it; that velvety timbre, that strange, magnetic vibration, the mere sound of which could draw tears to the eyes of the listener. She was the nightingale still.

At last came the overture to "Tannhäuser." Frau Kinkel became uneasy. "Now keep yourself well in hand," she said, looking at me with an expression betraying some anxiety as to the outcome. The opening "Pilgrim's Chorus," as it rose from the orchestra, pleased me much, without, however, impressing me as something overpowering. But when the violins set in with that weird and constantly growing tumult of passion, drowning the pious notes of the "Pilgrim's Chorus" under the wild outcries of an uncanny frenzy, then sinking into whining moans of exhaustion, I could hardly restrain myself. I felt as if I should jump up and shout. Frau Kinkel observed my emotion, put her hand upon my own as if to hold me down to my seat, and whispered: "Oh, oh, I see how it takes you, too. But do you not hear that it is all wrong?" I could not answer, but continued to listen with rapture. I did not hear that it was all wrong; and if I had noticed anything that was wrong under the accepted rules of thorough-bass, I should not have cared. My good friend Frau Kinkel noticed well what had happened to me. She looked at me sadly and said with a sigh, "I see, I see! You are now a captive, too. And so it goes. What will become of our art?"

Indeed, I was a captive, and I remained one. I shall never forget my first impressions of "Parsifal," which I enjoyed many years later. The performances at Bayreuth were then still on their highest level. The whole atmosphere of the town and the neighboring country was charged with artistic enthusiasm and exaltation. The crowds of visitors from all parts of the civilized world had come almost like pilgrims to a shrine. People went to Wagner's Opera House as true believers go to church. When the audience was assembled in the severely plain building, and the lights were turned down, an almost startling silence fell upon the house. The multitude held its breath in reverential expectation. Then came the solemn tones of the orchestra, floating up from the depth of its mysterious concealment. Then the parting of the curtain revealed the scene of the sacred lake. The suffering Amfortas entered with his companions of the Holy Grail, and the mystic action, as it unrolled itself, the appearance of the youthful Parsifal, and the killing of the sacred swan, all wrapped in majestic harmonies, held our hearts spellbound. But all this was but a feeble prelude to what followed. The changing scene became gradually enveloped in darkness, made more mysterious by the swinging peals of mighty cathedral bells. As by magic, the great temple hall of the Castle of the Holy Grail was before us, flooded with light. And then, when the knights of the Grail marched down its aisles and took their seats, and the blond-locked pages, fair as angels, and the king of the Grail appeared, bearing the miraculous cup, and the chorus of the boys came streaming down from the lofty height of the Cupola—then, I have to confess, tears trickled down my face, for I now beheld something like what I had imagined Heaven to be when I was a child.

CHAPTER IX

The Rise of Abraham Lincoln

WHEN we returned to America, in May, 1856, the public mind seemed to be in a state of high political animation. The hotels and the railroad cars and the steamboat decks were buzzing with eager discussions of the slavery question and the impending presidential campaign. My German neighbors in Watertown, Wisconsin, were almost all Democrats. As a rule, the foreign immigrants had drifted into the Democratic party, which presented itself to them as the protector of the political rights of the foreign-born population, while the Whigs were suspected of "nativistic" tendencies, hostile to the foreign born. Sitting on a dry-goods box in front of one of the stores on the "Main Street" of Watertown, I had many an arduous, but, of course, good-natured talk on the political situation with groups of fellow-townsmen, without, however, at first accomplishing much more for the anti-slavery cause than that I occasionally called forth a serious shaking of heads or an admission that the slavery question was indeed a matter very much worth thinking about.

But what I read in the newspapers of the invasions of the Territory of Kansas by the pro-slavery "border ruffians" of Missouri, and of their high-handed and bloody attempts to subjugate the Free-State settlers there, deeply agitated me. In June, the national conventions of the great political parties were held. That of the Democrats met at Cincinnati, in its platform approved the opening of the Territories to slavery under the guise of "popular sovereignty," and nominated Buchanan and Breckinridge as its candidates; that of the young Republican party met at Philadelphia, in its platform demanded the exclusion of slavery from the Territories that had been dedicated to freedom, reaffirmed the principles of the Declaration of Independence, and nominated, as its standard-bearers, Frémont of California and Dayton of New Jersey. The Republican platform sounded to me like a bugle-

133

call of liberty, and the name of Frémont, "the Pathfinder," surrounded by a halo of adventurous heroism, mightily stirred the imagination. Thus the old cause of human freedom was to be fought for on the soil of the new world. The great final decision seemed to be impending.

I was eager to take part in the contest. But at the same time a feeling came upon me that I was still sadly incompetent for the task. I had indeed studied the slavery question in its various aspects to the best of my ability. But every step in widening my knowledge painfully convinced me that I had very much more to learn. I had no experience in American politics. My acquaintance with public men was extremely limited. Would I not, when standing before the public, sometimes find myself speaking of things of which I knew very little or nothing? How could I expect to be able to answer the questions that might be put to me? While I was in that troubled state of mind, I was surprised by the visit of a gentleman I had never heard of. It was Mr. Harvey, a member of the State Senate of Wisconsin, one of the Republican leaders—(the same Mr. Harvey who subsequently was elected Governor of Wisconsin during the Civil War, and found his death in the Mississippi River when visiting Wisconsin troops in the field). I was very much astonished and felt myself greatly honored when I was told how distinguished a public man my visitor was. I found in him a gentleman of agreeable manners and persuasive address, and he told me in most winning tones that he had heard of me as a person of education sympathizing with the anti-slavery cause, and that he thought I could render valuable service in the pending campaign. I frankly revealed to him my mental trouble about the insufficiency of my equipment for such a task. He ventured to "guess" that I probably knew more about the question at issue than many of those who were publicly discussing it, and he asked me whether I would not make a little speech in German at a mass-meeting to be held in a few days at Jefferson, a country town near by. No, I could not think of it, for I was not prepared. Would I not, then, at least come and hear him speak at that meeting? Of course I would, with great pleasure. So I went, without the slightest anticipation of what was to happen. It was an open-air meeting, attended by a large crowd of country people. Mr. Harvey invited me to a seat on the platform and introduced me to the local magnates. He spoke with uncommon eloquence. His arguments were lucid, logical, and strong, and he closed with an exceedingly impressive peroration. When the applause following his speech had subsided, the chairman of the meeting coolly rose and said: "I have now the great pleasure of introducing

Mr. Carl Schurz of Watertown, who has fought for liberty in his native country and who has come to us to do the same in his adopted home, etc., etc. He will address his fellow citizens of German birth in their own native language." Well, well! I felt myself blush all over; but what could I do? I stammered a few initial words about the entirely unexpected honor, and then, for half an hour or more, I blurted out what happened to come into my mind about the slavery question, about the significance of the decision to be rendered, and about the duty we had to perform as American citizens to this Republic, and as citizens of the world to mankind. After the first sentences the words came easily and my hearers seemed to be well pleased. This was my first political speech in America. The ice was broken. Mr. Harvey triumphed over my diffidence. Invitations to address meetings poured in upon me from all sides and kept me busy during the whole campaign.

I did not yet trust myself to make a public speech in English, and therefore in that campaign addressed only German audiences in their own language. But I gathered very valuable experiences in coming face to face with a great variety of human beings which gave me ample opportunity for studying their ways of thinking and the motives which would be likely to govern their action, and also for weighing the different available methods to reach their minds and hearts by argument and appeal. I met simple-minded farmers in little country school-houses or court-rooms,—men who so far had more or less passively followed the accustomed party lead, and were slow to change, but who honestly and earnestly meant to find out what was right and how to do it, and who sat before me with serious faces, not seldom with a puzzled expression when I happened to say something they had never thought of; men who would listen quietly without giving any sign of assent or dissent, except an occasional nod or shake of the head, and who, when, after the close of the speech, applause came forth, would join in it, sometimes heartily, sometimes with timid reticence, and sometimes not at all. I met quick-witted townspeople who had been more or less used to political activity and were acquainted with the current language of political discussion, and who would promptly grasp the point of an argument or the catch-words or battle-cries of party and instantly respond with applause or signs of disapproval. I met the ingrained partisans of the opposite creed who would, some from personal interest, some from mere traditional prejudice, stubbornly close their ears and minds to every argument going against their side, and vociferously, not seldom with a sort of fanatical ferocity, resent and repel everything that seemed to threaten the power or prestige of their party, and who, in some instances, had established a sort of partisan lordship and sought to exercise a political terrorism over their neighbors.

These impressions made me shape my speeches so that they were arguments for my cause, not for a party—or only in so far for my party as it was a means to further my cause—unceasingly admonishing my hearers not to be mere blind followers of any leadership, whatever its name might be, but to think for themselves, honestly seeking to discover what was right and best for the common welfare, not indeed to reject advice, but to weigh it and then courageously to do that which, according to their conscientiously formed convictions, would be most apt to serve the cause of justice and the true interests of the country. This injunction I constantly repeated in endless variations.

On the whole, the campaign of 1856 was to me a very happy experience. There is an exhilarating inspiration in the consciousness of standing for a good cause, in being entirely right in one's fight, and of doing some service, be it ever so little. It belongs to the most genuine felicities of life; and that felicity I heartily enjoyed. How many votes I won for Frémont, I do not know. But I was so thoroughly convinced of the justice of my cause and of the truthfulness of my arguments that I thought I must have won many.

In the autumn of 1857, the Republicans of Watertown sent me as a delegate to the Republican State Convention that had to nominate candidates for the State offices. A great surprise awaited me there. I found that the leading party managers had selected me as the Republican candidate for the office of Lieutenant Governor. It was no doubt the work of my friend Senator Harvey. I cannot say that I was without ambition, and the nomination for the Lieutenant Governorship was an honorable distinction which I could not fail to appreciate. It flattered me greatly. But I was not at ease. I really did not desire official position at that time, and I seriously doubted my ability to discharge the duties of the place with credit. Moreover, I was not yet a citizen of the United States, lacking a few weeks of the five years required for the title to full citizenship. But I was told that I need not trouble myself about my fitness for the office, that its duties were not very exacting, and that I could easily acquire the knowledge of parliamentary law to enable me to preside over the State Senate. And as to the question of citizenship, there was nothing in the Constitution and the laws requiring that a candidate for such an office should be a full citizen; I would have my papers of citizenship when elected, and that was enough. I soon perceived that my nomination was intended as a bid to draw the

German vote to the Republican party, and as it would serve the anti-slavery cause, if it had that effect, I accepted.

But I had my misgivings. Would not the nomination of a young and comparatively unknown new-comer for so conspicuous and honorable a place, while it might attract some German voters, displease many voters of American birth? Besides, the thought of making a campaign for my principles in which I had a personal stake as a candidate for office was uncomfortable. The campaign—at least my share in it— was not nearly as spirited as that of 1856, the Frémont campaign, had been. However, it was to me a good exercise, as I then made my first public speeches in English, the peroration of one of which, a somewhat florid piece of oratory, had the honor of being published in some Eastern papers. My misgivings were justified by the result. While the Republican candidate for the Governorship, Mr. Alexander Randall, was elected by a small majority, I was defeated by one hundred and seven votes. Of course, my defeat was a disappointment, but I did not take it much to heart. In fact I accepted it rather as something like a relief which would permit me to continue undisturbed my harmless and enjoyable life on my farm, among my family, my friends, and my books.

The year 1858 was one of great developments. It revealed Abraham Lincoln to the American people. The very atmosphere of the country was quivering with excitement. The famous Dred Scott decision, that political pronunciamento coming from the bench of the Federal Supreme Court, which the pro-slavery interest had expected finally to settle the burning question in its favor, only served to shake the moral prestige of the judiciary, and to make the slavery question more than it had been before, a question of power. In Kansas, civil war had been followed by shameless fraud and revolting intrigue. The Free State party there was steadily gaining in numbers and moral strength, but the Federal Administration used its power in the efforts to force slavery upon that Territory so openly and unscrupulously that several of its own officers refused to obey it, and Senator Douglas himself recoiled from the use that was being made of the weapons he had put into the hands of the slave power by his repeal of the Missouri Compromise and his doctrine of "Popular Sovereignty," according to which not Congress, but only the people of a Territory should have the power to exclude slavery therefrom.

The Dred Scott decision must have made him feel that the two horses he attempted to ride were going in directly opposite directions. That decision declared that Congress had no Constitutional power to prohibit slavery in the Territories and that the slave-holder had, therefore, under the Constitution a right to take his slaves into any Territory and keep them there. The slave-power concluded at once that then the slave-holder was, under the Constitution, entitled to a protection of that right, no matter whether the inhabitants of a Territory liked slavery or not. But what would then become of Douglas's boasted "Popular Sovereignty," which his adherents in the North tried to make people believe would work to keep slavery out of the Territories?

But this theoretical discussion was not all that pestered the "Little Giant." The pro-slavery interest attempted to smuggle Kansas into the Union as a Slave State under the notorious Lecompton Constitution, which had been framed by the pro-slavery minority in Kansas fraudulently organized as a "Convention." It had not been submitted to a fair vote of the people, but had been eagerly welcomed by the pro-slavery cabal controlling the Buchanan Administration, and recommended to Congress for acceptance as the rightful constitution of Kansas. This attempt brought Douglas face to face with the question whether he would surrender his principle of "Popular Sovereignty" and the new State of Kansas to the slave-power and thus irretrievably ruin himself at the North, or repudiate the fraud by which Kansas was to be made a Slave State, and thus, just as irretrievably, forfeit the favor of the South, which he had hoped would lift him into the presidential chair. And it so happened that just at that time his term in the Senate expired and he had to appeal to the people of Illinois for a re-election. There he encountered the avenging angel in the person of Abraham Lincoln.

Lincoln and Douglas had met in public debate before—that is, the Whigs, and later the Republicans of Illinois, had regarded Lincoln as the fittest man to answer Douglas's speeches on the stump, and he had acted as their spokesman. But these discussions had hardly attracted, beyond the boundaries of Illinois, the attention they merited. It was only when the Republican State Convention of Illinois, on the 16th of June, 1858, passed, by unanimous acclamation, a resolve declaring Abraham Lincoln to be "the first and only choice of the Republicans of Illinois for the United States Senate as the successor of Stephen A. Douglas," that the eyes of the whole American people were turned upon the combat between the two men as an action which gravely concerned them all.

To be invited to serve as an aid—however humble—to one of those champions, I valued as a high honor; and that honor came to me unexpectedly. The Republican State Committee of Illinois asked me to make some speeches in their campaign, and, obeying that call, I found myself for the first time on a conspicuous field of political action. I was to appear first at a mass meeting in Chicago, and to speak in English. I took the matter very seriously, and resolved to do my best. I did not appeal to the sentimental sympathies of the audience by dilating upon the injustice and cruelties of the system and the suffering of the bondmen, but, in calm language, I sought to set forth the inherent incompatibility of slavery with free institutions of government, the inevitable and far-reaching conflicts which the existence of slavery in a democratic republic was bound to produce, and the necessity of destroying the political power of slavery in our republic if the democratic character of its institutions was to endure. The speech was not original as to its fundamental ideas; but its manner of treating the subject was largely received as something new, and it was published in full not only by the Chicago press but also by several Eastern papers—a distinction of which I was very proud. I then addressed several meetings, mostly German, in the interior of the State, in a similar strain. One of the appointments called me to Quincy on the day when one of the great debates between Lincoln and Douglas was to take place there, and on that occasion I was to meet Abraham Lincoln myself. On the evening before the day of the debate, I was on a railroad train bound for Quincy. The car in which I traveled was full of men who discussed the absorbing question with great animation. A member of the Republican State Committee accompanied me and sat by my side.

All at once, after the train had left a way station, I observed a great commotion among my fellow-passengers, many of whom jumped from their seats and pressed eagerly around a tall man who had just entered the car. They addressed him in the most familiar style: "Hello, Abe! How are you?" and so on. And he responded in the same manner: "Good-evening, Ben! How are you, Joe? Glad to see you, Dick!" and there was much laughter at some things he said, which, in the confusion of voices, I could not understand. "Why," exclaimed my companion, the committee-man, "there's Lincoln himself!" He pressed through the crowd and introduced me to Abraham Lincoln, whom I then saw for the first time.

I must confess that I was somewhat startled by his appearance. There he stood, overtopping by several inches all those surrounding him. Although measuring something over six feet myself, I had, standing quite near to him, to throw my head backward in order to look into his eyes. That swarthy face with its strong features, its deep furrows, and its benignant, melancholy eyes, is now familiar to every American by numberless pictures. It may be said that the whole civilized world knows and loves it. At that time it was clean-shaven, and looked even more haggard and careworn than later when it was framed in whiskers.

On his head he wore a somewhat battered "stove-pipe" hat. His neck emerged, long and sinewy, from a white collar turned down over a thin black necktie. His lank, ungainly body was clad in a rusty black dress coat with sleeves that should have been longer; but his arms appeared so long that the sleeves of a "store" coat could hardly be expected to cover them all the way down to the wrists. His black trousers, too, permitted a very full view of his large feet. On his left arm he carried a gray woolen shawl, which evidently served him for an overcoat in chilly weather. His left hand held a cotton umbrella of the bulging kind, and also a black satchel that bore the marks of long and hard usage. His right he had kept free for handshaking, of which there was no end until everybody in the car seemed to be satisfied. I had seen, in Washington and in the West, several public men of rough appearance; but none whose looks seemed quite so uncouth, not to say grotesque, as Lincoln's.

He received me with an off-hand cordiality, like an old acquaintance, having been informed of what I was doing in the campaign, and we sat down together. In a somewhat high-pitched but pleasant voice he began to talk to me, telling me much about the points he and Douglas had made in the debates at different places, and about those he intended to make at Quincy on the morrow.

When, in a tone of perfect ingenuousness, he asked me—a young beginner in politics—what I thought about this and that, I should have felt myself very much honored by his confidence, had he permitted me to regard him as a great man. But he talked in so simple and familiar a strain, and his manner and homely phrase were so absolutely free from any semblance of self-consciousness or pretension to superiority, that I soon felt as if I had known him all my life and we had long been close friends. He interspersed our conversation with all sorts of quaint stories, each of which had a witty point applicable to the subject in hand, and not seldom concluding an argument in such a manner that nothing more was to be said. He seemed to enjoy his own jests in a childlike way, for his unusually sad-looking eyes would kindle with a merry twinkle, and he himself led in the laughter; and his laugh was so genuine, hearty, and contagious that nobody could fail to join in it.

When we arrived at Quincy, we found a large number of friends waiting for him, and there was much hand-shaking and many familiar salutations again. Then they got him into a carriage, much against his wish, for he said that he would prefer to "foot it to Browning's," an old friend's house, where he was to have supper and a quiet night. But the night was by no means quiet outside. The blare of brass bands and the shouts of enthusiastic, and not in all cases quite sober, Democrats and Republicans, cheering and hurrahing for their respective champions, did not cease until the small hours.

The next morning the country people began to stream into town for the great meeting, some singly, on foot or on horseback, or small parties of men and women, and even children, in buggies or farm wagons; while others were marshaled in solemn procession from outlying towns or districts with banners and drums, many of them headed by maidens in white with tri-colored scarfs, who represented the Goddess of Liberty and the different States of the Union, and whose beauty was duly admired by everyone, including themselves. On the whole, the Democratic displays were much more elaborate and gorgeous than those of the Republicans, and it was said that Douglas had plenty of money to spend for such things. He himself also traveled in what was called in those days "great style," with a secretary and servants and a numerous escort of somewhat loud companions, moving from place to place by special train with cars specially decorated for the occasion, all of which contrasted strongly with Lincoln's extremely modest simplicity. There was no end of cheering and shouting and jostling on the streets of Quincy that day. But in spite of the excitement created by the political contest, the crowds remained very good-natured, and the occasional jibes flung from one side to the other were uniformly received with a laugh.

The great debate took place in the afternoon on the open square, where a large, pine-board platform had been built for the committee of arrangements, the speakers, and the persons they wished to have with them. I thus was favored with a seat on that platform. In front of it many thousands of people were assembled, Republicans and Democrats standing peaceably together, only chaffing one another now and then in a good-tempered way.

As the champions arrived they were demonstratively cheered by their adherents. The presiding officer agreed upon by the two parties called the meeting to order and announced the program of proceedings. Mr. Lincoln was to open with an allowance of one hour, and Senator Douglas was to follow with a speech of one hour and a half, and Mr. Lincoln was to speak half an hour in conclusion. The first part of Mr. Lincoln's opening address was devoted to a refutation of some things Douglas had said at previous meetings. This refutation may, indeed, have been required for the settlement of disputed points, but it did not strike me as anything extraordinary, either in substance or in form. Neither had Mr. Lincoln any of those physical advantages which usually are thought to be very desirable, if not necessary, to the orator. His voice was not musical, rather high-keyed, and apt to turn into a shrill treble in moments of excitement; but it was not positively disagreeable. It had an exceedingly penetrating, far-reaching quality. The looks of the audience convinced me that every word he spoke was understood at the remotest edges of the vast assemblage. His gesture was awkward. He swung his long arms sometimes in a very ungraceful manner. Now and then he would, to give particular emphasis to a point, bend his knees and body with a sudden downward jerk, and then shoot up again with a vehemence that raised him to his tip-toes and made him look much taller than he really was—a manner of enlivening a speech which at that time was, and perhaps still is, not unusual in the West, but which he succeeded in avoiding at a later period.

There was, however, in all he said, a tone of earnest truthfulness, of elevated, noble sentiment, and of kindly sympathy, which added greatly to the strength of his argument, and became, as in the course of his speech he touched upon the moral side of the question in debate, powerfully impressive. Even when attacking his opponent with keen satire or invective, which, coming from any other speaker, would have sounded bitter and cruel, there was still a certain something in his utterance making his hearers feel that those thrusts came from a reluctant heart, and that he would much rather have treated his foe as a friend.

When Lincoln had sat down amid the enthusiastic plaudits of his adherents, I asked myself with some trepidation in my heart, "What will Douglas say now?" Lincoln's speech had struck me as very clear, logical, persuasive, convincing even, and very sympathetic, but not as an overwhelming argument. Douglas, I thought, might not be able to confute it, but by the cunning sophistry at his command, and by one of his forceful appeals to prejudice, he might succeed in neutralizing its effect. No more striking contrast could have been imagined than that between those two men as they appeared upon the platform. By the side of Lincoln's tall, lank, and ungainly form, Douglas stood almost like a dwarf, very short of stature, but square-shouldered and broad-chested, a massive head upon a strong neck, the very embodiment of force, combativeness, and staying power. I have drawn his portrait when describing my first impressions of Washington City, and I apprehend it was not a flattering one. On that stage at Quincy he looked rather natty and well groomed in excellently fitting broadcloth and shining linen. But his face seemed a little puffy, and it was said that he had been drinking hard with some boon companions either on his journey or after his arrival. The deep, horizontal wrinkle between his keen eyes was unusually dark and scowling. While he was listening to Lincoln's speech, a contemptuous smile now and then flitted across his lips, and when he rose, the tough parliamentary gladiator, he tossed his mane with an air of overbearing superiority, of threatening defiance, as if to say: "How dare anyone stand up against me?" As I looked at him, I detested him deeply; but my detestation was not free from an anxious dread as to what was to come. His voice, naturally a strong baritone, gave forth a hoarse and rough, at times even something like a barking, sound. His tone was, from the very start, angry, dictatorial, and insolent in the extreme. In one of his first sentences he charged Lincoln with "base insinuations," and then he went on in that style with a wrathful frown upon his brow, defiantly shaking his head, clenching his fists, and stamping his feet. No language seemed to be too offensive for him, and even inoffensive things he would sometimes bring out in a manner which sounded as if intended to be insulting; and thus he occasionally called forth, instead of applause from his friends, demonstrations of remonstrance from the opposition. But his sentences were well put together, his points strongly accentuated, his argumentation seemingly clear and plausible, his sophisms skillfully woven so as to throw the desired flood of darkness upon the subject and thus beguile the untutored mind, his appeals to prejudice unprincipled and reckless, but shrewdly aimed, and his invective vigorous and exceedingly trying to the temper of the assailed party. On the whole, his friends were well pleased with his performance, and rewarded him with vociferous cheers.

But then came Lincoln's closing speech of half an hour, which seemed completely to change the temper of the atmosphere. He replied to Douglas's arguments and attacks with rapid thrusts so deft and piercing, with humorous retort so quaint and pat, and with witty illustrations so clinching, and he did it all so good-naturedly, that the meeting, again and again, broke out in bursts of delight by which even many of his opponents were carried away, while the scowl on Douglas's face grew darker and darker.

When the debate at Quincy was over, the champions were heartily cheered by their partisans, the assemblage dissolved peaceably, the brass bands began to play again, several of them within hearing of one another, so as to fill the air with discordant sounds, and the country people, with their banners and their maidens in white, got in motion to return to their homes, each party, no doubt, as it usually happens in such cases, persuaded that the result of the day was in its favor. I took my leave of Mr. Lincoln and was not to meet him again until about twenty months later.

I was deeply impressed by the democratic character of the spectacle I had witnessed in Illinois. On the whole it had strengthened my faith in the virtue of the democratic principle, although it had also made me more sensible of some of the dangers attending its practical realization. Here were two men, neither of whom had enjoyed any of the advantages of superior breeding or education. One of them, Lincoln, had in fact risen from home conditions so wretched that a faithful description of them severely taxes our credulity—conditions ordinarily apt to clog the intellect and to impede the development of all finer moral sensibilities. Neither of the two men had received any regular schooling calculated in any manner to prepare a person for the career of a statesman. Neither of them had in any sense been particularly favored by fortune. Neither of them had, in working his way upward from a low estate, any resource to draw on but his own native ability and spirit. But here they were, in positions before the country in which their ambitions could, without any overleaping, aim at the highest honors of the Republic. One of them, Douglas, had risen by rapid but regular political advancement to a Senatorship of the United States, and had, by his contact with the great world, acquired, if not the true refinement, at least some of the outward polish of "good society." His rise had been effected, perhaps, not altogether by blameless means, but at any rate mainly by the force of his own intellect and the exercise of his own energies. The other, Lincoln, had not been quite so successful in achieving official station, but he had won a singular influence over the minds of large numbers of people by the power of his own mind and the virtues of his own character—and this while the outward rusticity of his early life still clung to him, and was in a large sense a part of his being. Each one of them was truly a child of the people. Each had won his remarkable eminence because each had, in his way, by his own effort, deserved it. And these men now contended for the mastery by appealing to the intelligence and the patriotism of the people—the one, perhaps, largely by the arts of the demagogue, seeking to befog the popular understanding where he could not, to his advantage, honestly enlighten it; the other, perhaps, by candid truth-telling and grave appeals to conscience—but both by addressing themselves to the minds of the people, whose opinion, lawfully expressed, was by both recognized to be the only legitimate source of all power.

The debates were hardly over when I was urgently called to another field. As the anti-slavery movement was disintegrating both the old Whig party and the old Democratic party at a fast rate, the "Native American" sentiment burst forth in one of its periodical manifestations. That sentiment was originally—in greatest part at least—directed against the Catholic influence—against "Romanism," as the favorite phrase ran—but it demanded a curtailment of the political rights of the whole foreign-born element without distinction of origin or religious creed. A secret society, called the "Know-nothings," was organized with all the paraphernalia of rituals and oaths and vows and passwords which seem to have a peculiar charm for people of weak minds and susceptible imaginations, and the "order" spread rapidly all over the Northern States.

In Massachusetts, where the "American" movement had won control of the whole State government, the Legislature adopted for submission to a vote of the people an amendment to the State Constitution, providing that foreign-born persons should not have the right of voting until two years after they had become citizens of the United States. This was the famous "two-years' amendment" which at the time created much excitement among the foreign-born population, and was eagerly seized upon by Democratic newspapers and stump-speakers as a premonitory indication of the fate which awaited the foreign born if the Republican party should come into power. And this warning was all the more likely to make an impression, as the State of Massachusetts was recognized as the high school of the anti-slavery movement.

Among the Republican leaders who became especially alarmed at this state of things was Henry Wilson, one of the United States Senators from Massachusetts, whom I came to know at a later period. He was what is commonly called "a man of the people." Without the advantage of a higher education—his early connection with the shoe business in Natick had earned him the nickname of "the Natick cobbler"—he had worked himself up to a position of influence in politics. He had won the confidence of the anti-slavery men by his sincere and very active devotion to that cause. His eloquence did not rise to a high level, but became impressive by the ingenuous force with which it portrayed his convictions. He justly enjoyed the reputation of being a thoroughly honest and well-meaning man. There was something childlike in his being, even in his political dealings, although he may have considered himself, and to a certain extent he was, a skillful political manager. He certainly was a very watchful and busy one. The anti-slavery sentiment filled his whole soul. Beyond that cause he took very little interest in other political questions; at least he judged them by their relation to it, and only in that relation they became important or unimportant in his eyes. Everybody liked him; and everybody was attracted by the sympathetic warmth of his nature; and everybody trusted the goodness of his motives, although not always his discretion. There was a rumor that, believing he could aid the anti-slavery cause by countenancing the nativistic movement, he had secretly joined one of the Know-nothing lodges. Whether this rumor was correct or not, I do not know. He probably did not care much whether foreign-born citizens were permitted to vote a year or two earlier or a year or two later, provided they cast their votes against the slavery cause. Certain it is that as soon as the nativistic movement threatened to endanger the anti-slavery cause, he turned against it and anxiously looked for a way to defeat the "two-years' amendment" in Massachusetts.

Senator Wilson consulted with Edward L. Pierce, who many years later wrote the great biography of Charles Sumner, and became a warm and dear friend of mine, and the two joined in inviting me to come to Massachusetts and help them undo the mischief. The ostensible occasion was the celebration by a public dinner of the anniversary of Thomas Jefferson's birthday—a celebration which was in harmony with the recent revival of Jeffersonian States' rights principles in the agitation against the fugitive slave law. But the real object was to rally prominent anti-slavery men for a demonstration against the mischievous nativistic tide. Of this I was duly informed. As soon as the invitation arrived, my friend Byron Paine insisted that I must accept it. So I went.

The dinner took place at the Parker House in Boston, and was a notable affair. The principal figures in it were John A. Andrew, who was to be the illustrious war-governor of Massachusetts, Senator Henry Wilson, Governor Boutwell, Frank Bird, Edward L. Pierce, his brother, Henry L. Pierce, Samuel Bowles, the brilliant editor of the *Springfield Republican,* and several of the anti-slavery leaders of the State. The speeches which were delivered vied with one another in denouncing the fugitive slave law as one of the ruthless invasions of the rights and liberties of the American citizen.

This was my introduction to Boston, and to me it was a most happy one. Not only did I keenly enjoy the cordiality which met me wherever I turned, but the whole atmosphere of the city, the general physiognomy of the population were exceedingly congenial to me. I thought I saw a light of intelligence on the faces of all the passers-by on the streets, which impressed me as if every milkman on his wagon and every citizen hurrying to his task with his tools under his arm must be something like a Harvard graduate in disguise. No doubt my enthusiasm ran a little ahead of my judgment; but I had good reason to be intensely delighted with the persons whose acquaintance I was fortunate enough to make. It could hardly be otherwise. For instance, I was invited to a dinner party at the house of Mr. Gardner Brewer, one of the patrician houses of the town. I met there several of my friends of the Jefferson birthday dinner, also, for the first time, Longfellow and Banks. But I was seated at the table by the side of a little gentleman whose name had escaped me when I was presented to him. He was very kind to me, and soon I found myself engaged with him in a lively conversation which gradually drew the attention of the whole table, all the guests listening to him. His talk was so animated, bubbling and sparkling, and at the same time there was so kindly and genial a flow of wit and wisdom, that I sat there in a state of amazed delight. I had never heard anything like it. After a while I asked my neighbor on the other side: "Pray, who is the wonderful man?" "You do not know him?" he answered. "Why, this is Dr. Oliver Wendell Holmes."

I visited Boston often after those days in 1859, and then I had sometimes the happiness of sitting as a guest at the same table with the other members of the famous circle of Boston's, or rather America's, great celebrities—Longfellow, Emerson, Lowell, Agassiz, Holmes, Norton, Field, Sumner, and others of their companionship, and of hearing them converse among themselves—not with an effort of saying remarkable things, but with the natural, unpretending, and therefore most charming simplicity of truly great minds. I never saw Whittier at one of those dinners. But being a warm admirer of Whittier's powerfully moving anti-slavery poems, I wished very much to behold the poet's face and to hear his voice. Therefore, I eagerly accepted, on one of my visits to Boston, the offer of one of Whittier's friends to take me to Amesbury, the village where he lived, and to introduce me to him. When we called at his very modest frame house, the typical New England village house painted white with green shutters, we were told that he was not at home, but might possibly be found at the post-office. At the post-office we were told that he had been there, but had probably gone to the drug store. At the drug store we found him quietly talking with a little company of neighbors assembled around the stove—for it was a cold winter day. I was almost sorry to break into that tranquil chat between the poet and his village familiars, for I was satisfied with looking at him as he stood there, tall and slim, with his fine, placid face, all goodness and unpretending simplicity, so superior to those surrounding him, and yet so like them. My friend introduced me to him as a co-worker in the anti-slavery cause, and he received me very kindly. We had a little exchange of questions and answers not remarkable, and he offered to take us to his house. But we could not accept the invitation, as we had to hurry back to the train for Boston. I left him with a feeling as if the mere meeting with him had been a blessing—a breath of air from a world of purity and beneficence.

To no member of that famous circle I felt myself more attracted than to Longfellow, and he, too, seemed to look upon me with a friendly eye. He kindly invited me to visit him whenever I might come within hailing distance. And how delightful were those hours I spent with him from time to time in the cozy intimacy of his old colonial house in Cambridge, the historic Washington headquarters. We usually sat together in the little room on the right hand of the hall, the room with the round book-covered table in it. He then used to bring in a bottle of old Rhine wine and a couple of long German student pipes, which, I fear, he did not enjoy smoking very much, although he pretended to enjoy it, because, no doubt, he thought I did; and then he talked of German poetry and poets, and of the anti-slavery cause for which he cherished a warm, although quiet, interest, and of Charles Sumner, whom he loved dearly, as I did. Longfellow was one of the most beautiful men I have ever known, and he grew more beautiful every year of his advancing old age—with his flowing white hair and beard and his grand face of the antique Jupiter type —not indeed a "Jupiter tonans," but a fatherly Zeus holding a benignant hand over the world and mankind. He was by no means a brilliant conversationalist—not to be compared with Oliver Wendell Holmes—but his talk, although not remarkable for wit or eloquence, had to me a peculiar fascination. It produced, upon me at least, the impression of modestly withholding behind it a great store of serene reserve power, and it flowed on so placidly as to make me feel as if I were in a gently rocking boat floating down a tranquil stream meandering through green meadows. His very being seemed to be enveloped in an atmosphere of peace and noble sympathy. I have seen him quietly entering social gatherings of men and women when everybody seemed at once to become sensible of the mellow sunshine radiating from his presence, and all faces, old and young, turned to him with an expression of something like joyous affection.

CHAPTER X

Campaigning and Lecturing

In the autumn of 1859 I was on duty not only in Wisconsin, where it was my special business to allay the dissatisfaction caused among my friends by the action of the State Convention which I have described, but I was also urgently asked to make some speeches in Minnesota, where the first State election was to be held in November. I obeyed the call. I found myself put down in the plan of campaign for one or two speeches a day, with an itinerary spreading over a large part of the State.

Once, I was to speak at a place called by the committeeman instructing me, the "City of Lexington," the center of a large farming district. It was marked with a big dot on the map. A buggy was assigned to me with a young man as a driver who "knew the road." I should have to start about daybreak in order to reach my destination in time for the afternoon meeting. There I would meet the Hon. Galusha Grow, the well-known Representative from Pennsylvania in Congress. This was all the committeeman could tell me. It was a glorious sunrise, and soon I found myself on the open prairie, swept by the exhilarating morning breeze. The empty spaces between farms became larger and larger, human habitations scarcer. Now I saw a number of Indian papooses sitting in a row on the fence of a lonesome settlement, and an Indian wigwam near by. Then, before me, the vast plain, apparently boundless and without a sign of human life; here and there a little strip of timber along a water course; the road a mere wagon track. It was delightful to breathe. I heartily enjoyed the bracing freshness of this Western atmosphere. After we had traveled on for two or three hours, it occurred to me to ask my companion whether he had ever been at the "City of Lexington," and when we would be likely to get there. I was surprised to find that he knew as little of the City of Lexington as I did. He had simply been told to follow "this road," in a westerly direction, and we should get there sometime.

Presently a buggy hove in sight, coming from the opposite direction. Two men were seated in it, one of whom hailed me with, "Hello, stranger! Please stop a moment!" We stopped. A tall gentleman jumped down from the other vehicle and, saluting me, said: "I wonder whether you are not Mr. Carl Schurz?" "Yes, that is my name." "I am Frank Blair from St. Louis, Missouri," said he. His name was well-known to me as one of the bravest anti-slavery men in that slave State—himself the son of Francis P. Blair, who had been one of the confidential friends and advisers of President Andrew Jackson. "A committeeman told me last night," he said, "that you were in this part of the country, and when I saw you in that buggy, I made a happy guess. Very glad to meet you. Let us sit down in the grass and have some lunch. I have a bottle of claret, and some sandwiches, enough for both of us." So we sat down, and this was the way in which I made the acquaintance of the famous Frank Blair, one of the most gallant and successful anti-slavery leaders in the South, who, later, after the breaking out of the Civil War, bore such a splendid part in the movement saving St. Louis and the State of Missouri to the Union, who then became a major general in the Union Army, then, being discontented with the Republican reconstruction policy, went over to the Democrats, and was nominated by them for the vice-presidency in 1868; took a somewhat sinister part in the "Liberal-Republican" Convention at Cincinnati in 1872, and whom I met again in the Senate of the United States. Our meeting on the Minnesota prairie was exceedingly pleasant. We laughed much about the fun of this wild campaign, and rejoiced together in the prospects of our cause.

Before we parted I inquired of Mr. Blair's driver whether he knew where the City of Lexington was. He had only heard of it, but guessed that if we followed "this road" westward, we should "strike it." So our buggy trundled on over "this road" several hours longer, when we entered a belt of timber on a creek bottom, and suddenly found ourselves in front of a cluster of log houses, the largest of which seemed to be a tavern. Near its door a man was lounging on a wooden bench, whittling a stick. I asked him whether we were on the right road to the City of Lexington and what the distance might be. "Why," said he, with a contemptuous drawl, "this is the City of Lexington. Be you one of the chaps that's to lecture here this afternoon?" I confessed that I was, and at the same moment another buggy drove up, from which a traveler alighted, in whom, from some picture I had seen, I recognized

the Hon. Galusha Grow from Pennsylvania, the speaker of the National House of Representatives that was to be. I found in him an exceedingly jovial gentleman, in the prime of life, and inclined to look at
the bright or humorous side of everything. His search for the City of
Lexington had been no less arduous than mine, and we had a hearty
laugh at our discovery.

No sooner were the elections over than I had to start out on an extensive lecture-tour to make up by its earnings for money spent and
private affairs neglected, during the political season of the year, and
to accumulate something in advance for the coming great campaign of
1860.

While visiting Boston on a lecturing tour I had occasion to attend
one of those "Conservative Union Meetings," which were held to
warn the people against anything like an active anti-slavery movement
and to lead them back to the paths of ancient whiggery. It was held in
Faneuil Hall, and Edward Everett and Caleb Cushing were the principal speakers. I had never heard either of these two distinguished men
before, and was prepared for a powerful onset of argument and appeal.
But my expectations were disappointed. In the first place, Mr. Everett's introduction to the audience produced an almost comical effect.
It was a raw winter-day and Mr. Everett had evidently, before venturing out, been carefully armed against the inclemencies of the weather.
While the chairman made an eulogistic little speech presenting to
those assembled their illustrious fellow-citizen, Mr. Everett stood behind him being peeled out of an endless variety of wraps—an operation performed by an attendant, which caused him to turn himself
around several times. This spectacle of the unwinding of Mr. Everett
started a pretty general titter among the audience, which at last was
stopped by the applause following the close of the chairman's intro-
ductory speech. Mr. Everett's argument was the well-worn plea of
patriotic apprehension. It was very finely expressed, every sentence
of faultless finish, every gesture well pointed and appropriate. But
there was a coldness of academic perfection about it all which lacked
the robustness of true, deep, aggressive feeling. The audience ap-
plauded many times, but, as far as I could judge, without any real burst
of enthusiasm. When Mr. Everett sat down the general verdict seemed
to be that, as usual, he had made a very fine speech, and that he was a
most honorable and patriotic gentleman.

The impression produced by Mr. Caleb Cushing was very different.
While speaking he turned his left shoulder to the audience, looking at
his hearers askance, and with a squint, too, as it seemed to me, but I

may have been mistaken. There was something like a cynical sneer in his manner of bringing out his sentences, which made him look like Mephistopheles alive, and I do not remember ever to have heard a public speaker who stirred in me so decided a disinclination to believe what he said. In later years I met him repeatedly at dinner tables which he enlivened with his large information, his wit, and his fund of anecdote. But I could never quite overcome the impression he had made upon me at that meeting. I could always listen to him with interest, but never with spontaneous confidence.

My lecturing engagements left me time for a short visit at Washington. Congress was then in a state of excitement, the like of which we can now hardly imagine. The morning after my arrival I took breakfast with my friend, Mr. John F. Potter, the Representative of the First Congressional District of Wisconsin. He asked me to accompany him to the Capitol, where he promised to take me on the floor of the House of Representatives, if he could. Before we started I saw him buckle on a belt with a pistol and a bowie-knife, to be worn under his clothes. "You seem surprised," he said. "This is my regular morning toilet when I go to the House. You know I am no ruffian, but a peaceable citizen. We do not know what may happen." Then he explained to me that the Northern anti-slavery men might expect an attack at any time, not so much from the Southern Representatives themselves on the floor, as from a gang of Southern desperadoes gathered in the galleries. "They may open on us at any time," said Mr. Potter. "But when they begin to shoot we mean to be prepared to shoot back. A number of our friends go armed just as I do." I had already been told that Senator Wade from Ohio, having been threatened by Southern men, one day appeared in the Senate with a brace of large horse pistols, which he quietly put on the lid of his desk within sight of everybody; and when he was sure they had been noticed, he calmly shut them up in his drawer, ready to hand, and leaned back in his chair, looking around with a grim smile. Whether the story is true, I am not quite certain. But it was widely believed, for it looked very much like "old Ben Wade," and, no doubt, it fitted the situation.

On my return trip westward I had to keep a lecturing appointment at Columbus, Ohio. Mr. Salmon P. Chase, who was then Governor of that State, had written me a very kind letter offering me the hospitality of his house, and I had accepted, highly appreciating the honor. I arrived early in the morning, and was, to my great surprise, received at the uncomfortable hour by the Governor himself, and taken to the breakfast room. His daughter Kate, who presided over his household, he said, would be down presently. Soon she came, saluted me very kindly, and then let herself down upon her chair with the graceful lightness of a bird that, folding its wings, perches upon the branch of a tree. She was then about eighteen years old, tall and slender, and exceedingly well formed. Her features were not at all regularly beautiful according to the classic rule. Her little nose, somewhat audaciously tipped up, would perhaps not have passed muster with a severe critic, but it fitted pleasingly into her face with its large, languid but at the same time vivacious hazel eyes, shaded by long dark lashes, and arched over by proud eyebrows. The fine forehead was framed in waving gold-brown hair. She had something imperial in the pose of the head, and all her movements possessed an exquisite natural charm. No wonder that she came to be admired as a great beauty and broke many hearts. After the usual polite commonplaces, the conversation at the breakfast table, in which Miss Kate took a lively and remarkably intelligent part, soon turned upon politics, and that conversation was continued during a large part of the forenoon in the Governor's library. I had conceived a very profound respect for Mr. Chase's ability as well as his character. All his speeches on the slavery question were well known to me, and I greatly admired their argumentative lucidity and strength, and no less the noble elevation of sentiment pervading them. His personality, too, when I saw him on the floor of the Senate from the gallery a few years before, had impressed me powerfully. More than anyone else he looked the great man. And now, when I sat with him in the confidential atmosphere of his den, and he asked me to give him my view of the political situation, I felt as if a great distinction had been conferred upon me, and, at the same time, a responsibility which I was not altogether eager to take. His bearing in public gave Chase the appearance of a somewhat cold, haughty, and distant man. Without the least affectation or desire to pose, he was apt to be superbly statuesque. But when in friendly intercourse he opened himself, the real warmth of his nature broke through the icy crust, and one received the impression that his usual reticence arose rather from something like bashful shyness than from a haughty sense of superiority. His dignity of deportment never left him, even in his unbending moods, for it was perfectly natural and unconscious. It really belonged to him like the majestic figure that nature had given him. There was something very captivating in the grand simplicity of his character as it revealed itself in his confidences when he imparted them with that almost childlike little lisp in his deep voice, and I can well understand how intimate friends could conceive a sentimental affection for him and preserve it through the changes of time, even when occasionally they ceased to approve his course.

With this remarkable man, then, I sat alone in his cosy work-room, and he avowed to me with a frankness which astonished but at the same time greatly fascinated me, his ardent desire to be President of the United States, and to be nominated for that office by the coming Republican National Convention. He said that I would undoubtedly be sent by the Republicans of Wisconsin as a delegate to that convention, and that he wished very much to know what I thought of his candidacy. It would have given me a moment of sincerest happiness could I have answered that question with a note of encouragement, for nothing could have appeared to me more legitimate than the high ambition of that man, and I felt myself very strongly drawn to him personally. But I could not, and I esteemed him too highly to flatter him or to treat him to ambiguous phrases. I candidly told him that I was too inexperienced in American politics to estimate the number of votes he might command in the convention, but that I had formed a general judgment of the situation, which I expressed in this wise: "If the Republican Convention at Chicago have courage enough to nominate an advanced anti-slavery man, they will nominate Seward; if not, they will not nominate you." The Governor was silent for a moment, as if he had heard something unexpected. Then he thanked me for having so straightforwardly given him my opinion, which, possibly, might be correct. But, without casting the slightest reflection upon Seward's character and services, he gave me to understand that he could not see why anti-slavery men should place him second in the order of leadership instead of first—a point which I could not undertake to argue.

The Governor carried on the conversation in the best of temper, although I had evidently disappointed him, and he remained as cordial in his demeanor as before. Still, I thought I observed a note of sadness in his tone. At that period I had studied the history of the country enough to know that the "presidential fever" was a troublesome ailment, and sometimes fatal to the peace of mind and the moral equilibrium of persons attacked by it. But I had never come in contact with a public man who was, in the largest sense of the term, possessed by the desire to be President, even to the extent of honestly believing that he owed it to the country and that the country owed it to him that he should be President, and who had to make the utmost moral effort to keep that idea from obscuring his motives and controlling his whole conduct. Chase was one of the noblest victims of that disease, and he suffered terribly from it—not as though it had corrupted his principles and vitiated his public morals, for he remained true to the high aims of his public life; but because he constantly indulged in hopes and delusions which always proved deceptive. His repeated disappointments pierced him and rankled in him like poisoned arrows; and he was incessantly tortured by the feeling that his country did not do justice to him, and that his public life was a failure. It was a pathetic spectacle.

I remained in friendly relations with Mr. Chase as long as he lived, and our intercourse always became really confidential whenever we had occasion to exchange opinions. This was not infrequent when he was in President Lincoln's Cabinet and at the beginning of his career as Chief Justice. He always knew that I thought his ambition hopeless and his efforts to accomplish its aim futile. But this never affected our personal friendship, for he knew also that I esteemed him very highly and cherished for him a sincere affection.

CHAPTER XI

The Campaign of 1860

THE Republicans of Wisconsin were very kind to me. In the spring of 1860, their State Convention appointed me as one of their delegates to the Republican National Convention to be held at Chicago in May. The delegation elected me its chairman to announce its votes on the floor of the convention, to make, in its name, such statements or declarations as might become necessary, and generally to represent it whenever such representation was called for.

There was no real antagonism among us to Abraham Lincoln of Illinois. He was universally recognized as a true anti-slavery leader who had done our cause very great service. We esteemed him most highly, but we did not favor his nomination, because we were for Seward, as the current phrase then was, "first, last, and all the time."

But I must confess that my enthusiasm for Seward received a little chill, even before the convention met. Immediately after our arrival at Chicago, we from Wisconsin thought it our duty to report ourselves at the headquarters of the New York delegation to ask for suggestions as to what we might do to further the interests of our candidate. But we did not find there any of the distinguished members of that delegation whom we most wished to see—William M. Evarts, George William Curtis, Henry J. Raymond, Governor Morgan, and others. We found only the actual chief manager of the Seward interest, Mr. Thurlow Weed, and around him a crowd of men, some of whom did not strike me as desirable companions. They were New York politicians, apparently of the lower sort, whom Thurlow Weed had brought with him to aid him in doing his work. What that work consisted in I could guess from the conversations I was permitted to hear, for they talked very freely about the great services they had rendered or were going to render. They had marched in street parades with brass bands and Seward banners to produce the impression that the whole country was ablaze with enthusiasm for Seward. They had treated members of other delegations with no end of champagne and cigars, to win them for Seward, if not as their first, then at least as their second choice, to be voted for on the second or third ballot. They had hinted to this man and that man supposed to wield some influence, that if he could throw that influence for Seward, he might, in case of success, count upon proper "recognition." They had spent money freely and let everybody understand that there was a great lot more to spend. Among these men Thurlow Weed moved as the great captain, with ceaseless activity and noiseless step, receiving their reports and giving new instructions in his peculiar whisper, now and then taking one into a corner of the room for secret talk, or disappearing with another through a side door for transactions still more secret. I had heard much of Thurlow Weed as a man of mysterious powers; as a political wizard able to devise and accomplish combinations beyond the conception of ordinary mortals; as the past-master of political intrigue and stratagem; as the profoundest judge of men's abilities, virtues, and failings; as the surest calculator of political chances and results; and as the guide, superintendent, and protecting genius of William H. Seward's political career. This may sound like exaggeration, but he certainly had acquired the reputation of the most skillful political manager—others called it "wire-puller"—of his time. While everybody recognized his extraordinary ability, the opinions about his political virtue were divided. His opponents denounced him as a selfish and utterly unscrupulous trickster, while his friends emphasized the fact that he secured offices for ever so many friends, but never any for himself, except a public printer's place which was profitable in revenue, but very modest in rank. In this respect, therefore, his ambition passed as disinterested. His singular zeal for the furtherance of Seward's political welfare and the singular intimacy that existed between the two not seldom alarmed Seward's political friends, but it cannot be said that Thurlow Weed turned Seward's rise in influence and power to his own material advantage.

I was appointed a member of the Committee on Resolutions that had to draw up the Republican platform, and in that committee was permitted to write the paragraph concerning the naturalization laws so that the Republican party be washed clean of the taint of Know-nothingism. This was done in moderate but unequivocal terms, which produced an excellent effect in the campaign. I also took part in formulating the anti-slavery declarations of the platform, but there an unintentional omission occurred which led to a dramatic scene in the convention. While the platform severely denounced the policy of the Administration with regard to Kansas, repudiated all the theories upon which rested the right of the slave-holder to carry his slave property into the Territories, as well as Douglas's spurious "popular-sovereignty" doctrine, denied the authority of Congress, of a Territorial Legislature, or of any individuals to give legal existence to slavery in any Territories of the United States, branded the reopening of the slave trade as "a crime against humanity, and a burning shame to our country and age," thus covering all points in actual issue, it failed to mention specifically the great principles enunciated in the Declaration of Independence as our political creed and as the moral basis of our free institutions. When the draft of the platform was read to the convention, enthusiastic applause greeted almost every sentence of it, and an impatient call for a vote followed from all parts of the vast assembly. But amid this noise arose above the heads of the multitude the venerable form of Joshua R. Giddings of Ohio. Everybody knew him as one of the veteran champions of the anti-slavery cause. He had pleaded for that cause with undaunted courage and fidelity when even in many parts of the North no one could do so without danger. It was the religion of his life. No sooner had the clamor for a vote sufficiently calmed down to let him be heard, than he expressed himself painfully surprised that the Republican platform, that solemn promulgation of its political faith to be put forth by the party of freedom, should not contain a word of recognition of the Declaration of Independence.

There are always, in such Conventions, even those that are not controlled by machine power, many persons impatient at anything that threatens to interfere with the despatch of business as proposed by the committees; and so it was at Chicago. No sooner had Mr. Giddings stopped speaking, than the tumult of voices burst forth again with a stormy clamor for an immediate vote, and, carried away by the whirlwind, the Convention, heedlessly it may well be supposed, rejected the amendment. Then Mr. Giddings, a look of distress upon his face, his white head towering above the crowd, slowly made his way toward the door of the hall. Suddenly from among the New York delegation a young man of strikingly beautiful features leaped upon a chair and demanded to be heard. The same noisy demonstration of impatience greeted him, but he would not yield. "Gentlemen!" he said in a tone of calm determination, "this is a convention of free speech, and I have been given the floor. I have but a few words to say to you, but I shall say them, if I stand here until to-morrow morning!" Another tumultuous protest of impatience, but he firmly held his ground. At last the clamor yielded to his courage, and silence fell upon the great assembly. Then his musical voice rang out like a trumpet call. Was this, he said, the party of freedom met on the border of the free prairies to advance the cause of liberty and human rights? And would the representatives of that party dare to reject the doctrine of the Declaration of Independence affirming the equality of men's rights? After a few such sentences of almost defiant appeal, he renewed, in a parliamentary form, the amendment moved by Mr. Giddings, and with an overwhelming shout of enthusiasm the convention adopted it.

When the young orator sat down his name passed from mouth to mouth. It was George William Curtis. I had never seen him before. As he stood there in that convention, towering over the vast multitude, his beautiful face radiant with resolute fervor, his singularly melodious voice thrilling with impassioned anxiety of purpose, one might have seen in him an ideal, poetic embodiment of the best of that moral impulse and that lofty enthusiasm which aroused the people of the North to the decisive struggle against slavery. We became friends then and there, and we remained friends to the day of his death.

After the close of the Convention, Mr. Evarts is reported to have said in a tone of mournful irony: "We New Yorkers have lost our candidate, but we have at least saved the Declaration of Independence." I have often thought, in the light of later events, that what they saved was worth much more than what they lost. As the Convention progressed it became more and more evident every hour that Seward, whose support came mainly from New York, New England, and the Northwest, was not only not gaining, but rather losing, in strength.

When on the third day of the Convention the balloting began, the contest was already decided. After the first ballot, which gave the several delegations the required opportunity for casting the complimentary votes for the "favorite sons" of their States, the opposition to Seward, obeying a common impulse, concentrated upon Abraham Lincoln, and the third ballot gave him the majority. Much has been said about the superior volume and fierceness of the shouting for Lincoln in the packed galleries and its effect upon the minds of the delegates. But that is mere reporters' talk. The historic fact is that, as the Convention would not take the risks involved in the nomination of Seward, it had no other alternative than to select Lincoln as the man who satisfied the demands of the earnest anti-slavery men without subjecting the party to the risks thought to be inseparable from the nomination of Seward. That the popular demonstrations for Lincoln in and around the Convention were, indeed, well planned and organized, is true. But they were by no means a decisive factor. Without them the result would have been the same.

When on the third ballot, Lincoln came so near a majority that his nomination appeared certain, delegates, before the result was declared, tumbled over one another to change their votes in his favor. The Wisconsin delegation did not change its vote. Together with New York, Michigan, Minnesota, and parts of other delegations, we stood solidly for Seward until Mr. Evarts, the chairman of the New York delegation, with a speech of genuine pathos and admirable temper, moved to make Mr. Lincoln's nomination unanimous. To this we heartily assented.

While the victory of Mr. Lincoln was being announced to the outside world by the boom of a cannon which had been placed on the roof, and not only the great convention hall, but, as it appeared, the whole City of Chicago shook with triumphant cheers for Lincoln, my thoughts involuntarily turned to Chase, who I imagined, sat in a quiet office room at Columbus with a telegraph near by clicking the news from Chicago. Not only had the prediction made to him a few months before become true, but it had become more terribly true than I myself had anticipated. Of the votes, about 670 cast in the Convention, he had never received more than 49, and even that beggarly number had dwindled down to 24½ on the last ballot. Not even his own State had given him its full strength. No doubt he had hoped, and hoped and hoped against hope—no American afflicted with the presidential fever ever ceases to hope—and now came this disastrous, crushing, humiliating defeat. I saw that magnificent man before me, writhing with the agony of his disappointment, and I sympathized with him most profoundly. I should have pitied him, had I dared to pity such a man. But would not this distressing experience teach him the wisdom of not staking the happiness of his life upon the winning of that prize? Alas, it did not. He continued to nurse that one ambition so that it became the curse of his life to his last day. It sometimes painfully distorted his judgment of things and men. It made him depreciate all the honors and powers bestowed upon him. When he was Secretary of the Treasury and, later, Chief Justice of the Supreme Court, the finest opportunities for enviable distinction were open to him, which, indeed, he achieved, but he restlessly looked beyond for the will-o'-the-wisp which deceitfully danced before his gaze. Many years later, when he had been touched by a slight paralytic stroke which somewhat impaired his speech and the freedom of his limbs, I saw him at an evening reception in his house, when his futile efforts to appear youthfully vigorous and agile were pathetically evident. Gossip had it that the reception was given for the very purpose of convincing the political society of Washington that he was physically as fit to be President as ever. He was indeed a great man; but, like Henry Clay and Daniel Webster, how much greater and how much more useful would he have been had he been content with his real greatness!

I had the honor of being appointed a member of the committee that was sent to Springfield to carry to Mr. Lincoln the official announcement of his nomination. At every railway station we passed in daylight we were received with demonstrations of joy. Mr. Lincoln received us in the parlor of his modest frame house—a rather bare-looking room; in the center the customary little table with a white marble top, and on it the silver-plated ice-water pitcher and the family Bible or the photograph album; and some chairs and a sofa ranged along the walls. There the Republican candidate for the Presidency stood, tall and ungainly in his black suit of apparently new but ill-fitting clothes, his long tawny neck emerging gauntly from his turn-down collar, his melancholy eyes sunken deep in his haggard face. Most of the members of the committee had never seen him before, and gazed at him with surprised curiosity. He certainly did not present the appearance of a statesman as people usually picture it in their imagination. Standing up with folded hands, he quietly, without visible embarrassment or emotion, listened to the dignified little speech addressed to him by Mr. Ashmun, the president of the Convention, and then he responded with a few appropriate, earnest, and well-shaped sentences, expressing his gratitude for the confidence reposed in him, and his doubts of his own abilities, and his trust in a helping Providence. Then followed some informal talk, partly of a jovial kind, in which the hearty simplicity of Lincoln's nature shone out, and after the usual hand-shaking the committee took its leave. One of its members, Mr. Kelley of Pennsylvania, remarked to me as we passed out of the house: "Well, we might have done a more brilliant thing, but we could hardly have done a better thing."

I heard similar utterances from other members in which, however, an undertone of resignation and of suppressed doubt was perceptible. Some of them, who were entirely unused to Western men and Western ways, and who, on this occassion, saw Mr. Lincoln for the first time, could not quite conceal their misgivings as to how this single-minded man, this child of nature, would bear himself in the contact with the great world and in the face of the large and complicated problems, for grappling with which he had apparently so scant an equipment. Indeed, a few days after the adjournment of the Chicago Convention, some symptoms of dissatisfaction and of coldness towards Mr. Lincoln became perceptible even in certain circles of Western Seward enthusiasts, who could not reconcile themselves to what they called the ignominious slaughter of the greatest Republican leader. Having myself been an ardent advocate of Seward's nomination, I thought I could address an effective appeal to the discontented and I did so in my speech at the ratification meeting in Milwaukee.

The campaign was hardly opened when the whole North seemed to get into commotion. It looked as if people, especially in the smaller cities and towns and the country districts, had little else to do than to attend meetings, listen to speeches, march in processions, and carry torches after night-fall.

While "stumping" in Illinois I had an appointment to address an afternoon open-air meeting in the capitol grounds in Springfield, Mr. Lincoln's place of residence. He asked me to take dinner with him at his house. At table we conversed about the course and the incidents of the campaign, and his genial and simple-hearted way of expressing himself would hardly permit me to remember that he was a great man and a candidate for the presidency of the United States. He was in the best of humor, and we laughed much. The inevitable brass band took position in front of the house and struck up a lively tune, admonishing us that the time for the business of the day had arrived. "I will go with you to the meeting," said Mr. Lincoln, "and hear what you have to say." The day was blazing hot. Mr. Lincoln expressed his regret that I had to exert myself in such a temperature, and suggested that I make myself comfortable. He indeed "made himself comfortable" in a way which surprised me not a little, but which was thoroughly characteristic of his rustic habits. When he presented himself for the march to the capitol grounds I observed that he had divested himself of his waistcoat and put on, as his sole garment, a linen duster, the back of which had been marked by repeated perspirations and looked somewhat like a rough map of the two hemispheres. On his head he wore a well-battered "stovepipe" hat which evidently had seen several years of hard service. In this attire he marched with me behind the brass band, after us, the local campaign committee and the Wide-Awakes. Of course, he was utterly unconscious of his grotesque appearance. Nothing could have been farther from his

mind than the thought that the world-conspicuous distinction bestowed upon him by his nomination for the presidency should have
obliged him to "put on dignity" among his neighbors. Those neighbors who, from the windows and the sidewalks on that hot afternoon,
watched and cheered him as he walked by in the procession behind
the brass band, may have regarded him, the future President, with a
new feeling of reverential admiration, or awe; but he appeared before
and among them entirely unconcerned, as if nothing had happened,
and so he nodded to his acquaintances, as he recognized them in the
crowd, with a: "How are you, Dan?" or "Glad to see you, Ned!"
or "How d'ye do, Bill?" and so on—just as he had been accustomed to
do. Arrived at the place of meeting, he declined to sit on the platform,
but took a seat in the front row of the audience. He did not join in
the applause which from time to time rewarded me, but occasionally
he gave me a nod and a broad smile. When I had finished, a few voices
called upon Mr. Lincoln for a speech, but he simply shook his head,
and the crowd instantly respected the proprieties of the situation, some
even shouting: "No, no!" at which he gratefully signified his assent.
Then the brass band, and the committee, and the Wide-Awakes, in
the same order in which we had come, escorted us back to his house,
the multitude cheering tumultuously for "Lincoln and Hamlin," or
more endearingly for "Old Abe."

A large part of my work, my specialty, consisted in addressing meetings of German-born voters in their and my native language. This
took me into the States of Wisconsin, Illinois, Indiana, Ohio, Pennsylvania, and New York—not only into the large cities, but into small
country towns and villages, and sometimes into remote agricultural
districts, where I found my audiences in school-houses and even in
roomy barns or in the open air; and these were the meetings that I enjoyed most of all. It was a genuine delight to me thus to meet my
country-men who remembered the same old Fatherland that I remembered as the cradle of us all, and who had come from afar to find new
homes for themselves and their children in this new land of freedom
and betterment—to meet them, I say, face to face, without the noise
and formality of a large assemblage, and to talk to them in a conver-
sational, familiar way, without any attempt at oratorical flourish, about
the pending questions to be decided and the duties we owed under
existing circumstances to the great Republic that had received us so
hospitably, and about the high value of the blessings we enjoyed and
had to preserve, and how we could do no greater honor to our old
Fatherland than by being conscientious and faithful citizens of the

new. There they sat for an hour or two, hard-working farmers, and small tradesmen, and laborers, with earnest and thoughtful faces, some of quick perception and others of more slowly working minds, listening with strained attention, sometimes with a puzzled expression, which made me go over the same ground again and again, in clearer language and with different illustrations; they sat, often without a sign of applause except now and then a nod or a mere look of intelligent agreement—until the close of the speech, when they would throng around me for a hand-shake, and not seldom with requests for a little more elucidation of this or that point, which they thought of using in discussing the matter with their neighbors.

That one of my speeches which perhaps attracted most attention in the campaign of 1860 was wholly devoted to a dissection of Senator Stephen A. Douglas, the presidential candidate of the Northern wing of the Democratic party. In preparing this argument I debated with myself the question how far it was permissible to attack a political opponent personally, in the discussion of public interests. I came to the conclusion that it was entirely permissible and fair if the personality of that opponent was brought forward to give strength to his cause, and especially if that personality exercised an influence through false pretense. This, as it seemed to me, was in the highest degree the case with Senator Douglas. He posed as the "champion of free labor," while he had caused the Missouri Compromise to be repealed and slavery to be admitted into Territories until then dedicated to freedom, and while he openly sought to win the support of the Southern people by telling them that his policy of "popular sovereignty" and "non-intervention" would give them the best chance to get more Slave States. He posed as the great representative of true democracy and popular rights, while he advocated police measures to restrain all discussion adverse to slavery which might have done honor to the most despotic government of the old world. He was extolled by his partisans as "the greatest of living statesmen," while he advanced, in support of the institution of slavery, theories of government so glaringly absurd and childish that the merest schoolboy should have been ashamed of them. And he did all these things with an aggressive assurance which produced upon many people the impression that he was really a superior being who might be taken at his own valuation. He was, in my eyes, the most formidable and most dangerous demagogue in America. I thought it would be a meritorious work to prick this imposing bubble, especially as his prestige was the only thing that threatened to take from Mr. Lincoln the votes of some of the Northern

States and thus to defeat his election. I went at my task with zest, summoning all I could command of power of statement, of sarcasm, fancy, and humor, and the result was an analysis of Douglas's theories and career which I could not have made more scorching, merciless, and amusing.

The speech was to be delivered in the large hall of the Cooper Institute in New York. On the evening of the meeting I dined with Governor Morgan, who was chairman of the Republican National Committee, and some prominent Republicans of New York, at the Astor House. On the way from the Astor House to the Cooper Institute, Governor Morgan, with whom I drove, asked me how long I expected to speak. I answered: "About two hours and a half." "Good heavens!" exclaimed the Governor. "No New York audience will stand a speech as long as that!" He seemed to be seriously alarmed. I explained to him that the speech I was prepared to make was a connected argument which I had to present to the public in its entirety or not at all, and that, therefore, if I could not be permitted to deliver the whole of it, some excuse must be found for my not speaking at all that evening. The Governor seemed much distressed. At last he submitted, but with the air of one who was resolved to meet an inevitable disaster with fortitude.

The great hall of the Cooper Institute was crowded to suffocation, the atmosphere of the assemblage proved thoroughly sympathetic, and I not only held my audience but achieved that night, as a "stump-speaker," the greatest success of my career. The bursts of applause and laughter were such that, now and then, I had to stop for minutes at a time. The face of Governor Morgan, who sat near me, lost its anxious gloom and grew brighter and brighter as I went on to my second and even to my third hour. On one of the seats of the front row I noticed an old gentleman with flowing white hair and large spectacles, who held an umbrella in his hand. At first he looked rather drowsy, but gradually he seemed to wake up and his face beamed with pleasure. He joined in the general applause by pounding with his umbrella on the floor, at first gently, and then with constantly increasing violence. I was not half through with my speech when the ferrule of the old gentleman's umbrella broke. But that did not disturb him in the least. In his enthusiasm he continued to pound the floor with all his strength. At last the stick of the umbrella went to pieces, so that he no longer could make any noise with it. But then, when I brought out a point which particularly stirred him, or a cheer went up whose contagion he could not resist, the old gentleman would fling up the wrecked umbrella and wave it over his head like a victorious banner, much to the amusement of the multitude. Owing to the many interruptions my speech occupied more than three hours, but Governor Morgan no longer found fault with its length. An immense number of pamphlet copies of this speech were circulated, and I was told that it cost Mr. Douglas many votes. I have to confess that of my printed speeches this has remained one of my favorites.

The campaign-committees kept me very hard at work in several States until the day of the election. I was too tired to take any part in the Republican jubilations after Abraham Lincoln's victory. But rest at my quiet Wisconsin home was soon cut short by my necessities. I found myself compelled, a week or two after the election, to set out on lecturing tours for the purpose of replenishing somewhat my drained exchequer. On my journeys East and West I met with strange experiences. The news of the success of the Republican party had hardly gone through the land when political demonstrations took place in some of the Southern States which made it appear that the threats of secession, to which of late years we had become accustomed, were, after all, something more than mere bluster and gasconade. The danger of a disunion movement, with consequences difficult to foresee, loomed up in portentous reality. A chill swept over the North. The anti-slavery enthusiasm of the campaign was suddenly hushed. The question which but yesterday had agitated men's minds and fired men's hearts, whether it was not right and just and good policy to exclude slavery from the Territories and to put that remnant of barbarism upon the course of ultimate extinction, was suddenly crowded into the background by the apparently much more pressing question: what might be done to avert the awful calamity of a great civil conflict that seemed to hang over the country like a gloomy storm-cloud. People wore very sober faces, and inquired each other's opinions with a tremor of anxiety in their voices.

Moreover, news came from the South that the instigators and leaders of the secession movement did not wish any compromise, and that to them the election of the Republican president was really not the cause, but merely a *welcome opportunity* for their separation from the Union and for the realization of their long-cherished ideal of an independent confederacy of Slave States. The only question still undecided was whether those leaders could carry the great mass of their people with them. The probability was that they would be able to do so, for in such cases the most extreme counsel is apt to appeal most powerfully to the popular ear. President Buchanan's message at the opening of the session of Congress was highly characteristic. He argued in substance that while no State had a constitutional right to secede from the Union, yet, if a State did so, there was nowhere any power to keep it in the Union. President Buchanan was the very personification of the political species then known as the "Northern man with Southern principles," that is, a Northern politician always ready to do the bidding of the slave-holding interest. I had been introduced to Mr. Buchanan with a multitude of other people at a White-House reception and taken a good look at him while after the hand-shaking he conversed with some Senators. He was a portly old gentleman with a white head, always slightly inclined to one side, and a cunning twinkle in his eye which seemed to say that although he might occasionally not appear to be of your opinion, yet there was a secret understanding between him and you, and that you might trust him for it. He always wore a white neckerchief like a divine. His moral weakness was of the wise-looking kind. He could pronounce the commonplace sophistries of the pro-slavery Democracy with all the impressiveness of unctuous ponderosity. He had rendered the slave-power abject service in the Kansas affair, again and again putting forth statements of fact which he could not possibly believe to be true, and constitutional doctrines that could be supported only by the most audacious shifts of logic. He was mindful of the fact that he owed the presidency to the trust of the slave-power in his fidelity to its behests. So far he had justified that trust to the full of his ability and of his opportunities. No Southern pro-slavery fanatic could have served the slave-holding interest with more zeal and—considering his position as a Northern man—with more self-denial. By forfeiting the good opinion of his neighbors he had really made himself a martyr to the cause of slavery. But when his Southern masters now went so far as to strike out for the dissolution of the Union, the destruction of the Republic itself, his situation became truly desperate. He may have prayed in his heart that now at least they might have mercy upon a poor Northern man in the presidency of the Republic. But they would use him for their purposes to the last. When he attempted to balk, his courage went only to the length of quibbling about constitutional paradoxes. Thus he satisfied neither side, but won the contempt of both. In his Cabinet he had three Secretaries—of the Treasury, of War, and of the Interior—of whom he should have known that they conspired with the secessionists. He permitted them to remain at the head of their departments until they thought they had exhausted all the resources for mischief which their official power gave them. What he really did accomplish was to encourage the promoters of the secession movement by his confession of constitutional impotency, and to give them ample time for undisturbed preparation while the National Government stood by, idle. He recoiled from active treason, but had not courage enough for active patriotism. Thus Mr. Buchanan, to whom fortune offered one of the finest chances to win a great name by simply doing his plain duty with resolution and energy, managed to make himself the most miserable presidential figure in American history.

It was thought important, in view of the troublous state of things, that as large as possible a number of Republicans be present in Washington at the time of Mr. Lincoln's inauguration, and I found a great many friends, old and new, when I arrived there on March 1st. The air was still thick with rumors of "rebel plots" to assassinate Mr. Lincoln, or to capture him and carry him off before he could take hold of the reins of government. He had stolen a march upon what conspiracy there may have been, by entering the National Capital unexpected and unobserved on the morning of February 23d, and was, no doubt, well guarded. The multitude of Republicans assembled in the city were not satisfied that the danger was over, and saw treasonable designs in every scowling face observed on the streets or in the windows—of which indeed there were a good many. But the inauguration passed off without disturbance. I was favored with a place in front of the great portico of the Capitol, from which I could distinctly see and hear every part of the official function. I saw Lincoln step forward to the desk upon which the Bible lay—his rugged face, appearing above all those surrounding him, calm and sad, but so unlike any other in that distinguished assemblage that one might well have doubted how they could work together. I saw Senator Douglas standing close by him, his defeated antagonist, the "little giant" of the past period, who, only two years before, had haughtily treated Lincoln like a tall dwarf. I witnessed the remarkable scene when Lincoln, about to deliver his inaugural address, could not at once find a convenient place for his hat, and Douglas took that hat and held it like an attendant, while Lincoln was speaking. I saw the withered form of Chief Justice Taney, the author of the famous Dred Scott decision, that judicial compend of the doctrine of slavery, administer the oath of office to the first President elected on a distinct antislavery platform. I saw, standing by, the outgoing President, James Buchanan, with his head slightly inclined on one side, and his winking eye, and his white neck-cloth—the man who had done more than any other to degrade and demoralize the National Government and to encourage the rebellion, now to retire to an unhonored obscurity, and to the dreary task of trying to make the world believe that he was a better patriot and statesman than he appeared to be. I heard every word pronounced by Abraham Lincoln's kindly voice, of that inaugural address which was to be a message of peace and good will, but the reception of which in the South as a proclamation of war showed clearly that no offer of compromise, indeed, that nothing short of complete acceptance of their scheme of an independent slave-holding empire would have satisfied the Southern leaders. Their answer to the inaugural was increased energy in the formation of the Confederate Government, and in agitating the cause of secession in the Southern States that had not yet seceded.

While these things were going on, I saw President Lincoln repeatedly, and he always received me with great cordiality. We spoke together as freely as we had before he was President. Our conversations turned upon questions of policy and upon the qualifications and claims of applicants for office whom I had recommended. My own case was never mentioned between us until he, with evident satisfaction, announced to me that I had been nominated for the position of Minister of the United States to Spain. The Senate confirmed my nomination without unusual delay. I was curious to know whether Senator Douglas, whom I had so bitterly attacked during the campaign, had offered any objection, and I was informed that he had not. But there had been, as I learned later from Mr. Potter, some objection to my nomination on the part of Mr. Seward, the Secretary of State. He argued that, as I had been engaged in revolutionary movements in Europe at a comparatively recent period, my appearance in a diplomatic capacity at a European court might not be favorably received, and that this was of importance at a critical time when we had especial reason for conciliating the good will of foreign governments. Mr. Lincoln—as my informant told me—replied that I could be trusted to conduct myself discreetly; at any rate, that he did so trust me; that it was not for the government of this Republic to discriminate against men for having made efforts in behalf of liberty elsewhere—efforts with which every good American at heart sympathized; that it might be well for European governments to realize this fact; and finally, that the political significance of my appointment would be entitled to much consideration. He was strongly supported in this view by Mr. Chase, the Secretary of the Treasury, and Mr. Montgomery Blair, the Postmaster General. When Mr. Lincoln took so peremptory a stand, Mr. Seward at last yielded, but not with good grace. Indeed, the matter gave him occasion for a singular display of temper. One day when Mr. Potter, accompanied by another Republican member of Congress from Wisconsin, discussed the subject with Mr. Seward in his office at the State Department, and incidentally remarked that the failure to bestow such a distinction upon me would be a severe disappointment to a good many people, Mr. Seward jumped up from his chair, paced the floor excitedly, and exclaimed:

"Disappointment! You speak to me of disappointment. To me, who was justly entitled to the Republican nomination for the presidency, and who had to stand aside and see it given to a little Illinois lawyer! You speak to me of disappointment!"

Whenever in later years I reflected upon that part of my career, I have inwardly reproached myself for not anticipating at that time Mr. Seward's view of the matter, although it was kept secret from me while the question was still pending. I certainly ought to have done so. But I have to confess that my pride—or I might perhaps more properly call it my vanity—was immensely flattered by the thought of returning to Europe clothed in all the dignity of a Minister Plenipotentiary and Envoy Extraordinary of the United States only a few years after having left my native land as a political refuge. When, however, I heard of the discussions that had preceded my appointment, I did not enjoy that triumph as I had thought I should. Even while receiving public and private congratulations in unexpected abundance, I was secretly troubled by a lurking doubt as to whether the office I had obtained was really one that I should hold, and whether the fact that my friends had sought it for me with my knowledge and approval, was not really equivalent to having asked for it myself. In this state of mind I left Washington for my home in Wisconsin.

I had not been there many days when the portentous news of the rebel attack on Fort Sumter in Charleston Harbor startled the country. As soon as possible I reported myself to Mr. Lincoln at the White House. He seemed surprised, but glad to see me. I told him why I had come, and he approved. In his quaint way he described to me the anxieties he has passed through since the rebel attack on Fort Sumter and before the first Northern troops reached Washington. He told me of an incident characteristic of the situation which I wish I could repeat in his own language. I can give only the substance. One afternoon after he had issued his call for troops, he sat alone in his room, and a feeling came over him as if he were utterly deserted and helpless. He thought any moderately strong body of secessionist troops, if there were any in the neighborhood, might come over the "long bridge" across the Potomac, and just take him and the members of the Cabinet—the whole lot of them. Then he suddenly heard a sound like the boom of a cannon. "There they are!" he said to himself. He expected every moment somebody would rush in with the report of an attack. The White House attendants, whom he interrogated, had heard nothing. But nobody came, and all remained still. Then he thought he would look after the thing himself. So he walked out, and walked, and walked, until he got to the Arsenal. There he found the doors all open and not a soul to guard them. Anybody might have gone in and helped himself to the arms. There was perfect solitude and stillness all around. Then he walked back to the White House without noticing the slightest sign of disturbance. He met a few persons on the way, some of whom he asked whether they had not heard something like the boom of a cannon. Nobody had heard anything, and so he supposed it must have been a freak of his imagination. It is probable that at least a guard was sent to the Arsenal that evening. The confusion of those days must have been somewhat like that prevailing at the time of the capture of Washington in the War of 1812.

In the course of our conversation I opened my heart to Mr. Lincoln about my troubles of conscience. I told him that since recent events had made a warlike conflict with the seceding States certain, it was much against my feelings to go to Spain as Minister and to spend my days in the ease and luxury of a diplomatic position, while the young men of the North were exposing their lives in the field, in defense of the life of the Republic; that, having helped, as a public speaker, to bring about the present condition of things, I thought I would rather bear my share of the consequences; that I had seen some little field service in the revolutionary conflicts of my native country, and had ever since made military matters a favorite subject of study, and that I should be glad to resign my mission to Spain and at once join the volunteer army.

Mr. Lincoln listened to me with attention and evident sympathy. Then, after a moment of silence, he said that he fully understood and appreciated my feelings, but that he would not advise me to give up the Spanish mission. He thought that this diplomatic position might eventually offer me a greater field of usefulness. The war might be over very soon. Many people, whose opinions were entitled to respect, thought so. Mr. Seward was speaking of sixty or ninety days. He himself was not at all as sanguine as that, but he might be wrong. However, in a few weeks we would, as to that point, see more clearly.

I then laid before Mr. Lincoln a plan I had formed, as follows: in the impending war an efficient cavalry force would undoubtedly be needed. The formation and drilling of cavalry troops composed of raw material would require much time. But I was confident that there were in the City of New York and vicinity many hundreds of able-bodied immigrants from Germany who had served in German cavalry regiments, and who had only to be armed and put upon horses to make cavalrymen immediately fit for active service. There were also, to command them, a sufficient number of experienced cavalry officers trained in the Prussian or some other German army. I thought that I, being somewhat known among the German-born citizens of the country, was a suitable person to organize such a regiment if the government gave me proper authority. Mr. Lincoln was very much pleased with my project, and sent me at once to Mr. Cameron, the Secretary of War, to discuss with him the necessary arrangements. Mr. Cameron was also very much pleased, but thought it necessary that I should submit the matter to General Scott, the commanding general of the army, before final action was taken.

I had never seen General Scott, but had heard him described as a somewhat pompous old gentleman, not inclined to tolerate opinions on military matters in any way differing from his own. Looking forward to an interview with him on such subjects with some misgiving, I asked Mr. Cameron for a letter of introduction, setting forth as strongly as possible my claim to kind attention, so that the General might not at once put me down as a mere intruder seeking a favor for himself. Thus armed, I approached the General, who, after having read my letter, invited me to take a chair. But when I explained my scheme to him, his face assumed a look of stern and somewhat impatient authority. His question whether I had any practical experience in the organizing and drilling of mounted troops was of ill omen. When I had confessed that I had no such experience, he replied that he had concluded so from my proposition. If we were to have any war at all, he added, it would be a short one. It would be over long before any volunteer cavalry troops could be made fit for active service in the field. Moreover, the theater of that war would be Virginia, and the surface of Virginia was so cut up with fences and other obstructions as to make operations with large bodies of cavalry impracticable. The regular dragoons he had were quite sufficient for all needs.

I saw, of course, the utter uselessness of any attempt I might make further to argue the matter with such an authority. When I reported my conversation with General Scott to Mr. Lincoln and Mr. Cameron, they both agreed that the old gentleman was taking too narrow a view of present exigencies. I promptly received the desired authority for raising the regiment, and departed for the City of New York. I found the people of New York in the full blaze of the patriotic emotions excited by the firing upon Fort Sumter and the President's call for volunteers. There were recruiting stations in all parts of the town. The formation of regiments proceeded rapidly. Wealthy merchants were vying with each other in lavish contributions of money for the fitting out of troops, and numberless women of all classes of society were busy stitching garments or bandages for the soldiers, or embroidering standards. There was hardly anything else talked about in public places, in the clubs, and in family circles. The whole town constantly resounded with patriotic speeches and martial music. Party spirit seemed to be fairly lifted off its feet by the national enthusiasm. Men who but yesterday had cursed every Republican as a "rank abolitionist" and every abolitionist as an enemy of the country, and who had vociferously vowed that no armed body of men should be permitted to pass through the City of New York for the purpose of "making war upon a sovereign State," now, like Daniel E. Sickles in the East, and John A. Logan in the West, rushed to arms themselves. There were, doubtless, not a few persons in the Northern States who harbored sentiments of bitter hostility to the new administration and to the cause it represented; but that hostility, which at a later period found vent in the so-called "Copperhead" movement, was, in the spring and early summer of 1861, either awed into silence, or its utterances were at least so feeble as to be hardly audible in the roar of the patriotic storm. It was a genuine uprising of a people with all its noble inspirations. For once there was a true spirit of equality and fraternity in this great popular impulse to rescue the Republic. Social distinctions were forgotten. The rich merchant's son found it quite natural to shoulder his musket by the side of his porter, or to be drilled by his clerk who happened to have learned the manual of arms as a member of a militia company. Nor was the foreign-born citizen less zealous than the native.

In New York, I found that many of the German cavalrymen I had counted upon had already enlisted in the infantry regiments then forming. But there were enough of them left to enable me to organize several companies in a very short time, and I should certainly have completed my regiment in season for the summer campaign, had I not been cut short in my work by another call from the government. I received a letter from the Secretary of State informing me that circumstances had rendered my departure for my place at Madrid eminently desirable, and that he wished me to report myself to him at Washington as soon as possible. This was a hard blow. So I had to leave the country at that critical period and to go on my diplomatic errand after all. But hard as it was, I had to obey. I took it as a just punishment for ever having yielded to the vain thought of appearing in Europe as an American Minister Plenipotentiary. I promptly secured the transfer of my recruiting authority to Colonel McReynolds of Michigan, and left New York for Washington. My regiment was fully organized by my successor before the lapse of many weeks, and won an excellent reputation in the field as the First New York Volunteer Cavalry Regiment, commonly called the "Lincoln Cavalry." Thus it turned out that for once General Scott's military judgment was at fault. The war was not over before the volunteer cavalry could take the field, and the fences and other obstructions on the surface of Virginia did not prevent it from rendering good service.

As the South gathered strength, the North became impatient for action, and the administration was blamed for its slowness in getting ready for the decisive blow. Washington fairly buzzed with criticism, for the most part unjust because it did not take into account that the government did not find ready to its hand, but had to create, the means by which "action" could have been made effective. But the question was frequently asked in that atmosphere of discontentment, whether Abraham Lincoln was really the man to cope with a situation bristling with problems so perplexing. This question nobody seemed at that time ready to answer. Those who visited the White House—and the White House appeared to be open to whosoever wished to enter—saw there a man of unconventional manners, who, without the slightest effort to put on dignity, treated all men alike, much like old neighbors; whose speech had not seldom a rustic flavor about it; who always seemed to have time for a homely talk and never to be in a hurry to press business, and who occasionally spoke about important affairs of State with the same nonchalance—I might almost say, irreverence—with which he might have discussed an every-day law case in his office at Springfield, Illinois. People were puzzled. Some interesting stores circulated about Lincoln's wit, his quaint sayings, and also about his kindness of heart and the sympathetic loveliness of his character; but, as to his qualities as a statesman, serious people who did not intimately know him were inclined to reserve their judgment.

I had the good fortune of coming nearer to Charles Sumner in these days. Since the members from the seceding States had left the United States Senate, the Republicans commanded a majority in that body, and Sumner was by common consent made chairman of the Committee on Foreign Relations, a position for which he was unquestionably by far the fittest man among his colleagues. He knew Europe, and followed with intelligent understanding the political developments of the Old World. He showed a kind interest in my own experiences and observations and we had frequent conversations about kindred subjects. He found that he could speak to me on such things with a feeling that, having had some European experience myself, I would more easily understand him than most of those with whom he had intercourse; and thus a certain confidentiality grew up between us, which, in the course of time, was to ripen into genuine friendship.

Sumner had never seen Lincoln before he arrived in Washington. The conditions under which Lincoln had risen into prominence in the West were foreign to Sumner's acquaintance—perhaps even to his imagination. When he met Lincoln for the first time he was greatly amazed and puzzled by what he saw and heard. He confessed as much as this to me. Lincoln was utterly unlike Sumner's ideal of a statesman. The refined New Englander, who, after having enjoyed a thorough classical education, had seen much of the great world at home and abroad, and conceived an exalted idea of the dignity of an American Senator and of a President of the great American Republic, could hardly understand this Western product of American democracy. In the conversations he had with the President he, indeed, noticed, now and then, flashes of thought and bursts of illuminating expression which struck him as extraordinary, although, being absolutely without any sense of humor, he often lost Lincoln's keenest points. But on the whole he could not get rid of his misgivings as to how this seemingly untutored child of nature would master the tremendous task before him. He had, indeed, by Mr. Lincoln's occasional utterances, been confirmed in his belief that the President was a deeply convinced and faithful anti-slavery man; and since the destruction of slavery was uppermost in Sumner's mind as the greatest object to be accomplished, he found comfort in that assurance.

But he was much troubled by what he called the slow working of Mr. Lincoln's mind and his deplorable hesitancy in attacking the vital question. He profoundly distrusted Seward on account of his compromising attitude at the critical period between the election and Mr. Lincoln's inauguration, and also on account of the mysterious, delphic utterances Mr. Seward now occasionally gave forth. But he had great faith in Chase, whose anti-slavery principles he regarded as above all temptation, and whose influence with the President, he hoped, would neutralize Seward's.

But Chase, as I concluded from conversations I had with him, was not in a state of mind that would make the establishment of confidential relations between him and Lincoln easy. He did not give his disappointment as a defeated aspirant to the presidency so vehement an expression as Seward did, but he felt it no less keenly. Neither did he venture upon so drastic a demonstration of his underestimate of Lincoln's character and ability as Seward had done by his memorandum of April 1st; but I doubt whether his opinion of the President was much higher than Seward's had been before Lincoln's gentle but decisive victory over him. I concluded this, not from what Chase said, but rather from what he did not say when the conversation turned upon the President. This feeling only intensified Chase's natural reserve of manner, and, as became evident in the course of time, the relations between Chase and Lincoln always remained such as will exist between two men who, in their official intercourse, do not personally come near to each other and are not warmed into confidential heartiness.

When I called upon Mr. Lincoln to take leave, he received me with the old cordiality and expressed his sincere regret that, after all, I had to go away before this cruel war was over; but as Seward wanted it, I must go, of course, and he hoped it would all be for the best. We had some conversation about the state of affairs as it had developed itself since I had seen him last. He expressed the intensest gratification at the enthusiastic popular response to his call for volunteers, and at the patriotic attitude taken by so many leading Democrats. He warmly praised the patriotic action of the Germans of St. Louis in the taking of Camp Jackson. The criticism to which the administration was being subjected affected him keenly, but did not irritate him against those who exercised it. He always allowed that those who differed from us might be as honest as we were. He thought if the administration had so far "stumbled along," as was said, it had, on the whole, "stumbled along in the right direction." But he expressed great anxiety as to the attitude of foreign countries, especially England and France, with regard to our troubles, and this anxiety was much increased by the British Queen's proclamation of neutrality, the news of which had recently arrived. He gave me to understand that he deplored having given so little attention to foreign affairs and being so dependent upon other people's judgment, and that he felt the necessity of "studying up" on the subject as much as his opportunities permitted him. I did not know then that only a short time before he had found himself obliged very seriously to modify one of Mr. Seward's despatches to Mr. Charles Francis Adams, our Minister in England, in order to avoid complications that might have become very grave. Neither did Mr. Lincoln drop any hint of this to me, but he said that he wanted me, when in Europe, to watch public sentiment there as closely as possible, and he added: "Remember now when you are abroad, that, whenever anything occurs to you that you want to tell me personally, or that you think I ought to know, you shall write me directly."

Before parting I told Mr. Lincoln that I had a German brother-in-law with me in Washington, Mr. Henry Meyer, a young merchant from Hamburg, and an ardent friend of this country, who would be proud to pay his respects to the President. Could I bring him for a moment? "Certainly," said Mr. Lincoln, "bring him to-morrow about lunch time and lunch with me. I guess Mary (Mrs. Lincoln) will have something for us to eat." Accordingly the next day I brought my brother-in-law, who was greatly astonished at this unexpected invitation to lunch with the President, and much troubled about the etiquette to be observed. I found it difficult to quiet him with the assurance that in this case there was no etiquette at all. But he was still more astonished when Mr. Lincoln, instead of waiting for a ceremonious bow, shook him by the hand like an old acquaintance and said in his hearty way that he was glad to see the brother-in-law of "this young man here," and that he hoped the Americans treated him well. Mrs. Lincoln, "Mary," as the President again called her—was absent, being otherwise engaged, and there were no other guests. So we had Mr. Lincoln at the table all to ourselves. He seemed to be in excellent spirits, asked many questions about Hamburg, which my brother-in-law, who spoke English fluently, answered in an entertaining manner, and Mr. Lincoln found several occasions for inserting funny stories, at which not only we, but he himself, too, laughed most heartily. As we left the White House, my companion could hardly find words to express his puzzled admiration for the man who, having risen from the bottom of the social ladder to one of the most exalted stations in the world, had remained so perfectly natural and so absolutely unconscious of how he appeared to others—a man to whom it did not occur for a single moment that a person in his position might put on a certain dignity to be always maintained, and who bore himself with such genial sincerity and kindliness that the dignity was not missed, and that one would have regretted to see him different.

A few days later I was afloat on my way to Spain.

CHAPTER XII

Madrid and Washington

I STOPPED in London long enough to call upon the American Minister, Mr. Charles Francis Adams, for the purpose of obtaining from him the latest information about the attitude of European powers concerning the United States. I had never seen Mr. Adams before. The appearance of the little bald-headed gentleman with the clean-cut features and blue eyes, to whom I introduced myself with some diffidence as a colleague, reminded me strongly of the portraits I had seen of President John Quincy Adams, his father. What I had read of the habitual frigidity of the demeanor of the father served me to interpret rightly the manner in which the son received me. He said that he was very glad to see me, in a tone which, no doubt, was intended for kindness. It was certainly courteous. But there was a lack of warmth and a stiffness about it, which, as I afterwards told one of Mr. Adams's sons, to his great amusement, made me feel as though the temperature of the room had dropped several degrees. Of course, Mr. Adams could have no reason for desiring to chill me, and I concluded that this prim frigidity was purely temperamental and normal. When we began to talk about public business, he did, indeed, not exactly "warm up," but he spoke to me with a communicativeness which touched me as confidential and therefore complimentary. He told me very minutely the story of the "precipitate" proclamation of neutrality by the British Government and of the "unofficial" reception of the "Confederate Commissioners," and described to me in a manner which betrayed grave apprehensions on his part, the unfriendly, if not positively hostile, influences he had to contend with—influences the strength of which depended in a great measure upon the strength of the wide-spread belief that the existence of slavery was not involved in our home struggle.

I left Mr. Adams with the highest impression of his patriotism, of the clearness and exactness of his mind, of the breadth of his knowledge, and his efficiency as a diplomat, History has since pronounced its judgment on his services. He was, in the best sense of the term, a serious and sober man. Indeed, he lacked some of the social qualities which it may be desirable that a diplomat should possess. While he kept up in London an establishment fitting the dignity of his position as the representative of a great republic, and performed his social duties with punctilious care, he was not a pleasing after-dinner speaker, nor a shining figure on festive occasions. He lacked the gifts of personal magnetism or sympathetic charm that would draw men to him. Neither had he that vivacity of mind and that racy combativeness which made his father, John Quincy Adams, so formidable a fighter. But his whole mental and moral being commanded so high a respect that every word he uttered had extraordinary weight, and in his diplomatic encounters his antagonists not only feared the reach and exactness of his knowledge and the solidity of his reasoning, but they were also anxious to keep his good opinion of them. He would not trifle with anything, and nobody could trifle with him. His watchfulness was incessant and penetrating without becoming offensive through demonstrative suspiciousness, and his remonstrances commanded the most serious attention without being couched in language of boast or menace. The dignity of his country was well embodied in his own. It is doubtful whether a fitter man could have been found to represent this Republic during the great crisis in its history near a government the attitude of which was to us of such vital importance.

In Paris I saw our Minister, Mr. Dayton, whose account of the uncertainty of the French Emperor's policy with regard to the United States was decidedly disquieting. My wife wished to pay a visit to our relatives at Hamburg, and it was thought best that she should remain there with our children until the autumn, when the summer heat at Madrid would be over. I therefore set out for Spain alone. At Madrid I was received by Mr. Perry, the Secretary of Legation, a gentleman five years older than I, of very prepossessing appearance and pleasant address. My arrival relieved him of considerable anxiety. He informed me that Queen Isabella was on the point of leaving Madrid for Santander, a seaside place, and that if I had not arrived before her departure, my official reception would have had to be delayed for several weeks. He had conferred upon this matter with the Minister of Foreign Affairs, Don Saturnino Calderón Collantes, and the Queen had consented to receive me at the royal palace that very evening at half-past nine o'clock. Mr. Perry impressed upon me that this arrangement was to be accepted by me as a great favor. He had secured quarters for me at the hotel "de los Embajadores." After my installment there we went together to the office of the American Legation, which was situated at some distance in the Calle de Alcalá. I sat down to compose the little speech with which I was to present my letter of credence, addressed by the President to the Queen of Spain. This done, I put some official papers which I had brought with me into the desk assigned to me. Mr. Perry then took me to the foreign office for my first official call, and then to the hotel where I was to rest while he showed the draught of my speech to the Minister of Foreign Affairs. On the way to the hotel Mr. Perry remarked something about the official dress in which we were to appear that evening. It being at that time still the rule that the Ministers of the United States should wear a certain uniform at foreign courts—a richly embroidered dress-coat with correspondingly orna-mented trousers, a cocked hat, and a court-sword—I had ordered those articles at the establishment of a tailor at Paris who seemed to have the custom of American diplomats, but they were not ready when I left Paris for Madrid. They were to be sent after me in a few days. I could, therefore, appear before the Queen only in an ordinary gentleman's evening attire.

Mr. Perry seemed to be much disturbed by this revelation. He did not know how the "Introductor de los Embajadores," a high court-official who had to supervise the ceremonial of such state functions, would take it. He feared that there would be difficulty. However, he would lay the state of things before that dignitary and do his best to arrange matters. An hour or two later Mr. Perry returned with the report that the Introductor de los Embajadores, a very solemn and punctilious grandee, had at first grown pale at the idea of a foreign minister being received by her Majesty in plain evening clothes. He doubted whether such a thing had ever happened in the history of the Spanish monarchy, and whether it was compatible with the dignity of the Spanish throne. Mr. Perry then hurried to the Minister of Foreign Affairs, who succceeded in persuading the Introductor de los Em-bajadores that the exigencies of the situation would justify a departure from ever so solemn a rule, but as that official still insisted that he could not permit such a departure without special permission from her Maj-esty, the matter was hurriedly submitted by the Minister to the Queen, who graciously consented. This crisis being happily passed, I was to rest in peace until nine in the evening, when Mr. Perry was to call for me with a carriage to take me to the palace.

At the appointed hour Mr. Perry arrived and found me in faultless evening attire, ready for action. I had only to put the "letter of credence" to be presented to the Queen, in my pocket. But—good heavens!—where was that letter of credence? Not to be found! Could it have been among the papers which I had locked up in my desk at the office of the Legation? It must have been so. But what was now to be done? To drive to the Legation and from there to the palace was impossible. We could not have arrived at the palace until half an hour after the time appointed by the Queen. That the Queen should be made to wait for a foreign gentleman in plain evening clothes could not be thought of. Only a bold stroke could save the situation; and such a stroke I resolved upon. I took a newspaper and put it carefully folded into a large envelope of the official size which I inscribed to "Doña Isabella, Queen of Spain." This envelope I would hand to her Majesty at the ceremonial, and I asked Mr. Perry to have a short aside with the Minister of Foreign Affairs for the purpose of informing him of what had happened, of excusing me as best he could, and of requesting him not to open the envelope in her Majesty's presence, after she had handed it to him. The real letter of credence would surely be presented to him the next morning. Fortunately Mr. Perry, who had a Spanish wife and spoke the language perfectly, was well acquainted with Don Saturnino, and so we hoped that this new crisis would be safely passed, too.

Thus armed and equipped we drove to the palace. At the foot of the great staircase stood two halberdiers in gorgeous mediæval costume to guard the passage to the rooms of state. When they saw me in plain evening dress, the dignity of the Spanish throne must have occurred to them, too, for they crossed their halberds and refused to let us ascend. Mr. Perry wore the uniform of a Secretary of Legation, but this did not satisfy the halberdiers, who looked at me with evident disapproval and suspicion. Mr. Perry, putting on a proud and indignant mien, and assuming a tone of command, called upon one of the flunkeys who stood on the stairs, instantly to run up and report to the Introductor de los Embajadores the outrage that had been inflicted on the Minister of the United States. The Introductor came rushing down with an expression of consternation on his face, threw apart the crossed halberds with his own hands, poured forth a torrent of Spanish words which obviously were meant for apologies, and we ascended the great staircase in triumph.

In the hall of state we found Sir John Crampton, the new British minister, with his staff, who was also to present his credentials. As he had called at the foreign office a little earlier than I, he was entitled to precedence. The Minister of Foreign Affairs was also on hand; and, as we were waiting for the Queen, Mr. Perry had time to communicate to him in a few hurried words our embarrassment concerning the letter of credence and the expedient I had resorted to. The Minister looked grave, but nodded. A door was flung open, a gorgeously attired official shouted something into the hall, and the Queen appeared, a portly dame with a fat and unhandsome but good-natured looking face. Sir John Crampton went through the ceremony, and as I looked on I could study his performance as a model for what I had to do. When my turn came, I made as good a bow as Sir John had made, delivered my little speech in English, of which the Queen did not understand a word, and presented the envelope containing a newspaper to the Queen, who held the precious object in her hand while she delivered a little speech in Spanish to me, of which I did not understand a word, whereupon she, with a grand swing, turned the envelope unopened over to the Minister of Foreign Affairs. He took it, bowing profoundly. While he did so, I caught Don Saturnino's eye and saw a knowing smile flitting across his features. Then, according to custom, the Queen spoke to me conversationally in French, expressing the hope that I was well and would be pleased with Spain, and I said something polite in response. Then another bow, and the ceremony was over.

But I was told that I was to present myself also to the King, Don Francisco de Assisi. He was, in fact, only the Prince Consort to the Queen, but had, by an arrangement of courtesy, received the title of "King" and "his Majesty" on the occasion of his marriage to the Queen. His only political function consisted in his presenting himself to the world as the official father of Isabella's children. The affair of Isabella's marriage had created great excitement in Europe, in the early forties, owing to the anxiety of some powers lest some other power gain an advantage by a family alliance with the Spanish dynasty. It was at last thought safest that Isabella marry some Spanish Bourbon, and then Don Francisco appeared to be the only available candidate, although he was a very disagreeable person to Isabella herself. Thus the ill-matched couple were united in wedlock for so-called "state reasons."

The "King" was not present in the great hall where the foreign ministers were received by the Queen, and I was conducted through long corridors to his apartments. Suddenly a door was opened, and I almost stumbled over a very little man standing on the threshold of a small, dimly lighted room. I was greatly surprised to find myself the next moment presented to this little person as "his Majesty, the King." The conversation that followed, carried on in French, was simple in the extreme. The King spoke in a cracked soprano voice, somewhat like the scream of a young hen. He said that he was very glad to see me, that he hoped my long journey all the way from America to Spain had been a pleasant one, and he hoped especially that I had not been very seasick. Did I ever get very seasick? I was happy to assure his Majesty that my journey had been throughout a pleasant one, and that I had not at all been seasick, and I hoped his Majesty was in good health. His Majesty replied that he was entirely well, but he thought never to get seasick was a rare thing. It was a great gift of nature—a very valuable gift indeed. After this utterance, our theme seemed to be exhausted, and I was permitted to withdraw. When thinking over the events of the day before falling asleep, my introduction into diplomatic life in Madrid appeared to me very much like an act in an opera bouffe—a comical prelude to serious business.

The following day I delivered the genuine letter of credence to Don Saturnino Calderón Collantes, and had a long conversation with him. He was a little gentleman, with large features, somewhat stern when in repose, and looked rather like a high-grade schoolmaster than a political leader, or a Castilian Caballero. He spoke French with the accent peculiar to the Spaniards, but fluently enough to make conversation easy. Although somewhat inclined to be solemn in his attitude, he had sense of humor enough to appreciate the ludicrousness of yesterday's proceedings with the pretended letter of credence, and referred to it with a twinkle in his eye. It was rather an advantage to me to have that funny reminiscence in common with him, for to have been engaged together in a secret adventure of that sort is apt to put men upon a footing a little more confidential than it would have been without such an occurrence.

It is impossible to describe the gloom cast upon our Legation by the news of the disastrous battle of Bull Run. I well remember the day when it struck us in Madrid like a bolt of lightning from a clear sky. I had, indeed, not anticipated an easy and very speedy suppression of the insurrectionary movement. Although bound to present our case in the most favorable light, I had not, in my representation to the Spanish Government, indulged in any oversanguine prophesies for the near future—mindful of the rule that it is unwise to make confident predictions upon the fulfillment of which your credit depends, unless you are perfectly sure of the fulfillment. I had, therefore, confined myself to insistence upon the immense superiority of our resources, which would command ultimate success. This was tenable enough.

But the disaster at Bull Run, as my despatches indicated and the newspapers elaborately described it, went far beyond what we had thought possible. It not only was a disaster, but it appeared as a disgrace. It put in doubt the fighting capacity of the Northern soldier.

My longing to go back to the United States grew stronger every day. The elegant ease of my life in Spain chafed me like a reproach. It became more and more intolerable to me to think of leading a lounging existence at this post with an activity more apparent than real, while those with whom I had worked for the anti-slavery cause were painfully struggling against adverse fate, many at the hourly peril of their lives. All my time not demanded by my official duties—which left me much leisure—was devoted to the study of military works. The campaigns of Frederick the Great, of the Archduke Charles, and of Napoleon, and the works of Jomini and Clausewitz, together with minor books on tactics, I had studied before. I now took the last French campaign in Italy that ended with the battle of Solferino, and some writings of Marshal Bugeaud. I even translated a new work on tactics from French into English, with the intention of publishing it, which, however, I never did. At the same time I made every possible effort to inform myself about the effect which the Bull Run disaster might have produced on public opinion in Europe.

I could not repress a shout of joy when at last an answer came from the President and the State Department granting me my leave of absence. My preparations for departure were soon made. My family being at Hamburg, I wished to join them there and to take them with me on a Hamburg steamer to America. To this end I had to cross Prussian territory. I called upon Count Galen, the Prussian Minister, to acquaint him with my desire to join my family at Hamburg, and to ask him whether he thought I could pass through Prussian territory without being noticed. He had no doubt of it, but to satisfy me, he would inquire of his government. The answer came promptly that instructions would at once be given to the officers concerned to extend to me every accommodation I might desire on my way. I so arranged my journey as to cross the Prussian frontier after dark, to pass over the Rhine at Cologne during the night, and to reach Hamburg the next forenoon. When I touched the Prussian frontier, a customs officer above the lower grade presented himself to me, ordered my luggage to pass unexamined, and asked for my wishes. My fellow-travelers seemed surprised at the official attention I received, and were evidently anxious to know what distinguished person it was they had the honor to travel with. I did not gratify their curiosity. Thus my reappearance in the Fatherland was exceedingly modest and untriumphant. But I was wide awake when my railroad train stopped in the station at Cologne, and I listened to the sound, so familiar from my boyhood days, of the church-clocks striking the hour, and when crossing the dear old Rhine I heard the rushing of its waters in the darkness.

Early in January I embarked with my family on the Hamburg steamship "Bavaria," a vessel of some 2500 or 3000 tons, which would be considered nowadays quite small for an ocean liner, but which was then of the usual size. We had a terrible voyage.

From New York I hurried at once to Washington, where I first reported to Mr. Seward at the State Department. Owing to the presence of some foreign diplomats waiting upon the Secretary, we cut our conversation short with the understanding that we would discuss matters more fully at some more convenient time. I then went to call upon Mr. Lincoln at the White House. He received me with the old cordiality.

I had frequent conversations with Senator Sumner at that period. His personality attracted me greatly. He was strikingly unlike all the public men surrounding him—just as Lincoln was, but in the opposite sense. Sumner was a born Puritan character, an aristocrat by instinct and culture, a democrat by study and reflection, a revolutionary power by the dogmatic intensity of his determination to impose his principles upon the world at any cost. There were many who thought that these two men, being so essentially different, could not possibly work together. But on the whole they did, and they were able to do so, because, however great the divergence of their views on some points, they believed in one another's sincerity. Sumner was a doctrinaire by character—an enlightened doctrinaire, yet an unbending and uncompromising one. His notions of right and wrong were absolute. When someone asked him whether he had ever looked at the other side of the slavery question, he answered: "There is no other side." No answer could have been more characteristic. Not that he was merely *unwilling* to see the other side of a question of that nature—he was *unable* to see it. The peremptoriness of his convictions was so strong, so absolute, I might say, that it was difficult for him to understand how anyone could seriously consider "the other side" without being led astray by some more obliquity. Of a very old and tried friend who favored a temporizing course toward the South after the election of Mr. Lincoln, he said, after a severe denunciation of that course, "However, I believe he is honest"—but said it in a way indicating that it had cost him a very great effort to reach such a conclusion. I know an instance in which

his bluntly ingenuous manner of saying such things gave great offense
to a family consisting of high-minded persons with whom he had been
on terms of intimate friendship for many years.

Mr. Lincoln was a constant puzzle to him. He frequently told me
of profound and wise things Mr. Lincoln had said, and then again of
other sayings which were unintelligible to him and seemed to him in-
consistent with a serious appreciation of the tasks before us. Being
entirely devoid of the sense of humor himself, Mr. Sumner frequently
—I might say almost always—failed to see the point of the quaint anecdotes or illustrations with which Lincoln was fond of elucidating his
argument, as with a flashlight. Mr. Sumner not seldom quoted such
Lincolnisms to me, and asked me with an air of innocent bewilderment,
whether I could guess what the President could possibly have meant.
To Sumner's mind the paramount object of the war was the abolition
of slavery. He had all his life been a peace man in the widest sense. His
great oration, delivered on the Fourth of July, 1846, on "The True
Grandeur of Nations," which introduced him to public life, had been
a panegyric on universal peace. In it he had proclaimed as his fundamental doctrine that "in our age, there can be no peace that is not
honorable, there can be no war that is not dishonorable." Thus in order
to support the government in the Civil War he had to compromise
with his own conscience, and he did this on the ground that it was a
war for the abolition of that slavery, which, to him, was the sum of all
iniquities. Only by extinguishing an evil worse than war itself could
this war be justified by him. Thus he was impatient at everything that
seemed to obscure that supreme object or to impede or delay its attainment. This impatience caused him to undervalue the reasons Mr.
Lincoln gave him for what Sumner called the "dilatoriness" of the
government in proclaiming an anti-slavery policy and in making a
direct attack upon the hateful institution. He was grievously disappointed when Lincoln thought it necessary, in order to conciliate the
feelings of the War Democrats and of the Border State Unionists, as
well as to keep the military commanders within the bounds of discipline, to disavow the partial emancipation orders of Generals
Frémont and Hunter, and he gave voice to that disappointment in
unsparing criticism. But he did not lose confidence in the man who
had said that "if slavery is not wrong, nothing is wrong"; and with unceasing persistency he plied the President with appeals in favor of
decisive measures and of speedy action. Lincoln warded off his ur-
gency by telling him: "Mr. Sumner, you are only six weeks ahead of
me." Sumner would argue that the emancipation of the slaves was a

simple necessity to the end of putting down the rebellion. Lincoln would reply that he saw the necessity coming, but, in order to keep our forces united, he wanted those, whose aid he needed to see that necessity, too. Many a time I saw Sumner restlessly pacing up and down in his room and exclaiming with uplifted hands: "I pray that the President may be right in delaying. But I am afraid, I am almost sure, he is not. I trust his fidelity, but I cannot understand him."

As to myself, I felt with Sumner, but at the same time I learned to understand Mr. Lincoln. He was perfectly sincere in saying that, as the head of the government, he regarded the saving of the Union, with or without the destruction of slavery, as the paramount object to be accomplished. He was equally sincere in believing that the destruction of slavery would turn out to be a necessary means for the salvation of the Union, aside from the desirability of that destruction on its own merits. Seeing the necessity of emancipation by the act of the government rapidly approaching, he wished, in the interest of the blacks as well as of the whites, that emancipation to be gradual, if it possibly could be made gradual under existing circumstances. Nor would he shrink from sudden emancipation if the circumstances so shaped themselves as to leave no choice. But he would delay the decisive step until he could be reasonably sure that it could be taken without danger of producing a fatal disintegration of the forces coöperating in the struggle for the Union. He reasoned that, if we failed in that struggle, a decree of emancipation would be like the Pope's bull against the comet. This reasoning was doubtless correct, but it caused hesitations and delays which were sorely trying to the composure of the more ardent among the anti-slavery men. I have to confess that I belonged to that class myself, and that I did not fully appreciate the wisdom of his cautious policy until it had borne its fruit. But being more conversant than Sumner was with the easy-going, unconventional way in which Western men, especially the self-educated among them, were wont to express their thoughts and sentiments, I was less disturbed by what Sumner sometimes interpreted as a lack of seriousness, an inclination to make light of grave things, in Lincoln's utterances. Thus Sumner's confidence in Lincoln's character and principles found itself often more heavily taxed than mine.

Lincoln had great respect for the superior knowledge and culture of other persons. But he did not stand in awe of them. In fact, he did not stand in awe of anybody or anything in the sense of a recognition of an apparent superiority that might have made him in the slightest degree surrender the independence of his own judgment or the freedom of his will. He would have approached the greatest man in the world—the greatest in point of mental capacity, or the greatest in point of station or power—with absolute unconcern, as if he had been dealing with such persons all his life. When he formed his Cabinet he chose the foremost leaders of his party, who at that period might well have been regarded as the foremost men of the country, without the slightest apprehension that their prestige or their ability might overshadow him. He always recognized the merit of others, but without any fear of detracting from his own.

There was no man in authority in the world whose opinion or advice he would have estimated by another standard than its intrinsic value as he judged it. There was not a problem to be solved capable of confusing his mind by its magnitude or dignity, or one that would have caused him to apply to it any other rules than those of ordinary logic and common sense. He therefore met great statesmen and titled persons with the absolutely natural, instinctive, unaffected self-respect of an equal; he regarded great affairs as simple business he had to deal with in the way of his public duty, and he loved to discuss them with his friends in simple and unceremonious language. They were not above even the play of his humor, although the principles and sympathies according to which he treated them were rooted deep and firm in his mind and heart.

It may well be said that while there was no man whose opinions were more truly his own, that is, even when suggested by others, formed by himself according to his general points of view and methods of reasoning, there was none more accessible to candid advice and more tolerant of adverse criticism. I have known public men in powerful position who would resent every disapproval of their acts or utterances as a personal affront, and treat every opponent as an enemy. Nothing would have been farther from Lincoln's impulses or habits of thought than to take offense at ever so great a difference of judgment between himself and anyone he considered sincere and well meaning. Whenever he found himself misjudged or even attacked by such a person, he would, instead of frowning upon him or excluding him from his intercourse, rather invite him to a friendly exchange of views, and reason with him and be reasoned with, by him. And if then no concord of opinion could be reached, there was at least a kindly agreement to disagree without any bitterness of feeling. Lincoln's patience in listening to adverse, not seldom very unjust criticism, became well known, and was sometimes severely, even unreasonably taxed, without ruffling the goodness of his heart or unsettling the equipoise of his mind. I have to confess that in one or two instances I was myself one of the sinners, and I shall describe the characteristic manner in which he then treated me in the order of my narrative.

At the time of which I now speak, Charles Sumner was one of the most difficult to satisfy among Mr. Lincoln's frequent visitors, because of the very sincerity with which the two men looked at the task of the hour from different points of view. But Lincoln regarded and esteemed Sumner as the outspoken conscience of the advanced antislavery element, the confidence and hearty coöperation of which was to him of the highest moment in the common struggle. While it required all his fortitude to bear Sumner's intractable insistence, Lincoln did not at all deprecate Sumner's public agitation for an immediate emancipation policy, even though it did reflect upon the course of the administration. On the contrary, he rather welcomed everything that would prepare the public mind for the approaching development.

Among the members of Congress with whom I had an opportunity of conversing, I found the Republicans mostly in favor of the adoption by the government of a stronger and more openly pronounced antislavery policy. There were exceptions, however—men who thought their constituents were not quite ready yet to make the "war for the Union" an "abolition war." In some cases these cautious politicians, as happens frequently, were more timid than the state of public sentiment among their people warranted. I went to New York for the purpose of examining the field outside of the reach of the official atmosphere. The impression I received was that party spirit had not remained as silent as it was during the days of the great uprising before my departure for Spain. Some of the Democratic leaders had resumed their old vocabulary in criticising the abolitionists in power. But many of the Democrats who had risen up for the defense of the Union in obedience to their patriotic impulses had gradually freed themselves from the ties of their old party allegiance, and heartily agreed that slavery, being the guilty cause of the whole mischief, must pay the due penalty and perish in the collision. This sentiment had become quite general outside of the circles of hide-bound Democratic partisanship, and among the friends whose advice I sought, it was agreed that the time had come for an open movement in outspoken advocacy of emancipation. To start this movement we organized an "Emancipation Society," and arranged to hold a public meeting on the 6th of March, in the great hall of the Cooper Institute.

I returned to Washington, and at once called upon Mr. Lincoln to report to him what I had seen and heard and what our friends proposed to do. "Good!" said he. "And at that meeting you are going to make a speech?"

"Yes."

"Well, now go home and sketch that speech. Do it as quickly as you can. Then come and show me your arguments and we will talk it over."

Without delay I went to work. To advocate emancipation on the ground that it would give us the support of the moral sentiment in all civilized countries, and thus deter governments, depending upon public opinion, from giving countenance and aid to those fighting for slavery, as I had done in my despatches to the government, would not have been fitting in a public appeal to the American people. I adopted a line of reasoning equally truthful, but starting from a different point of view. I deprecated the oversanguine anticipation of an early collapse of the military power of the Confederacy, and predicted an arduous and protracted struggle, which would indeed finally, but not quietly, lay the rebellion defeated and helpless, at our feet. But the defeat of the rebellion by means of force was not the only object. Beyond that we wanted to restore the Union of the States, the National Republic, based upon local self-government. This required not only the military reconquest of the States that had attempted to secede from the Union —not merely the holding together of those States by means of force such as is used by despotic governments, but it required a revival of that feeling of loyalty to the Union without which the Union could not endure under democratic institutions. There could be no doubt that the disunion sentiment in the South, and its offspring, the secession movement, were owing to the existence of slavery, an institution at war with our democratic principles, an institution which could not live unless it ruled, and would therefore always remain rebellious unless permitted to rule. If, therefore, we aimed at the restoration and maintenance of the Union under democratic government, the Southern people must be brought under the influence of conditions which made loyalty to the Union and to democratic principles their natural sentiment. In other words, the cause of the mischief, slavery, must cease to control their sympathies and aspirations. Slavery would exercise that control so long as it existed. It must, therefore, cease to exist. As initiatory measures to this end I proposed, first, the abolition of slavery in the District of Columbia, and wherever the National Government had immediate authority. Secondly, the confiscation, and, *ipso facto*, the emancipation of slaves belonging to persons engaged in the rebellion. And thirdly, the offer of a fair compensation to loyal Slave

States and loyal masters who would agree to some system of emancipation—this to be followed by such measures as might appear necessary to render the restoration of slavery impossible, and to take away from the Southern people all hope of such a restoration. I then reviewed the objections currently made to such a plan, and showed their futility, and closed with an appeal to the good sense, the patriotism, and the instinct of justice and honor of the American people.

This draft of my speech I took to Mr. Lincoln, and he asked me to read it to him. When I had finished he said: "Now, you go and deliver that speech at your meeting on the 6th of March. And maybe you will hear something from me on the same day."

Our meeting at the Cooper Institute was an imposing demonstration. The great hall was crowded to overflowing with an audience representative of all social classes. Many of the most prominent citizens of New York sat on the platform. Every allusion to the abolition of slavery as a necessity for the preservation of the Union, and as a moral deliverance and a consummation devoutly to be wished and sure to come, called forth outbursts of genuine enthusiasm. There was something like religious fervor in the proceeding—something of that spirit which impelled the singing of "Old Hundred" before the meeting dissolved. While the meeting was going on, the arrival of a despatch from Washington was announced—if I remember rightly, by Horace Greeley—with the remark that it "would greatly interest this audience." The despatch informed us that President Lincoln had on that day, the 6th of March, sent a special message to Congress, asking for the adoption of a joint resolution substantially to this effect: "That the United States ought to co-operate with any State which may adopt gradual abolishment of slavery, giving to each State pecuniary aid, to be used by such State, in its discretion, to compensate for the inconveniences, public and private, produced by such change of system."

The announcement was received by the whole assemblage with transports of joy. Everybody felt that, although the resolution proposed was in a high degree cautious and conservative, yet it indicated the true relation between the Civil War and slavery. Here the abolishment of slavery with compensation was distinctly pointed out as a measure of peace and reunion. If the Slave States rejected it, they would have to bear the consequences. In the argument accompanying the draft of the resolution the President said: "In my judgment, gradual, not sudden emancipation, is better for all. Such a proposition on the part of the government sets up no claim of a right by Federal authority to interfere with slavery within State limits, referring, as it does, the absolute control of the subject in each case to the State and its people immediately interested. In the annual message last December, I thought fit to say: 'The Union must be preserved; and hence, all indispensable means must be employed.' I said this, not hastily, but deliberately. War has been made, and continues to be, an indispensable means to this end. A practical reacknowledgment of the national authority would render the war unnecessary, and it would at once cease. If, however, resistance continues, the war must also continue; and it is impossible to foresee all the incidents which may attend and all the ruin which may follow it. Such as may seem indispensable, or may obviously promise great efficiency towards ending the struggle, must and will come."

The possibilities, or rather the probabilities, of the future were thus distinctly foreshadowed. Mr. Lincoln, naturally of a conservative cast of mind, was much in earnest when he spoke of gradual as preferable to sudden emancipation, and when, as he did on several occasions, he revived the old scheme of colonizing the emancipated negroes somewhere outside of the United States as a very desirable measure. Having been born in a slave-holding State, and grown up in a Negro-hating community, he foresaw more distinctly than other anti-slavery men did the race-troubles that would follow emancipation, and he was anxious to prevent, or at least to mitigate them. But events overruled his cautious and conservative policy, and urged him on to more radical measures. Congress adopted the resolution proposed by the President in his message of the 6th of March, but not one of the slave-holding States responded. Thus their last opportunity for securing a gradual abolishment of slavery with compensation to the owners was lost. Before the end of April, Congress enacted a law prohibiting slavery in the District of Columbia. The practice of surrendering to their owners slaves who had come into the lines of our armies—a practice which had long been kept up by some military commanders—ceased altogether. And the time was rapidly approaching when Abraham Lincoln, recognizing the necessities of the war, obeying the generous impulses of his heart, and feeling himself supported by the enlightened opinion of his fellow-citizens, issued that decree of practically general emancipation which has become his principal title to immortality in the history of the world.

CHAPTER XIII

Second Manassas

THREE days after the emancipation meeting of the 6th of March, I returned to Washington and made my report to Mr. Lincoln. He was in high spirits over the event which, on the preceding day, had taken place in Hampton Roads. It was the epoch-making naval battle between the "Merrimac" and the "Monitor"—the introduction of the ironclad war-vessel to the history of the world.

When I saw Mr. Lincoln the next day, his mind was still so full of the great event that it gave him evident delight to tell me the whole story. He described so vividly the arrival of the first tidings of disaster, and his own and the several Cabinet members' dismay at the awful prospect thus opened, and their sighs of relief when the telegraph announced the appearance of "the little cheese-box" which drove the rebel Goliath off the field, that I have been for years under the impression of having been personally in the President's room when it all happened, and when the despatches successively arrived. A careful scrutiny of circumstances convinced me at last—to my regret, I must confess—that I was not at the White House that day, but the day following. This is one of the cases which have made me very anxious to verify my memory by all attainable outside evidence in writing this story.

Before leaving Mr. Lincoln, I gave him as good a report as I could of our emancipation meeting on the 6th of March, and of the general situation in New York. Mr. Lincoln expressed his satisfaction with what had been done, and trusted that the public discussion of the subject would go on so as to familiarize the public mind with what would inevitably come if the war continued. He was not altogether without hope that the proposition he had presented to the Southern States in his message of March 6th would find favorable consideration, at least in some of the Border States. He had made the proposition in perfect good faith; it was, perhaps, the last of the kind; and if they repelled it, theirs was the responsibility. I remember how grave he looked when he said this. The merry twinkle, which had glimmered in his deep-set eyes when he told the story of the little cheese-box, had altogether given way to an expression of deep melancholy, as he added: "An awful responsibility either way."

The conversation then turned upon my own personal situation. I repeated to Mr. Lincoln that I wished to resign my position as Minister to Spain; that it was an intolerable thought to me to lead a life of ease and luxury and comparative idleness while the Republic was fighting for its life, and most of the men of my age were in the field at the post of danger; and that now, our relations with Spain being in a satisfactory condition, and my business of reporting to him on the public sentiment in Europe, and of lending a helping hand in quickening the anti-slavery current being substantially accomplished, I was anxious to enter the army. Mr. Lincoln said that, remembering how reluctantly I had gone abroad last June, he had thought about this himself, and had talked with Mr. Seward about it. Seward had told him that he was very well satisfied with my services; that I had won for myself a good position with the Spanish Government, and that he wanted me to go back to Madrid. Would I not consider the matter further for a week or two, or as long as I liked, and see Mr. Seward myself? This, of course, I could not decline to do. Mr. Seward, when I called upon him, was very kind, even complimentary; invited me and Mrs. Schurz to dinner, and urged me strongly not to give up the mission—which was very gratifying to me, inasmuch as originally he had, for very good reasons, opposed my appointment. But in all our conversations he did not with a single word mention the subject of slavery, an omission which I could not but think significant and disquieting.

The more maturely I debated with myself the question of returning to Spain, the more firmly I became convinced that, in such times, the true place for a young and able-bodied man was in the field, and not in an easy chair. I waited a reasonable time, so as to avoid the appearance of treating Mr. Lincoln's kindly admonition lightly, and then I told him that my mind was made up. "Well," said he, "I hope you have not forgotten that you are giving up a large salary and a distinguished and comfortable place to take one that pays little and will bring you plenty of work and discomfort and danger. Have you talked the matter over with that handsome, dear wife of yours?" Mr. Lincoln had seen Mrs. Schurz several times, and had apparently been much pleased with her appearance and conversation. "Yes," I said, "she thought it was pretty hard, but she is a good patriot." "If she agrees," said Mr. Lincoln, "then I do. I expected you to come to this decision, and I shall send your name to the Senate with the next batch of brigadiers, and I trust we can find you a suitable command." I was delighted, and thanked him most sincerely.

While I was waiting in Washington for my confirmation and assignment, I had again to undergo the tribulations of persons who are supposed to be men of "influence." The news had gone abroad that in America there was a great demand for officers of military training and experience. This demand could not fail to attract from all parts of the globe adventurous characters who had, or pretended to have, seen military service in one country or another, and who believed that there was a chance for prompt employment and rapid promotion. Washington at that period fairly swarmed with them. Some were very respectable persons, who came here well recommended, and subsequently made a praiseworthy record. Others belonged to the class of adventurers who traded on their good looks or on the fine stories they had concocted of their own virtues and achievements. Being myself of foreign birth, I was approached by many of those who came from Germany, or Austria, or France, with the expectation that I would naturally be disposed to make especial exertions in their behalf. In some cases, having satisfied myself as to their antecedents and qualifications, I willingly did so, and two of them, Major Hoffman, who had been an engineer officer in the Prussian army, which he had left for honorable cause, and who had then served with Garibaldi in his remarkable campaign for the liberation of Italy, and Captain Spraul, a former Bavarian officer, who had also joined Garibaldi, I caused to be appointed "additional aides-de-camp," a military grade especially created for such appointments, and took them upon my own staff, where they did excellent service. Hoffman remained in government employment as an engineer long after the close of the war. One of the best men that came here at that time was Captain Hubert Dilger, who had served in the artillery of the Grand Duchy of Baden. He greatly distinguished himself as one of the most brilliant artillery officers in our army, and I had the good fortune of having him in my command for a considerable time.

In other instances my experience was different. A young man, calling himself Count von Schweinitz, presented himself to me neatly attired in the uniform of an Austrian officer of Uhlans. He was very glib of tongue, and exhibited papers which had an authentic look, and seemed to sustain his pretensions. But there were occasional smartnesses in his conversation which made me suspicious. He may have noticed that I hesitated to trust him, for suddenly he ceased to press me with his suit. I learned afterwards that he had succeeded in obtaining some appointment, and also in borrowing considerable sums of money from two foreign Ministers. Finally it turned out that his mother was a washerwoman, that he had served an Austrian officer of Uhlans as a valet, and that as such he had possessed himself of his uniform and his master's papers.

Another foreign nobleman sought my intercession, of whose genuineness I soon became fully convinced. He was a young German count whose identity was vouched for by a member of the Prussian Legation. Moreover, there were no smartnesses at all in his talk. He had a long row of ancestors, whom he traced back for several hundred years. He was greatly impressed with the importance of this fact, and thought it would weigh heavily in securing him a position in our army. If he could only have an "audience" with the President, and lay his case before him, he believed the result could not be doubtful. He pursued me so arduously with the request for a personal introduction to Mr. Lincoln, that at last I succumbed and promised to introduce him, if the President permitted. The President did permit. The count spoke English moderately well, and in his ingenuous way he at once explained to Mr. Lincoln how high the nobility of his family was, and that they had been counts so-and-so many centuries. "Well," said Mr. Lincoln, interrupting him, "that need not trouble you. That will not be in your way, if you behave yourself as a soldier." The poor count looked puzzled, and when the audience was over, he asked me what in the world the President could have meant by so strange a remark.

Another saying of Mr. Lincoln, of a similar kind, made the rounds at the time, and was very much enjoyed. I cannot vouch for the truth of the anecdote, but it is so strikingly Lincolnesque that there is a strong probability in its favor. I have never seen it mentioned anywhere, and so I may be pardoned for inserting it here. It was to this effect: An Englishman, who had traveled far and wide over the United States, called upon Mr. Lincoln, and told him of the impressions he had received of various parts of the country. Speaking of social conditions and habits, he said, among other things, that to his astonishment he had heard that many gentlemen in America were in the habit of blacking their own boots. "That is true," said Mr. Lincoln, "but would gentlemen in your country not do that?" No; certainly not," the Englishman replied with emphasis. "Well!" said Mr. Lincoln, quietly, "whose boots do they black?"

It is not my purpose to give in what now follows anything pretending to be a valuable contribution to the military history of the Civil War. I shall rather confine myself to the description of some personal experiences, with occasional glimpses of important historical events.

As soon as I had received my order to report for duty to General Frémont in the Shenandoah Valley, I called upon Mr. Lincoln to take leave. He was most kind, wished me "good luck," and said at parting—as he had done when I started for Spain—that he wished me to write to him freely whenever anything occurred to me that I thought he ought to know. This I had soon occasion to do.

After a somewhat adventurous journey, I joined General Frémont's army at Harrisonburg, Virginia, on June 10th, 1862, and reported myself for duty. When Frémont was a candidate for the presidency in 1856, his personality had appeared surrounded by a romantic halo as the great "Pathfinder" who had opened a large and mysterious part of the continent to the knowledge of his countrymen, and who was thought to possess abilities of an extraordinary order. At the beginning of the Civil War, I heard him spoken of in Washington as one of the coming heroes of the conflict, in almost extravagant terms. I remember especially Mr. Montgomery Blair, the Postmaster General in Mr. Lincoln's administration, insisting that Mr. Frémont must at once be given large and important military command, and predicting that the genius and energy of this remarkable man would soon astonish the country. Frémont was, indeed, promptly made a major general in the regular army, and entrusted with the command of the Department of the West, including the State of Illinois and all the country from the Mississippi to the Rocky Mountains, with headquarters at St. Louis. But he sorely disappointed the sanguine expectations of his friends. He displayed no genius for organization. Frémont's headquarters seemed to have a marked attraction for rascally speculators of all sorts, and there was much scandal caused by the awarding of profitable contracts to persons of bad repute. But Frémont won the favor of advanced and impatient anti-slavery men by the issue of an order looking to the emancipation of slaves within his department, which Mr. Lincoln found himself obliged to countermand, seeing in it an act of military usurpation, and a step especially inopportune at a time when the attitude of some of the

Border States was still undetermined. But it gave Frémont a distinct political position and he was given another chance of service at the head of the Mountain Department.

But in that sphere of action he was no more fortunate. He was operating in West Virginia, protecting railroads and putting down guerrillas, when the renowned rebel general, Stonewall Jackson, made his celebrated raid into the Shenandoah Valley, driving Banks before him to the Potomac, and apparently threatening to cross that river, and to make an attack upon Washington. This, however, Jackson did not attempt, but having succeeded in gathering up stores and in disturbing the plans of the Washington government, he turned back and rapidly retreated up the Shenandoah Valley. Frémont was ordered to intercept, and, with the co-operation of Banks' and McDowell's troops, to "bag" him. This required some forced marches, which Frémont failed to execute with the expected promptness, a failure which excited the dissatisfaction of the administration in a marked degree. Frémont, having failed to "bag" Jackson, followed him up the Shenandoah. He had a sharp but indecisive engagement with the enemy at Cross Keys, near Harrisonburg, whereupon Jackson went on to rejoin the main rebel army near Richmond, and Frémont fell back to Harrisonburg with the intention of retiring further down the Shenandoah Valley to Mount Jackson.

I arrived at Harrisonburg late in the evening of June 9th, a day after the action at Cross Keys. There were confused reports about the result of the fight, some telling of a glorious victory, others of a bloody disaster. On the morning of the 10th, I started to join the army, but I soon met officers bringing the news that General Frémont had ordered a retrograde movement and would arrive in town in a few hours. Presently troops began to come in, marching in rather loose order. The men looked ragged, tired, and dejected. I heard a good deal of hard swearing in the ranks in various tongues, English, German, and Hungarian—signs of a sorry state of mind. A troop of neat-looking horsemen appeared, patiently making their way through the throng, and stopped at a house which, as I was informed, had been taken for General Frémont's headquarters. It was the General himself with his staff. As soon as they had dismounted, I presented myself with my order of assignment. To be admitted to General Frémont's presence was a matter attended with some ceremony. There had already been complaints at St. Louis, as I learned, that General Frémont was "difficult to be seen." He was surrounded by a body guard consisting mostly of Hungarians, brave soldiers who on occasion did excellent service, but who also contributed much to the somewhat unusual "style" which was kept up at Frémont's headquarters. As I afterwards observed, Frémont himself had a taste for that sort of thing. When I was finally introduced by Colonel Zagonyi, one of the Hungarian aides-de-camp, the General received me kindly, and at once promised to have a suitable command arranged for me without delay. It was my first meeting with Frémont. I saw before me a man of middle stature, elegant build, muscular and elastic, dark hair and beard slightly streaked with gray, a broad forehead, a keen eye, fine, regular features. It has been said that there was much of the charlatan in him, but his appearance at that time certainly betrayed nothing of the kind. There was an air of refinement in his bearing. His manners seemed perfectly natural, easy, and unaffected, without any attempt at posing. His conversation, carried on in a low, gentle tone of voice, had a suggestion of reticence and reserve in it, but not enough to cause a suspicion of insincerity. The whole personality appeared rather attractive—and yet, one did not feel quite sure.

Our first conversation was rather short and formal, but about an hour later he sent for me to give me an elaborate exposé of his recent operations and his present circumstances. He had received from Washington a telegraphic order to stay at Harrisonburg, while he thought it best to take his command further down the Shenandoah Valley into a more secure position. He considered himself still threatened by Stonewall Jackson, who was reported to have received heavy reinforcements, giving him a decided superiority in numbers. This report was incorrect, but it was credited by other Union commanders in that region. Frémont, therefore, thought it necessary to put his command in a position more easily defensible. Whether he knew or guessed that Mr. Lincoln wanted me to write to him, I do not know. At any rate I gave him no reason for thinking so. But he evidently wished me to form the most favorable judgment of his past action and of his purposes. What he told me of the miserable condition of his troops, I found to be but too true when I reviewed the regiments that were to constitute the two little brigades of my division.

As soon as we were settled at Mount Jackson, and I had, as well as I could in a few days, satisfied myself by personal observation as to the actual state of things, I availed myself of the privilege given me by Mr. Lincoln to report to him what I had seen and what I thought of it. While I could not justify the lack of celerity in Frémont's movements, I could conscientiously say that, if Frémont had marched more rapidly and succeeded in placing his forces athwart

Stonewall Jackson's line of retreat, he would probably not have been able to stop the enemy, very much superior numerically, commanded by the fiercest fighter of the South, but would have exposed himself to a disastrous defeat. To be sure, a very self-reliant and resolute commander would eagerly have taken the risk and strained every nerve to be on the decisive spot on time. Frémont evidently was not of that class.

Two weeks later, unity of command was effected. On June 26th, President Lincoln issued an order providing that "the forces under Generals Frémont, Banks, and McDowell, including the troops now under Brigadier General Sturgis at Washington, shall be consolidated and form one army, to be called the Army of Virginia," and to be under command of Major General Pope. Of this army the troops of the Mountain Department were to constitute the First Army Corps, to be commanded by Major General Frémont. Upon receipt of this order, General Frémont promptly asked the President to relieve him of his command, for the reason that the position assigned to him was "subordinate and inferior to those hitherto conceded" to him, and because the subordinate command to which he was now assigned would "virtually and largely reduce his rank and consideration in the service of the country." Secretary Stanton replied that the other Major Generals, Banks and McDowell, had cheerfully consented to serve under the orders of a junior in rank, but Frémont's request was at once complied with, and, as no other command was conferred upon him, he disappeared from the scene of military action. Two years later he emerged again from retirement for a little while as a candidate for the presidency, nominated by a small conventicle of radicals dissatisfied with Mr. Lincoln's administration. And later, he was heard of only as a business speculator, leading a precarious existence, vibrating between that of a multi-millionaire and a pauper. Finally he died in obscurity, leaving behind him a dim, shadowy myth of quondam glory as the great "Pathfinder" and the first Republican color-bearer.

In the place of Frémont, the President appointed General Franz Sigel as the commander of the First Army Corps of the Army of Virginia. The German-American troops welcomed Sigel with great enthusiasm, which the rank and file of the native American regiments at least seemed to share. He brought a splendid military reputation with him. He had bravely fought for liberty in Germany, and conducted there the last operations of the revolutionary army in 1849. He had been one of the foremost to organize and lead that force of armed men, mostly Germans, that seemed suddenly to spring out of the pavements of St. Louis, and whose prompt action saved that city and the State of Missouri to the Union. On various fields, especially at Pea Ridge, he had distinguished himself by personal gallantry as well as by skillful leadership. The popular war-cry, "fighting mit Sigel," had given his name an extraordinary vogue.

Thus General Sigel seemed to enter upon his field of activity in the East under the most propitious circumstances. But in the course of events I have become convinced that, as regards his personal interests as well as his usefulness, he made a great mistake in leaving the West. The very prestige he had won in the West exposed him to peculiar troubles and dangers in the East. There is no less professional jealousy among military men than there is among musicians or actors. This is human nature. That the officers of the regular army, the West-Pointers, when they saw so many civilian volunteers appointed to high grades and commands, should have been stirred to a grudging discontent, and that they should have clubbed together for the protection or advancement of the pretentions or claims of their class, may sometimes have been deplorably injurious to the public interest, but it was not surprising.

Moreover, General Sigel was not well fitted to meet the difficulties of such a situation. He possessed in a small degree that amiability of humor which will disarm ill-will and make for friendly comradeship. His conversation lacked the sympathetic element. There was something reserved, even morose, in his mien, which, if it did not discourage cheerful approach, certainly did not invite it. That sort of temperament is rather a misfortune than a fault, but in Sigel's case it served to render the difficulties of his situation more difficult at critical periods. However, his prospects seemed to be bright enough when he began his career in the East.

As to myself, after I obtained my command, I was busy studying and performing my various duties and endeavoring to win the respect and confidence of my officers and men. Some of the colonels in the army corps, especially those who had, in one country or another, received some sort of regular military training, were little edified when they saw me put over their heads, and I had reason for believing that in private they occasionally gave vent to their feelings. Among the minor officers and the rank and file, I enjoyed a certain popularity, but it was not of the military kind. These things, however, did not trouble me seriously. First, I earnestly endeavored to provide for the wants of my troops, and as we had the good fortune of several weeks' rest, during

which government supplies arrived, good cheer and contentment gradually returned to our camps. For this my men gave their new commander more credit than he deserved. At the same time I had occasion
to let my officers know that I knew something of our business. I inspected our picket lines by day and by night, and corrected several
mistakes in the placing of our outposts, which my colonels promptly
recognized to be necessary. On the 9th of July, we marched from
Mount Jackson across Thornton's Gap to Sperryville, and it was noticed by officers and men that the march of my command was conducted with more order and comfort than they had been accustomed
to. At Sperryville, as soon as the troops were sufficiently rested, I began a series of division drills under my personal command, including
the formation of my two brigades in column, deployment for action,
formation for attack, changes of front, and similar evolutions. One of
these drills was watched by General Sigel, who accidentally came by.
He was unusually profuse in commendation, and remarked that he
wished such things were more frequently done in the army. I was even
more pleased by a visit from Colonel Alexander von Schimmelfennig,
commanding the Seventy-fourth regiment, Pennsylvania Volunteers,
in my first brigade—the same Prussian officer Schimmelfennig who,
thirteen years before, had served in the revolutionary army of the
Palatinate, and who, in the winter of 1849–50, at Zurich, in Switzerland, had given me military instruction. Now he was my subordinate.
"Your division drill was very good," said he; "very good; where did
you learn these things?" "First from you," I replied, "and then from
the books you recommended to me to study, at Zurich, you remember." "Very good," he repeated, evidently pleased. "You have studied
well; now let us do as well when the bullets whistle."

I felt with great satisfaction that I had much advanced in the respect
and confidence of my officers and men. But the severest and most essential trial was still to come; and it came before many days. On the
8th of August we received marching orders. Although the subordinate
commanders knew little of the ulterior purposes of our movements,
the general situation of affairs was understood to have become critical.
McClellan's great Peninsular campaign dragged discouragingly on.
The Army of the Potomac no longer threatened Richmond, and General Lee, who in the meantime had been advanced to the head of the
Confederate army of Northern Virginia, felt himself free to enter with
his main forces upon offensive operations menacing Washington, and
to invade the North. General Halleck was put in the place of McClellan as General in Chief of the armies of the United States—an appoint-

ment which inspired the people and the troops with little confidence and no enthusiasm. The administration had selected for the command of the Army of Virginia General Pope, who, indeed, on some occasions had rendered fine service in the West, but whose elevation to so important a post caused much headshaking among military men. Halleck resolved to withdraw the Army of the Potomac from the Peninsula, and to bring it to Pope's aid.

At the very start General Pope managed to make an unfavorable impression by one of those indiscretions which an untried leader should be most careful to avoid. He issued a proclamation "to the officers and soldiers of the Army of Virginia," in which he said such things as these: "I have come to you from the West, where we have always seen the backs of our enemies; from an army whose business it has been to seek the adversary, and to beat him when he was found; whose policy has been attack and not defense. I presume that I have been called here to pursue the same system and to lead you against the enemy. It is my purpose to do so, and that speedily. Meantime I desire you to dismiss from your minds certain phrases which I am sorry to find so in vogue amongst you. I hear constantly of 'taking strong positions and holding them,' of 'lines of retreat,' and of 'bases of supplies.' Let us discard such ideas," and so on. There was in this a good deal of boasting not altogether well founded, and some almost contemptuous criticism of Eastern officers and soldiers not altogether merited, and likely to stir up among these a feeling of resentment. In less than two months the boaster was to repent of every word of it.

In July, Pope, having three army corps, Sigel's, McDowell's, and Banks's, at his disposal, was aiming at Gordonsville and Stanton, and thus at the railroad forming the important artery of communication between Richmond, the Confederate Capital, and the West, and pushed some of his forces, under Banks, forward to Culpepper. But Stonewall Jackson, with 25,000 men, advanced against Banks, who had only a greatly inferior force on the ground, and met him near Cedar Mountain. Sigel was ordered to hurry to the support of Banks. We broke camp at Sperryville on the afternoon of August 8th, and marched all night. The night was hot, but the next day much hotter.

After having rested a little while at Hazel River, we continued, in the morning, our march to Culpepper, where we arrived at 2 p. m. It was my first experience of a march with the thermometer up high in the nineties. It must have been well above eighty at the moment when the sun rose—like a huge, angry, red-hot ball. By nine o'clock his rays blazed down with inexorable fierceness. There was not a cloud in the sky, and no breath of air stirring. The dust raised up by the marching column hardly rose above the heads of the men, and enveloped them like a dense, dark, immovable fog bank, within which a black, almost indistinguishable mass struggled onward. As we expected to meet the enemy, I had instructed the commanding officers of brigades and of regiments to keep the marching column well closed up, and to prevent straggling as much as possible. No doubt, they did their best. But as the sun rose higher and the heat grew fiercer, discipline gave way. The men, burdened with their knapsacks and blankets, their guns, and their cartridge belts heavy with ammunition, their faces fairly streaming with sweat, their mouths and nostrils filled with an earthy slime, their breasts panting with almost convulsive gasps for breath, their eyes wide open with a sort of insane stare, dragged themselves along with painful effort. Each man feeling the heat increased by the nearness of his neighbor, and seeking to have the comfort of as much elbow room as possible, the army lost its orderly compactness and spread over the fields to an irregular breadth. Wherever there was a run of water, or a well, or a pool, hundreds would rush to it and tumble over one another to slake their ferocious thirst. Hundreds threw away their knapsacks, and even their blankets. Scores dropped by the wayside, utterly exhausted. Many of them lay there in fits of vomiting. I rode along the column to cheer up the marching men and to encourage those prostrate on the ground. Some of my German regiments had, early in the morning, been singing their native songs. I asked them to try again, and the attempt was actually made, but it failed dismally. Their throats were too much parched to have any music left in them. Among those who were lying down some had spirit enough to struggle up to their feet and salute and say: "Never mind, General, we shall get there somehow." Others were, as they said, about ready to give up and die, it might be here just as well as anywhere else; but march on, they could not. When about 2 o'clock p. m. we entered Culpepper, some of the regiments looked but little larger than mere color-guards. But during the short rest allowed us, those who had promised to "get there somehow" came bravely in, and even most of those who had been ready to give up and die rejoined their companies, so that when we resumed our march a short time later, we had almost fully regained the strength with which we had started from Sperryville the day before. The knapsacks and blankets that had been thrown away were picked up and brought on by the regimental train wagons following the column.

Between four and five o'clock we heard the booming of artillery in the direction of Cedar Mountain. It was the expected battle between Banks on our side and Stonewall Jackson on the Confederate side, and we were to hasten to the support of Banks. We had hardly marched two miles from our resting place when we met a number of straggling fugitives from the battlefield, who told us gruesome stories about "terrible slaughter," about "Banks's army having been all cut to pieces," and about the rebels being "close on their heels in hot pursuit." We tried to stop and rally the runaways, but with small success. A regiment with its colors and a number of officers came on in an evidently demoralized condition, but still maintaining something like order. There were, however, only some two or three hundred men in its ranks. The officer commanding it said that the battle was lost, that they had been overwhelmed and driven from the field by vastly superior numbers, and that he was without orders. Seeing our troops marching on in good shape, he seemed to take heart and stopped his hasty retreat. We learned that General Sigel, who was ahead of us with the advanced guard, General Milroy's brigade, had also succeeded in gathering up some of the dispersed troops and especially two batteries of artillery in full retreat, the commanders of which willingly placed themselves under General Sigel's orders. When we had caught up with General Sigel, the cannonading still going on, he put General Schenck's and my division in position, but the rebels ceased their attacks, and the fight stopped without our becoming actively engaged.

General Banks had indeed been badly beaten after a gallant struggle against a hostile army outnumbering him four to one, but the victorious Jackson, becoming aware of the strong reinforcements massing against him, withdrew across the Rapidan. On the 11th we had a day's truce between the two armies for the purpose of caring for the wounded and burying the dead. Confederate and Union officers met on the battlefield of Cedar Mountain and exchanged polite compliments. The famous cavalry general, "Jeb" Stuart, a figure of martial elegance, was one of the Confederate generals. I am sorry I did not have any conversation with him, for I could not help feeling myself attracted by that handsome young enemy, looking so gay and so brave.

Stonewall Jackson having withdrawn his forces across the Rapidan, our army took position along the course of that river, Sigel's corps forming the right wing. Meanwhile General Lee brought up the bulk of the Confederate forces from Richmond to unite them with Jackson's and then to overwhelm Pope in his exposed position. It became known that he planned a grand attack on Pope's right, whereupon Pope ordered a general retreat to the line of the Rappahannock. This movement was begun on the 18th. Our corps marched northward and reached Sulphur Springs on the 20th, where we crossed the Rappahannock and marched southward on its eastern bank, reaching, about noon of the 21st, the neighborhood of Rappahannock Station, where McDowell's corps was camped. At the same time the Confederate forces under Jackson, and behind him Longstreet's, were marching up the river on its western bank. It was our business to observe them closely and to keep them from crossing. McDowell had a fight on the 21st with a part of Longstreet's corps which lasted several hours and kept the enemy on the western side of the river.

On the 22d, our corps was at Freeman's Ford, and in order to inform himself about the enemy's strength and the movements on the other side of the river, and to disturb those movements if possible, Sigel ordered me to send a regiment of infantry across the river to reconnoiter. I selected Colonel Schimmelfennig's Seventy-fourth Pennsylvania. Schimmelfennig forthwith forded the river, the water reaching up to the belts of the men, ascended the rising open field on the other side, crossed a belt of timber, on top of it, and saw a large wagon train of the enemy moving northward with its flank apparently unguarded. He promptly captured eleven heavily laden pack-mules and several infantry soldiers, and also observed troops marching not far off. His booty he sent to me, with the request that the two other regiments of the brigade be thrown across to support him if he were to do anything further, and to secure his retreat in case the enemy should try to get between him and the river. The two regiments, the Sixty-first Ohio and the Eighth Virginia (loyalists), went over, led by General Bohlen, the brigade commander.

Although, in the regular order of things, I was not required as commander of the division to accompany the brigade in person, I followed an instinctive impulse to do so, this being my first opportunity to be with troops of my command under fire. I placed a mountain howitzer battery on an eminence to sweep the open field and the roads on the other side in case of necessity, and then I crossed with some members of my staff. Colonel Schimmelfennig's foresight in asking for help proved well founded. When he proceeded to subject the rebel wagon train to further annoyance, Trimble's brigade of Stonewall Jackson's rear-guard suddenly turned about and fell upon our right flank, and the two regiments brought to Schimmelfennig's aid were at once hotly engaged. The onset was fierce, and my Eighth Virginia broke and ran. My first service on the battlefield thus consisted in stopping and rallying broken troops, which I and my staff officers did with drawn swords and lively language. But now Hood's Texas brigade of Longstreet's vanguard following closely Jackson's wagon train rushed upon our left flank and threatened our rear.

The situation became serious. I then ordered the Seventy-ninth Pennsylvania and the Sixty-first Ohio, which had remained firm, to make a bayonet charge upon the enemy in front and toward the left, which was executed with drums beating and a great hurrah. The enemy recoiling a short distance, this gave us a little more freedom to extricate our regiments from the embrace of vastly superior numbers. Then we retreated. When our regiments were out of the woods they went down the field to the river at a somewhat accelerated pace. Forthwith our artillery opened to keep the enemy from venturing into the open, but they pushed a skirmish line to the edge of the woods to send their musket balls after us. General Bohlen fell dead from his horse, shot through the heart. I thought it would not do for the division commander and his staff officers to retreat in full view of his command at a gait faster than a walk. So we moved down the river in a leisurely way. I did not cross the ford until my regiments were all on the other side. When I rode up the bank the brigade drawn up there in line received me with a ringing cheer. I met General Sigel, who had watched the whole operation. His first word was: "Where is your hat?" I answered: "It must be somewhere in the woods yonder. Whether it was knocked from my head by a rebel bullet or the branch of a tree, I don't know. But let us say a rebel bullet. It sounds better." We had a merry laugh. "Well," said Sigel, "I am glad you are here again. When I saw you coming down that field at a walk under the fire from the woods, I feared to see you drop at any moment."

This occurrence itself served a good purpose in my relations to my men. From that moment on they were fully convinced that wherever I might order them to go, I would be ready to go myself. My standing with them was now well established. And many years later I had the satisfaction of reading in General Sigel's reminiscences the following sentence referring to this incident: "This was General Schurz's first fight in the American Civil War, and he acquitted himself very bravely." I may be forgiven if this sounds like a little bit of bragging. Every soldier is apt to indulge in that weakness after his first affair, and he will be likely to continue so if that first affair remains the only one. Further experience usually has a sobering effect.

This Freeman's Ford fight amounted to very little as it was. But it might have become of importance had it been followed up by a vigorous push of our forces assembled at and near Freeman's Ford to break

into the rebel column of march just at the point where Jackson's
wagon train passed along and only his rearguard and Longstreet's vanguard were within immediate supporting distance. Sigel at once reported to General Pope what had happened, but no further orders
came. I will not describe in detail all the marches and counter marches
which followed. Suffice it to say that the troops were moving day and
night with but slight interruptions for rest, and ill provided, the regimental wagons of the different corps as well as the ammunition and
provision trains having become almost inextricably mired. I remember
to have been at one time continually in the saddle for more than thirty
hours, only changing occasionally from a tired mount to a fresh one.
It was then that I learned to sleep on horseback.

The men were hungry and terribly fatigued, as repeated night
marches almost without rest will always fatigue the soldier. Moreover,
they were disquieted by strange rumors flying about—rumors which
proved true—that Stonewall Jackson, with a force of 26,000 men, had
worked his way through Thoroughfare Gap to the north of us, had
swooped all around Pope's flank—his famous "foot-cavalry," as his
infantry was called, having made a march of fifty miles in thirty-six
hours—and pounced upon Manassas Junction, where Pope's supplies
and ammunition were stored, helping himself to whatever he could use
and carry off, and burning the rest. "Jeb" Stuart's troopers, accompanying Jackson, had even raided Pope's headquarters at Catlett's Station. It was a brilliant stroke, but at the same time most hazardous, for
Pope's largely superior forces might have been rapidly concentrated
against him, with Longstreet, his only support, still far away.

There was again a chance to "bag Jackson." Indeed, at nine o'clock
of the evening of the 27th, Pope directed McDowell with Sigel "to
march rapidly on Manassas Junction with their whole force." But that
same night, Jackson left Manassas Junction and marched northward
to the old battlefield of Bull Run, there to take position and to await
the arrival of Longstreet, who was to join him by way of Thoroughfare Gap! After much confusion in the transmission of despatches and
orders, and a bloody collision between a part of Jackson's force and
General King's division of McDowell's corps on the evening of the
28th, it was at last ascertained where Jackson was. He was far from
being "bagged."

With his three divisions he stood immediately west of Bull Run and
north of the Gainsville-Centreville turnpike, expecting Longstreet,
with a force of about equal strength coming from Thoroughfare Gap,
to join his right wing within a few hours. The best we could do was

to beat him before Longstreet's arrival. Immediately against him Sigel's corps drew up, about 9000 men strong, south of the Gainsville-Centreville turnpike; on its left Reynolds' division near New Market; King's division on the road from Gainsville to Manassas, near Bethlehem Church, and Ricketts' division on the same road near Dawkin's Branch, under the command of General McDowell. Meantime some parts of the Army of the Potomac having come up from the Peninsula, had joined or were joining us. Of these Fitz-John Porter's corps, about 10,000 strong, stood further south on Dawkin's Branch, forming our extreme left. Heintzelman's corps, with the divisions of Hooker and Kearney, marching on from Centreville, was within supporting distance of our right. Reno's corps was also approaching and arrived on the 29th, while the corps of Sumner and Franklin were on their march toward Centreville. The corps of Banks was detached for the protection of our wagon trains. Not counting Banks, Franklin, and Sumner, Pope had about 60,000 men with at least 120 pieces of artillery at his disposal. His cavalry force had become well-nigh unserviceable by the operations of the preceding days.

The question whether a great battle should be fought by Pope at that time and on that spot, was open to two answers. One was in favor of falling back with his whole force to Centreville, where he would have found ample supplies of provisions and every other needful thing for his troops, as well as a reinforcement of two veteran army corps of about 10,000 men each. This would have greatly increased the fighting capacity of his troops and given us an almost overwhelming numerical superiority, obliging Lee either to abandon the field or to accept battle under very unfavorable conditions. On the other hand, there was the chance of catching and beating Jackson before Longstreet would arrive to reinforce him—a thing which might have been accomplished by a prompt, vigorous, and skillful use of the means at hand. Pope, who had bragged so lustily when he took command, may have thought that he could not afford to fall back upon the Army of the Potomac for help when the time for fighting had come, and the famous second battle of Bull Run was the result.

Will the reader be interested in the description of a Division Commander's personal experience in a battle?

It is about daybreak. My two little brigades are still in bivouac, finishing their scanty breakfast, crackers and thin coffee. This is all, for the regimental wagons are still mixed up with the general train. Then the troops fall into line, silently, without bugle signals, for we are in the immediate presence of the enemy. As the sun rises in a cloudless

August sky, they are ready to march. Looking round, I see to the right
and the left a considerable expanse of open ground with some slight
elevations and a few scattered houses surrounded by trees, houses already famous from the first battle of Bull Run; in front of me a little
affluent of Bull Run, called Young's Branch; beyond this, some patches
of timber, and farther on a long stretch of forest. General Sigel's corps,
about 9000 men strong, forms the right wing of our army, and my division, the right wing of Sigel's corps. I receive the order to advance
and attack. Not the slightest sign of the enemy is to be seen. He is supposed to be posted in the woods yonder, but just where and in what
strength, nobody knows. All is perfectly still. Neither do I hear anything stirring on my left, where I am to connect with Milroy's brigade,
nor beyond, where Schenck's division of Sigel's corps stands, nor beyond that, where several divisions of other corps are supposed to be.
However, my orders are positive and clear: "Advance at sunrise and
attack." Evidently I am to open the proceedings of the day. My command quickly fords Young's Branch, and on the other side I promptly
form it in order of battle, first line deployed, second line, 150 paces
behind in column, skirmish line well ahead, flanking party on the right;
right wing, Col. Schimmelfennig's brigade, left wing, Col. Krzyzanowski's, my artillery so placed as to command the edge of the forest
before me. I gallop along the front to say a last word to the commanding officers. The troops begin to cheer, but are promptly stopped
because we want no noise.

At a brisk pace the skirmishers pass the detached groups of timber
and enter the forest. The line of battle follows at the proper distance.
No sign of the enemy. A quarter of an hour elapses. Perfect stillness all
around. Are the enemy there at all? But hark!—two musket shots in
rapid succession, apparently near the spot where my skirmishers are
to join Milroy's. I hear the clear ringing of those two shots now. Then
a moment's silence, followed by a desultory rattle of musketry along
the line. No more doubt; we have struck the enemy. The rattle is increasing in liveliness and volume, but the enemy's skirmishers seem to
be falling back. "Seem to be"—for we can see very little. The woods
are thick, permitting no outlook to the front nor to the right or left,
beyond a few paces. Moreover, they are soon filled with white powder
smoke. I am impatient to advance my line of battle with greater
energy. But the troops, having marched forward through thick forest
with tangled underbrush, the ranks are broken up into irregular little
squads. The company officers, shouting and waving their swords, do
their utmost to hold their men together. Still they press on. I cannot

see anything except what is immediately around me. The troops are out of my hands. I am with Krzyzanowski's brigade, and conclude only from the firing I hear on my right, that Schimmelfennig's is in its place, hotly engaged. But lo! here is an aide-de-camp bringing me a message from Schimmelfennig: "All right so far, but the devil to pay ahead. Examine the two prisoners I send you." The prisoners stand before me—stalwart, wild-bearded, weather-beaten, ragged, simple-minded looking men. I examine them separately, and they tell the same story. Stonewall Jackson confronts us with two divisions, each about 8000 strong. This agrees with the reports we have received of his strength. Jackson expects Longstreet to join him inside of a few hours.

There is indeed "the devil to pay ahead." Stonewall Jackson, the most dashing rebel general, with at least 15,000 men of the best Confederate infantry, right before me, and I have, at best, 3000 muskets. What is to be done? Notify Sigel, and hope for reinforcements. Meanwhile, keep a cool head and a bold front. Perhaps Jackson does not know how weak I am. Meanwhile, my skirmishers have advanced well-nigh half a mile under the weird clatter of rebel bullets against leaves and tree trunks and branches. The line of battle, such as it is, is after them. But now the rattling fire of skirmishers changes into crashes of musketry, regular volleys, rapidly following each other. We have evidently struck Jackson's main position. Now, "Steady, men! Steady! Aim low; aim low!" My men still advance, although slowly. Another messenger from Schimmelfennig with ominous news. He has observed heavy bodies of troops in the open at some distance from his right, coming toward him. He does not know whether they are Confederate or Union troops. I send him the only regiment still unengaged of Krzyzanowski's brigade, to face the mysterious new-comers, and to find out who they are. The roar in my immediate front continues. Brave old Milroy, who commands on my left, startled by what he subsequently calls in his report the "tremendous fire of small arms" on my line, sends me two of his regiments to help me in what he considers my stress. At the same time, General Steinwehr, commanding the second division of Sigel's corps, hurries on with one of his regiments, the Twenty-ninth New York, which I can put in reserve. A third message from Schimmelfennig. The body of troops apparently threatening his right have disappeared again—no doubt a Union force coming from Centreville. I heave a deep sigh of relief, and call back the regiment I had sent to his aid. It comes none too soon. The rebels make a vicious dash against my center and throw it into confusion. But we succeed soon in restoring order, and with a vigorous counter-charge, we regain the ground we had won before.

It is now about ten o'clock—nearly five hours since we have gone into action. An officer announces to me that General Kearney of the Army of the Potomac has arrived in my rear and is looking for me. I find him in the open just outside of my woods—a strikingly fine, soldierly figure, one-armed, thin face, pointed beard, fiery eyes, his cap somewhat jauntily tipped on the left side of his head, looking much as we might expect a French general to look. He asks me about the state of the action and the position of my command, and requests me to shorten my front a little toward my left, so as to make room for his division on my right. I gladly promise this, and despatch orders to Schimmelfennig accordingly. Poor Kearney—he had not three days more to live.

Kearney has hardly left me when I hear a tremendous turmoil in the direction of my center—the rebel yell in its most savage form, and one crash of musketry after another. I conclude that the rebels are making another and more furious charge. I order the commander of the artillery to load his pieces with grape-shot, and the Twenty-ninth New York, held in reserve, to be ready for action. Not many minutes later, three of my regiments, completely broken, come tumbling out of the woods in utter confusion. A rebel force in hot pursuit, wildly yelling, gains the edge of the forest and is about to invade the open, when the artillery pours into them one discharge after another of grape, and the Twenty-ninth New York, volley after volley of musketry. The rebels are stopped, but still hold the edge of the woods. The Twenty-ninth advances, firing, and behind it, sword in hand, we rally the broken regiments. The routed men present a curious spectacle: some fierce and indignant at the conduct of their comrades; some ashamed of themselves, their faces distorted by a sort of idiotic grin; some staring at their officers with a look of helpless bewilderment, as if they did not understand what had happened, and the officers hauling them together with bursts of lively language, and an incidental slap with the flat of their blades. But the men are quickly rallied and reformed under their colors. A few encouraging words revive their spirits. "Never mind, boys! Such things may happen to the best of soldiers. Now, forward with a hurrah!" The hurrah is given, we rush upon the enemy, and the line we had occupied is promptly regained. On my right, Schimmelfennig's brigade remained perfectly firm, and Krzyzanowski's left had yielded but little.

Presently an officer of the corps staff comes at a gallop, he hands me a letter addressed by General Sigel to General Kearney, which I am to read and forward. Sigel requests Kearney to attack at once with his whole strength, as the rebel general, Longstreet, who is to join Jackson, has not yet reached the battlefield, and we have still a chance, the last, to beat Jackson alone. This is good sense. Instant action being necessary, I prepare at once for another charge, and hearken eagerly to hear Kearney's guns on my right. But I hear nothing. Probably Sigel's request conflicts with orders Kearney has received from his own immediate superiors. But construing Sigel's request as implying an instruction for myself, I order a general advance of my whole line, and put in every man I have. It is gallantly executed with a hurrah. The enemy yields everywhere. The brave Col. Soest of the Twenty-ninth New York falls at the head of his men, seriously wounded. On my left the fight comes to a stand at an old railroad embankment, nearly parallel with my front, which the enemy use as a breastwork, and from behind which they pour a galling fire. On my right, Schimmelfennig's brigade, by a splendid charge, gains possession of this embankment, and goes even beyond it, but is received there with so murderous a cross-fire of artillery and infantry that it has to fall back; but it holds the embankment firmly in its grip. General Sigel sends me two small mountain howitzers, which I put at once into the fire-line of my left brigade. With the aid of their effective short-range fire, that brigade, too, reaches the embankment and holds it. The enemy repeatedly dashes against it, but is hurled back each time with a bloody head.

But my hope that on my right the troops come from the Army of the Potomac under Kearney and Hooker, would attack at the same time, is sorely disappointed. Had their whole force been flung upon Jackson's left in conjunction with my attack in front, we might have seriously crippled Jackson before Longstreet's arrival. Now, if I have gained any advantage, I am far too weak to pursue it. The old story of the war—to be repeated again and again—time and strength and blood uselessly frittered away by separate and disconnected efforts of this and that body of troops, when well-concerted action of all of them together might have achieved great and perhaps decisive results.

While on my right all is quiet, I hear on my left, where Milroy, and, beyond him, Schenck's division stands, from time to time heavy firing, which sways forward and backward, from which I can only conclude that the fight is carried on with varying success.

It is about two o'clock of the afternoon, and the fight about my railroad embankment has dwindled into a mere exchange of shots between skirmishers, when I am advised by General Sigel that my division is to be relieved by the troops of Generals Kearney and Hooker, and that we are to be put into a reserve position. I cannot say that this news is entirely unwelcome on account of the condition of my regiments. They have been under fire for eight hours, almost without intermission. They have suffered the loss of a large number of officers and soldiers in killed and wounded. The men still in the ranks have well-nigh reached the point of utter exhaustion. Their stomachs are as empty as their cartridge boxes. The water in their tin flasks has long given out, and for hours they have been tortured by that agonizing thirst which nobody knows who has not, on a hot summer day, stood in the flaming fire-line of a battle without a drop of water to moisten his tongue.

Pursuant to General Sigel's order, I withdraw my regiments, one by one, as their places are filled by the men of the Army of the Potomac. I can truthfully say in my official report to my superiors: "Thus the possession of that part of the woods which my division had taken and held, was in good order delivered to the troops that relieved me." I had every reason to be proudly satisfied with the conduct of my officers and men.

My division being rallied in the open, a comfortable distance behind the line of battle, my first duty is to look after the wounded, of whom there are a great many. I have to confess that now, for the first time that day, I become conscious of a strong sympathetic emotion. While in action and absorbed by the duties of the moment, I had hardly noticed the falling of men near me, and their moans and exclamations. But now! The stretchers coming in dreadful procession from the bloody field, their blood-stained burdens to be unloaded at the places where the surgeons stand with their medicine chests and bandages, and their knives and uprolled sleeves and blood-smeared aprons, and by their sides ghastly heaps of cut-off legs and arms—and, oh! the shrieks and wailings of the wounded men as they are handled by the attendants, and the beseeching eyes of the dying boy who, recognizing me, says with his broken voice: "Oh, General! can you not do something for me?"—and I can do nothing but stroke his hands and utter some words of courage and hope, which I do not believe myself, and commend him to the special care of the surgeon and his men—and such scenes one after another—I feel a lump in my throat which almost chokes me.

Having seen my wounded cared for as well as I can, I visit my regiments bivouacking near by. The roar of the battle is still thundering hardly a mile away, but some of our supply wagons have found their way to our position and added, not much, indeed, but something in the way of more crackers and coffee and a little bacon to the bill of fare. And they have had a drink at the creek, and some had enjoyed the luxury of a dash of water in their faces. And now they are as gay as if the whole war were over and they might go home to-morrow. And their jokes about the gorgeousness of their meal, and the banterings about the "skedaddling" of some before the rebel yell, and their cheers when I praise their good conduct, which I most heartily do!

At last myself and my staff may sit down on the ground to a royal feast. And a royal feast it is. To-day's battle had its humorous incident. About noon, when the bullets were flying thick, I suddenly heard somebody shouting behind me with a stentorian voice: "Oh, General! Oh, General!" Looking round, I saw Schiele, my tent orderly, or body servant, brandishing a bulky object over his head. "What is it, Schiele?" I asked. "A ham, General! a ham! a ham!" cried Schiele jubilantly. "Where did you get it?" I asked. "I have found it, General!" he answered with a broad grin. I told him to go to the rear, and try not to get killed, and to hold on to the ham like grim death until we should have time to eat it. Schiele scampered off amid the laughter of the soldiers happening to be around. Schiele was "a character," and a great favorite with the whole division.

While we were thus feasting—ready, of course, at any moment to move wherever our help might be wanted—the battle was going on. The line taken by my small division of six regiments and those regiments sent to reinforce them, and held successfully during the day, was now occupied by two divisions of the Army of the Potomac, counting in all twenty-nine regiments, and commanded by two of the most renowned fighters of the army, Kearney and Hooker. They delivered during the afternoon various attacks upon the enemy, some of which were very brilliant, and actually succeeded in "doubling up" Stonewall Jackson's extreme left, without, however, producing decisive results. Toward evening they fell back into what had been substantially my position during the day. As to other parts of the field, the expected attack upon the enemy's right by Fitz John Porter, which subsequently caused so much bitter controversy, had not come off at all, and Longstreet's junction with Jackson, increasing more than twofold the strength of the enemy in our front, had not been prevented.

We slept on the battlefield among dead bodies of men and horses and the tattered fragments of vehicles and clothes and accouterments.

On the next morning, April 30th, General Sigel did me the honor of adding to my command another brigade under Col. Koltes, with a battery commanded by Captain Hubert Dilger, one of the most brilliant artillery officers of the army. I was proud of this mark of confidence. About 9 o'clock I was ordered to put my three brigades in the rear of Schenck's division, front toward Groveton, in a sort of reserve position, from which we could overlook a large part of the battlefield —an undulating plain with some low hilltops and patches of timber; upon our right the stretch of forest in which my division had fought the previous day, now occupied by Hooker, Reno, Stevens, Ricketts, and Kearney; before us, Fitz John Porter's command, which had been brought up early in the morning, facing a belt of woods; upon our left, Reynold's division and part of McDowell's corps. Of the enemy we saw, from our position, nothing except thick clouds of dust, which indicated a movement of large masses of troops toward our left.

As we were told, it was believed at General Pope's headquarters that the enemy had been "badly cut up" the previous day and had begun his retreat during the night, and that to demoralize him still further, we had only to pursue him with vigor. At about two o'clock, Porter moved forward to attack. But he had hardly passed the belt of timber immediately before him when we heard a fearful roar of artillery and infantry, indicating that he had struck, not a mere rear guard, but the enemy in full force and in position to receive him. For half an hour we watched in anxious expectancy. Then we observed the signs of a disastrous repulse of the attack—disordered swarms of men coming out of the woods, first thin and scattered, then larger disbanded squads, some at a full run, others at a hurried walk; then shattered companies, or battalions, or skeleton regiments crowding around their colors and maintaining something like organization; and, finally, still larger bodies retreating in better order, and higher officers surrounded by their staffs, struggling to steady the retreat and to rally the straggling men.

The situation was serious indeed. As we afterward learned, that part of Porter's command which was repulsed by the Confederates had made its attack with great spirit and gallantry, but had been met by the cross-fire of a numerous and skillfully posted artillery, and a hail-storm of musketry from advantageous positions so murderous, that their charge was hopeless. Moreover, this was another of those efforts the chances of whose success were reduced to nothing by the lack of support and co-operation by other bodies of troops.

Having repulsed this charge, the enemy was expected to take the offensive. Sigel moved forward Schenck's division to a stronger position near Dugan's Farm, and ordered me to close up behind it. By four o'clock Porter's retreating troops had well uncovered our front, when McLean's and Stahel's brigades of Schenck's division, followed by my command, pushed bravely on under a heavy artillery fire of the enemy, which cost us many men. But, by five o'clock, the enemy disclosed his main attack on the left wing of our army, which could not hold its ground against the superior forces the enemy had massed at that point. I had to put in Koltes' and Krzyzanowski's brigades to protect Schenck's left. The contest grew extremely sharp. Koltes fell dead at the head of his regiments, Krzyzanowski's horse was shot under him, and Schenck had to be carried wounded from the field. The ground was thickly strewn with our dead. When Sigel observed that the left wing of the army was being constantly pressed back, and the left of his corps was uncovered and furiously assailed by the enemy's infantry in front, and enfiladed by his artillery so that, in our position, we were substantially fighting alone against overwhelming odds, he ordered me to withdraw my division to the next range of low hills near the "stone house." I had left Schimmelfennig's brigade with Dilger's battery on my right in reserve, and they now covered the retrograde movement, which was executed in perfect order. Especially Captain Dilger distinguished himself by receiving the pursuing enemy in several positions with grape shot at short range, obliging him twice to turn back, and then following his brigade unmolested. My command come out of the trial sadly thinned, but in a state of firm organization. I could say in my official report: "My men stood like trees until the instruction to retire reached them, and then they fell back slowly and in perfect order."

When I reached the rising ground indicated to me, a singular spectacle presented itself. I found General McDowell with his staff on horseback, standing still, and around them a confused mass of men, partly in an organized, partly in a disbanded state, and among them army wagons, ambulances, and pieces of artillery, streaming to the rear. Nobody seemed to make any effort to stem the current or to restore order. I noticed a fully equipped battery of six guns moving with the crowd, and succeeded in inducing the commanding officer, who told me that he had somehow become separated from his brigade and was without orders, to disentangle his pieces from the confusion and place them on a nearby knoll. He did this willingly, and opened upon the enemy's guns immediately opposite. On the left of the army the fighting was still going on, the enemy steadily gaining ground.

Sigel ordered me to send a brigade to the aid of Milroy, who was still engaged there, hard pressed. I brought forward Schimmelfennig's brigade, which plunged resolutely into the ragged fire-line, and not finding Milroy, whose forces had become much scattered, did good service on the right of Sykes and Reno.

The enemy's artillery seemed to sweep the whole battlefield. For two hours we had been under a continuous shower of shot and shell, with only an irregular response from our side. As the dusk of evening came on, the enemy's fire, artillery as well as musketry, rapidly slackened, and soon ceased altogether. On the left of the army the fight came to a complete standstill. The enemy, although successful, had no doubt suffered not much less than we had, and got into that state of disorder resulting from the mixing up of different divisions, brigades, and regiments, which is almost always caused by the action of great masses on the battlefield. In a talk about the situation which, at that moment, I had with General Sigel, we agreed that the enemy, upon arriving at the foot of the rising ground which we were then occupying, were probably too exhausted to continue the assault, and would perhaps also be exhausted enough to yield to a vigorous offensive movement on our part. We might, indeed, have found enough bodies of troops in a good state of organization to execute such an attack. However, the arrival of General Pope's instruction ordering a general retreat, and the fact that a large portion of the army was already on its way to Centreville, put an end to the question. But it has since been held by military critics of high authority that General Pope might have remained on the battlefield without much danger, that he might have brought on, during the night, from Centreville, the 20,000 men of Sumner's and Franklin's corps, which would have given him a superiority of numbers, and that thus the formal confession of defeat and the consequent demoralization of the army and the injury to the Union cause might have been avoided. My personal experience of the condition of the battlefield that night seems to speak for this theory.

About eight o'clock General Sigel directed me to withdraw Schimmelfennig's brigade, and to march with my whole division to the hilly ground between Young's Branch and Bull Run, where I joined the rest of our army corps. There we waited in the dark for two hours, my first brigade furnishing the guards and pickets. The enemy did not molest us in the least. After having received a report that, as far as could be ascertained, the rest of the army, with their wagons and ambulances, had crossed Bull Run, General Sigel ordered the corps to take up its march to Centreville. We passed over the Stone Bridge between eleven o'clock and midnight. On the east side of the bridge we once more took position, General Stahel on the right of the road and I on the left, front towards the creek, with Dilger's guns to command the bridge. As we were forming, we discovered a small body of troops bivouacking there, a battalion of the Pennsylvania Bucktail Regiment, under Colonel Kane, who had become detached from his brigade, and had picked up and kept with him several stray pieces of artillery. He was delighted to meet us, and willingly reported to General Sigel for orders. One of General McDowell's officers coming that way told us that we were threatened by the enemy on our left, but no enemy made his appearance. General Sigel gave the order to march on toward Centreville, my first brigade, under Colonel Schimmelfennig, to form the rear guard, and to destroy the bridge. Some little time after one o'clock we set fire to the wooden part of the bridge and marched off. We rejoined General Sigel and the bulk of the corps, on the road at three o'clock, bivouacked until five, because the road before us was obstructed, reached Centreville about seven, and went into camp among the intrenchments built by the Confederates a year before.

Thus I may claim the honor of having, with my command, covered the retreat from the Bull Run battlefield of the main part of our army, which retired by way of the Stone Bridge—that is, as much as any "covering" was necessary. I am aware that General Sykes was charged with that business, but I have the best reason for believing that General Sykes, no doubt thinking that all other troops had left the battlefield before him, crossed Bull Run a considerable time before I did. My command was the last to arrive at Centreville, which fact, as no troops could have passed by it on the road, seems to be conclusive.

The rest at Centreville was short. The enemy, instead of molesting us on the Warrenton-Centreville turnpike, moved a strong column around our flank by way of the Little River turnpike, to strike us at Fairfax Court-House, and to cut off as large a part of our army as possible from the fortifications of Washington. The outcome was the fierce fight at Chantilly, in which two of our bravest Generals, Kearney and Stevens, lost their lives, but the Confederates were stopped.

The whole army was to be put under the protection of the fortifications of Washington, there to be reorganized, and to this end McClellan was set to work again—a kind of work for which he had proved himself well fitted.

The night march of Sigel's corps from Centreville to Fairfax Court-House is like a nightmare in my recollection. By some blunder of the staff, two large bodies of troops were put on the same road at the same time, and that in the dark. In a moment they became inextricably mixed. All orderly command ceased. The road was so densely crowded with men and guns and caissons and wagons and ambulances, that those who were marching absolutely lost the freedom of their movements. One was simply pushed on from behind or stopped by some obstruction ahead. Nor was it possible to march alongside the road, for there the fields or woods were filled with all sorts of vehicles, a great many of them broken down, and by groups of soldiers, who had straggled from the edges of the column, had gathered around little fires and were frying their bacon or heating water for their coffee. I was on horseback in the midst of the column, with one of my staff-officers by my side, who, for a wonder, had succeeded in remaining with me. Our horses would walk on a few paces, half a dozen at the most, then would be forced to stand still, sometimes for minutes, by some stoppage in front. Having had my feet in the stirrups almost constantly for several days and nights, my heels began to ache almost insufferably. I tried to relieve the pain by letting my legs hang down, or by throwing one or the other across the pommel of the saddle, but it was of no avail. Neither could I dismount in order to walk, for the throng around me was too dense to permit it. Indeed, had I succeeded in getting off the horse, I could not have mounted again. So we crawled on, being alternately pushed and stopped, at the rate of a good deal less than a mile an hour, until finally we reached Fairfax Court-House long after sunrise. There we found soldiers stationed at the cross-roads and the street corners, crying out the numbers of regiments at the top of their voices—and the men belonging to those regiments struggled out of the column with many kicks and curses, to be directed to their colors. It required many hours thus to disentangle the confused mass, and then to give the sorely jaded troops a short rest.

The next day, about the dusk of evening, my command reached the spot within the circle of entrenchments surrounding Washington, where it was to go into camp. Riding at the head of my column, I met on the road an officer in general's uniform, attended, if I remember rightly, by only one aide-de-camp and one orderly. Although I had never before seen him, I recognized General McClellan. I observed with some surprise how trim and natty he looked in his uniform. Even the yellow sash around his waist was not wanting. There was a strange contrast between him and our weather-beaten, ragged, and grimy officers and soldiers. In a pleasant voice he asked me to what corps I belonged and what troops I commanded, and then directed me to my camping place. And thus ended my part in the campaign of the "Army of Virginia."

CHAPTER XIV

Chancellorsville

O N the 17th of September, the battle of Antietam was fought, in which McClellan might have made a victory of immense consequence, had he not, with his usual indecision and procrastination, let slip the moments when he could easily have beaten the divided enemy in detail. As it was, General Lee came near being justified in calling Antietam a "drawn battle." He withdrew almost unmolested from the presence of our army across the Potomac. But the battle of Antietam became one of the landmarks of human history by giving Abraham Lincoln the opportunity for doing the great act which crowned him with eternal fame. There is something singularly pathetic in the story —and it is a true story—that Abraham Lincoln, harassed by anxious doubts as to whether the issue of the Emancipation Proclamation, already once postponed, would not cause dangerous dissension among the Northern people, at last referred the portentous question to the arbitrament of heaven, and vowed in his heart to himself and "to his Maker" that the proclamation should certainly come forth, if the result of the next battle were in favor of the Union. And so, after the battle of Antietam, the great proclamation, in Lincoln's heart sanctioned by the decree of Providence, did come forth, and it made our Civil War not only a war for a political Union, but also a war against slavery before all the world.

At the North the Emancipation Proclamation was used by Democratic politicians to denounce the administration for having turned the "War for the Union" into an "abolition war," and much seditious clamor was heard about the blood of white fellow-citizens being treacherously spilled for the sole purpose of robbing our Southern countrymen of their negro property, and all this in direct violation of the Federal Constitution and the laws. While this agitation, on the whole, affected only Democratic partisans, it served to consolidate their organization, to turn mere opposition to the Republican administration into opposition to the prosecution of the war. On the other hand, it greatly inspired the enthusiasm of the anti-slavery people, and gave a new impetus to their activity. Moreover, it produced a powerful impression in Europe. It did not, indeed, convert the enemies of the American Union in England and France; but it created so commanding a public sentiment in favor of our cause that our enemies there could not prevail against it.

But the political situation at the North assumed a threatening aspect. Hundreds of thousands of Republican voters were in the army, away from home. Arbitrary arrests, the suspension of the writ of habeas corpus, and similar stretches of power had disquieted and even irritated many good men. But—more than this—our frequent defeats in the field and the apparent fruitlessness of some of our victories, like that of Antietam, had a disheartening effect upon the people. Our many failures were largely ascribed to a lack of energy in the administration. The consequence was, that at the November elections in 1862, the Democrats achieved some startling successes, winning the States of New York and New Jersey, and a good many congressional districts in various other important States, and boastfully predicting that the next time they would obtain the control of the National House of Representatives.

It was under these circumstances that I wrote from my camp to Mr. Lincoln, giving voice to the widespread anxiety as I understood and felt it. I thought myself all the more at liberty to do so since Mr. Lincoln, when I joined the army, had asked me personally to write to him freely whenever I had anything to say that I believed he should know. I have never again seen that letter, and do not clearly remember all it contained. One of its main points probably was that, in view of the suspicions current in the army and among the people, the administration should select for the discharge of important duties only men whose hearts were in the struggle and who could, therefore, be depended upon. Perhaps I intimated also that the government had been too lax in that respect. Mr. Lincoln's prompt reply took me to task for my criticism in his peculiar clean-cut, logical style, and there was in what he said an undertone of impatience, of irritation, unusual with him—this time, no doubt, induced by the extraordinary harassment to which he was subjected from all sides.

EXECUTIVE MANSION,
WASHINGTON, NOV. 24, 1862.

GENERAL CARL SCHURZ:

My Dear Sir—I have just received and read your letter of the 20th. The purport of it is that we lost the late elections, and the Administration is failing, because the war is unsuccessful, and that I must not flatter myself that I am not justly to blame for it. I certainly know that if the war fails, the Administration fails, and that I will be blamed for it, whether I deserve it or not. And I ought to be blamed if I could do better. You think I could do better; therefore you blame me already. I think I could not do better; therefore I blame you for blaming me. I understand you now to be willing to accept the help of men who are not Republicans, provided they have "heart in it." Agreed. I want no others. But who is to be the judge of hearts, or of "heart in it"? If I must discard my own judgment, and take yours, I must also take that of others; and by the time I should reject all I should be advised to reject, I should have none left, Republicans or others—not even yourself. For be assured, my dear sir, there are men who have "heart in it" and think you are performing your part as poorly as you think I am performing mine. I certainly have been dissatisfied with the slowness of Buell and McClellan; but before I relieved them I had great fears I should not find successors to them who would do better; and I am sorry to add that I have seen little since to relieve those fears. I do not clearly see the prospect of any more rapid movements. I fear we shall at last find out that the difficulty is in our case rather than in particular generals. I wish to disparage no one—certainly not those who sympathize with me; but I must say I need success more than I need sympathy, and that I have not seen the so much greater evidence of getting success from my sympathizers than from those who are denounced as the contrary. It does seem to me that in the field the two classes have been very much alike in what they have done and what they have failed to do. In sealing their faith with their blood, Baker, and Lyon, and Bohlen, and Richardson, Republicans, did all that men could do; but did they any more than Kearney, and Stevens, and Reno, and Mansfield, none of whom were Republicans, and some at least of whom have been bitterly and repeatedly denounced to me as secession sympathizers? I will not perform the ungrateful task of comparing cases of failure. In answer to your question, Has it not been publicly stated in the newspapers, and apparently proved as a fact, that from the commencement of the war the enemy was continually supplied with information by some of the confidential subordinates of as important an officer as Adjutant General Thomas? I must say "No," as far as my knowledge extends. And I add that if you can give any tangible evidence upon the subject, I will thank you to come to this city and do so.

Very truly your friend,

A. LINCOLN.

Two or three days after Mr. Lincoln's letter had reached me, a special messenger from him brought me another communication from him, a short note in his own hand asking me to come to see him as soon as my duties would permit; he wished me, if possible, to call early in the morning before the usual crowd of visitors arrived. At once I obtained the necessary leave from my corps commander, and the next morning at seven I reported myself at the White House. I was promptly shown into the little room up-stairs which was at that time used for Cabinet meetings—the room with the Jackson portrait above the mantel-piece—and found Mr. Lincoln seated in an arm chair before the open-grate fire, his feet in his gigantic morocco slippers. He greeted me cordially as of old and bade me pull up a chair and sit by his side. Then he brought his large hand with a slap down on my knee and said with a smile: "Now tell me, young man, whether you really think that I am as poor a fellow as you have made me out in your letter!" I must confess, this reception disconcerted me. I looked into his face and felt something like a big lump in my throat. After a while I gathered up my wits and then I explained to him my impressions of the situation and my reasons for writing to him as I had done. He listened with silent attention and when I stopped, said very seriously: "Well, I know that you are a warm anti-slavery man and a good friend to me. Now let me tell you all about it." Then he unfolded in his peculiar way his view of the then existing state of affairs, his hopes and his apprehensions, his troubles and embarrassments, making many quaint remarks about men and things. I regret I cannot remember all. Then he described how the criticisms coming down upon him from all sides chafed him, and how my letter, although containing some points that were well founded and useful, had touched him as a terse summing up of all the principal criticisms and offered him a good chance at me for a reply. Then, slapping my knee again, he broke out in a loud laugh and exclaimed: "Didn't I give it to you hard in my letter? Didn't I? But it didn't hurt, did it? I did not mean to, and therefore I wanted you to come so quickly." He laughed again and seemed to enjoy the matter heartily. "Well," he added, "I guess we understand one another now, and it's all right." When after a conversation of more than an hour I left him, I asked whether he still wished that I should write to him. "Why, certainly," he answered; "write me whenever the spirit moves you." We parted better friends than ever.

While Sigel's corps was camped within the defenses of Washington, events of great importance took place. A fortnight after the battle of Antietam, one of the bloodiest days of the war, which McClellan claimed as a great victory, the President visited the Army of the Potomac, which was still lying idle in Maryland. After his return to Washington the President ordered General McClellan to move forward, but McClellan procrastinated in his usual way three weeks longer, while the government as well as the Northern people fairly palpitated with impatience. When McClellan at last had crossed the Potomac and then again failed in preventing the Confederate army from crossing the Blue Ridge and placing itself between the Army of the Potomac and Richmond, the President removed him from his command and put General Burnside in his place.

The selection of Burnside for so great a responsibility was not a happy one. He was a very patriotic man whose heart was in his work, and his sincerity, frankness, and amiability of manner made everybody like him. But he was not a great general, and he felt, himself, that the task to which he had been assigned was too heavy for his shoulders.

The complaint against McClellan having been his slowness to act, Burnside resolved to act at once. The plan of campaign he conceived was to cross the Rappahannock at Fredericksburg, and thence to operate upon Richmond. His army of about 120,000 officers and men, which was then in splendid condition, he divided into three grand divisions and a reserve corps—the "Right Grand Division," under General Sumner, to consist of the Second and Ninth corps; the "Center Grand Division," under General Hooker, to consist of the Third and Fifth corps; and the "Left Grand Division," to consist of the First and Sixth corps, under General Franklin. The "Reserve Corps" was to consist of the Eleventh corps and some other troops, under the command of General Sigel. The whole campaign was a series of blunders, mishaps, ill-conceived or ill-executed plans, and finally a horrible butchery, costing thousands of lives. On the 17th of November, Sumner's corps arrived at Falmouth opposite Fredericksburg, and the rest of the army followed within two days. But the pontoon trains for crossing the river did not appear until the 25th. Meanwhile

General Lee had drawn his forces together and strongly fortified his position for defense. Only on the 11th of December, Burnside began laying his pontoon bridges and crossing his troops for the attack. Sigel's "Reserve Corps" remained on the left bank of the river, where we could overlook a large part of the battlefield—the open ground beyond the town of Fredericksburg stretching up to Marye's Heights, from which Lee's entrenched batteries and battalions looked down. In the woods on our left, where Franklin's Grand Division had crossed and from where the main attack should have been made, the battle began December 13th, soon after sunrise, under a gray wintry sky. Standing inactive in reserve, we eagerly listened to the booming of the guns, hoping that we should hear the main attack move forward. But there was evidently no main attack, the firing was desultory and seemed to be advancing and receding in turn. At eleven o'clock Burnside ordered the assault from Fredericksburg upon Marye's Heights, Lee's fortified position. Our men advanced with enthusiasm. A fearful fire of artillery and musketry greeted them. Now they would stop a moment, then plunge forward again. Through our glasses we saw them fall by hundreds, and their bodies dot the ground. As they approached Lee's entrenched position, sheet after sheet of flame shot forth from the heights, tearing fearful gaps in our lines. There was no running back of our men. They would sometimes stop or recoil only a little distance, but then doggedly resume the advance. A column rushing forward with charged bayonets almost seemed to reach the enemy's ramparts, but then to melt away. Here and there large numbers of our men, within easy range of the enemy's musketry, would suddenly drop like tall grass swept down with a scythe. They had thrown themselves upon the ground to let the leaden hail pass over them, and under it to advance, crawling. It was all in vain. The enemy's line was so well posted and protected by a canal and a sunken road and stone walls and entrenchments skillfully thrown up, and so well defended, that it could not be carried by a front assault. The early coming of night was most welcome. A longer day would have been only a prolonged butchery. And we, of the reserve, stood there while daylight lasted, seeing it all, burning to go to the aid of our brave comrades, but knowing also that it would be useless. Hot tears of rage and of pitying sympathy ran down many a weather-beaten cheek. No more horrible and torturing spectacle could have been imagined.

Burnside, in desperation, thought of renewing the attack the next day, but his generals dissuaded him. During the following night, aided by darkness and a heavy rainstorm, the army recrossed the Rappahannock without being molested by the enemy. This was one of the instances in which even so great a general as Robert E. Lee failed to see his opportunity. Had he followed up his success with a prompt and vigorous dash upon our shattered army immediately in front of him, he might have thrown our retreat into utter confusion and driven the larger part of our forces helplessly into the river.

General Burnside bore himself like an honorable man. During the battle he had proposed to put himself personally at the head of his old corps, the Ninth, and to lead it in the assault. Reluctantly he desisted, yielding to the earnest protests of his generals. After the defeat he unhesitatingly shouldered the whole responsibility for the disaster. He not only did not accuse the troops of any shortcomings, but in the highest terms he praised their courage and extreme gallantry. He blamed only himself. His manly attitude found a response of generous appreciation in public opinion, but the confidence of the army in his ability and judgment was fatally injured. The number of desertions increased alarmingly, and regimental officers in large numbers resigned their commissions. A little later 85,000 men appeared on the rolls of the army as absent without leave. Burnside, deeply mortified, at once resolved upon another forward movement to retrieve his failure. He intended to cross the river at one of the upper fords, but a severe rainstorm set in and made the roads absolutely impassable. The infantry floundered in liquid mud almost up to the belts of the men, and the artillery could hardly be moved at all. I remember one of my batteries being placed where we camped overnight on ground which looked comparatively firm, but we found the guns the next morning sunk in sandy mud up to the axles, so that it required all the horses of the battery to pull out each piece. The country all around was fairly covered with mired wagons, ambulances, pontoons, and cannons. The scene was indescribable. "Burnside stuck in the mud" was the cry ringing all over the land. It was literally true.

A further advance was not to be thought of, and, as best he could, Burnside moved the army back to its camps at or near Falmouth. It was fortunate that the condition of the roads rendered Lee just as unable to move as Burnside was, for the demoralization of the Army of the Potomac had reached a point almost beyond control. The loyal people throughout the land were profoundly dejected. There seemed to be danger that the administration would utterly lose the confidence of the country. A change in the command of the Army of the Potomac was imperatively necessary, and the President chose General Hooker.

If Burnside lacked self-confidence, Hooker had an abundance of it. He had been one of the bitterest critics of McClellan and Burnside, and even of the administration—perhaps the loudest of all. He had even talked of the necessity of a military dictatorship. But he had made his mark as a division and corps commander and earned for himself the name of "Fighting Joe." The soldiers and also some—although by no means all—of the generals had confidence in him. Lincoln, as was his character and habit, overlooked all the hard things Hooker had said of him, made him commander of the Army of the Potomac in view of the good things he expected him to do for the country, and sent him, with the commission, a letter full of kindness and wise advice. Hooker was a strikingly handsome man,—a clean-shaven, comely face, somewhat florid complexion, keen blue eyes, well-built, tall figure, and erect soldierly bearing. Anybody would feel like cheering when he rode by at the head of his staff. His organizing talent told at once. The sullen gloom of the camps soon disappeared, and a new spirit of pride and hope began to pervade the ranks. By the 30th of April, the Army of the Potomac attained an effective force of more than 130,000 men, with over 400 pieces of artillery, ready for duty in the field.

Hooker abolished the "Grand Divisions," the chiefs of which were otherwise disposed of. Sigel, having commanded the "Reserve Corps," which had passed for the fourth "Grand Division," left the Army of the Potomac. The reasons why he did so he never discussed with me. I know, however, that his relations with his superior officers on the Eastern field of action had never been congenial.

General Hooker selected Major General Howard as commander of the Eleventh Corps. In various writings I have since seen it stated that General Hooker made that appointment to prevent me from remaining at the head of the corps. I had been promoted to a major-generalship on March 14, 1863, and when Sigel left, the command of the corps fell temporarily to me as the ranking officer, and Sigel strongly recommended me for the permanent command. It appeared to me perfectly natural that under existing circumstances a regular army officer of merit should be put into that place, and I therefore welcomed General Howard with sincere contentment. He was a slender, dark-bearded young man of rather prepossessing appearance and manners; no doubt a brave soldier, having lost an arm in one of the Peninsular battles; a West Point graduate, but not a martinet, and free from professional loftiness. He did not impress me as an intellectually strong man. Our personal relations grew quite agreeable, and even cordial, at least on my side. But it soon became apparent that the regimental officers and the rank and file did not take to him. They looked at him with dubious curiosity; not a cheer could be started when he rode along the front. And I do not know whether he liked the men he commanded better than they liked him.

My command remained the same—the Third Division of the Eleventh Corps, but it was strengthened by the addition of some fresh regiments. There was the Eighty-second Illinois, commanded by no less a man than Colonel Friedrich Hecker, the most prominent republican leader in the Germany of 1848, now an ardent American patriot and anti-slavery man, no longer young, but in the full vigor of ripe manhood. There was also the Twenty-sixth Wisconsin, mainly composed of young men of the best class of German-born inhabitants of Milwaukee. There was, finally, the One Hundred and Nineteenth New York, commanded by Colonel Elias Peissner, a professor at Union College, Schenectady. His face bore a very striking resemblance to Ludwig I., King of Bavaria, and rumor had it that he was a natural son of that eccentric monarch, who in his day cultivated art and poetry along with his amours. I have good reason for believing that, in this instance, rumor spoke the truth. Colonel Peissner was a gentleman of the highest type of character, exquisite refinement, large knowledge, and excellent qualities as a soldier. And in his lieutenant colonel, John T. Lockman, whom I have cherished as a personal friend to this day, he had a worthy companion. Of my two brigade commanders, Schimmelfennig had been made a brigadier general, as he well deserved. Krzyzanowski was less fortunate. The President nominated him too for that rank, but the Senate failed to confirm him—as was said, because there was nobody there who could pronounce his name.

By the middle of April Hooker was ready to move. His plan was excellent. Lee occupied the heights on the south side of the Rappahannock skirting the river to the right and left of Fredericksburg in skillfully fortified positions. Hooker set out to turn them by crossing the upper Rappahannock so as to enable him to gain Lee's rear. A cavalry expedition under General Stoneman, intended to turn Lee's left flank and to fall upon his communications with Richmond, miscarried, but this failure, although disagreeable, did not disturb Hooker's general scheme of campaign. On the morning of April 27th, the Eleventh, Twelfth, and Fifth Corps started for Kelly's Ford, 27 miles above Fredericksburg, which they reached on the afternoon of the 28th. I remember those two days well. The army was in superb condition and animated by the highest spirits. Officers and men seemed to feel instinctively that they were engaged in an offensive movement promising great results. There was no end to the singing and merry laughter relieving the fatigue of the march. A pontoon bridge was thrown across the river, and our corps crossed before midnight. The Seventeenth Pennsylvania cavalry regiment was sent ahead to clear the country immediately opposite.

Something singular happened to me that night. While it was still light, one of General Howard's staff officers pointed out to me a strip of timber at some distance on the other side of the river, at the outer edge of which I was to stay until morning. Between that timber and the river there was a large tract of level, open ground,—meadow or heath, perhaps three-quarters of a mile across,—which I was to traverse. When I set out at the head of my division to pass the pontoon bridge, General Howard gave me a cavalryman as a guide who "knew the country perfectly." Meanwhile a dense fog had arisen over the open ground in which we could distinguish nothing a few paces ahead. With the guide who "knew the country perfectly" at my side, I marched on and on for a full hour without reaching my belt of timber, which I ought to have reached in much less than half that time. I asked my guide whether he knew where we were. He stammered that he did not. Almost at the same moment I heard a well-known voice say something emphatic a short distance ahead of me. It was Colonel Hecker, whose regiment, the Eighty-second Illinois, was, as I knew, at the tail of my column. A short investigation revealed the fact that my whole division was standing on the open ground in a large circle, and that we had been marching round and round in the fog for a considerable time. We struck matches, examined our compasses, and then easily found our way to my belt of timber, which was close by. There I halted again to ascertain my location, and seeing the glimmer of a light through the window of what I found to be a little house near at hand, I dismounted and went in, accompanied by Brigadier General Schimmelfennig, to look at our maps. We had hardly entered the lighted room, when one of my orderlies rushed in, excitedly exclaiming: "There is rebel cavalry all around. They have already taken Captain Schenofsky prisoner." Captain Schenofsky, a Belgian officer, whom the government had assigned to my staff, was one of my aides whom I had ordered to look for the Pennsylvania cavalry regiment supposed to be ahead of us. The orderly had seen him "run right into a bunch of rebels," who promptly laid hold of him. As fast as we could we hurried back to our column, which we found in a curious condition. The men, having marched all day and several hours of the night, had dropped down where they stood, overwhelmed by fatigue. With the greatest effort we tried to arouse some of them to form something like out-posts, and as this was a slow and rather unsuccessful proceeding, I and my officers as well as the brigade staffs, stood guard ourselves, revolver in hand, until day broke. Then it turned out that the Pennsylvania cavalry regiment which was to clear the ground and to cover our front, had gone astray—we could not ascertain where—and that rebel scouting parties had been hovering closely around us.

After our two days' march up stream on the northern bank of the Rappahannock, we now had two days' march down stream on its southern side. We forded the Rapidan, and on the afternoon of April 30th, we reached the region called the Wilderness. We stopped about two miles west of Chancellorsville. The following night four army-corps camped in that vicinity, the Eleventh, Twelfth, and Fifth, which had come down from Kelly's Ford, and the Second, under General Couch, which had crossed at United States Ford as soon as that ford was uncovered by our advance,—a force of 50,000 men. This flanking movement had been masked by an operation conducted by General Sedgwick, who crossed the Rappahannock a few miles below Fredericksburg with a force large enough to make Lee apprehend that the main attack would come from that quarter. This crossing accomplished, the Third Corps under Sickles joined Hooker at Chancellorsville. Until then, Thursday, April 30th, the execution of Hooker's plan had been entirely successful, and with characteristic grandiloquence the commanding general issued on that day the following general order to the Army of the Potomac: "It is with heartfelt satisfaction that the commanding general announces to the army that the operations of the last three days have determined that our enemy must ingloriously fly, or come out from behind his defenses and give us battle on our own ground, where certain destruction awaits him—the operations of the Fifth, Eleventh, and Twelfth Corps have been a succession of splendid achievements."

The impression made upon the officers and men by this proclamation was by no means altogether favorable to its author. Of course, they were pleased to hear themselves praised for their achievements, but they did not forget that these had so far consisted only in marching, not in fighting, and that the true test was still to come. They hoped indeed that the Army of the Potomac, 130,000 strong, would prove able to beat Lee's army, only 60,000 strong. But it jarred upon their feelings as well as their good sense to hear their commanding general gasconade so boastfully of having the enemy in the hollow of his hand,—that enemy being Robert E. Lee at the head of the best infantry in the world. Still we all hoped, and we explored the map for the important strategical point we would strike the next day. But the "next day" brought us a fearful disappointment.

On the morning of Friday, May 1st, Hooker ordered a force several divisions strong, to advance towards Fredericksburg and the enemy's communications. Our corps, too, received marching orders, and started at 12 o'clock M. But the corps was hardly on the road in marching formation when our movement was stopped and we were ordered back to the position we had occupied during the preceding night. What did this mean? General Hooker had started out to surprise the enemy by a grand flank march taking us into the enemy's rear. We had succeeded. We had surprised the enemy. But the fruits of that successful surprise could be reaped only if we followed it up with quick and vigorous action. We could not expect a general like Lee to stay surprised. He was sure to act quickly and vigorously, if we did not. And just this happened. When we stopped at Chancellorsville on the afternoon of Thursday, April 30th, we might, without difficulty, have marched a few miles farther and seized some important points, especially Bank's Ford on the Rappahannock, and some commanding positions nearer to Fredericksburg. It was then that Lee, having meanwhile divined Hooker's plan, gathered up his forces to throw them against our advance. And as soon as, on Friday, May 1st, our columns, advancing toward Fredericksburg, met the opposing enemy. Hooker recoiled and ordered his army back into a defensive position, there to await Lee's attack. Thus the offensive campaign so brilliantly opened was suddenly transformed into a defensive one. Hooker had surrendered the initiative of movement, and given to Lee the incalculable advantage of perfect freedom of action. Lee could fall back in good order upon his lines of communication with Richmond, if he wished, or he could concentrate his forces, or so much of them as he saw fit, upon any part of Hooker's defensive position which he might think most advantageous to himself to attack. As soon as it became apparent that Hooker had abandoned his plan of vigorous offensive action, and had dropped into a merely defensive attitude, the exuberant high spirits which so far had animated the officers and men of the Army of the Potomac turned into head-shaking uncertainty. Their confidence in the military sagacity and dashing spirit of their chief, "Fighting Joe," was chilled with doubt. The defensive position into which the Army of the Potomac was put could hardly have been more unfortunate. It was in the heart of the "Wilderness." That name designated an extensive district of country covered by thick woods of second growth with tangled underbrush of scrub oak and scrub pine. There were several clearings of irregular shape which afforded, in spots, a limited outlook. But they were surrounded by gloomy woods, which were not dense enough to make the approach of a hostile force impossible, but almost everywhere dense enough to conceal it.

The westernmost of the clearings, or openings, in the wilderness occupied by our army was Talley's farm, crossed by the "Old Turnpike" running east and west from Fredericksburg to Orange Court-house. Along that turnpike the first division of the Eleventh Corps, under General Devens, was strung out, the first brigade of which, Colonel Gilsa's, was posted west of the clearing on the road; dense woods on all sides. To protect the right flank and rear, two of Colonel Gilsa's regiments were placed at a right angle with the road, and two pieces of artillery in the road. The rest of the brigade was on the road itself, facing south, with thickets in front, flank, and rear. The second brigade, under General McLean, also facing south, on the road, with the same thicket in its rear, the southern front protected by hastily constructed breastworks. Four pieces of artillery, Dieckmann's battery, were posted on the Talley farm, also facing south. Next came my division, partly also strung out in the road, facing south, breastworks in front and thickets in the rear, partly in reserve on a large opening containing Hawkins' farm, an old church in a little grove, and Dowdall's Tavern, a wooden house situated on the Pike, where the Corps Commander, General Howard, had his headquarters. On that clearing, near Dowdall's Tavern, another road, coming from the southwest, called the Plank-road, joined the turnpike at a sharp angle, and at that angle Dilger's battery was placed, also facing south. Connecting with Dilger's left was Colonel Buschbeck's brigade of the Second, Steinwehr's division, with Captain Wiedrich's battery, behind a rifle pit, also facing south; General Barlow's brigade with three batteries of reserve artillery stood near the eastern border of the opening as a general corps reserve.

Thus the Eleventh Corps formed the extreme right of the army. East of it there was another body of thick woods through which the turnpike led to the third great opening, in the eastern part of which stood the Chancellor house, in which General Hooker had established his headquarters. On the left of the Eleventh Corps, the Third (Sickles) and the Twelfth (Slocum) were posted, and further east the rest of the army in positions which I need not describe in detail.

Early on Saturday morning, May 2d, General Hooker with some members of his staff rode along his whole line and was received by the troops with enthusiastic acclamations. He inspected the position held by the Eleventh Corps and found it "quite strong."

The position might have been tolerably strong if General Lee had done General Hooker the favor of running his head against the breast-works by a front attack. But what if he did not? "Our right wing," as I said in my official report, "stood completely in the air, with nothing to lean upon, and that, too, in a forest thick enough to obstruct any free view to the front, flanks or rear, but not thick enough to prevent the approach of the enemy's troops. Our rear was at the mercy of the enemy, who was at perfect liberty to walk right around us through the large gap between Colonel Gilsa's right and the cavalry force stationed at Ely's Ford." As we were situated, an attack from the west or northwest could not be resisted without a complete change of front on our part. To such a change, especially if it was to be made in haste, the formation of our forces was exceedingly unfavorable. It was almost impossible to maneuver some of our regiments, hemmed in as they were on the old turnpike by embankments and rifle pits in front and thick woods in the rear, drawn out in long deployed lines, giving just room enough for the stacks of arms and a narrow passage; this turnpike road being at the same time the only line of communication we had between the different parts of our front. Now, the thing most to be dreaded, an attack from the west, was just the thing coming.

The firing we had heard all along the line of our army during the preceding day, May 1st, indicated that the enemy was "feeling our front" along its whole length. Toward evening the enemy threw some shells from two guns placed on an eminence opposite General Devens' left. General Schimmelfennig, the commander of my first brigade, was ordered to push forward a regiment for the purpose of capturing or at least dislodging those pieces. That regiment, after a sharp little skirmish, came back with the report that the guns had departed. The night passed quietly.

But next morning, May 2d, not long after General Hooker had examined our position, I was informed that large columns of the enemy could be seen from General Devens' headquarters moving from east to west on a road running nearly parallel with the plank-road, on a low ridge at a distance of about a mile or more. I hurried to Talley's, where I could plainly observe them as they moved on, passing gaps in the woods, infantry, artillery, and wagons. Instantly it flashed upon my mind that it was Stonewall Jackson, the "great flanker," marching towards our right, to envelop it and attack us in flank and rear. I galloped back to corps headquarters at Dowdall's Tavern, and on the way ordered Captain Dilger to look for good artillery positions fronting west, as the corps would, in all probability, have to execute a change of front. I reported promptly to General Howard what I had seen, and my impression, which amounted almost to a conviction, that Jackson was going to attack us from the west.

In our conversation I tried to persuade him that in such a contingency we could not make a fight in our cramped position facing south while being attacked from the west; that General Devens' division and a large part of mine would surely be rolled up, telescoped, and thrown into utter confusion unless the front were changed and the troops put upon practicable ground; that, in my opinion, our right should be withdrawn and the corps be formed in line of battle at a right angle with the turn-pike, lining the church grove and the border of the woods east of the open plain with infantry, placing strong échelons behind both wings, and distributing the artillery along the front on ground most favorable for its action, especially on the eminence on the right and left of Dowdall's Tavern. In such a position, sweeping the opening before us with our artillery and musketry, and checking the enemy with occasional offensive returns, and opposing any flanking movements with our échelons, we might be able to maintain ourselves even against greatly superior forces, at least long enough to give General Hooker time to take measures in our rear, according to the exigencies of the moment.

I urged this view as earnestly as my respect for my commanding officer would permit, but General Howard would not accept it. He clung to the belief which, he said, was also entertained by General Hooker, that Lee was not going to attack our right, but was actually in full retreat toward Gordonsville. I was amazed at this belief.

Some time before noon, General Howard told me that he was very tired and needed sleep; would I, being second in command, stay at his headquarters, open all despatches that might arrive, and wake him in case there were any of urgent importance. Shortly after, a courier arrived with a despatch from General Hooker calling General Howard's attention to the movement of the enemy toward our right flank, and instructing him to take measures to resist an attack from that quarter. At once I called up General Howard, read the despatch aloud to him and put it into his hands. We had exchanged only a few words about the matter when another courier, a young officer, arrived with a second despatch of the same tenor. At a later period I saw the document in print and recognized it clearly as the one I had read and delivered to General Howard on that eventful day. It runs thus:

Headquarters, Army of the Potomac,
Chancellorsville, May 2d, 1863, 9:30 a. m.

MAJOR GENERALS SLOCUM AND HOWARD:

I am directed by the Major General commanding to say that the disposition you have made of your corps has been with a view to a front attack of the enemy. If he should throw himself upon your flank, he wished you to examine the ground and determine upon the position you will take in that event, in order that you may be prepared for him in whatever direction he advances. He suggests that you have heavy reserves well in hand to meet this contingency. The right of your line does not appear to be strong enough. No artificial defenses worth naming have been thrown up, and there appears to be a scarcity of troops at that point, and not, in the general's opinion, as favorably posted as might be. We have good reason to suppose that the enemy is moving to our right. Please advance your pickets as far as may be safe, in order to obtain timely information of their approach.

J. H. VAN ALEN,
Brig. Gen. and Aide-de-Camp.

To my utter astonishment I found, many years later, in a paper on "The Eleventh Corps at Chancellorsville," written by General Howard for the *Century Magazine*, the following sentence: "General Hooker's circular order to 'Slocum and Howard' neither reached me nor, to my knowledge, Colonel Meysenburg, my adjutant general." How he could have forgotten that I had read and delivered to him that identical despatch I find it difficult to understand, especially as it touched so vital a point, and its delivery was followed by another animated discussion between us, in which I most earnestly—although ineffectually—endeavored to convince him that in case of such an attack from the west, our right, as then posted, would be hopelessly overwhelmed.

We were standing on the porch of Dowdall's Tavern. I saw Major Whittlesey, one of General Howard's staff-officers, coming out of the woods opposite, not far from the turnpike. "General," I said, "if you draw a straight line from this point over Major Whittlesey's head, it will strike Col. Gilsa's extreme right. Do you not think it certain that the enemy, attacking from the west, will crush Gilsa's two regiments, which are to protect our right and rear, at the first onset? Is there the slightest possibility for him to resist?" All General Howard had to say was: "Well, he will have to fight," or something to that effect. I was almost desperate, rode away, and, on my own responsibility, took two regiments, the Fifty-eighth New York and the Twenty-sixth Wisconsin, from my second line facing south and placed them facing west on Hawkins' farm in the rear of Gilsa's forlorn right, with a third regiment, the Eighty-second Ohio, a little further back, so that, when the attack on our flank and rear came, there should be at least a little force with a correct front. When I reported this to General Howard, he said that he did not object. This was all, literally all, that was done to meet an attack from the west, except the tracing of a shallow rifle pit, the embankment of which reached hardly up to a man's knees, running north and south, near Dowdall's Tavern, and the removal of the reserve artillery, three batteries, to the border of the woods on the east of the open ground. As for the rest, the absurdly indefensible position of the corps remained unchanged.

A little after 3 p. m. we were startled by two discharges of cannon followed by a short rattle of musketry, apparently near Gilsa's position. Could this already be Jackson's advance? I jumped upon my horse and rode with all speed to the spot from which the noise came. No, it was not Jackson's advance. I found that only a few rebel cavalrymen had shown themselves on the old turn-pike west of our right, and that the two pieces of artillery posted on the road had been fired off without orders. Evidently Jackson was still feeling our lines. But my horse was surrounded by regimental officers of Devens' division, telling me with anxious faces that their pickets had, time and again during the day, reported the presence of large bodies of rebel troops at a short distance from their right flank, and that, if an attack came from that quarter, they were not in a position to fight. What did I think? I was heartsick, for I could not tell them what I did think, for fear of producing a panic. Neither would I deceive. So I broke away from them and hurried to General Devens to try whether I could not get him to aid me in another effort to induce General Howard to order a change of front. To my surprise I found him rather unconcerned. He had reported all his information to corps headquarters, he said, and asked for instructions, and the officer carrying his message had been told there that General Lee seemed to be in full retreat. He, Devens, thought that at corps headquarters they were better informed than he was, and that he could only govern himself by the instructions received from his superior.

To corps headquarters I returned to make another effort. There General Howard met me with the news that he had just been ordered by General Hooker to send Barlow's brigade to the aid of General

Sickles, who had, about noon, set out with his corps to attack and capture Stonewall Jackson's rearguard with his wagon trains—and that
was the meaning of the cannonading we had heard since noon. This,
General Howard added, was clear proof that General Hooker did not
expect us to be attacked in flank by Jackson, for, if he really expected
anything of the kind, he would certainly not at that moment deprive
the Eleventh Corps of its strongest brigade, the only general reserve it
had. I replied that, if the rebel army were really retreating, there would
be no harm in a change of front on our part; but that, if the enemy
should attack us on our right, which I still anticipated, then would the
withdrawal of Barlow's brigade make a change of front all the more
necessary. But all my reasoning and entreating were in vain, and
General Howard rode off with Barlow's brigade on what proved to be
a mere wild-goose-chase, to see, as he said, that the brigade be well
put in.

   There we were, then. That the enemy was on our flank in very
great strength had become more certain every moment. Schimmelfennig had sent out several scouting parties beyond our regular pickets.
They all came back with the same tale, that they had seen great masses
of rebel troops wheeling into line; that they had even heard the commands of rebel officers. The pickets and scouts of McLean and Gilsa
reported the same. My artillery captain, Dilger, returned from an adventurous ride. He had made a reconnoissance of his own, had been
right among the rebels in Gilsa's front, had been chased by them, had
been saved from capture by the speed of his horse, had been at army
headquarters at the Chancellor house where he told his experience to a
major belonging to the staff, had been told by him to go to his own
corps with his yarn, and had finally come back to me. In fact, almost
every officer and private seemed to see the black thunder-cloud that
was hanging over us, and to feel in his bones that a great disaster was
coming—all felt it, except the corps commander and, perhaps, General
Devens, who permitted his judgment to be governed by the corps
commander's opinion. Could there be better reason for this unrest?
Within little more than rifle-shot of our right flank there stood Stonewall Jackson with more than 25,000 men, the most dashing general of
the Confederacy with its best soldiers, forming his line of battle, which
at the given word was to fold its wings around our feeble flank; and
within his grasp the Eleventh Corps—originally 12,000 strong, but reduced to 9,000 men by the detachment of its strongest brigade and
main reserve, and its commanding general gone away with that brigade; and, to cap the climax, hardly a Federal soldier within two miles

on its left and rear, to support it in case of need, for Sickles' corps and a large part of Slocum's had moved into the woods after Jackson's wagon train—and in addition to all this, the larger part of the corps so placed as to be helpless against an attack from the west. It may fairly be said that, if there had been a deliberate design, a conspiracy, to sacrifice the Eleventh Corps—which, of course, there was not—it could not have been more ingeniously planned. This was the situation at 5 o'clock of the afternoon.

At last the storm broke loose. I was with some of my staff at corps headquarters, waiting for General Howard to return, our horses ready at hand. It was about 5:20 when a number of deer and rabbits came bounding out of the woods bordering the opening of Hawkins' farm on the west. The animals had been started from their lairs by Jackson's advance. Ordinarily such an appearance of game might have been greeted by soldiers in the field with outbreaks of great hilarity. There was hardly anything of the kind this time. It was as if the men had instinctively understood the meaning of the occurrence. A little while later there burst forth a heavy roar of artillery, a continuous rattling of musketry, and the savage screech of the "rebel yell" where Gilsa stood, and then happened what every man of common sense might have foreseen. Our two cannon standing in the road threw several rapid discharges into the dense masses of the enemy before them, and then the men made an effort to escape. But the rebel infantry were already upon them, shot down the horses, and captured the pieces. Gilsa's two regiments, formed at a right angle with the turn-pike, were at once covered with a hail of bullets. They discharged three rounds—it is a wonder they discharged as many—and then, being fired into from front and from both flanks at close quarters, they had either to surrender or beat a hasty retreat. They retreated through the woods, leaving many dead and wounded on the field. Some of Gilsa's men rallied behind a reserve regiment of the first division, the Seventy-fifth Ohio, whose commander, Colonel Riley, had been sensible and quick enough to change front, and to advance, without orders, to help Gilsa. But they were promptly assailed in front and flank by several rebel regiments, and completely wrecked, Colonel Riley being killed and the adjutant wounded. Meanwhile the enemy had also pounced upon the other regiments of the first division, which were deployed in the turn-pike. These regiments, being hemmed in on the narrow road between dense thickets, and being attacked on three sides, many of the men being shot through their backs, were not able to fight at all. They were simply telescoped and driven down the turn-pike in utter confusion.

While this happened, a vigorous attempt was made to form a line of defense which in some way might stem the rout of our sacrificed regiments and impede the progress of the enemy. As soon as I heard the firing on our right I despatched an aide-de-camp to Colonel Krzyzanowski to turn about all his regiments and front west. For the same purpose I hurried to the point where the plank-road and the turn-pike united. There I found General Schimmelfennig already at work. Our united efforts succeeded in changing the front of several regiments, and in forming something like a line facing the attack, but not without very great difficulty. Several pieces of the artillery of the first division, as well as some wagons and ambulances, came down the turn-pike at a full run, tearing lengthwise through the troops still deployed in line on the road. They were followed by the telescoped regiments of the first division in the utmost confusion. We had scarcely formed a regiment in line fronting west, when that rushing torrent broke through its ranks, throwing it into new disorder. Thus it could happen to General Devens to state in his report that, being carried by, wounded, he failed to see any second line behind which his dispersed troops might have rallied, while, after seeing him taken to the rear, we held that point twenty minutes. For, in spite of the terrible turmoil which almost completely wrecked two of my best veteran regiments, we did succeed, in the hurry, in forming a line, somewhat irregular and broken, to be sure, near the church-grove, consisting of the Sixty-first Ohio, One Hundred and Nineteenth New York, One Hundred and Fifty-seventh New York, and the Eighty-second Illinois, and, farther to the right, the Eighty-second Ohio, the Fifty-eighth New York, and the Twenty-sixth Wisconsin, the regiments I had placed front west earlier in the afternoon. Captain Dilger quickly moved his six guns a little distance back upon higher ground, where he could sweep the turn-pike and the plank-road. He poured shot and shell into the enemy's battalions as they advanced on the heels of the wrecked regiments of our first division. On they came, with fierce yells and a withering fire of musketry, widely overlapping our lines on both sides. At their first onset, the noble Colonel Peissner of the One Hundred and Nineteenth New York dropped dead from his horse, but Lieutenant-Colonel Lockman held his men bravely together. My old revolutionary friend, Colonel Hecker of the Eighty-second Illinois, who had grasped the colors of his regiment to lead it in a bayonet charge, was also struck down, wounded by a rebel bullet, and was taken behind the front. Major Rolshausen, who promptly took command of the regiment, met the same fate. A multitude of our dead and wounded strewed the field. But in spite of the rain of bullets coming from front, right, and left, these regiments held their ground long enough to fire from twenty to thirty rounds.

On my extreme right, separated from the line just described by a wide gap, which I had no forces to fill, things took a similar course. A short time after the first attack a good many men of Colonel Gilsa's and General McLean's wrecked regiments came in disorder out of the woods. A heavy rebel force followed them closely with triumphant yells and a rapid fire. The Fifty-eighth New York, a very small regiment, and the Twenty-sixth Wisconsin received them firmly. Captain Braun, in temporary command of the Fifty-eighth New York, was one of the first to fall, mortally wounded. The regiment, exposed to flanking fire from the left, where the enemy broke through, and most severely pressed in front, was pushed back after a desperate struggle of several minutes. The Twenty-sixth Wisconsin, a young regiment that had never been under fire, maintained the hopeless contest for a considerable time with splendid gallantry. It did not fall back until I ordered it to do so. Colonel Krzyzanowski, the brigade commander, who was with it, asked for immediate reinforcements, as the Twenty-sixth Wisconsin, being nearly enveloped on all sides, could not possibly maintain its position longer. Not having a man to send, I ordered the regiment to fall back to the edge of the woods in its rear, which it did in perfect order, facing about and firing several times as it retired.

In the meantime, the enemy completely turned my left flank, and had not the rebel general, Colquitt, who commanded a force of seventeen regiments to execute that flanking movement, made the mistake of stopping his advance for a while, believing that his right was threatened, a large part of the Eleventh Corps might have been captured before it could have reached the open ground surrounding the Chancellor house. But the Confederate force which actually did attack my left was far more than strong enough to press back the One Hundred and Nineteenth New York, and to fall upon the left of Captain Dilger's battery. Captain Dilger kept up his fire with grape and canister to the last moment. He gave the order to limber up only when the enemy's infantry was already between his pieces. His horse was shot under him, and the two wheel-horses and a lead-horse of one of his guns were killed. After an ineffectual effort to drag this piece along with the dead horses hanging in the harness, he had to abandon it to the enemy. The rest of the battery he sent to the rear, with the exception of one piece, which he kept in the road, firing against the pursuing enemy from time to time as he retreated.

The rebels were now pressing forward in overwhelming power on our right and left, and the position in and near the church-grove could no longer be held. We had to fall back upon the shallow rifle pit running north and south near Dowdall's Tavern, which had been dug when General Howard had a dawning suspicion that we might be attacked by Jackson from the west. This rifle pit was partly occupied by Colonel Buschbeck's brigade of our second division. It stood on the extreme left of the corps, had ample time to change front, and was therefore in perfect order. On its left several companies of the Seventy-fourth Pennsylvania, of the Sixty-first Ohio, and the One Hundred and Nineteenth New York took position, and on its right the Eighty-second Ohio and the fragments of other regiments. Several pieces of the reserve artillery were still firing over the heads of the infantry.

It was there that I found General Howard again, who meanwhile had come back from Barlow's detached and wandering brigade and rejoined his corps about the time when Jackson's attack on our right flank began, or soon after. He was bravely engaged in an effort to rally the broken troops, and exposed himself quite freely. I did my best to assist him. So did General Schimmelfennig. But to reorganize the confused mass of men belonging to different regiments was an extremely difficult task under the constant attack of the enemy. I succeeded once in gathering a large crowd, and, placing myself at its head, led it forward with a hurrah. It followed me some distance, but was again dispersed by the enemy's fire pouring in from the front and from both flanks. One of my aides was wounded on that occasion. Two or three similar attempts had the same result. The enemy advancing on our right and left with rapidity, the artillery ceased firing and withdrew, and the rifle pit had to be given up. As I said before, it was too shallow to afford any protection to the men behind it. The infantry fell back into the woods, the density of which naturally caused renewed disorder among regiments and companies that had remained well organized, or had been successfully rallied. I joined Captain Dilger with his one gun on the road to Chancellorsville. He was protected by two companies of the Sixty-first Ohio. His grape and canister checked the enemy several times in his pursuit. When I entered the woods I looked at my watch. It was 7:15 o'clock. The fight of the 9,000 men of the Eleventh Corps, so posted as to present their unprotected flank to the enemy, against Stonewall Jackson's 25,000 veterans had, therefore, lasted, at the lowest reckoning, one and one-half hours. Not a man nor a gun came to their aid during their hopeless contest. They had to retreat a mile and a half before they met a supporting force. But when this was found, the wrecked corps was soon fully reorganized, each regiment around its colors and under its own officers before 11 o'clock.

Early next morning, Sunday, May 3d, we were put on the extreme left of the army. I rode to General Hooker's headquarters to ask him that we be given another opportunity for showing what we could do, after the disaster of the previous evening. He seemed to be in a very depressed state of mind, and said he would try. But we remained on the extreme left, with nothing but slight skirmishing in our front, until the army recrossed the Rappahannock on the morning of May 6th.

I must now permit myself a few remarks on the progress of the battle after the discomfiture of the Eleventh Corps. It is a curious story, full of psychological puzzles. As I have already stated, there was behind us no supporting force, within two miles. Only Birney's division of the Third Corps was near the Chancellor house, the rest of the Third Corps and the Twelfth Corps had disappeared from the ground between the Chancellor house and Dowdall's long before. Jackson's march toward our right had been observed early in the morning. It was ascertained to be a movement in great force. It could mean only one of two things: either a retreat of Lee's army, or an attack on our right flank and rear. In either case a prompt attack, also in great force, on Jackson's flank naturally suggested itself. It was a great opportunity to interpose between Lee and Jackson and beat them in detail. Sickles was ordered, at his own request, to make an attack, but the order to move in any force was given only at noon—several hours too late—and Sickles was instructed to push on "with great caution," instead of with the utmost celerity and vigor. The result was that Sickles did not reach Jackson's line of march until Jackson, with the exception of a small rear guard, was miles away. The second result was that all the troops which might have supported the Eleventh Corps in case of a flank attack, and even the reserve brigade of that corps itself, were immersed in the woods in front, about two miles from where, as the event turned out, they were most needed. Instead of beating Lee and Jackson in their state of separation, this movement only completed the absolute isolation of the right flank of our own army.

When at last Jackson's overwhelming assault had wrecked the helpless Eleventh Corps, there was no other power of resistance between Jackson's triumphant force and the Chancellor house—the very heart of the position of the Army of the Potomac—but the remnants of the Eleventh Corps in a disorganized condition, and what troops could be hastily summoned from other points. As already mentioned, Berry's division, standing north of the Chancellor house, was promptly thrown forward. Captain Best, the chief of artillery of the Twelfth Corps still on the ground, soon had his guns trained upon the advancing Confederates. The retreating batteries of the Eleventh Corps joined him. Several divisions that had been engaged in the bootless chase after Jackson's rear guard and wagon train in the woods were brought up in a hurry. But other circumstances coöperated to help us over the critical situation. Although the moon shone brightly, it grew dark in the shadows of the forest, and, moreover, the first two lines of the Confederates, owing partly to the temporary resistance of the Eleventh Corps, partly to the breaking of the formations in their advance through tangled woods, had fallen into great confusion, which was increased by the murderous fire now bursting from the hastily-formed Federal front. Thus some time was consumed in restoring order in the Confederate brigades. But Jackson was still hotly intent upon pressing his advantage in getting into Hooker's rear. Then fate stepped in with an event of great portent. The victorious Confederates lost their leader. Returning from a short reconnaissance outside of his lines, Stonewall Jackson was grievously wounded by bullets coming from his own men, and died a few days later. The attack stopped for that night.

The next morning, Sunday, May 3d, found the Army of the Potomac, about 90,000 men of it under General Hooker's immediate command, strongly entrenched in the vicinity of the Chancellor house, and about 22,000 men, under General Sedgwick, near Fredericksburg, moving up to attack General Lee in his rear. Never did General Lee's genius shine more brightly than in the action that followed. He proved himself, with his 60,000 men against nearly double that number, a perfect master of that supreme art of the military leader: to appear to have superior forces at every point of decisive importance. First he flung Jackson's old corps, now under the command of General "Jeb" Stuart, against some of Hooker's breastworks in the center, carrying one line of entrenchments after another by furious assaults. Then, hearing that Sedgwick had taken Marye's Heights and was advancing from Fredericksburg, he detached from his front against Hooker a part of his force large enough to overmatch Sedgwick, and drove that general across the Rappahannock. Then he hurried back the divisions that had worsted Sedgwick to make his own forces superior to Hooker's at the point where he wished to strike. Hooker meanwhile seemed to be in a state of nervous collapse. On the second day of the battle, standing on the porch of the Chancellor house, he was struck by a wooden pillar as it fell, knocked down by a cannon ball. For an hour he was senseless, and then recovered. But before and after the accident his mental operations seemed to be equally loose and confused. I have spoken of some curious psychological puzzles presented by the conduct of some commanders in this battle. There was Hooker, "Fighting Joe," literally spoiling for the conflict, and having successfully initiated an emphatically offensive campaign, suddenly losing all his enterprise and dash, as soon as he came into the presence of the enemy, and dropping into a tame defensive which utterly dampened the morale of his army. On the 2d of May, he warned Slocum and Howard of Jackson's dangerous movement on our right flank, and then, on the very same evening, he indulged in the preposterous delusion that Lee and Jackson were retreating on a road parallel to our front; on the 3d of May, he permitted himself to be pounded by the Confederates wherever they chose, from one position into another, and to be literally cooped up in his entrenchments by a greatly inferior force without making any effort to bring into action some 35,000 to 40,000 men of his own who had hardly fired a shot, and stood substantially idle all the time; and finally, he knew nothing better than to recross the Rappahannock and to say that, really, he had not fought any battle because one-half of his army had not been under fire—although he had lost over 17,000 men.

There has been much speculation as to whether those who accused General Hooker of having been intoxicated during the battle of Chancellorsville, were right or wrong. The weight of the testimony of competent witnesses is strongly against this theory. It is asserted, on the other hand, that he was accustomed to the consumption of a certain quantity of whiskey every day; that, during the battle of Chancellorsville, he utterly abstained from his usual potations for fear of taking too much, inadvertently, and that his brain failed to work because he had not given it the stimulus to which it had been habituated. Whichever theory be the correct one—certain it is that to all appearances General Hooker's mind seemed, during those days, in a remarkably torpid condition. On no similar theory can we explain General Howard's failure to foresee the coming of Jackson's attack upon our right flank—for he was a man of the soberest habits. How, in spite of the reports constantly coming in, in spite of what, without exaggeration, may be called the evidence of his senses, he could finally conclude, on the 2d of May, that Jackson, instead of intending to attack, was in full retreat, I have never been able to understand, except upon the theory that his mind simply failed to draw simple conclusions from obvious facts.

Our corps remained inactive on the left flank of the army all through the 3d, 4th, and 5th of May. Eager to be led to the front again, all we could do was to listen anxiously to the din of battle near us, straining our senses to discern whether it approached or receded. In fact, it approached, indicating that our army was giving up position after position, and that the battle was going against us. At last, on the evening of the 5th, we received orders to be ready to move at 2 o'clock the next morning. We understood it to be a general retreat across the river. During the afternoon a heavy rain began to fall, which continued into the night. Wet through to the skin, we shivered until 1:20 o'clock, when, without the slightest noise, the troops were formed into line, ready to wheel into column of march. So we stood without moving from 2 until 6 o'clock. At last the order to march came. We had to withdraw from the presence of the enemy unobserved, and in this we succeeded.

When we reached the large clearing at United States Ford, where the river was bridged for the army to cross, an appalling spectacle presented itself. The heavy rains had caused a sudden rise in the river, which threatened to sweep away the pontoon bridges. There were three of them, one of which was taken up to strengthen the others. General Hooker with his staff had already passed over the preceding evening. The artillery, also, except that of the corps covering the retreat, had crossed during the night. But here on that open ground on the river bank was the infantry, probably some 70,000 to 80,000 men, packed together so close that there was hardly an interval between the different organizations wide enough to permit the passage of a horse, waiting to file away in thin marching columns, regiment after regiment, over the bridges. Had the enemy known of this, and succeeded in planting one battery in a position from which it might have pitched its shells into this dense, inarticulate mass of humanity, substantially helpless in its huddled condition, the consequences would have baffled the imagination. A wild panic would have been unavoidable, and a large part of the Army of the Potomac would have perished in the swollen waters of the Rappahannock. But General Lee did not disturb our retreat, and by 4 o'clock in the afternoon the whole army was safely over. It is not too much to say that every officer and man of it greeted the northern river bank with a deep sigh of relief.

But no sooner were we settled in camp again than we of the Eleventh Corps had to meet a trial far more severe than all the dangers and fatigues of the disastrous campaign. Every newspaper that fell into our hands told the world a frightful story of the unexampled misconduct of the Eleventh Corps; how the "cowardly Dutchmen" of that corps had thrown down their arms and fled at the first fire of the enemy; how my division, represented as first attacked, had led in the disgraceful flight without firing a shot; how these cowardly "Dutch," like a herd of frightened sheep, had overrun the whole battlefield and come near stampeding other brigades or divisions; how large crowds of "Eleventh Corps Dutchmen" ran to United States Ford, tried to get away across the bridges, and were driven back by the provost guard stationed there; and how, in short, the whole failure of the Army of the Potomac was owing to the scandalous poltroonery of the Eleventh Corps. I was thunderstruck. We procured whatever newspapers we could obtain—papers from New York, Washington, Philadelphia, Boston, Pittsburg, Cincinnati, Chicago, Milwaukee—the same story everywhere. We sought to get at the talk of officers and men in other corps of the army—the verdict of condemnation and contempt seemed to be universal. Wherever, during the night from the 2d to the 3d of May, any confusion had occurred—and there had been much—or any regiment been broken and thrown into disorder—it was all the Eleventh Corps. Only two prominent generals, Couch and Doubleday, were heard from as expressing the opinion that there might be another side to the story. All the rest, as far as we could learn, vied with one another in abusive and insulting gibes. The situation became unendurable. Would not justice raise its voice?

On the 10th of May I received a letter from General Schimmelfennig. It ran thus:

> GENERAL: The officers and men of this brigade of your division, filled with indignation, come to me, with newspapers in their hands, and ask if such be the reward they may expect for the sufferings they have endured and the bravery they have displayed. The most infamous falsehoods have been circulated through the papers in regard to the conduct of the troops of your division in the battle of the 2d inst. It would seem as if a nest of vipers had but waited for an auspicious moment to spit out their poisonous slanders upon this heretofore honored corps. Little would I heed were these reports but emanations from the prurient imaginations of those who live by dipping their pens in the blood of the slain, instead of standing up for the country, sword and musket in hand; but they are dated, "Headquarters of General Hooker," and they are signed by responsible names.

He then went on, stating what had actually happened, and concluded as follows:

General, I am an old soldier. To this hour I have been proud to command the brave men in this brigade; but I am sure that unless these infamous falsehoods be retracted and reparation made, their good-will and soldierly spirit will be broken, and I shall no longer be at the head of the same brave men whom I have heretofore had the honor to lead. In the name of truth and common honesty, in the name of the good cause of our country, I ask, therefore, for satisfaction. If our superior officers be not sufficiently in possession of the facts, I demand an investigation; if they are, I demand that the miserable penny-a-liners who have slandered the division, be excluded, by a public order, from our lines, and that the names of the originators of these slanders be made known to me and my brigade, that they may be held responsible for their acts.

A. SCHIMMELFENNIG, Brigadier-General.

On May 12th, I sent up my official report. It contained a sober and scrupulously truthful recital of the events of the 2d of May—at least, scrupulously correct according to my knowledge and information—and closed with these words: "I beg leave to make one additional remark. The Eleventh Corps, and, by error or malice, especially the third division, have been held up to the whole country as a band of cowards. My division has been made responsible for the defeat of the Eleventh Corps, and the Eleventh Corps for the failure of the campaign. Preposterous as this is, yet we have been overwhelmed by the army and the press with abuse and insult beyond measure. We have borne as much as human nature can endure. I am far from saying that on May 2d everybody did his duty to the best of his power. But one thing I will say, because I know it: these men are not cowards. I have seen most of them fight before this, and they fought as bravely as any. I am also far from saying that it would have been quite impossible to do better in the position the corps occupied on May 2d, but I have seen with my own eyes troops who now affect to look down upon us with sovereign contempt, behave much worse under circumstances far less trying. Being charged with such an enormous responsibility as the failure of a campaign involves, it would seem to me that every commander has a right to a fair investigation of his conduct and of the circumstances surrounding him and his command on that occasion. I would, therefore, most respectfully and most urgently ask for permission to publish this report—every statement contained therein is strictly truthful, to the best of my knowledge and information. If I have erred in any particular, my error can easily be corrected. But if what I say is true, I deem it due to myself and those who serve under me, that the country should know it."

In order to avoid every possible objection to the publication of my report, I had been studiously moderate in my description of occurrences and circumstances; I had refrained from accusing anybody of anything; I had even mentioned with the greatest mildness of statement my urgent efforts to induce General Howard to make the necessary change of front. In spite of all this, the permission to publish my report was refused. General Hooker wrote: "I hope soon to be able to transmit all the reports of the recent battles, and meanwhile I cannot approve of the publication of one isolated report."

I appealed to Mr. Stanton, the Secretary of War—of course, through the regular military channels—repeating my request that my report be published as soon as it reached the War Department, and adding that, if the publication of my report should be deemed inexpedient, I urgently asked for the calling of a court of inquiry to investigate publicly "the circumstances surrounding my command on the 2d day of May, the causes of its defeat, and my conduct on that occasion." General Howard's endorsement on this letter was as follows: "Respectfully forwarded. With reference to the court of inquiry asked for, I recommend that the request be granted. I do not know of any charges against General Schurz from any official quarter, but I do not shrink from a thorough investigation of all the circumstances connected with the disaster of May 2d. O. O. Howard, Major-General." This could be interpreted as meaning that, as to me, a court of inquiry was not necessary, there being no official charges against me; and as to him, he did not shrink from a thorough investigation of the event, but did not ask for it. The result was that the court of inquiry was not granted. The only answer I received was from General Halleck: "Publication of partial reports not approved till the general commanding has time to make his report." The general commanding, General Hooker, never made any report; mine was simply buried in some pigeonhole. My request for a court of inquiry was not even mentioned. I could not publish my report without permission, for that would have been a breach of military discipline. So I found myself completely muzzled.

While thus the official world seemed determined to take no notice of our distress, the flagrant injustice done us created much excitement among the German-born people of this country. Some prominent German-American citizens in New York called a mass-meeting —so far as I know entirely without incitement or suggestion from members of the Eleventh Corps—and expressed their indignation at the scandalous treatment meted out to us. The leaders of that movement had taken steps to inform themselves from official sources, and it was easy for them to show, first, that the Eleventh Corps was not a German corps, that not one-half of its men, in fact, only a little more than one-third, belonged to that nationality; second, that it was not my division, but a division commanded by General Devens, a native Massachusetts man, that was first overthrown and put to flight; third, that it was not a German brigade that yielded "almost without firing a shot," but one composed entirely of American regiments—General McLean's—and very brave regiments, too, that made no fight because they were so placed that they positively could not fight; fourth, that regiments of my division which were not telescoped on the turnpike, as well as Buschbeck's brigade, composed mainly of Germans, did make a fight, and a stubborn one, too, detaining Jackson's overwhelming force for more than an hour; fifth, that the story of the Eleventh Corps throwing down their arms and running away like sheep was a lie cut out of the whole cloth, it being proved that after the battle only seventeen muskets were missing in Gilsa's brigade, and only fifteen in Schimmelfennig's, rather less than the average after any severe engagement; sixth, that the story about large crowds of Eleventh Corps men seeking to escape across the bridges at United States Ford was also utterly false, it being testified by General Patrick, who had charge of the provost guard at the bridges and on the roads leading to them, that the stragglers or skulkers arrested there had not been Eleventh Corps men. And so on.

But while such demonstrations and showings might make an impression upon a comparatively small number of unprejudiced persons, they did not in any perceptible degree affect our standing in the army and in the press. As a last resort, I applied for a hearing before the Congressional "Committee on the conduct of the War."

But when this application, too, remained without a response, I found myself driven to the conclusion that there was, in all the official circles concerned, a powerful influence systematically seeking to prevent the disclosure of the truth; that a scapegoat was wanted for the remarkable blunders which had caused the failure of the Chancellorsville campaign, and that the Eleventh Corps could plausibly be used as such a scapegoat—the Eleventh Corps, which had always been looked at askance by the Army of the Potomac as not properly belonging to it, and which could, on account of the number of its German regiments and officers, easily be misrepresented as a corps of "foreigners," a "Dutch corps," which had few friends, and which might be abused, and slandered, and kicked with impunity. But for this, why was my demand for a court of inquiry ignored?

Not for my own sake, but in the name of thousands of my comrades I asked for nothing but a mere opportunity by a fair investigation of the facts to defend their honor, not against a mere anonymous letter, but against the most infamous slanders and insults circulated from mouth to mouth in the army, and throughout the whole country by the press; when that opportunity was denied me, was there not ample reason for the conclusion that there was a powerful influence working to suppress the truth, and that the Eleventh Army Corps, and especially the German part of it, was to be systematically sacrificed as the scapegoat?

It might have been expected that one general, at least, who knew the truth as to where the responsibility for the disaster rested, would have spoken a frank and sympathetic word to remove the stain of ignominy from the slandered troops. It would have been much to the honor of the corps commander, General O. O. Howard, had he done so promptly. He would have stood before his countrymen as Burnside did when, after the bloody defeat at Fredericksburg, he frankly shouldered the responsibility for that calamity, and exonerated his officers and men; or as, two months after the battle of Chancellorsville, General Lee did on the the third day of the battle of Gettysburg when that great soldier said to his distressed men, looking up to him: "It is my fault, my men! It is my fault!" Alas, the attitude of our corps commander was different. In a council of war during the night of the 2d to the 3d of May, as was reported, he complained of the "bad conduct" of his corps. In his official report on the battle he spoke of the density of the woods preventing the whereabouts of the enemy from being discovered by scouts and patrols and reconnoissances—an assertion glaringly at variance with the facts, for the scouts and patrols saw and reported the advance of Jackson. He actually spoke of a "panic produced by the enemy's reverse fire, regiments and artillery being thrown suddenly upon those in position," and of a "blind panic and a great confusion at the center and near the plank-road," about "a rout which he and his staff officers struggled to check,"—but not a word about a large part of the corps being so posted that it could not fight; not a word to take the responsibility for the disaster from the troops; not a word to confess that he was warned early in the day, and repeatedly as the day advanced, of what was coming; not a word to take the stigma of cowardice from his corps.

Even twenty-three years later, when he contributed an article on the Eleventh Corps at Chancellorsville to the "War Series" of the *Century Magazine,* he sought to sustain the impression that the troops, rather than their commander, were chargeable with the disaster. He had nothing better to say than: "We had not a *very good* position, it is true, but we did expect to make a good strong fight should the enemy come." Not a very good position, forsooth! As if there could be a worse and more absurd position than one presenting flank and rear unprotected to the enemy! As if anyone had a right to expect a "good strong fight" with the certainty of being telescoped and wrecked in every possible way! "Should the enemy come!" As if the general commanding had not been most pointedly warned, again and again, that the enemy most surely was coming! General Howard, in that article, said further: "General Schurz was anxious." This is true. I was anxious, indeed. And it would have been much better for the corps, for the whole army, and for himself, had General Howard been as anxous as I was. But General Howard does not say that I explained to him again and again why I was anxious, and that I most urgently warned him of the things which would come, and which actually did come. He did not emphasize that I was not only anxious, but also right. He positively denied having received General Hooker's "Howard and Slocum" despatch, warning him of the danger threatening his right, which I had personally read and delivered to him; and then he adds: "But Generals Schurz and Steinwehr, my division commanders, and myself, did precisely what we should have done, had that order come." This again is a misstatement, for, as my official report explained, I proposed entirely to withdraw the corps from its exposed position fronting south, and to form it fronting west, on the eastern side of the Dowdall clearing—a proposition which General Howard rejected.

To justify that rejection he argues in his *Century* article: "In his report after the battle General Schurz says: 'Our right ought to have been drawn back towards the Rappahannock, to rest on that river at or near the mouth of the Hunting Run, the corps abandoning so much of the plank-road as to enable it to establish a solid line.' This position, which Schurz recommended in his report, was the very one into which Hooker's whole army was forced two days afterward. He was so cramped by it that he did not dare to take the offensive." I must be pardoned for saying that this is incomprehensible, for I did not recommend "this" position for the whole army, but for the Eleventh Corps—not for 90,000 men, but for 12,000. It is a pity that the General insisted upon presenting, by such statements, so sorry a spectacle. I am sincerely grieved that I have to say all this. I owe it not only to myself but to the much maligned men under my command.

CHAPTER XV

Gettysburg

THE story of the Gettysburg campaign has so often and so elaborately been rehearsed, that it is hardly possible to add anything of value to the familiar tale. I shall, therefore, put down only some individual impressions and experiences which may be of interest at least to the circle of my personal friends.

We did not know that we were marching towards the most famous battlefield of the war. In fact, we, I mean even the superior officers, had no clear conception as to where the decisive battle of the campaign was to take place. Only a few days before, General Hooker had left the command of the Army of the Potomac—he had been made to resign, as rumor had it—and General Meade had been put into his place. Such a change of commanders at the critical period of a campaign would ordinarily have a disquieting effect upon officers and men. But in this case it had not, for by his boastful proclamation and his subsequent blunders and failures at Chancellorsville, General Hooker had largely forfeited the confidence of the army, while General Meade enjoyed generally the repute, not of a very brilliant, but of a brave, able and reliable officer. Everybody respected him. It was at once felt that he had grasped the reins with a firm hand. As was subsequently understood, neither he nor General Lee desired or expected to fight a battle at Gettysburg. Lee wished to have it at Cashtown, Meade on Pipe Creek. Both were drawn into it by the unexpected encounter of the Confederate general Heth, who hoped to find "some shoes" for his men in the town of Gettysburg, and a Federal cavalry general on reconnaissance, both instructed not to bring on a general engagement, but rather cautioned against it. When we left Emmitsburg at 7 a. m. we were advised that the First Army Corps, under General Reynolds, was ahead of us, and there was a rumor that some rebel troops were moving toward Gettysburg, but that was all. At

255

10:30, when my division had just passed Horner's Mills, I received an order from General Howard to hurry my command forward as quickly as poissible, as the First Corps was engaged with the enemy in the neighborhood of Gettysburg. This was a surprise, for we did not hear the slightest indication of artillery firing from that direction. I put the division to the "double quick," and then rode ahead with my staff. Soon I met on the road fugitives from Gettysburg, men, women and children, who seemed to be in great terror. I remember especially a middle-aged woman, who tugged a small child by the hand and carried a large bundle on her back. She tried to stop me, crying out at the top of her voice: "Hard times at Gettysburg! They are shooting and killing! What will become of us!" Still I did not hear any artillery fire until I had reached the ridge of a rise of ground before me. Until then the waves of sound had passed over my head unperceived.

I found General Howard on an eminence east of the cemetery of Gettysburg, from which we could overlook a wide plain. Immediately before us was Gettysburg, a comfortable-looking town of a few thousand inhabitants. Beyond and on both sides of it, stretching far away was an open landscape dotted with little villages and farmhouses and orchards and tufts of trees and detached belts of timber; two creeks, Willoughby's Run on the left and Rock Creek on the right; radiating from the town westward and eastward, well-defined roads—counting from right to left the Hanover road, the York Pike, the Gettysburg and Hanover railroad, the Hunterstown road, the Harrisburg road, the Carlisle road, the Mummasburg road, the Cashtown and Chambersburg Pike, the Hagerstown road, and behind us the roads on which our troops were coming—the Emmitsburg road, the Taneytown road, and the Baltimore road. The elevated spot from which we overlooked this landscape was Cemetery Hill, being the northern end of a ridge which terminated due south in two steep, rocky knolls partly wooded, called the Round Tops—half a mile distant on our right a hill called Culp's Hill, covered with timber; and opposite our left, about a mile distant, a ridge running almost parallel with Cemetery Ridge, called Seminary Ridge, from the Lutheran Seminary buildings on its crest—the whole a smiling landscape inhabited by a peaceable people wont to harvest their crops and to raise their children in quiet and prosperous contentment.

From where we stood we observed the thin lines of troops, and here and here puffy clouds of white smoke on and around Seminary Ridge, and heard the crackle of the musketry and the booming of the cannon, indicating a forward movement of our First Corps, which we knew to be a little over 8000 men strong. Of the troops themselves we could see little. I remember how small the affair appeared to me, as seen from a distance in the large frame of the surrounding open country. But we were soon made painfully aware of the awful significance of it. The dead body of General Reynolds, the commander of the First Corps, was being carried away from the field. He had been too far forward in the firing-line and the bullet of a Southern sharpshooter had laid him low. So the action had begun with a great loss. He was known as an officer of superior merit, and in the opinion of many it was he that ought to have been put at the head of the Army of the Potomac. General Reynolds' death devolved the command of the First Corps upon General Doubleday, the command of all the troops then on the field upon General Howard, and the command of the Eleventh Corps upon me.

The situation before us was doubtful. We received a report from General Wadsworth, one of the division commanders of the First Corps, that he was advancing, that the enemy's forces in his front were apparently not very strong, but that he thought that the enemy was making a movement towards his right. From our point of observation we could perceive but little of the strength of the enemy, and Wadsworth's despatch did not relieve our uncertainty. If the enemy before us was only in small force, then we had to push him as far as might seem prudent to General Meade. But if the enemy was bringing on the whole or a large part of his army, which his movement toward General Wadsworth's right might be held to indicate, then we had to look for a strong position in which to establish and maintain ourselves until reinforced or ordered back. Such a position was easily found at the first glance. It was Cemetery Hill on which we then stood and which was to play so important a part in the battle to follow. Accordingly General Howard ordered me to take the First and Third Divisions of the Eleventh Corps through the town and to place them on the right of the First Corps, while he would hold back the Second Division under General Steinwehr and the reserve artillery on Cemetery Hill and the eminence east of it, as a reserve.

About 12:30 the head of the column of the Eleventh Corps arrived. The weather being sultry, the men, who had marched several miles at a rapid pace, were streaming with perspiration and panting for breath. But they hurried through the town as best they could, and were promptly deployed on the right of the First Corps. But the deployment could not be made as originally designed by simply prolonging the First

Corps' line, for in the meantime a strong Confederate force had arrived on the battlefield on the right flank of the First Corps, so that to confront it, the Eleventh had to deploy under fire at an angle with the First. General Schimmelfennig, temporarily commanding my (the Third) Division, connected with the First Corps on his left as well as he could under the circumstances, and General Francis Barlow, commanding our First Division, formerly Devens', deployed on his right. General Barlow was still a young man, but with his beardless, smooth face looked even much younger than he was. His men at first gazed at him wondering how such a boy could be put at the head of regiments of men. But they soon discovered him to be a strict disciplinarian, and one of the coolest and bravest in action. In both respects he was inclined to carry his virtues to excess. At the very time when he moved into the firing line at Gettysburg I had to interfere by positive order in favor of the commander of one of his regiments, whom he had suspended and sent to the rear for a mere unimportant peccadillo. Having been too strict in this instance, within the next two hours he made the mistake of being too brave.

I had hardly deployed my two divisions, about 6000 men, on the north side of Gettysburg, when the action very perceptibly changed its character. Until then the First Corps had been driving before it a comparatively small force of the enemy, taking many prisoners, among them the rebel general Archer with almost his whole brigade. My line, too, advanced, but presently I received an order from General Howard to halt where I was, and to push forward only a strong force of skirmishers. This I did, and my skirmishers, too, captured prisoners in considerable number. But then the enemy began to show greater strength and tenacity. He planted two batteries on a hillside, one above the other, opposite my left, enfilading part of the First Corps. Captain Dilger, whose battery was attached to my Third Division, answered promptly, dismounted four of the enemy's guns, as we observed through our field-glasses, and drove away two rebel regiments supporting them. In the meantime the infantry firing on my left and on the right of the First Corps grew much in volume. It became evident that the enemy's line had been heavily reinforced, and was pressing upon us with constantly increasing vigor. I went up to the roof of a house behind my skirmish line to get a better view of the situation, and observed that my right and center were not only confronted by largely superior forces, but also that my right was becoming seriously overlapped. I had ordered General Barlow to refuse his right wing, that is to place his right brigade, Colonel Gilsa's, a little in the right rear of his other brigade, in order to use it against a possible flanking movement by the enemy.

But I now noticed that Barlow, be it that he had misunderstood my order, or that he was carried away by the ardor of the conflict, had advanced his whole line and lost connection with my Third Division on his left, and in addition to this, he had, instead of refusing, pushed forward his right brigade, so that it formed a projecting angle with the rest of the line. At the same time I saw the enemy emerging from the belt of woods on my right with one battery after another and one column of infantry after another, threatening to envelop my right flank and to cut me off from the town and the position on Cemetery Hill behind.

I immediately gave orders to the Third Division to re-establish its connection with the First, although this made still thinner a line already too thin, and hurried one staff officer after another to General Howard with the urgent request for one of his two reserve brigades to protect my right against the impending flank attack by the enemy. Our situation became critical. As far as we could judge from the reports of prisoners and from what we observed in our front, the enemy was rapidly advancing the whole force of at least two of his army-corps—A. P. Hill's, and Ewell's, against us, that is to say, 40,000 men, of whom at least 30,000 were then before us. We had 17,000, counting in the two brigades held in reserve by General Howard and not deducting the losses already suffered by the First Corps. We had at that moment less than 14,000 men in the open field without the slightest advantage of position. We could hardly hope to hold out long against such a superiority of numbers, and there was imminent danger that, if we held out too long, the enemy would succeed in turning our right flank and in getting possession of the town of Gettysburg, through which our retreat to the defensive position on Cemetery Hill would probably have to be effected. For this reason I was so anxious to have one of the reserve brigades posted at the entrance of the town to oppose the flanking movement of the enemy which I saw going on.

But, before that brigade came, the enemy advanced to the attack along the whole line with great impetuosity. Gilsa's little brigade, in its exposed position "in the air" on Barlow's extreme right, had to suffer the first violent onset of the Confederates, and was fairly crushed by the enemy rushing on from the front and both flanks. Colonel Gilsa, one of the bravest of men and an uncommonly skillful officer, might well complain of his fate. Here, as at Chancellorsville, he was in a position in which neither he nor his men could do themselves justice, and he felt keenly the adverse whims of the fortunes of war. General Barlow, according to his habit always in the thickest of the fight, was seriously wounded, as happened to him repeatedly, and had to leave the command of the division to the commander of its second brigade, General Adelbert Ames. This brigade bravely endured an enfilading fire from two rebel batteries placed near the Harrisburg road. But it was forced back when its right flank was entirely uncovered and heavy masses of rebel infantry pressed upon it.

About four o'clock, the attack by the enemy along the whole line became general and still more vehement. Regiment stood against regiment in the open fields, near enough almost to see the white in one another's eyes, firing literally in one another's faces. The slaughter on both sides was awful. At that moment it was reported that the right wing of the First Corps, which had fought heroically all day, had been pressed back, and one of General Doubleday's aides-de-camp brought me a request for a few regiments to be sent to his assistance. Alas, I had not a man to spare, but was longing for reinforcements myself, for at the same time I received a report that my Third Division was flanked on its left, on the very spot where it should have connected with the First, General Doubleday's corps. A few minutes later, while this butchery was still going on, an order reached me from General Howard directing me to withdraw to the south side of the town and to occupy a position on and near Cemetery Hill.

While I was doing my utmost, assisted by my staff officers, to rally and re-form what was within my reach of the First Division, for the purpose of checking the enemy's advance around my right, and to hold the edge of the town, the reserve brigade I had so urgently asked for, the First Brigade of the Second Division, Eleventh Corps, under Colonel Coster, at last arrived. It came too late for that offensive push which I had intended to make with it in order to relieve my right, if it had come half, or even quarter of an hour earlier. But I led it out of the town and ordered it to deploy on the right of the junction of the roads near the railway station, which the enemy was fast approaching. There the brigade, assisted by a battery, did good service in detaining the enemy long enough to permit the First Division to enter the town without being seriously molested on its retreat. The Third Division was meanwhile still sustaining the murderous contest. To break off an engagement carried on at long range, is comparatively easy. But the task becomes very difficult and delicate in a fight at very close quarters. Still, the Third Division, when ordered to do so, fell back in good form, executing its retreat to the town, fighting, step by step, with great firmness. I said in my official report: "In this part of the action, which was almost a hand-to-hand struggle, officers and men showed the highest courage and determination. Our loss was extremely severe. The Second Brigade, Third Division, lost all its regimental commanders; several regiments nearly half their number in killed and wounded." Among the mortally wounded was Colonel Mahler of the Seventy-fifth Pennsylvania, who had been a revolutionary comrade of mine in the German fortress of Rastatt, in 1849. Now with death on his face he reached out his hand to me on the bloody field of Gettysburg, to bid me a last farewell. I came out unscathed, but my horse had a bullet hole clean through the fatty ridge of the neck just under the mane.

It has been represented by some writers, Southerners, that the Union forces on the first day of the battle of Gettysburg were utterly routed and fled pell-mell into the town. This is far from the truth. That there were a good many stragglers hurrying to the rear in a disorderly fashion, as is always the case during and after a hot fight, will not be denied. Neither will it be denied that it was a retreat after a lost battle with the enemy in hot pursuit. But there was no element of dissolution in it. The retreat through the town was of course more or less disorderly, the streets being crowded with vehicles of every description, which offered to the passing troops exceedingly troublesome obstructions. It is also true that Eleventh Corps men complained that when they entered the town, it was already full of First Corps men, and vice versa, which really meant that the two corps became more or less mixed in passing through. It is likewise true that many officers and men, among others General Schimmelfennig, became entangled in cross streets, and alleys without thoroughfare, and were captured by the enemy pressing after them. But, after all, the fact remains that in whatever shape the troops issued from the town, they were promptly reorganized, each was under the colors of his regiment, and in as good a fighting trim as before, save that their ranks were fearfully thinned by the enormous losses suffered during the day.

As we ascended Cemetery Hill from the town of Gettysburg we met General Hancock, whom General Meade had sent forward to take command of the field. The meeting of Generals Hancock and Howard is thus described by Major E. P. Halstead of the staff of the First Corps, who had been sent by General Doubleday to ask General Howard for reinforcements: "I returned to where General Howard sat, just as General Hancock approached at a swinging gallop. When near General Howard, who was then alone, he saluted, and with great animation, as if there was no time for ceremony, said General Meade had sent him forward to take command of the three Corps [the First, Eleventh, and his own, the Second]. General Howard replied that he was the senior. General Hancock said: 'I am aware of that, General, but I have written orders in my pocket from General Meade, which I will show you if you wish to see them.' General Howard said: 'No; I do not doubt your word, General Hancock, but you can give no orders here while I am here.' Hancock replied: 'Very well, General Howard, I will second any order that you have to give, but General Meade has also directed me to select a field on which to fight this battle in the rear of Pipe Creek.' Then casting one glance from Culp's Hill to Round Top, he continued: 'But I think this the strongest position by nature upon which to fight a battle that I ever saw, and if it meets your appro- bation I will select this as the battlefield.' General Howard responded: 'I think this a very strong position, General Hancock, a very strong position.' 'Very well, sir, I select this as the battlefield,' said General Hancock, and immediately turned away to rectify our lines."

This story is told by Major Halstead in the *Century* series of "Battles and Leaders," and he adds this remark: "There was no person present besides myself when the conversation took place between Howard and Hancock. A number of years since I reminded General Hancock of that fact and what I had heard pass between them. He said that what I have repeated here was true, and requested a written statement, which I subsequently furnished him."

That the appearance of Hancock as commander of the field should have sorely touched Howard's pride, is well intelligible, especially as he could hardly fail to understand it as an expression of want of confi- dence in him on the part of General Meade.

It was about 3:20 of the afternoon when General Buford sent a dis- patch to General Meade in which he said: "In my opinion there seems to be no directing person." This was too severe on General Howard, who, in fact, had given several directions which were unquestionably correct. But it, no doubt, expressed the prevailing impression, and under these circumstances the appearance of General Hancock at the front was a most fortunate event. It gave the troops a new inspiration. They all knew him by fame, and his stalwart figure, his proud mien, and his superb soldierly bearing seemed to verify all the things that fame had told about him. His mere presence was a reinforcement, and everybody on the field felt stronger for his being there. This new in- spiration of self-reliance might have become of immediate importance, had the enemy made another attack—an eventuality for which we had to prepare. And in this preparation Howard, in spite of his heart-sore, coöperated so loyally with Hancock that it would have been hard to tell which of the two was the commander, and which the subordinate.

The line was soon formed. The Second Brigade, Colonel Orlando Smith's of Steinwehr's division, was already in position on the Cemetery Hill, fronting the town and occupying the nearest houses. Coster's brigade, and next the First Division, under Ames, were posted on the right, and my division, the Third, on his left on the cemetery itself. The First Corps was placed on my left, except Wadsworth's division, which was sent to the extreme right to occupy Culp's Hill. The batteries were put in proper position, and breastworks promptly constructed wherever necessary. All this was accomplished in a very short time. This done, General Hancock sat down on a stone fence on the brow of the hill from which he could overlook the field, on the north and west of Gettysburg, occupied by the Confederates. I joined him there, and through our fieldglasses we eagerly watched the movements of the enemy. We saw their batteries and a large portion of their infantry columns distinctly. Some of those columns moved to and fro in a way the purpose of which we did not clearly understand. I was not ashamed to own that I felt nervous, for while our position was a strong one, the infantry line in it appeared, after the losses of the day, woefully thin. It was soothing to my pride, but by no means reassuring as to our situation, when General Hancock admitted that he felt nervous, too. Still he thought that with our artillery so advantageously posted, we might well hold out until the arrival of the Twelfth Corps, which was only a short distance behind us. So we sat watching the enemy and presently observed to our great relief that the movements of the rebel troops looked less and less like a formation for an immediate attack. Our nerves grew more and more tranquil as minute after minute lapsed, for each brought night and reinforcements nearer. When the sun went down the Twelfth Corps was on the field and the Third Corps arriving.

There has been much speculation as to whether the Confederates would not have won the battle of Gettysburg had they pressed the attack on the first day after the substantial overthrow of the First and Eleventh Corps. Southern writers are almost unanimous in the opinion that Lee would then without serious trouble have achieved a great victory. It is indeed possible that had they vigorously pushed their attack with their whole available force at the moment when the First and Eleventh Corps were entangled in the streets of the town, they might have completely annihilated those corps, possessed themselves of Cemetery Hill, and taken the heads of the Federal columns advancing toward

Gettysburg at a disadvantage. But night would soon have put an end to that part of the action; that night would have given General Meade time to change his dispositions, and the main battle would in all likelihood have been fought on Pipe Creek instead of Gettysburg, in the position which General Meade had originally selected.

Nor is it quite so certain, as Southern writers seem to think, that the Confederates would have had easy work in carrying Cemetery Hill after the First and Eleventh Corps had passed through the town and occupied that position. When they speak of the two corps as having fled from the field in a state of utter demoralization, they grossly exaggerate. Those troops were indeed beaten back, but not demoralized or dispirited. Had they been in a state of rout such as Southern writers describe, they would certainly have left many of their cannon behind them. But they brought off their whole artillery save one single dismounted piece, and that artillery, as now posted, was capable of formidable work. The infantry was indeed reduced by well-nigh one-half its effective force, but all that was left, was good. Besides, the Confederates, too, had suffered severely. Their loss in killed and wounded and prisoners was very serious. Several of their brigades had become disordered during the action to such an extent that it required some time to re-form them. It is therefore at least doubtful whether they could have easily captured Cemetery Hill before the arrival of heavy reinforcements on our side. Another disputed point is whether we did not make a great mistake in continuing the bloody fight north of the town too long.

Thirty-eight years after the event I was called upon by Mr. John Codman Ropes, the eminent historian of the Civil War, who unfortunately for the country had died before finishing his work. He had then the history of the battle of Gettysburg in hand and wished to have my recollections as to certain details. In the course of our conversation I asked him what his criticism was of our conduct on the first day. He said that on the whole we fought well and were obliged to yield the field north and east of the town, but that we committed a great mistake in not retreating to our second position south and west of Gettysburg an hour and perhaps two hours earlier. The same opinion was expressed by General Doubleday in his official report. In referring to about that time of the day he says: "Upon taking a retrospect of the field it might seem, in view of the fact that we were finally forced to retreat, that this would have been the proper time to retire; but to fall back without orders from the commanding general might have inflicted lasting disgrace upon the corps—nor would I have retreated without the knowl-

edge and approbation of General Howard, who was my superior officer. Had I done so, it would have uncovered the left flank of his corps.
If circumstances required it, it was his place, not mine, to issue the
order. General Howard, from his commanding position on Cemetery
Hill, could overlook all the enemy's movements as well as our own, and
I therefore relied much upon his superior facilities for observation to
give me timely warning of any unusual danger."

That General Howard ought to have given the order to retreat at
an earlier period of the action will, in the light of subsequent events,
seriously be doubted. He may, in the first place, well have hesitated to
retreat without orders from General Meade for reasons perhaps not
quite as good, but nearly as good, as those given by General Doubleday for not having retreated without orders from General Howard.

But there was another consideration of weightier importance.
Would not the enemy, if we had retreated two hours, or even one hour
earlier, have been in better condition, and therefore more encouraged
to make a determined attack upon the cemetery that afternoon,—and
with better chance of success? The following occurrence subsequently
reported, indicates that he would. Three or four companies of my regiments, led by Captain F. Irsch, became separated from the main body
while retreating through the streets of Gettysburg. Hotly pressed by
the pursuing enemy, they threw themselves into a block of buildings
near the market place, from which they continued firing. A rebel officer approached them under a flag of truce, and summoned them to
surrender. Captain Irsch defiantly refused, saying that he expected
every moment to be relieved, as the Army of the Potomac was coming
on. The rebel officer replied that the whole town was in the possession
of the Confederates, and he offered Captain Irsch "safe conduct" if he
would look for himself. The Captain accepted, and saw on the market
place General Ewell on horseback, at the moment when an officer
approached him (General Ewell) in hot haste, and said to him within
the Captain's hearing that General Lee wished him, General Ewell,
forthwith to proceed to attack the Federals on Cemetery Hill, whereupon General Ewell replied in a low voice, but audible to Captain
Irsch, that if General Lee knew the condition of his, Ewell's, troops,
after their long march and the fight that had just taken place, he would
not think of such an order, and that the attack could not be risked.
This story, which I have from Captain Irsch himself and which is cor-
roborated by other evidence, would seem to show that by continuing
as long as we did, our fight in the afternoon, in spite of the losses we
suffered, we rendered the enemy unable, or at least disinclined, to

undertake a later attack upon Cemetery Hill, which might have had much more serious results. There is, therefore, very good reason for concluding that General Howard rendered valuable service in not ordering the retreat as early as General Doubleday thought he ought to have ordered it.

I remember a picturesque scene that happened that night in a lower room of the gate house of the Gettysburg Cemetery. In the center of the room a barrel set upright, with a burning tallow candle stuck in the neck of a bottle on top of it; around the walls six or seven generals accidentally gathered together, sitting some on boxes but most on the floor, listening to the accounts of those who had been in the battle of the day, then making critical comments and discussing what might have been and finally all agreeing in the hope that General Meade had decided or would decide to fight the battle of the morrow on the ground on which we then were. There was nothing of extraordinary solemnity in the "good-night" we gave one another when we parted. It was rather a commonplace, business-like "good-night," as that of an ordinary occasion. We of the Eleventh Corps, occupying the cemetery, lay down, wrapt in our cloaks, with the troops among the gravestones. There was profound stillness in the graveyard, broken by no sound but the breathing of men and here and there the tramp of a horse's foot; and sullen rumblings mysteriously floating on the air from a distance all around.

The sun of the 2nd of July rose brightly upon these two armies marshalling for battle. Neither of them was ready. But as we could observe the field from Cemetery Hill, the Confederates were readier than we were. The belts of timber screening their lines presented open spaces enough, in which we could see their bayonets glisten and their artillery in position, to permit us to form a rough estimate of the extent of the positions they occupied and of the strength of their forces present. There was a rumor that Lee's army was fully as strong as ours— which, however, was not the case—and from what we saw before us, we guesed that it was nearly all up and ready for action. We knew, too, that to receive the anticipated attack, our army was, although rapidly coming in, not nearly all up. It was, indeed, a comforting thought that Lee, who, as rumor had it, had wished and planned for a defensive battle, was now obliged to fight an aggressive one against our army established in a strong position. Yet we anxiously hoped that his attack would not come too early for our comfort. Thus we watched with not a little concern the dense columns of our troops as they approached at a brisk pace on the Taneytown road and the Baltimore Pike to wheel into the positions assigned to them. It was, if I remember rightly, about 8 o'clock when General Meade quietly appeared on the cemetery, on horseback, accompanied by a staff officer and an orderly. His long-bearded, haggard face, shaded by a black military felt hat the rim of which was turned down, looked careworn and tired, as if he had not

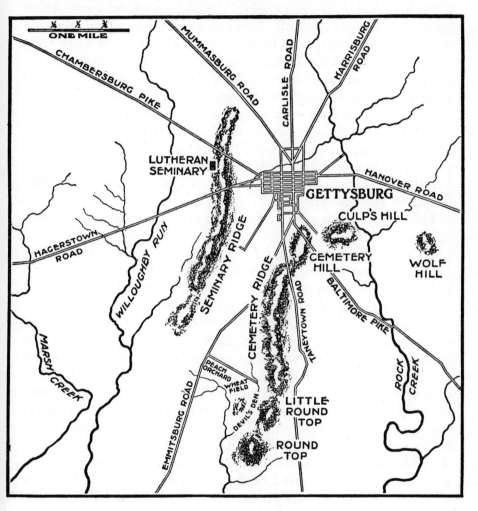

ONE MILE

CHAMBERSBURG PIKE

MUMMASBURG ROAD

CARLISLE ROAD

HARRISBURG ROAD

LUTHERAN SEMINARY

HANOVER ROAD

GETTYSBURG

CULP'S HILL

HAGERSTOWN ROAD

WILLOUGHBY RUN

SEMINARY RIDGE

CEMETERY HILL

WOLF HILL

BALTIMORE PIKE

MARSH CREEK

CEMETERY RIDGE

TANEYTOWN ROAD

EMMITSBURG ROAD

PEACH ORCHARD

WHEAT FIELD

DEVILS DEN

LITTLE ROUND TOP

ROCK CREEK

ROUND TOP

THE BATTLEFIELD OF GETTYSBURG

slept that night. The spectacles on his nose gave him a somewhat magisterial look. There was nothing in his appearance or his bearing —not a smile nor a sympathetic word addressed to those around him —that might have made the hearts of the soldiers warm up to him, or that called forth a cheer. There was nothing of pose, nothing stagey, about him. His mind was evidently absorbed by a hard problem. But this simple, cold, serious soldier with his business-like air did inspire confidence. The officers and men, as much as was permitted, crowded around and looked up to him with curious eyes, and then turned away, not enthusiastic, but clearly satisfied.

With a rapid glance he examined the position of our army, which has often, and quite correctly, been likened to a fishing hook, the long shank of which was formed by Cemetery Ridge, running south from the cemetery to Round Top; the head by the cemetery itself, and the hook, receding toward the southeast, by the woods of Culp's Hill. The General nodded, seemingly with approval. After the usual salutations I asked him how many men he had on the ground. I remember his answer well. "In the course of the day I expect to have about 95,000— enough, I guess, for this business." And then, after another sweeping glance over the field, he added, as if repeating something to himself: "Well, we may fight it out here just as well as anywhere else." Then he quietly rode away.

The Second Corps of our army had arrived about seven; two divisions of the Fifth about the same time; several brigades of the Third Corps came up about nine; the Artillery Reserve and the large ammunition train was parked in the valley between Cemetery Ridge and Culp's Hill by eleven; the Sixth Corps under Sedgwick reached Rock Creek after a march of thirty-four miles, about four of the afternoon. Thus our line was gradually filled. But the forenoon passed without any serious attack from the Confederates. There were only, as the two armies "felt" one another, occasional sputterings of musketry and abrupt discharges of cannon, like growling barks of chained watchdogs when you approach them too closely. At last, between three and four, the expected attack came. Our position had its weak points. On our extreme right the Twelfth Corps under General Slocum held Culp's Hill—Wadsworth's division of the First Corps joined the Twelfth Corps to the Eleventh under Howard, which occupied the cemetery, forming the bend of the fishing hook; to the left of the Eleventh on Cemetery Ridge, the "long shank," stood Doubleday's division of the First, then the Second Corps under Hancock, and on its left the Third under Sickles, which, to gain a higher and apparently more advantageous position, was moved forward on the Cemetery Ridge line to a peach orchard, hence become famous, the two divisions of the corps forming a projecting angle, provoking attack. The Round Tops on the left of the Third Corps were unoccupied. These were the weak points which General Lee's keen eyes quickly perceived. Our

Fifth Corps stood in reserve, and our Sixth Corps under Sedgwick had not yet arrived. Lee's army formed a large semicircle fronting our lines —Ewell's Corps on its left, facing Culp's Hill and Cemetery Hill; A. P. Hill's Corps in the center, occupying Seminary Ridge and facing part of Cemetery Ridge held by the Second and the Third Corps, and Longstreet's facing our left.

It was from Longstreet's Corps, therefore, that the attack upon our weak points came. A brisk cannonade preceded it, which, to judge by the missiles which whirred over our heads, was partly directed upon Cemetery Hill, and to which the batteries near us replied at a lively rate. Then we heard a confused noise on our left, a continuous rattle of musketry, discharges of artillery now thundering with rapid vehemence; then slackening as if batteries were silenced; then breaking out again with renewed violence; and from time to time something like an echo of a Union cheer or a rebel yell. Owing to a projecting spur of Cemetery Ridge, we on the cemetery itself could not see what was happening on our extreme left—nothing but the rising clouds of white smoke. Neither did the sounds we heard indicate which side had the advantage in the battle. But looking to our rear we observed how regiment after regiment was taken from our right wing to be hurried as quickly as possible toward the left of the army as reinforcement. The fire grew more furious from minute to minute, and about half after six, the roar of the battle actually seemed to indicate that our line was yielding. A moment later Captain Dilger of my artillery, who had gone to the ammunition train to get a new supply, came galloping up Cemetery Hill in great agitation with the report that the enemy had overwhelmed the Third Corps in the peach orchard and pressing after our flying troops had pierced our left center; that his musket balls were already falling into our ammunition train, and that unless the rebels were beaten back at once, they would attack us in the rear and take us prisoners in half an hour. It was a moment of most anxious suspense. But it did not last long. Loud and repeated Union cheers on our left, which could be heard above the din of battle, told us that relief had come in time and had rolled back the hostile wave. General Meade had skillfully used the advantage afforded us by the "interior line" in rapidly shifting forces from one point to another as the necessities of the moment required, and thus succeeded in meeting the assault of the enemy with superior numbers. As evening came the battle on the left sank into a lull and we were assured that, although the enemy had gained some ground, we had won a secure lodgment on the Round Tops, owing to General Warren's keen discernment of the situation, and our line from there to Cemetery Hill was substantially restored.

In the meantime the enemy, noticing the withdrawal of some of our troops from Culp's Hill, had tried to capture that vitally important position. But there, too, although the enemy possessed himself of some of the breastworks left by the brigades that had been called away to assist in beating back the attack on our left, he was checked by our troops left in position, especially General Greene's brigade—the same General Greene who lived in New York to reach, in honor and health, the age of ninety odd years—which heroically maintained itself alone until succored by reinforcements, among which were several of my regiments. A part of my First Brigade was sent to strengthen General Ames, who was hard pressed, and some of the Second Brigade pushed to the support of General Wadsworth, which they did very efficiently —for which thanks were returned.

But the dangers of the day were not yet ended. It was already dark when we on Cemetery Hill were suddenly startled by a tremendous turmoil at Wiedrich's and Ricketts' batteries placed on a commanding point on the right of Cemetery Hill. General Howard and I were standing together in conversation when the uproar surprised us. There could be no doubt of its meaning. The enemy was attacking the batteries on our right, and if he gained possession of them he would enfilade a large part of our line toward the south as well as the east, and command the valley between Cemetery Ridge and Culp's Hill, where the ammunition trains were parked. The fate of the battle might hang on the repulse of this attack. There was no time to wait for superior orders. With the consent of General Howard I took the two regiments nearest to me, ordered them to fix bayonets, and, headed by Colonel Krzyzanowski, they hurried to the threatened point at a double-quick. I accompanied them with my whole staff. Soon we found ourselves surrounded by a rushing crowd of stragglers from the already broken lines. We did our best, sword in hand, to drive them back as we went. Arrived at the batteries, we found an indescribable scene of mêlée. Some rebel infantry had scaled the breastworks and were taking possession of the guns. But the cannoneers defended themselves desperately. With rammers and fence rails, hand spikes and stones, they knocked down the intruders. In Wiedrich's battery, manned by Germans from Buffalo, a rebel officer, brandishing his sword, cried out: "This battery is ours!" Whereupon a sturdy artilleryman responded: "No, dis battery is *unser*," and felled him to the ground with a sponge-staff. Our infantry made a vigorous rush upon the invaders, and after a short but very spirited hand-to-hand scuffle tumbled them down the embankment. As General Hunter said in his contribution to the *Century* series: "The Dutchmen showed that they were in no way inferior to their Yankee comrades, who had been taunting them ever since Chancellorsville." Our line to the right, having been reinforced by Carroll's brigade of the Second Corps, which had hurried on in good time, also succeeded in driving back the assailants with a rapid fire, and the dangerous crisis was happily ended. I could say with pride in my official report that during this perilous hour my officers and men behaved splendidly. During the night the regiments that had been withdrawn from my command to give aid elsewhere, returned to their former positions.

The net result of the second day's battle was, on the whole, not encouraging to either side. The Confederates had gained some ground —the position of the Emmitsburg road on their right and some Union breastworks on Culp's Hill on their extreme left; but they had also failed in several of their attacks, and become aware how difficult it would be to break the Union lines at any point in a manner to secure a decisive result. On the other hand, our army had lost some ground, but at the same time made its position stronger by the secure occupation of the Round Tops and the rectification of its line between them and Cemetery Hill. But both armies had suffered enormous losses in killed, wounded, and prisoners, and the commander of each, as has appeared from subsequent revelations, profoundly wished he were well out of the mess, while neither could see how he could do else than continue on the line on which he had begun. A council of the corps commanders held by General Meade that night was unanimous in that decision.

At dawn of day on the 3rd of July we were roused from sleep by a fierce rattle of musketry in the woods of Culp's Hill. As already mentioned, the withdrawal of several brigades from our right to assist our left in the fights of the preceding day had enabled the enemy to get possession of several breastworks abandoned by the Twelfth Corps. General Meade decided that for the security of our right flank those positions must be retaken, and the Twelfth Corps went at the task with great spirit. It was a little battle of its own, of which, owing to the woods on the field of action, we could see nothing except the columns of troops sent from the center and the left wing of our army to the assistance of the right. But the firing was incessant, both of artillery and musketry, now and then swelling into a great roar, stimulating the imagination of the distant listeners into nervous activity as to what might be happening under that cloud of white smoke hovering over Culp's Hill. About half past ten the firing ceased, and it was reported that the Twelfth, aftter a six hours' stubborn fight, not too bloody on our side, had retaken the positions held by the enemy during the night.

And then came that interval of perfect stillness of which most of the descriptions of the battle of Gettysburg have so much to say. That the battle should have come to a short stop would have surprised nobody. But when that stop lengthened from minute to minute, from half hour to half hour, and when it settled down into a tranquillity like the peaceful and languid repose of a warm midsummer morning in which one might expect to hear the ringing of the village church-bells, there was something ominous, something uncanny, in these strange, unexpected hours of profound silence so sharply contrasting with the bloody horrors which had preceded, and which were sure to follow them. Even the light-hearted soldiers, who would ordinarily never lose an opportunity for some outbreak of an hilarious mood, even in a short moment of respite in a fight, seemed to feel the oppression. Some sat silently on the ground munching their hard-tack, while others stretched themselves out seeking sleep, which they probably would have found more readily had the cannon been thundering at a distance. The officers stood together in little groups discussing with evident concern what this long-continued calm might mean. Could it be that Lee, whose artillery in long rows of batteries had been silently frowning at us all the morning, had given up his intention to make another great attack? If not, why had he not begun it at an earlier hour, which unquestionably would have been more advantageous to him?

Suddenly the riddle was solved. About one o'clock the long hush was broken by the booming of two guns fired in rapid succession on the enemy's right, where Longstreet's Corps stood. And at once this signal was answered by all the batteries of the Confederate army, about 130 cannon, that could be brought to bear upon Cemetery Hill and the ridge joining it to the Round Tops. Instantly about 80 pieces of our artillery—as many as could usefully be posted in our line facing west and northwest—took up the challenge, and one of the grandest artillery duels in the history of wars followed. All that I had ever read in battle-stories of the booming of heavy guns out-thundering the thunders of heaven, and making the earth tremble, and almost stopping one's breath by the concussions of the air—was here made real, in terrific effect. The roar was so incessant and at times so deafening that when I wished to give an order to one of my officers I had to put my hands to my mouth as a speaking trumpet and shout my words into his ear. Fortunately the enemy had aimed their artillery a little too high, so that most of its missiles passed over our heads. But enough of them struck the ground on the cemetery and exploded there, to scatter death and destruction among the men immediately around, and to shatter gravestones and blow up ammunition caissons. But as most of them flew over us, rushing, screaming, whirring, and as they burst above, and sent down their deadly fragments, they added to the hellish din a peculiarly malicious noise of their own. How would the men endure this frightful experience? One of the hardest trials of the courage and steadfastness of the soldier is to stand still and be shot at without being able to reply. This ordeal is especially severe when the soldier is under a heavy artillery fire which, although less dangerous than that of musketry, is more impressive on the nerves. It bewilders the mind of the bravest with a painful sense of helplessness as against a tremendous power, and excites to peculiar vivacity the not unnatural desire to get into a safer place out of range. As a matter of course we ordered the troops to lie down flat on the ground, so as to present the smallest possible target. But when I observed the effect of the dropping of a shell right into the midst of a regiment which caused some uneasy commotion, I thought it my duty to get upon my feet and look after it. I found that it had a very steadying and cheering effect upon the men to see me quietly walking up and down in front smoking a cigar. I could not speak to them, for the incessant roar of the cannonade would not let them hear me. But I noticed that many of them returned my smile in a sort of confidential way when I happened to catch their eyes, as if to say: "It is not jolly, but we two will not be frightened by it." Indeed it was not jolly, for I felt as if the enemy's projectiles rushing over me were so near that I might have touched them with my riding-whip held up at full length of my arm. But observing the good effect of my promenade in front, I invited, by gesture, some of the regimental officers to do likewise. They promptly obeyed, although, I suppose, they liked the stroll no more than I did.

The furious bombardment had lasted more than an hour when the excellent Chief of Artillery of the Army of the Potomac, General Hunt, passed along the line the order to "cease firing"; not all the batteries to become silent at once, but one after another. The intention, and the actual effect, was, not only to prevent the further useless expenditure of ammunition, but principally to make the enemy believe that our artillery was in great part seriously crippled and would no longer be able to offer effective resistance to a vigorous attack. In fact the actual effect of the enemy's grand bombardment of our lines had been very trifling. A few pieces had been dismounted, but they were easily replaced from the reserve artillery. A few caissons had been exploded, but there was plenty of ammunition left. Some men and some horses had been killed or wounded, but their number was astonishingly small considering the awfulness of the turmoil, and there was nothing of the terror and demoralization which the enemy, no doubt, had expected to produce. To judge by my own command, which occupied one of the positions most exposed to the enemy's fire, we had suffered very little in killed and wounded, and I did not hear of a single man that had skulked away from the ranks.

But the enemy seemed to think differently. As our batteries grew silent, so did his. And then came forth that famous scene which made the battle of Gettysburg more dramatic than any other event of the Civil War, and which more nearly approached the conception of what a battle is in the imagination of persons who have never seen one. I will describe only what we observed of it from the crest of Cemetery Hill.

From a screen of woods opposite our left center emerged a long line of Confederate infantry, mounted officers in front and behind; and then another, and another—about 15,000 men. The alignment was perfect. The battle-flags fluttered gaily over the bayonets glittering in the sunlight. The spectacle has often been truly likened to a grand holiday parade on a festive ground. A mile of open field separated them from our line of defense. They had hardly traversed onetenth of that distance when they became fully aware that those of them who had counted upon our artillery having been much disabled, had grievously deceived themselves. No sooner had the attacking column appeared on the open than our batteries, which had in the meantime been re-formed and well supplied with ammunition, opened upon them from the front and from the right and left, with a terrific fire. Through our field-glasses we could distinctly see the gaps torn in their ranks, and the ground dotted with dark spots—their dead and wounded. Now and then a cheer went up from our lines when our men observed some of our shells striking right among the advancing enemy and scattering death and destruction around. But the brave rebels promptly filled the gaps from behind or by closing up on their colors, and unshaken and unhesitatingly they continued their onward march. Then the Confederate artillery behind them, firing over their heads, tried to silence our batteries or at least to attract their fire so as to divert it from the infantry masses advancing in the open field. But in

vain. Our cannon did not change their aim, and the number of dark
spots dotting the field increased fearfully from minute to minute. So
far not a musket had been discharged from behind the stone fences
protecting our regiments. Now the assailants steadily marching on
seemed to disappear in a depression of the ground, where they stopped
for a little while to readjust their alignment. But when they emerged
again, evidently with undismayed courage, and quickened their pace
to make the final plunge, a roar of cannon and a rattle of musketry, so
tremendous, received them that one might have thought any force
coming against it would have been swept from the face of the earth.
Still the attacking lines, although much thinned and losing their
regularity, rushed forward with grim determination. Then we in the
cemetery lost sight of them as they were concealed from our eyes by
the projecting spur of the ridge I have already spoken of.

Meanwhile a rebel force, consisting apparently of two or three brigades, supporting the main attack on its left, advanced against our
position on Cemetery Hill. We had about thirty pieces of artillery in
our front. They were ordered to load with grape and canister, and to
reserve their fire until the enemy should be within four or five hundred
yards. Then the word to fire was given, and when, after a few rapid
discharges, the guns "ceased" and permitted the smoke to clear away,
all we saw of the enemy was the backs of men hastily running away,
and the ground covered with dead and wounded. Our skirmishers
rushed forward, speeding the pace of fugitives and gathering in a multitude of prisoners.

But on our left the struggle, which from the cemetery we could not
see, still continued. We could only hear a furious din which seemed
to be stationary. Could it be that the rebels were breaking our lines?
With nervous anxiety we turned our eyes upon the valley behind us.
But there we saw, not fugitives or skulkers from our positions, but columns of troops hurrying to the scene of the decisive conflict. This was
reassuring. At last, looking again at the field which had been traversed
by the splendid host of assailants, we saw, first little driblets, then
larger numbers, and finally huge swarms of men in utter disorder
hurrying back the way they had come, and then, soon after, in hot pursuit, clouds of blue-coated skirmishers from our front rushing in from
both sides, firing and capturing prisoners. This spectacle could have
but one meaning. The great attack had failed disastrously. That magnificent column that had so proudly advanced upon us, was not only
defeated, but well-nigh annihilated. A deep sigh of relief wrung itself

from every breast. Then tremendous cheers arose along the Union lines, and here and there the men began to sing "John Brown's Soul." The song swept weirdly over the bloody field.

The general feeling in our ranks was that we had won a victory, and that we had now to reap its fruits. The instinct of the soldiers demanded a prompt, aggressive movement upon the enemy, and I think the instinct of the soldiers was right. The strongest of our army corps, the Fifth, kept in reserve, was substantially intact. Hardly any of the other corps had suffered so much as to be incapable of vigorous action. Their spirits were elated to genuine enthusiasm by the great event of the day. An order for a general advance seemed to be the natural outcome of the moment, and many men in the ranks fairly cried for it. But it did not come. Our skirmishers followed the retreating enemy for a certain distance, and then returned with their prisoners without having touched the positions from which the attacking force had emerged. Then two or three batteries of rebel artillery galloped forth from the belt of timber which screened the enemy's scattered forces. They advanced a short distance, unlimbered, fired a few discharges, limbered up again, and galloped back—probably to make us believe that the enemy, although repulsed, was still on the ground in fighting trim. (I do not remember having seen this fact stated in any of the histories of the battle of Gettysburg, but I observed it with my own eyes, and the impression is still vivid in my memory.)

Soon darkness and deep silence fell upon the battlefield. Officers and men, utterly exhausted by the fatigues and excitements of the past three days, just dropped down on the ground. In a moment my people around me were soundly asleep among the shattered gravestones. About two o'clock in the morning I was suddenly aroused by a sharp but short rattle of musketry, the sound coming clearly from the plain on the north side of the town. It lasted only a few seconds—then complete stillness again. What could it mean? Only that the enemy was withdrawing his pickets, and some of our outposts sent a volley after them. This was my own opinion, and that of my officers. The next minute we were fast asleep again, and woke up only when daylight was upon us. Early in the morning I sent a detachment of my second brigade, under my chief of staff, Lieutenant Colonel Otto, into the town to reconnoiter. They took prisoners over 250 rebel stragglers, who remained behind while the enemy had during the night quietly evacuated Gettysburg. I at once rode in with some staff-officers and orderlies to satisfy myself whether there were any wounded men left in the houses or on the fields beyond, where my troops had been engaged on the first day of the battle. Then I enjoyed a most delightful surprise.

Of all the losses we had suffered in the first day's bloody battle, that of my old friend Schimmelfennig went nearest to my heart. He had not only been an officer of exceptional ability, but my military instructor in the old German days, and a dear personal friend. We did not know what had become of him—whether he lay dead on the field, or had been wounded, or made a prisoner by the enemy. Some of his officers had last seen him in the thickest of the fight, and how, when the order to retreat was given, he had left the field in the rear of his command. Further, their accounts did not go. Now, when early in the morning after the three-days' struggle I entered the town—what should I see? In the door of one of the houses on the main street, General Schimmelfennig, alive and waving his hat to me. "Halloh!" he shouted. "I knew you would come. I have been preparing for you. You must be hungry. I found some eggs in this house and saved them for you. We shall have them fried in a few minutes. Get off your horse and let us take breakfast together." It was a jolly repast, during which he told us his story. When, during that furious fight of the first day, the order to retreat reached him, he did his best to take his command out of the fire-line in as orderly a shape as possible—a very difficult operation under any circumstances—and, therefore, left the field in the rear of his troops. But when he reached the town he found the streets crowded with a confused mass of artillery and vehicles of all sorts, and disorganized men. Somehow he was crowded into a blind lane, and suddenly ran against a high fence, barring his progress, while some rebel infantrymen, in hot pursuit, were yelling close behind him. To clear the tall fence on horseback was impossible. He therefore dismounted and climbed over it. While he was on the top rail, his pursuers came up to him, and one of them knocked him on the head with the butt of his gun. The blow did not hurt him much, but he let himself drop on the other side of the fence as if he were dead, or at least stunned. Fortunately, he wore an ordinary cavalry overcoat over his general's uniform, so that no sign of his rank was visible. The rebel soldiers, thus taking him for a mere private, then passed by him. After a little while he cautiously raised his head and discovered that he was alone in a little kitchen garden, and that within a few yards of him there was a small stable or shed that might serve him as a temporary shelter. He crawled into it, and found a litter of straw on the ground, as well as some bread crumbs and other refuse, which seemed to have been intended for pigs. Soon he heard voices all around him, and from the talk he could catch he concluded that the rebels had taken possession of the town and were making preparations for its defense.

There he lay, then, in his pig-sty, alone and helpless, surrounded on all sides by enemies who might have discovered him at any moment, but fortunately did not, and unknown to the inhabitants of the house to which the kitchen garden belonged. He had nothing to eat except the nauseous scraps he found on the ground, and nothing to drink except the few drops that were left in his field flask. And in this condition he lay from the afternoon of the 1st of July until the early morning of the 4th. But worse than hunger and thirst during those two and a half days and three nights was his feverish anxiety concerning the course of the battle. There was an ill-omened silence during the first night and the early forenoon of the second day. Had our army withdrawn? From the noises he heard he could only conclude that the enemy held the town of Gettysburg in force. But the roar of cannon and the rattle of the musketry during the afternoon assured him that our army was present in force, too. Only he could not tell which side had the advantage, or whether there was any advantage achieved by either side. And so it was on the third day, when the battle seemed to rage furiously, at different times and at different points, apparently neither advancing nor receding, until late in the afternoon the artillery became silent, and a mighty Union cheer filled the air. Then his hope rose that something favorable to us had happened. Still, he was disquieted again by the continued presence of the rebel infantry around him, until late in the night he heard something like the passing around of an order among them in a low voice, whereupon they seemed quietly to slink away. Then perfect stillness. At break of day he ventured his head out of the pig-sty, and finding the kitchen garden completely deserted, he went into the house, the inhabitants of which greeted him first with some apprehension, but then, upon better knowledge of the situation, with great glee. A happy moment it was to me when I could telegraph to Mrs. Schimmelfennig, who was with my family at Bethlehem, Pa., that her husband, who had been reported missing after the first day's battle, had been found, sound and safe!

No contrast could have been gloomier than that between the light-hearted hilarity of our breakfast and my visit to the battlefield immediately following it. The rebels had removed many if not most of their dead, but ours lay still in ghastly array on the ground where they had fallen. There can be no more hideous sight than that of the corpses on a battlefield, after they have been exposed a day or more to the sun in warm weather—the bodies swollen to monstrous size, the faces bloated and black, the eyes bulging out with a dead stare, all their features puffed out almost beyond recognition, some lying singly or in rows, others in heaps, having fallen over one another, some in attitudes of peaceful repose, others with arms raised, others in a sitting posture, others on their knees, others clawing the earth, many horribly distorted by what must have been a frightful death-struggle. Here I stood on the ground occupied by my division during that murderous conflict, around me the dead bodies of men who, but three days ago, had cheered me when I rode along their front, and whose greetings I had responded to with sincere affection, the features of some of whom I now succeeded in recognizing after a painful effort; some officers whom I had known well, with whom I had talked often, and who now lay here, struck down in the flower of their young manhood, now horrible to look at like the rest—and over yonder, only a few paces away, some Confederate dead, whom their comrades had left on the field, now looking just like our men, and having in all probability died with the same belief in the justice of *their* cause. Was it possible that any of them should have been sincerely convinced of the righteousness of the cause they fought for—the cause of slavery? I had to say to myself that it was possible, and in many cases even certain; for did I not know from history that in many religious wars men had cut one another's throats with the fierceness of fanatical conviction concerning differences of opinion on doctrinal points which to-day would call forth from any educated person only a smile of pity? I rode away from this horrible scene in a musing state of mind, finally composing myself with the reaffirmed faith that in our struggle against slavery we could not possibly be wrong; that there was an imperative, indisputable necessity of fighting for our cause; that the belief of the rebels in the righteousness of their cause might be ever so sincere, and that they might individually deserve ever so much credit for that sincerity, but that their error stood offensively in the way of justice, and that their challenge had to be met.

There were more harrowing experiences in store for me that day. To look after the wounded of my command, I visited the places where the surgeons were at work. At Bull Run, I had seen only on a very small scale what I was now to behold. At Gettysburg the wounded—many thousands of them—were carried to the farmsteads behind our lines. The houses, the barns, the sheds, and the open barnyards were crowded with moaning and wailing human beings, and still an unceasing procession of stretchers and ambulances was coming in from all sides to augment the number of the sufferers. A heavy rain set in during the day—the usual rain after a battle—and large numbers had to remain unprotected in the open, there being no room left under roof. I saw long rows of men lying under the eaves of the buildings, the water pouring down upon their bodies in streams. Most of the operating tables were placed in the open where the light was best, some of them partially protected against the rain by tarpaulins or blankets stretched upon poles. There stood the surgeons, their sleeves rolled up to the elbows, their bare arms as well as their linen aprons smeared with blood, their knives not seldom held between their teeth, while they were helping a patient on or off the table, or had their hands otherwise occupied; around them pools of blood and amputated arms or legs in heaps, sometimes more than man-high. Antiseptic methods were still unknown at that time. As a wounded man was lifted on the table, often shrieking with pain as the attendants handled him, the surgeon quickly examined the wound and resolved upon cutting off the injured limb. Some ether was administered and the body put in position in a moment. The surgeon snatched his knife from between his teeth, where it had been while his hands were busy, wiped it rapidly once or twice across his blood-stained apron, and the cutting began. The operation accomplished, the surgeon would look around with a deep sigh, and then—"Next!"

And so it went on, hour after hour, while the number of expectant patients seemed hardly to diminish. Now and then one of the wounded men would call attention to the fact that his neighbor lying on the ground had given up the ghost while waiting for his turn, and the dead body was then quietly removed. Or a surgeon, having been long at work, would put down his knife, exclaiming that his hand had grown unsteady, and that this was too much for human endurance—not seldom hysterical tears streaming down his face. Many of the wounded men suffered with silent fortitude, fierce determination in the knitting of their brows and the steady gaze of their bloodshot eyes. Some would even force themselves to a grim jest about their situation or about the "skedaddling of the rebels." But there were, too, heart-rending groans and shrill cries of pain piercing the air, and despairing exclamations, "Oh, Lord! Oh, Lord!" or "Let me die!" or softer murmurings in which the words "mother" or "father" or "home" were often heard. I saw many of my command among the sufferers, whose faces I well remembered, and who greeted me with a look or even a painful smile of recognition, and usually with the question what I thought of their chances of life, or whether I could do anything for them, sometimes, also, whether I thought the enemy were well beaten. I was sadly conscious that many of the words of cheer and encouragement I gave them were mere hollow sound, but they might be at least some solace for the moment.

There are people who speak lightly of war as a mere heroic sport. They would hardly find it in their hearts to do so, had they ever witnessed scenes like these, and thought of the untold miseries connected with them that were spread all over the land. He must be an inhuman brute or a slave of wild, unscrupulous ambition, who, having seen the horrors of war, will not admit that war brought on without the most absolute necessity, is the greatest and most unpardonable of crimes.

In the course of the day the great tidings came that General Grant had taken Vicksburg and made the whole garrison of that Confederate stronghold prisoners of war. That was a great victory—a complete victory—and great was the cheering along our lines when we heard of it. But there was also among many of the officers of the Army of the Potomac, deep-down, a depressing consciousness that ours was not, what it might have been, a complete victory. To be sure, we had fought a great battle—and fought it bravely; our losses were enormous, over twenty-five per cent. of the whole force, and the losses of the enemy could hardly be less; we had disastrously repulsed a fierce attack of the Confederates and inflicted upon them a terrible blow. But now, on the day after that great event, there stood the enemy—having, indeed, withdrawn from the field fought over during the preceding three days, but only to concentrate his forces in a strong defensive position on that very Seminary Ridge from which he had been directing his offensive movements—there he stood, within sight of us, within cannonshot, grimly daring us to attack him, and we did not move. The situation seemed almost humiliating when we remembered that the day before, after the repulse of Pickett's charge, with three hours of daylight to spare, we might, by a resolute and vigorous counter-charge by our whole disposable force, have achieved a real victory over Lee's army, a victory which might have stopped this mainstay of the Confederacy of most of its power of mischief. I have always esteemed General Meade's character so highly that I am loath to join his critics on any point. But I have always understood it to be one of the first of the rules of war—which, in fact, are nothing but the rules of common sense applied to the business of war—that when you have dealt the enemy a blow which destroys his strength at some important point, and which confuses and demoralizes him so as to make him stagger— or, as the pugilists say, to render him "groggy"—you must follow up your advantage to the best of your ability, so as to reap its fruits. That we had dealt such a blow to Lee's army by the repulse of Pickett's charge we could see with our eyes. The attacking force of the rebels had not only been hurled back, but what was left of it had been turned into a disorderly and demoralized mob—that is, it had been substantially annihilated as a fighting body, much more apt to continue running than to offer effective resistance—for the time being, at least. On the other hand, we had one army corps that had hardly been engaged at all, and several others which, in spite of the losses they had suffered, were in good fighting form and in unusually fine fighting spirits; for at that moment the Army of the Potomac—what had not often happened to it before—felt victory in its bones. In one word, the chances of success would have been decidedly and largely in our favor. It was one of those rare opportunities in war promising great results, but, to win them, demanding instant resolution. There being no instant resolution the great opportunity was lost. Lee was given ample time to rally and re-form his shattered host, and, contracting his lines, to establish himself in his strong defensive position on Seminary Ridge. There he stood—a whole day longer, like a wounded lion—wounded, but still defiant.

He gave the order to retreat across the Potomac on the afternoon of July 4th. There we had another opportunity to win great results by a vigorous pursuit. Lee's retreat was a difficult one, owing to his encumbrances and the heavy rains spoiling the roads. But our pursuit was not vigorous. We started the next day, exerted hardly any pressure at all upon his rear, marched by circuitous routes more or less parallel with Lee's line of retreat, and when, after several days, we caught up with him in an entrenched position, we put off the attack long enough to give him time to withdraw his whole army across the river without any serious loss. Thus it happened that General Lee saved from the battlefield at Gettysburg an army still capable of giving many anxious hours to the defenders of the Union. Indeed, the political value of the results achieved at Gettysburg can hardly be overestimated. Had Lee defeated us on that battlefield, and marched with his victorious hosts upon Baltimore and Washington, there would have been complications of incalculable consequence. The lines of communication between the seat of our government and the North and West might have been seriously interrupted. A new secession movement might possibly have been started in Maryland. The disloyal partisan elements in the Northern States might have been greatly encouraged to aggressive activity. New attempts might have been made in England and France to bring about the recognition of the Southern Confederacy by those powers, and eventual intervention in its favor. I am far from believing that all this would have resulted in the final breaking down of the Union cause, for the North would no doubt have risen to a supreme effort, but our situation would certainly have been beset with most perplexing troubles for a time, and the war might have been materially prolonged. On the other hand, Lee's failure at Gettysburg—if we call it only that—had dashed the highest hopes of the Southern people. The invasion of the North and the attempt to transplant the war upon Northern soil had so decidedly miscarried that so ambitious a plan would hardly again be thought of. The hope of supplying the meager and constantly dwindling resources of the South with rich Northern spoil had to be given up forever. Moreover, Lee's army, which so far had thought itself invincible, and looked upon the Northern soldiers with haughty contempt, had been seriously weakened in the self-reliance which had inspired its daring in many battles. Thenceforth it felt itself on the defensive. And the defensive, although still formidable, was bound gradually to grow weaker as the Confederacy found it more and more difficult to fill the widening gaps in the ranks of its armies, and to furnish its fighting forces with the necessaries of warfare.

It has been a common saying that the capture of Vicksburg, giving us the free command of the Mississippi, and the battle of Gettysburg, forcing the best Southern army back upon Southern soil, broke the backbone of the rebellion. This is substantially true. But it is equally true that, had our success at Gettysburg been so followed up as to destroy Lee's army, or at least to render it unable to keep the field, the war would probably have been a year shorter.

When General Lee had recrossed the Potomac, our army leisurely followed rather than pursued him upon the old, well-trodden field of operations in Virginia. An amusing little adventure happened to me on that occasion. When we were passing through Loudoun County, Virginia, my division had the rear of the marching column, and I observed on a ridge of ground on our left, running nearly parallel with our line of march, at a distance of about two miles, groups of horsemen, who would quickly disappear again after having for a moment shown themselves. Owing to the distance we could not make out through our glasses whether they looked like Union or rebel cavalry, or guerrillas, of whom there were a good many in that part of Virginia, under their famous chief, Colonel Mosby. But it was my own opinion, as well as that of my staff-officers, that they must be detachments of Union cavalry, charged with the duty of guarding the flank of the army on its march. This would have been the correct thing. Not having any cavalry to investigate the matter at a distance, I had to content myself with pushing out a little farther my infantry flanking parties and my rear guard. That night we camped at a place called Mountsville, where we were to rest two or three days. The next morning it was reported to me that Mosby's guerrillas were hovering all around us, and had already picked up some army vehicles and sutlers' wagons, as well as a number of stragglers.

At once I ordered out several strong infantry patrols to scour the country in all directions, and one of them I accompanied myself for the special purpose of establishing an outpost at a mill situated on a water-course, near which I had noticed on yesterday's march several loiterers of suspicious appearance. I rode ahead of the patrol, accompanied by an officer of my staff, two orderlies, and my staff bugler. Light-heartedly we enjoyed the freshness of the morning.

To get to the mill we had to pass through a little defile—a narrow, sunken road, slightly descending, and bordered on each side by an abrupt rise of ground covered with trees and underbrush. We had hardly entered this defile, when, at the lower end of it, perhaps two hundred yards ahead of us, we observed a troop of horsemen, ten or twelve of them, who advanced toward us. They looked rather ragged, and I took them for teamsters or similar folk. But one of my orderlies cried out: "There are the rebels!" And true enough, they were a band of Mosby's guerrillas. Now they came up at a gallop, and in a minute they were among us. While we whipped out our revolvers, I shouted to my bugler: "Sound the advance, double-quick!" which he did; and there was an instant "double-quick" signal in response from the infantry patrol, still hidden by the bushes, but close behind us. We had a lively, but, as to my party, harmless conversation with revolvers for a few seconds, whereupon the guerrillas, no doubt frightened by the shouts of the patrol coming on at a run, hastily turned tail and galloped down the road, leaving in our hands one prisoner and two horses. We sped after them, but as soon as they had cleared the defile they scattered over the fields, and were soon lost to sight in the ravines and among the timber-belts around.

CHAPTER XVI

Chattanooga

A<small>T</small> last, on the 25th day of September, 1863, the Eleventh Corps was cut loose from the Army of the Potomac and despatched, together with the Twelfth, both under the command of General Hooker, to the western field of operations. General Rosecrans had maneuvered the rebel general, Bragg, out of Chattanooga, but suffered a grievous defeat on September 19th and 20th at Chickamauga, where the Army of the Cumberland was saved from total destruction only by the heroic firmness of General Thomas.

On the 1st and 2nd of October, my command arrived at Bridgeport, Alabama, on the Tennessee River. About the 20th of October we learned, first by rumor, and then by official announcement, that General Grant had taken command of the "Military Division of the Mississippi," including the field of operations of the Army of the Cumberland; that General Rosecrans had been removed from the command of that army, to be superseded by General Thomas; and that General Sherman was hurrying on from the West with large reinforcements. On the 27th we broke camp and started on our march from Bridgeport to Chattanooga. The road was in a dreadful condition. There were so many carcasses of mules and horses lying on and alongside of it, that I thought if they were laid lengthwise they would easily cover the whole distance. In the afternoon of the 28th we arrived in Lookout Valley, near Brown's Ferry, about three miles from Chattanooga. The commanding form of Lookout Mountain frowned down upon us, with a rebel battery on top. We presumed that there must be a rebel force at its foot, but it was hidden from us by dense woods. There were with us two divisions of the Eleventh Corps, General Steinwehr's and mine, except some detachments, and part of General Geary's division of the Twelfth Corps, which, however, was left behind with a wagon train at a small hamlet called Wauhatchie, about three miles distant. The road from Wauhatchie to Brown's Ferry was bordered on the enemy's eastern side by steep ridges, intersected by gaps and ravines, through one of which ran a country road leading to Kelly's Ferry, and through another the track of the Memphis and Charleston Railroad. On the western side of the Wauhatchie road there was a valley about one-half mile wide, covered partly with cornfields, partly with timber and underbrush, and bordered by the Raccoon Mountains. On our march we saw nothing of the enemy except little squads of cavalry, who vanished at our approach, and a small infantry force in the woods near Wauhatchie, which disappeared after having fired a few shots, when it saw some of our regiments deploy for attack. Besides, the rebel battery posted on the top of Lookout Mountain pitched some shells at us, without effect. But from the same height the enemy could easily observe every one of our movements, and it occurred to some of us that the separation by nearly three miles of bad road of Geary's small force from ours was really an invitation to an attack under circumstances very favorable to the enemy. However, such was the disposition made by General Hooker, and all we could do was to surround ourselves by strong picket lines, well thrown out, to guard against a surprise. So we went into bivouac.

All remained quiet until about midnight, when we were disturbed by a few shots fired on our picket line. Then profound stillness again, which, however, lasted only about half an hour. Then very lively firing was heard in the direction of Wauhatchie. This evidently meant something more serious. We could not doubt that the enemy was attacking Geary in order to overwhelm him, and thus to break the line of communication we had established. Prompt action was necessary. The troops abruptly waked from their first and best sleep, tumbled out of their blankets with alacrity, and were under arms in a few minutes, ready to march.

Soon General Hooker rode up—as it seemed to me in a somewhat excited state of mind—and ordered me to hurry my division to the relief of Geary. This was the order I had expected. Instantly I put myself at the head of Tyndale's brigade, which was the nearest at hand, and marched off on the road to Wauhatchie, sending my chief-of-staff to my other two brigades, with the order to follow me. The moon shone brightly, only now and then obscured by passing clouds. We could see ahead on the open ground tolerably well. But the shadows of the dense woods we entered were all the darker. Having thrown out a skirmish line to the front, and flanking parties towards the hills, we pressed on with the utmost possible expedition on the road, which was very bad. The musketry fire ahead of us at Wauhatchie grew more lively and was punctuated with occasional discharges of artillery which, to judge from the sound, came from Geary's battery. Evidently, Geary was hard pressed, and we accelerated our speed. We had advanced only a few hundred yards when we received a heavy volley of musketry from one of the darkly wooded hills on our left. One of my aides, riding by my side, was wounded and had to be carried to the rear. Several men in the marching column were also hit. Without orders some scattering shots were fired in reply from our side, which were promptly stopped, and we pushed on without delay, anxious as I was to reach Geary, and confident that our forces behind would at once take care of the enemy on my left and rear who had tried to molest us. This, indeed, was done by a brigade of the second division which in splendid style stormed and cleared the hill from which the volley had come.

But it seemed probable that the whole row of hills along which the road to Wauhatchie ran, was occupied by rebel troops to guard the flank and rear of those who attacked Geary, and I reinforced my flanking parties. We soon struck a slight turn towards the hills in the road where it was especially muddy and difficult. I directed the column to march straight ahead through what appeared to me an open field, expecting to reach Geary more quickly. But my advance skirmishers soon ran into a miry bog covered with low brush, which appeared to be impassable, and we were obliged to regain the road by a movement to the left. This was done without any loss of time. Until then General Howard had been with me off and on during the march. Now, accompanied by an aide, he rode on to Geary to tell him that help was near.

Then one of those confusing disarrangements occurred which occasionally will happen in campaigns or battles, and which sometimes produce much mischief and cause excited controversies among the interested parties. I had hardly reached the road again, when through staff officers sent after me, I received the information that my second and my third brigades which, according to my orders, were to follow Tyndale's, and which, therefore, I firmly expected to be at my heels, were not following me at all, but were kept back—one by General Hooker's personal direction, and the other by an order delivered by one of General Hooker's staff officers that it should accompany a lot of prisoners to Chattanooga. I was much surprised, but would have hurried on to Geary with Tyndale's brigade alone, had not at that moment one of General Hooker's aides-de-camp, Lieutenant Oliver, come with an order from General Hooker that I should take and occupy with one brigade the hill on my left next to the railroad gap. I replied to Lieutenant Oliver that I was ordered by General Hooker personally to push through to Geary, that I had just been informed of my other two brigades having been stopped by General Hooker's direction, and that if I occupied the hill on my left with the only brigade I had on hand, I would have no troops at all to push on to Geary. Lieutenant Oliver answered that General Hooker wanted the hill on my left taken, and he repeated the order. This was puzzling. However, it naturally occurred to me that circumstances might have changed. The firing at Wauhatchie had for a while slackened and then died out altogether. It was evident that Geary, after a fierce fight, had succeeded in repulsing the rebel attack. But there was still more firing going on in my rear near the hill from which the volley had been thrown upon us. The enemy might perhaps have made a new movement, making it most important that the gaps in the row of hills be in our possession. Finally, although General Hooker had personally ordered me to push through to Geary, his last order, brought by his aide-de-camp, was that I should take and occupy with one brigade the hill immediately on my left, and according to all military rules, it was the last order that counted. I asked, therefore, General Tyndale to arrest the march to Geary, and to take and occupy the hill with his brigade.

This was done. Our skirmishers ascended the dark woods, silently. There was a moment of remarkable stillness. Then we heard about half way up a ringing voice calling out: "What regiment do you belong to?" Another voice, a little further away, responded, naming a Georgia regiment. Thereupon promptly followed a shot and then a rattle of musketry. Then three of our regiments rushed up after our skirmishers, the firing became more lively, and soon our men were on the crest and descended the opposite slope, the enemy yielding as our men steadily advanced. The affair occupied not much more than a quarter of an hour, but it cost us two killed, one of them a captain, and ten wounded. The importance of our occupation of the hill consisted in its commanding one of the passes through that chain of ridges. Our troops had, therefore, to be put in proper position to sustain an attack, the immediate vicinity to be explored by scouts, pickets to be well thrown out on front and flanks, and a reserve to be properly placed—arrangements which require some time, especially in the dark and on densely wooded and uneven ground, not permitting anything to be discerned with certainty, even at a very short distance. While these things were being done, Lieutenant Oliver, who had left me soon after the fight, had ample time to report to his chief all that had happened, and General Hooker had ample time to send me further instructions if my doings were in any respect not in accordance with his wishes, or if he desired me to do anything beyond. But as I received no word from him I naturally believed that I had acted to General Hooker's entire satisfaction; and as the firing had ceased along the whole line, and everything seemed be in the best of order, I hastened to report to General Hooker myself, and to look after my other two brigades held back by him.

I found General Hooker in the midst of my brigades, which stood there with grounded arms. Expecting a word of commendation in response to my salute, I was beyond measure astonished when in a harsh voice and in that excited manner which I had observed in him an hour or two before, he asked me why I had not carried out his order to march my division to the relief of Geary. Mastering my feelings, I quietly replied that I had tried to do so; that I had marched off at the head of my advance brigade; that I then had received his positive order while en route to take and occupy a certain hill with one brigade; that I had ordered my other two brigades to follow me, but that they had been held back by superior orders; that therefore I had no troops to take to Geary. There was a moment's silence. He broke it by repeating that he had given me the order to march to Geary two hours before, and that I should do it now. I asked him whether my two brigades held back by his superior orders were now at my disposal again. He answered that they were, and rode away. I doubted, and my officers, too, whether he was in his senses.

At once we were in motion, Colonel Hecker's brigade leading. On the road Colonel Hecker told me what had happened. He had promptly obeyed the instruction brought to him by my chief-of-staff, to follow my second brigade, Colonel Krzyzanowski's, in marching to Wauhatchie. A little while after the head of our column had been fired upon from the hill on our left, he observed that Krzyzanowski's brigade halted, presumably by order. But he, Colonel Hecker, having received no such order, continued his march, passing by Krzyzanowski's brigade through an open field. He had hardly done so when Major Howard, of General Hooker's staff, brought him, too, a positive order to halt at the cross-roads, one branch of which led to Chattanooga, and to form his brigade front towards the hills. He had not time to do so when General Hooker himself appeared, and Major Howard said: "Here is General Hooker himself." General Hooker asked: "What troops are these?" Hecker answered: "Third Brigade, Third Division, Eleventh Corps." General Hooker asked further: "Where is General Schurz?" Hecker replied: "In the front; one of his aides has just been carried by here, wounded." General Hooker then instructed Hecker so to form his brigade that it could easily change front towards the right—the valley—if necessary. He thereupon inquired about the troops standing nearest to Hecker, and was informed that it was the Second Brigade, Colonel Krzyzanowski's, of my division, and saying to Colonel Hecker: "You stay here!" he rode over to Krzyzanowski's brigade and remained with it a considerable time. Indeed, it was between it and Hecker's brigade, within speaking distance of both, where I found him when I returned from Tyndale's position. This was the report Hecker gave me. It was subsequently proved to be absolutely correct in every detail. It made the words addressed by General Hooker to me more and more inexplicable. I could understand how the sudden appearance of the enemy on the range of hills between us and Chattanooga should have produced upon his mind the impression that the main action that night would have to be fought not at Wauhatchie, but in the immediate vicinity of our camp, and how that impression should have led him to throw into the hills or to keep in his own hand the troops he had ordered to the relief of Geary. But that he should not have appreciated what he had done in changing his dispositions, even after he had been informed of it, and that he should have blamed anybody for the confusion but himself, was not so easy to explain, except upon the supposition that he wanted a scapegoat for the mistake he had made in leaving Geary in so recklessly exposed a situation, which might have resulted in a very serious disaster, had the rebels attacked with a larger force. However, I consoled myself with the hope that when after a good sound sleep he reviewed the events of the night quite soberly, General Hooker would find it to be the best policy to recognize the truth and tell it.

As soon as I had free disposition of my two brigades again, both Hecker and Krzyzanowski were promptly dispatched to Geary, and the gap between him and Tyndale was properly filled. In the course of the next morning I saw General Grant for the first time. Unexpectedly he had come over with General Thomas to inspect our lines. As his coming had not been announced, his appearance among us was a surprise, and there was no demonstration, no cheering, among the soldiers, because they did not know that this modest-looking gentleman was the victorious hero of many battles. There was absolutely nothing of the fuss-and-feathers style, nothing of the stage or picture general about him. His head was covered with the regulation black felt hat. He wore a major-general's coat, but it was unbuttoned and unbelted. He carried no sword. On his hands he had a pair of shining white cotton gloves, and on his feet low shoes which permitted a pair of white socks to be seen, all the more as his trousers had perceptibly slipped up. He smoked a large black cigar with great energy, and looked about him in a business-like way with an impassable face. I had no opportunity for coming into personal contact with him at that time, as the cavalcade passed by at a brisk gait.

At last General Grant was ready to strike. Bragg had foolishly detached Longstreet's corps to overwhelm Burnside at Knoxville, and thus had dangerously weakened himself. Sherman had arrived with several divisions of his army, and on November 22nd the Eleventh Corps received orders to leave Lookout Valley and to march to Chattanooga, where we joined the Army of the Cumberland. I shall not attempt a description of the battle of Missionary Ridge, with all its dramatic and picturesque incidents, but confine myself to my own personal experiences, one of which is of some psychological interest.

When after a quiet sleep I woke up about daybreak on November 23rd, my first thought was that on that day I would be killed. It was as if a voice within me told me so with solemn distinctness. I tried to shake off the impression and to laugh at my weakness in listening to that voice a single moment. But while I met my companions and went about the performance of my duties in the accustomed way, the voice would always come back: "This day I shall be killed." Once I actually came very near sitting down to write a "last letter" to my wife and children, but a feeling of shame at my superstitious emotion came over me, and I desisted. Still the voice would not be silent. I busied myself with walking about among my troops to see that they were in proper fighting trim for the battle which we expected to open at any moment, but the voice followed me without cessation. I made a strong effort to appear as cheerful as usual, so that my officers should not notice the state of my mind, and I think I succeeded. But what I could not conceal was a restless impatience that the impending action should begin. Still the whole forenoon passed without any serious engagement—only a cannon shot now and then, and here and there a little crackle of picket firing. The breastworks and batteries of the enemy on the steep crest of Missionary Ridge on our left and opposite our center, and on Lookout Mountain on our right, frowned down upon us, apparently impregnable; and we stood inactive, looking at them.

At last, about noon, two divisions of the Army of the Cumberland in our left center were ordered to advance, and in a short space of time they took the first line of the enemy's rifle pits at the foot of the mountains. Although the voice within still spoke, I felt a little relief when I heard the real thunder of battle immediately in front. But my command stood there two hours more with grounded arms waiting for orders. At last at two o'clock a staff officer galloped up with the instruction that I should take position in the woods on the left of those divisions, between Orchard Knob and the Tennessee River, connecting on my right with General Wood, and on my left with the second division of our Corps. "Now is the time," said the voice within. In deploying my command and making the prescribed connection I had no difficulty—only a slight skirmish fire, the enemy readily yielding when I pushed my skirmishers as far ahead as Citico Creek. But there was a rebel battery of artillery placed on the slope of Missionary Ridge opposite Orchard Knob, invisible to us on account of the woods, which threw shells at us, and apparently had a correct range. Shells would come over to us from it in slow order, probably about two a minute. A practiced ear could gauge their course in coming rather accurately by their whirring noise. Having made my alignment with the neighboring divisions on the right and left, I was halting on horseback with my staff, between my skirmishers and my line of battle, in momentary expectation of further orders, when I heard a shell, as I judged, coming straight towards me. "This is the one," I said to myself. The few moments I heard it come seemed very long. It did strike the ground under my horse, causing the animal to give a jump, broke the forelegs of the horse of one of my orderlies immediately behind me, and then struck an embankment about twenty yards in the rear of me, and exploded, without hurting anyone. The effect was electric. The voice within me said: "This was the one, but it did not kill me after all." Instantly the premonition of death vanished, and my usual spirits returned. I never had such an experience again; but I have in vain tried to find an explanation for the one I have had.

The share of my division in the actual fighting in the battle of Missionary Ridge was rather slight. It would have been our fortune to take part in the conquest of Lookout Mountain, the so-called "battle above the clouds"—had not an unexpected mixing of General Hooker's troops with other commands transferred us from Lookout Mountain to Chattanooga. But as it was, we could only watch it from afar as during the afternoon the little puffs of smoke enlivened the brush on the rugged mountain slope, and after dark the musketry flickered through it like swarms of fireflies. The steady advance of our fire-line in this spectacular fashion greatly cheered the whole army. Late the same afternoon I received an order from General Grant to support the forces on my right and left in case of an attack, but, unless myself attacked, to do nothing that might bring on a general engagement. As there was nothing but slight skirmishing in my front and that of my neighbors, this order was easily executed. The night passed quietly. At sunrise the next day, the 25th of November, I was ordered to drive the enemy out of his rifle pits in my front, which was done with ease.

It was General Grant's plan that Sherman should assault the extreme right of Bragg's army placed on the northern end of Missionary Ridge at Tunnel Hill, and then drive the enemy from the flank out of his position on the crest. Sherman did succeed in crossing the Tennessee River at the appointed place on the right of the enemy, and in dislodging the rebel forces from the heights immediately before him; but advancing, he discovered to his chagrin that the heights he had carried were separated from the enemy's strong position on Tunnel Hill by a deep and precipitous ravine which was a very serious obstacle to his progress. In the course of the morning I received orders to join General Sherman, the second division of our Corps having preceded me. About 2 p. m. I took position on Sherman's left. I then met the General personally for the first time. I found him sitting on a stone fence overlooking the great ravine separating him from the enemy's fortifications on Tunnel Hill, which bristled with cannon and bayonets.

General Sherman was anxiously watching the progress of Ewing's division of the Fifteenth Corps, reinforced by two or three regiments of Buschbeck's brigade of the Eleventh, as it struggled up the slope toward the rebel entrenchments above, under very heavy fire of the enemy. They were evidently laboring hard. General Sherman received me very cordially and asked me to sit by him. At once we were engaged in lively conversation as if we had been old acquaintances. The General was in an unhappy frame of mind, his hope of promptly overwhelming the enemy's right flank and thus striking the decisive blow of the battle having been dashed by the discovery of the big ravine in his way. It was a stinging disappointment. He gave vent to his feelings in language of astonishing vivacity,—at least, it astonished me, as I had never seen or heard him before. I expected every moment that he would order me to "go in" with my whole division in support of Ewing's charge. But he preferred that my command should remain in reserve on his left to provide for the emergency of a rebel attack from that quarter. The result as to my command was that it stood there inactive, only now and then attracting a shell from the rebel position across the ravine, as my troops showed themselves. So the afternoon wore on. After a short stay on the stone fence Sherman restlessly walked away, and I did not see him again that day. Ewing's attack advanced more and more slowly, but came near reaching the rebel entrenchments on the crest, when toward dusk it seemed to be arrested by the increasing intensity of the rebel fire, and dropped back down the hill. From the direction of Chattanooga, the center of the position of our army, we heard a tremendous roar, and saw thick clouds of white smoke rising into the air, but we did not know what it signified. It might have meant an unsuccessful attack on Missionary Ridge, like Ewing's, but on a grander scale and perhaps with more disastrous results. Thus we on the extreme left, were rather in a depressed state of mind when the shadows of evening fell and the battlefield grew more and more silent.

The great victory of Missionary Ridge was announced to us in an almost casual way. There was immediately behind my line of battle a little dilapidated Negro cabin, in which our headquarter orderlies had constructed, out of planks found lying around, something like a table, with a bench on each side. There I sat down with my staff officers to "supper"—coffee, hard-tack, and, perhaps, a slice of bacon. We had hardly begun our repast when my division-surgeon dismounted outside, came in and joined the revelers. He was a somewhat monosyllabic gentleman, and gave us only a "good evening." After a while I asked him: "Where do you come from, doctor?"

"Just from Chattanooga, sir."

"Looked for medical stores, I suppose."

"Yes, sir."

"There was a tremendous noise around there. What was it?"

"Fighting, sir."

"Fighting—where?"

"On the hillside, sir. Boys went up nicely."

"What hillside?"

"They call it Missionary Ridge, I believe, sir."

"What? Our boys went up Missionary Ridge? Did they get to the top? Now be a little more lively, doctor!"

"Yes, sir, we could see them climb up there, and there was much waving of hats and cheering."

"What? Got to the top? And the rebels ran away?"

"I heard some officers say so at headquarters."

"By Jove, then we have won the battle!"

"I guess so, sir!" said the doctor quietly.

The rest of us jumped up without finishing our supper and hurriedly ran out for more news. Then we heard from afar a swelling wave of cheers rolling along our lines toward us, and in a few minutes we had the whole glorious story. It was an amazing tale. Sherman's attack on the enemy's right having come to a standstill, several divisions of the Army of the Cumberland in our center were ordered to advance. It was at first not intended to attempt the actual storming of Missionary Ridge—a fortified position which seemed well-nigh impregnable by a front attack—but rather to make a threatening demonstration cal- culated to induce Bragg to withdraw forces from his right to his center, and thus to facilitate Sherman's task. But the brave men of our Army of the Cumberland, once launched, could not be held back. With irresistible impetuosity, without orders,—it may almost be said against orders,—they rushed forward, hurled the enemy's advanced lines out of their defenses on the slope, scaled the steep acclivity like wild-cats, suddenly appeared on the crest of the ridge, where the rebel host, amazed at this wholly unlooked-for audacity, fled in wild con- fusion, leaving their entrenched artillery and thousands of prisoners behind them. It was a soldier's triumph, one of the most brilliant in history.

The next two days we took part in the pursuit of the discomfited enemy, which resulted in the capture of more guns—bringing up the total to 42 pieces—of more prisoners, amounting to 6000 in all, and of large numbers of vehicles and stores, and in vast destruction of property. And then we set out under General Sherman's command on an expedition to Knoxville, East Tennessee, for the relief of Gen- eral Burnside, who was hard pressed by General Longstreet's corps.

According to alarming reports, Burnside was in sore need of speedy help. It seemed to be a matter of days how long he would be able to hold out. The distance to be covered in a hurry was 120 miles. We marched in the lightest kind of order—no tents, no wagon trains, the men carrying only their blankets and knapsacks, if they had any, with something to eat in their haversacks, and plenty of ammunition in their cartridge boxes. But they were in fine spirits after the great victory, and bore the fatigue of the forced march with excellent cheer. We usually started about daybreak and went into camp about dark, having in the meantime crossed rivers and creeks with or without bridges, and mountain passes, sometimes over roads hardly worthy of the name. We saw no enemy in our front except some cavalry detachments sent out not to fight, but to observe. Whenever they came within range, a shell or two from our guns made them scamper off.

On this march I witnessed a little scene which was characteristic of the "fun" which we higher officers occasionally indulged in. One frosty morning I noticed a rather decent-looking house by the road-side, from the chimney of which a blue cloud of smoke curled up. In the front yard two orderlies were holding saddled horses. I concluded that there must be general officers inside, and, possibly, something to eat. Seduced by this thought, I dismounted, and found within, toasting their feet by a crackling wood fire, General Sherman and General Jefferson C. Davis, who commanded a division in the Fourteenth Corps attached to Sherman's command,—the same General Jeff. C. Davis, who, at the beginning of the war, had attracted much attention by the killing of General Nelson in the Galt House at Louisville. General Sherman kindly invited me to sit with them, and I did so. A few minutes later General Howard entered. He enjoyed the repu-tation of great piety, and went by the name of "the Christian soldier." General Sherman greeted him in his brusque way, exclaiming: "Glad to see you, Howard! Sit down by the fire! Damned cold this morn-ing!" Howard, who especially abhorred the use of "swear words," answered demurely: "Yes, General, it is *quite* cold this morning." Sherman may have noticed a slight touch of reproof in this answer. At any rate, I observed a wink he gave General Davis with his left eye, while a sarcastic smile flitted across his features. It became at once clear what it meant, for Davis instantly, while talking about some indiffer-ent subject, began to intersperse his speech with such a profusion of "damns" and the like, when there was not the slightest occasion for it, that one might have supposed him to be laboring under the intensest excitement, while really he was in perfectly cold blood. In fact, as I afterward learned, General Davis was noted for having mastered the vocabulary of the "Army in Flanders" more completely than any other man of his rank. Howard made several feeble attempts to give a different turn to the conversation, but in vain. Encouraged by repeated winks and also a few sympathetic remarks from Sherman, Davis in-exorably continued the lurid flow of his infernalisms, until finally Howard, with distress painted all over his face, got up and left; where-upon Sherman and Davis broke out in a peal of laughter. And when I ventured upon a remark about Howard's sufferings, Sherman said: "Well, that Christian soldier business is all right in its place. But he needn't put on airs when we are among ourselves."

A few weeks later, when the Knoxville campaign was over, Sher-man addressed a letter to Howard thanking him, most deservedly, for the excellent services rendered by him on that expedition, and praising him as "one who mingled so gracefully and perfectly the polished Christian gentleman and the prompt, zealous, and gallant soldier."

When I read this, I remembered the scene I have just described, and imagined I saw a little twinkle in Sherman's eye.

On December 5th, not many miles from Knoxville, we were informed that Longstreet had not waited for the arrival of our forces of relief, but effected his retreat toward Virginia. Thus our expedition had accomplished its purpose. It was a victory achieved by the soldiers' legs. We were allowed a day's rest, and then started on our way back, the same 120 miles and a little more, to our old camp in Lookout Valley. We could march more leisurely, but the return seemed harder than the advance had been. There was not the same spirit in it. Our regular food supplies were entirely exhausted. We had "to live upon the country." We impressed what live stock we could, which was by no means always sufficient. The surrounding population, Union people, were friendly, but poor. Roasted wheat and corn had to serve for coffee, molasses found on the farms, for sugar. But far worse than this, the clothing of the men was in tatters, the shoes worn and full of holes. Perhaps one-fourth of the men had none at all. They protected their feet by winding rags around them. Their miseries were increased by occurrences like this: One day our march was unusually difficult. We passed through a hilly country. The roads were in many places like dry, washed-out beds of mountain torrents, full of boulders, large and small. The artillery horses could not possibly pull their pieces and caissons over these obstacles. They had to be unhitched, and infantry detachments were called upon to help the artillerymen lift their guns and appurtenances over the rocks. This operation had to be repeated several times during the day. Thus the marching column was stopped time and again without affording the soldiers any real rest. On the contrary, such irregular stoppages for an uncertain length of time are apt to annoy and fatigue the marching men all the more. At last, toward dusk of the evening, I struck on our route a large meadow-ground through which a clear stream of water flowed. There was plenty of wood for fires near by. The spot seemed to be made for camping. My orders as to how far I was to march, were not quite definite. I was to receive further instructions on the way. My troops having been on their feet from early morning and having marched under the difficulties described, were tired beyond measure. They just dragged themselves painfully along. I resolved to rest them on this favored spot if permitted, and despatched a staff officer to corps-headquarters, two or three miles ahead, to obtain that permission. Meanwhile, waiting for an answer which I did not doubt would be favorable, camping places were assigned to the different brigades.

After the lapse of about an hour, when a large part of my command had come in and were beginning to build fires and to prepare such food as they had, my officer returned from corps-headquarters with the positive order that I must, without loss of time, continue my march and proceed about three miles farther, where a camping place would be assigned to me. I thought there must be some mistake, as, according to reports, there was no enemy within many miles, and I despatched a second staff officer to represent to corps-headquarters that to start my men again would be downright cruelty to them, and I begged that they be allowed to stay for the night where they were, unless there were real necessity for their marching on. In due time the answer came that there was such necessity. Now nothing was to be done but to obey instantly. My division bugler sounded the signal. There arose something like a sullen groan from the bivouac, but the men emptied the water, which was just beginning to boil in their kettles, upon the ground, and promptly fell into line. We had hardly been on the way half an hour when a fearful thunderstorm broke upon us. The rain came down in sheets like a cloudburst, driving right into our faces. In a few minutes we were all drenched to the skin. I wore a stout cavalry overcoat with cape, well lined with flannel, over my uniform. In an incredibly short time I felt the cold water trickle down my body. My riding boots were soon full to overflowing. One may imagine the sorry plight of the poor fellows in rags. They had to suffer, too, not only from the water coming down from above, but also from water coming from below. We were again passing through a hilly district. The road ran along the bottom of a deep valley with high ridges on both sides. From these the rain-water rushed down in streams, transforming the road into a swelling torrent, the water reaching up to the knees of the men, and higher. Meanwhile the thunder was rolling, the lightning flashing, and the poor sufferers stumbling over unseen boulders under the water, and venting their choler in wild imprecations.

At last, after having struggled on in this way for about two hours, we emerged from the wooded hills into a more open country—at least I judged so, as the darkness seemed to be a little relieved. The storm had ceased. Riding at the head of my column, I ran against a horseman standing in the middle of the road. "What troops are these?" he asked. "Third Division, Eleventh Corps." He made himself known as an officer of the corps staff. My advance patrol had somehow missed him and gone astray. He brought me an order to put my command into camp "right here on both sides of the road." I asked him what it was that made my march in this dreadful night necessary, but he did not know. It was so dark that I could not distinguish anything beyond half a dozen feet. I did discover, however, that on "both sides of the road" there were plowed fields. There was water from the rain standing in the furrows and the ridges were softened into a thick mire. And there my men were to camp. My staff officers scattered themselves to find a more convenient, or less dismal, location for the men, but they soon returned, having, in the gloom, run into camps occupied by other troops. Nothing remained but to stay where we were. The regiments were distributed as well as possible in the darkness. The men could not stretch themselves out on the ground because the ground was covered or soaked with water. They had to sit down on their knapsacks, if they had any, or on their heels, and try to catch some sleep in that position. About midnight the wind shifted suddenly and blew bitterly cold from the north, so bitterly, indeed, that after a while our outer garments began to freeze stiff on our bodies. I thought I could hear the men's teeth chatter. I am sure mine did. There we sat, now and then dropping into a troubled doze, waiting for day to dawn. As soon as the first gray of the morning streaked the horizon, there was a general stir. The men rose and tossed and swung their limbs to get their blood into circulation. The feet of not a few were frozen fast in the soil, and when they pulled them up, they left the soles of such shoes as they had, sticking in the hardened mud. The pools of water left by the rain were covered with solid crusts of ice, and the cold north wind was still blowing. I started my command as soon as possible in order to get the men into motion, intending to have them prepare their breakfast further on in some more congenial spot. The ranks were considerably thinned, a large number of the men having strayed away from the column and trudged on in the darkness of the night. As we proceeded we saw them crawl out from houses or barns or sheds or heaps of corn-straw or whatever protection from the weather they had been able to find. The hard-frozen and stony road was marked with streaks of blood from the feet of the poor fellows who limped painfully along.

And finally it turned out that all this had been for nothing. Headquarters had been disturbed by a rumor that the enemy was attempting a cavalry raid in our direction, which might have made a drawing together of our forces necessary. But the rumor proved quite unfounded. I have told the story of that dismal night so elaborately to show my reader that even in an ordinary campaign, not to be compared with the retreat of Napoleon's army from the Russian snow-fields, soldiers are sometimes exposed to hardships not always necessary, which in their effects are now and then no less destructive than powder and lead.

But on the whole the expedition to Knoxville for the relief of Burnside had been a decided success. The forced marches were well planned, and executed with exemplary precision and spirit. Congratulatory orders and complimentary letters were flying about in great profusion. General Sherman wrote one to General Howard in which he, with justice, commended his conduct very highly, and charged him "to convey to General Schurz and Colonel Buschbeck and to all your officers the assurance of my official and personal respect." General Howard, in his turn, was quite eloquent in praise of the Eleventh Corps, and lauded its "division and brigade commanders for the energy and constancy they manifested during the campaign." In the course of his report he spoke with especial commendation of Colonel Hecker, who commanded my Third Brigade, and who had performed the most arduous duties with his characteristic spirit and efficiency. On the 17th of December we re-occupied our old encampments in Lookout Valley and looked forward to a comparatively quiet and comfortable winter.

But my repose and that of many of the officers in my command was disturbed in an entirely unexpected and exasperating manner. On the 10th of January, 1864, I found in a New York paper a reprint of General Hooker's official report on the engagement of Wauhatchie, which I have so elaborately described above because a knowledge of the details of the occurrence is needed for a just appreciation of what followed. In that report General Hooker praised the conduct of the troops under his command in the Wauhatchie affair very highly, and then added:

"I regret that my duty constrains me to except any portion of my command in my commendation of their courage and valor. The brigade dispatched to the relief of Geary, by orders delivered in person to the division commander, never reached him until long after the fight had ended. It was alleged that it lost its way, when it had a terrific infantry fire to guide it all over the way; and that it became involved in a swamp, where there was no swamp or other obstacle between it and Geary to delay it a moment in marching to the relief of its imperiled companions."

When I read this I was utterly amazed and indignant. I had often heard a murmur among the generals of the army that "Joe Hooker's character for truth and veracity was not good." But how he could have put into an official report statements so palpably false and so malicious was beyond my comprehension. It was cowardly at the same time, for if Hooker's allegations were true, or believed by him to be true, it was his obvious duty not only to call the division and the brigade commanders by name, but to cause them to be tried by court mar-tial for undutiful conduct in the presence of the enemy. What brigade was meant in the report as guilty of such conduct? Was it Tyndale's, which really had run into a bog, but which was promptly extricated, and then by General Hooker's own order, acknowledged by him, took and occupied a gap in the hills? Or was it Hecker's brigade, which, on its way to Geary's position, was held back by General Hooker himself and was permitted to proceed only long after Geary's fight had ceased, and had never been stopped by any swamp? I had hardly finished reading the report when my brave friend Colonel Hecker, pale with anger, rushed into my tent, paper in hand, and with quivering lip swore that he would rather die than submit to so infamous an outrage as this imputation. I suggested to Hecker that he address to me a written pro-test against this untruthful report, in the calmest language he could command, and a short statement of the facts, together with a demand for a court of inquiry, and I sat down at once to write a letter to Gen-eral Hooker containing an emphatic remonstrance against his report, in which I declared that, "*believing* that Colonel Hecker and his com-mand did on that occasion all they were ordered to do, and did it with conscientiousness and alacrity, I begged leave to assume the re-sponsibility for their conduct, if any mistakes or any violation of orders had been committed. If, indeed, anybody must be blamed, I would rather claim the blame entirely for myself, than permit it to fall, even by construction, upon my subordinate commanders and their men, who bear no responsibility in this matter and have always exe-cuted orders with promptness and spirit." I then asked, "respectfully and earnestly," that General Hooker properly exonerate Colonel Hecker and his brigade from the accusation cast upon them, or that a court of inquiry be granted to probe the matter to the bottom. Thus I made the cause of my subordinates my own, fully resolved to expose the calumny and calumniator and not to spare him.

The court of inquiry was granted, but with ill grace. In the first place it was ordered to include in its investigation all the operations connected with the fight at Wauhatchie, which would have required the collection of great masses of testimony obscuring the real issue and consuming endless time. I remonstrated, and the order was satisfac-torily changed. But in the second place the composition of the court might have been resented as an indignity to me. Among its members there was not a single officer of my rank, and all of them belonged to General Hooker's command. But this I permitted to pass without any protest, relying upon the justice of my cause. As I expected, the testimony of the many witnesses called demonstrated beyond the possibility of doubt or cavil the absolute truthfulness of the story as I have told it above: That General Hooker had ordered me to march my command to the relief of Geary; that I started at the head of Tyndale's brigade to execute this order, having directed my other two brigades to follow me; that then, being attacked near his camp, General Hooker disposed by later order of these two brigades for other purposes; that he ordered me to take and occupy a gap in the hills with the only brigade, Tyndale's, left me; that Colonel Hecker finally sent off to Geary, had acted strictly according to General Hooker's and my personal directions; that Hecker could not by any possibility have reached Geary before the end of his fight, because he was not let go by General Hooker himself until hours after Geary's fight had ended, and so on; in other words, that General Hooker's report was nothing but a muddled jumble of untruths.

General Hooker, when examined as a witness, had substantially nothing to say except that he must stand by his report. But having the privilege of summing up the case in my own behalf, I availed myself of the opportunity to give General Hooker a piece of my mind. I did this to my heart's content in a written statement which I read to the court, and which went on record. I reviewed the testimony with great care, exposing every fact in the case with the utmost clearness, and then paid General Hooker my compliments:

"There are two things which every conscientious man will be careful to guard against. The first is saying anything to the prejudice of another which he knows to be false, and the other is saying anything to the prejudice of another which he does not positively know to be true. And did General Hooker positively know his report to be true and just? He could not know to be just what is proved to be unjust. But would it have been impossible to ascertain the truth? I lived within five minutes' walk of his headquarters. My brigade commanders were all within call. I saw him almost every day, and a single question would have elicited a satisfactory explanation. The question was not asked. Five minutes' conversation with his own aides, Lieutenant Oliver and Captain Hall, would have removed the error. Was the error so dear to him that he shielded it with silence against the truth? But to me it is a mystery how that error could stand against the force of his own recollections. Were they, too, shut out when that paragraph was penned? They would, indeed, have ill-comported with the sensational dash with which the verbiage of the censure is flavored.

"Everybody that knows me, will tell you that here, as elsewhere, I have been and am the most forbearing and inoffensive of men. And even in this case, I would have abstained from all sharpness of criticism had I not, by a series of occurrences, been tortured into the conviction that, at last, I owed it to myself and to my companions to array on one occasion the whole truth in its nakedness against official and private obloquy." * * * *

The verdict of the court of inquiry appeared like an almost ludicrous effort to carry water on both shoulders. It is intelligible that the colonels composing that court should have hesitated to find their commander, General Hooker, guilty of a muddled head during the night of the Wauhatchie engagement in giving orders and then making the execution of those orders utterly impossible by subsequent orders, and of covering this fact by a palpable falsehood and a shameless slander of his subordinates in an official report. On the other hand, they were too honest to join General Hooker in his outrageous misrepresentation of facts and his calumnious assault. Thus they hit upon a finding according to which the facts were exactly as I had stated them; but General Hooker was right in wishing Geary speedily relieved, and in being displeased when this was not done as he had wished; and he held back my brigades, believing I had other troops to send to Geary. Tyndale was right in not marching to the relief of Geary, because he was ordered to occupy a certain hill. Hecker was right in doing what he did, because he was ordered to do so. And, finally, "General Schurz, as soon as he had received his orders from General Hooker, promptly set about carrying them into execution; the troops were quickly under arms; they turned out splendidly. The necessary orders answering the object and fitting the circumstances were given. The column was put in motion, and General Schurz took his proper place at its head. He had reason to assume, and act upon the assumption, that his entire command was following him; if any of his brigades failed to do so, they acted in disregard of orders, or were stopped by orders which were regarded as superior to those of General Schurz. General Schurz had official information upon which in the opinion of the court, he was authorized to rely and act; that the Second and Third Brigades of his division had been detached from his command, and were under orders direct from General Hooker, which orders were in conflict with the orders issued by him. In the opinion of the court, General Schurz has fully explained his delay in going to the relief of Geary, and his apparent disobedience of orders in this regard, and fully justified his conduct in the premises, and consequently it follows that he has exonerated himself from the strictures contained in General Hooker's official report." As to my vindication, the verdict could not have been more conclusive and emphatic.

I was told that General Hooker felt the substantial condemnation of his conduct very keenly, and spoke of it with intense bitterness. Although I remained under his command for several months longer, I never saw him again until about fifteen years later at a dinner at the White House. I was then Secretary of the Interior under President Hayes. General Hooker had been married in the meantime, and, visiting Washington with his wife, was invited to dine with the President. The President, knowing nothing of our past difficulties, invited me, too, thinking that it would be a pleasant meeting of old war comrades. I noticed, after dinner, that Hooker sought to have some private words with me, and I could not avoid him. "You know, General," he said, "that trouble about Wauhatchie between you and me was all owing to Howard's riding away from his command." "General," I answered— I fear somewhat coldly—"I do not see what Howard's riding away could have had to do with our quarrel." Some other guest intervening, there our conversation stopped.

At last I was advised that in the work of reorganization the Eleventh and Twelfth Corps had been consolidated under the name of the Twentieth Corps, that the Twentieth Corps was to be commanded by General Hooker, and I was assigned to the command of a so-called Corps of Instruction near Nashville, in which a number of newly levied regiments were to be made fit for active duty, and then, presumptively, to form part of the Army of the Cumberland, under General Thomas. Thus I was separated from General Hooker, but in a manner not at all according to my wishes and expectations. I had hoped to march with Sherman southward, but the position to which I was now assigned promised little active service, for nobody could then foresee the battle of Nashville. Still, I obeyed orders without protest or murmur. My camp was speedily established at Edgefield, on the northern side of the river, opposite Nashville, and several newly organized regiments from Western States, especially from Indiana, came in to fill it.

It was then that I made the acquaintance of Andrew Johnson, whom President Lincoln had made "Military Governor" of Tennessee. I called upon him at the State House in Nashville, and he received me not only with polite kindness, but with some evidence of a desire to cultivate intercourse with me. I was not quite clear in my own mind about the impression he made upon me. He had worked himself up from poverty and a low social position to political prominence by the energy of his character and a degree of ability which, if not brilliant, was at least higher than that of his political competitors in East Tennessee. By a bold and vigorous fight against all secession tendencies and against the arrogant pretensions of the slave-holding aristocracy, he became the most conspicuous representative and the leader of the loyal Union element of the South. His appearance was not prepossessing, at least not to me. His countenance was of a distinctly plebeian cast, somewhat like that of the late Senator Douglas, but it had nothing of Douglas' force and vivacity in it. There was no genial sunlight in it; rather something sullen, something betokening a strong will inspired by bitter feelings. I could well imagine him leading with vindictive energy an uprising of a lower order of society against an aristocracy from whose lordly self-assertion he had suffered, and whose pride he was bent upon humiliating. Nor did he as a "child of the soil," possess anything of that ingenuous, naïve, and lovable naturalness which never ceased to form one of the greatest charms of Lincoln's character. Johnson was by no means a man of culture. His education had been of the scantiest. Judging from his conversation, his mind moved in a narrow circle of ideas as well as of phrases. But his contact with the world had taught him certain things as to decent and correct appearance. As often as I saw him I found him clothed in the customary broadcloth of the higher politician in Washington, with immaculate linen; and I noticed also in his deportment, as far as I could observe it, an air, whether assumed or genuine, of quiet dignity. Yet I could not rid myself of the impression that beneath this staid and sober exterior there were still wild fires burning which occasionally might burst to the surface. This impression was strengthened by a singular experience. It happened twice or three times that, when I called upon him, I was told by the attendant that the Governor was sick and could not see anybody; then, after the lapse of four or five days, he would send for me, and I would find him uncommonly natty in his attire, and generally "groomed" with especial care. He would also wave off any inquiry about his health. When I mentioned this circumstance to one of the most prominent Union men of Nashville, he smiled, and said that the Governor had "his infirmities," but was "all right" on the whole.

My conversation with him always turned upon political subjects. He was a demonstratively fierce Union man—not upon anti-slavery grounds, but from constitutional reasons and from hatred of the slave-holding aristocracy, the oppressors and misleaders of the common people, who had resolved to destroy the Republic if they were not permitted to rule it. The constant burden of his speech was that this rebellion against the government of the Union was treason, and that treason was a crime that must be made odious by visiting condign punishment upon the traitors. To hear him expatiate upon this, his favorite theme, one would have thought that if this man ever came into power, the face of the country would soon bristle with gibbets, and foreign lands swarm with fugitives from the avenging sword of the Republic. And such sentiments he uttered not in a tone betraying the slightest excitement, but with the calmness of long-standing and unquestionable conviction. When, in the course of our conversations, I suggested, as I sometimes did, that there were in the reconstruction of the Union other objects to be accomplished fully as important as the punishment of the traitors, he would treat such suggestions with polite indulgence, at the same time insisting with undisturbed sternness, that the Union could not endure unless by a severe punishment of the traitors, treason were forever branded as the unpardonable crime. Indeed, this seemed to constitute the principal part of his political program for the future. No doubt, there were gentler and more amiable currents of feeling in Mr. Johnson's composition, known to his family, friends, and neighbors; but in our political talks at that time they did not manifest themselves. When, a short time after my first meeting with Mr. Johnson, the Republican National Convention nominated him as its candidate for the vice-presidency, I was, I must confess, one of those who received the news with a certain uneasiness of feeling.

CHAPTER XVII

Lincoln, Sherman, and the War's End

ALTHOUGH Lincoln, to the astonishment of his Republican opponents, who would not recognize any popular force behind him, had been renominated with substantial unanimity by the National Convention, the hostile movements in the Republican ranks did not cease. Senator Benjamin F. Wade, from Ohio, one of the oldest, most courageous, and most highly respected of the anti-slavery champions, and Henry Winter Davis, a member of the National House of Representatives from Maryland, a man of high character and an orator of rare brilliancy, rose in open revolt against Lincoln's reconstruction ideas, and issued a formal manifesto, in which, in language of startling vehemence, they assailed the integrity of his motives as those of a usurper carried away by lust of power. And then cries arose in the most unexpected quarters that Lincoln could not possibly be elected. Such men as Horace Greeley and Thurlow Weed, usually hostile to one another in Republican factional fights, united in the gloomy prediction that Lincoln would most surely be defeated; and men of similar importance, severally and as members of committees, plied Lincoln himself with urgent entreaties that he should withdraw from the contest and make room for another more promising candidate. Neither was there much encouragement in the popular temper as it manifested itself during the first two months after Lincoln's renomination. The people seemed to be utterly spiritless. They would hardly attend a mass-meeting, much less inspire the speaker with enthusiastic acclamations. This may have been partly owing to the fact that the Democrats had not yet held their National Convention, and there was, therefore, neither a candidate nor a declared policy of the opposite party to attack. But, surely, the administration party could not have been in a more lethargic and spiritless condition. Its atmosphere was thoroughly depressing.

I called upon Mr. Lincoln on a hot afternoon late in July. He greeted me cordially, and asked me to wait in the office until he should be through with the current business of the day, and then to spend the evening with him at the cottage on the grounds of the Soldiers' Home, which he occupied during the summer. In the carriage on the way thither he made various inquiries concerning the attitude of this and that public man, and this and that group of people, and we discussed the question whether it would be good policy to attempt an active campaign before the Democrats should have "shown their hand" in their National Convention. He argued that such an attempt would be unwise unless some unforeseen change in the situation called for it. Arrived at the cottage, he asked me to sit down with him on a lounge in a sort of parlor which was rather scantily furnished, and began to speak about the attacks made upon him by party friends, and their efforts to force his withdrawal from the candidacy. The substance of what he said I can recount from a letter written at the time to an intimate friend.

He spoke as if he felt a pressing need to ease his heart by giving voice to the sorrowful thoughts distressing him. He would not complain of the fearful burden of care and responsibility put upon his shoulders. Nobody knew the weight of that burden save himself. But was it necessary, was it generous, was it right, to impeach even the rectitude of his motives? "They urge me with almost violent language," he said, "to withdraw from the contest, although I have been unanimously nominated, in order to make room for a better man. I wish I could. Perhaps some other man might do this business better than I. That is possible. I do not deny it. But I am here, and that better man is not here. And if I should step aside to make room for him, it is not at all sure—perhaps not even probable—that he would get here. It is much more likely that the factions opposed to me would fall to fighting among themselves, and that those who want me to make room for a better man would get a man whom most of them would not want in at all. My withdrawal, therefore, might, and probably would, bring on a confusion worse confounded. God knows, I have at least tried very hard to do my duty—to do right to everybody and wrong to nobody. And now to have it said by men who have been my friends and who ought to know me better, that I have been seduced by what they call the lust of power, and that I have been doing this and that unscrupulous thing hurtful to the common cause, only to keep myself in office! Have they thought of that common cause when trying to break me down? I hope they have."

So he went on, as if speaking to himself, now pausing for a second, then uttering a sentence or two with vehement emphasis. Meanwhile the dusk of evening had set in, and when the room was lighted I thought I saw his sad eyes moist and his rugged features working strangely, as if under a very strong and painful emotion. At last he stopped, as if waiting for me to say something, and, deeply touched as I was, I only expressed as well as I could, my confident assurance that the people, undisturbed by the bickerings of his critics, believed in him and would faithfully stand by him. The conversation, then turning upon things to be done, became more cheerful, and in the course of the evening he explained to me various acts of the administration which in the campaign might be questioned and call for defense. As to his differences with members of Congress concerning reconstruction, he laid particular stress upon the fact that, looked at from a constitutional standpoint, the Executive could do many things by virtue of the war power, which Congress could not do in the way of ordinary legislation. When I took my leave that night he was in a calm mood, indulged himself in a few humorous remarks, shook my hand heartily, and said: "Well, things might look better, and they might look worse. Go in, and let us all do the best we can."

A few days after the election I read in the papers the report of a speech delivered by Lincoln in response to a serenade, in which he offered the hand of friendship to those who had opposed him in these words: "Now that the election is over, may not all, having a common interest, reunite in a common effort to save our common community? For my own part, I have striven, and will strive, to place no obstacle in the way. So long as I have been here, I have not willingly planted a thorn in any man's bosom. While I am deeply sensible of the high compliment of a re-election, it adds nothing to my satisfaction that any other man may be pained or disappointed by the result. May I ask those who were with me to join with me in the same spirit towards those who were against me?" When I read those noble words, which so touchingly revealed the whole tender generosity of Lincoln's great soul, the haggard face I had seen that evening in the cottage at the Soldiers' Home rose up vividly in my memory.

The election over, I reported to the War Department for such duty as might be assigned to me.

When I personally made my report, Secretary Stanton asked me to bear a confidential communication, not to be put on paper, to Mr.

Lincoln, who had gone to City Point, on the James River, in order to have easy and constant conference with General Grant. I found Mr. Lincoln in excellent spirits. He was confident that the fall of Richmond, and with it the total collapse of the rebellion, would come in the near future. Also of the political situation, of which he spoke with great freedom, he took a hopeful view, much in contrast with the depression of mind which he had shown at our last meeting during the presidential campaign. He felt that his triumphant re-election had given him a moral authority stronger than that which he had possessed before, and he trusted that this strengthened authority, used with discretion and in a friendly and magnanimous spirit, would secure to his opinions concerning the measures of reconstruction he thought it wise to adopt, a friendlier consideration on the part of the leading Unionists in Congress and in the country. He did not say this in terms, but I gathered it from the tone of his utterances. And here I may mention a story thoroughly characteristic of Lincoln's ways, which I heard in passing through Washington. Charles Sumner had formed a theory of State suicide which gave to the National Government absolute liberty of action as to the status of the States in rebellion and their reconstruction after the return of peace. This theory stood in sharp contrast to Lincoln's ideas, but Sumner clung to it with his peculiar tenacity. The difference of opinion between the two men was so radical and outspoken that at the time of Lincoln's second inauguration, an actual rupture of their personal relations was currently reported and widely believed. But in spite of their disagreements and jarrings, Lincoln at heart esteemed Sumner very highly, and Sumner, although sometimes seriously disturbed by Lincoln's acts or failures to act, had implicit confidence in the rectitude of his character and the justness of his ultimate aims. Now, when Lincoln heard of the rumor of his personal rupture with Sumner, he at once resolved to discredit it by an open demonstration. On the evening of the inauguration ball he suddenly appeared in his carriage with Mrs. Lincoln and Mr. Colfax, Speaker of the House of Representatives, at Mr. Sumner's house, and invited the Senator to join them. Being asked by the President, the Senator could not refuse. And then, arrived at the ball-room, the President further asked the Senator to offer Mrs. Lincoln his arm and to take her in. The Senator, with grave gallantry, complied, and appeared before all the assembled multitude, if not as a member of Lincoln's family, at least as one of his dearest and most honored friends. After this their difference of opinion continued, although much softened; but there was no more talk of a personal rupture between Lincoln and Sumner.

I spent the better part of a day with Mr. Lincoln on the steamboat off City Point, on which he lodged. When I was ready to leave, he asked me what conveyance I had to take me back to Washington. I answered, the government tug, on which I had come. "Oh," said he, "you can do better than that. Mrs. Lincoln is here, and will start back for Washington in an hour or two. She has a comfortable steamboat to carry her, on which there will be plenty of room for both of you, if you keep the peace. You can accompany her, if you like." Mrs. Lincoln joining in the invitation, I accepted.

Shortly after my return from City Point, I received an order from the War Department to report at once for duty to General Sherman at Goldsborough, North Carolina. I obeyed without delay. When I presented my order to General Sherman, he greeted me like an old friend, and ordered me to report to General Slocum for employment in the Army of Georgia. I found with General Slocum a pleasant reception, and as there was at the time no proper command vacant in the Army of Georgia, he appointed me temporarily as his chief-of-staff. From the very beginning our relations were hearty and confidential. There was a general feeling that the final collapse of the Confederacy, and with it the end of the war, could not be far distant. But it was supposed that Sherman's command, after having put itself in communication with General Grant's forces, would still have the honor of participating in the capture of Richmond and of Lee's army. With that view Sherman ordered his forces to be ready to move on the morning of April 11th. But that morning brought us the news that Richmond had fallen, and that General Lee was making an effort to effect a junction with General "Joe" Johnston's army, which was at some distance in our front. Thereupon General Slocum resolved to march directly upon Raleigh, hoping to strike Johnston at Smithfield. It was at the village of Smithfield that I heard rebel bullets whistle for the last time. It appeared that Johnston had left that place and marched to Raleigh, leaving a small rear-guard behind, with whom we had a very slight skirmish. On the 12th, while I was riding by General Slocum's side in the column of march, we observed a horseman galloping towards us, swinging his hat and shouting something to the troops, to which they responded with a wild hurrah. When he came near we understood his shout to be that "Grant had captured Lee's army."

Now there could no longer be any doubt that the end of the war was actually at hand. Indeed, hardly one day had elapsed after our arrival at Raleigh before a flag of truce brought a message from General Johnston, asking for a suspension of hostilities and a meeting between him and General Sherman for the arrangement of terms of surrender. The meeting was fixed for April 17th, at a point intermediate between the two armies. Just as he was leaving Raleigh on that morning, Sherman received a telegraphic message from Secretary Stanton, containing the announcement of the assassination of President Lincoln. While Sherman was gone to confer with Johnston the terrible news was kept secret from our troops, to be revealed to them by a general order the next day. I well remember the effect the announcement had upon them. The camps, which for two days had been fairly resounding with jubilation over the advent of peace, suddenly fell into gloomy stillness. The soldiers admired their great generals, and often saluted some of them with enthusiastic acclamations. But their President, their good "Father Abraham," they loved. Him they carried in their hearts as their personal friend and the friend of their homes and families. When the foul deed, by which he had been taken off, was made known to them, they did not vent their feelings in loud tones of anger and vengeance, but they sat around their camp-fires either silent or communicating their wrathful grief to one another in grim murmurs. But as I went around among them, and here and there caught their utterances, it occurred to me that now it was the highest time that the war should cease. If it had continued, and if these men had once more been let loose upon "the enemy's country," there would have been danger of vengeance taken for Abraham Lincoln's blood that might have made the century shudder.

Some years later, when I visited Germany again and met the Chancellor, Prince Bismarck, as well as several generals of the Prussian army who had studied the history of our Civil War, they plied me with questions about the organization, the spirit, and the efficiency of our volunteer army. What I told them was substantially what I have put into these pages. It amused them immensely, but, accustomed as they were to judge everything by the high standard of professional instruction and discipline of the Prussian army, they seemed unable to understand how an army like ours could fight. How would it cope with any of the regular armies of European powers arrayed against it on anything like equal terms in point of numbers? They listened to me with a polite smile when I expressed the opinion that no country had human material superior to ours as regards physical development, intelligence, and martial spirit; that in the long run our volunteers could outmarch any European troops, and surpass them in the endurance of any sort of fatigue; that our volunteers, with incredible skill and rapidity, would build roads, and extemporize serviceable railway bridges and viaducts, with nothing but nails and tools, such as axes and saws and hammers and picks and shovels, and pine trees near at hand, and a clever engineer to guide them—I had seen them do it—and that they would construct temporary entrenchments and defenses almost without tools—I had seen them do that, too, many times—and that, in my opinion, they would, in a conflict with a European army, perhaps at the beginning of a campaign suffer some reverses by the superiority of European drill and discipline, but soon become acquainted with the tactics of their adversaries, and prove decidedly superior in the long run, especially if the contest were to be fought out on American soil.

Here I may remark that of all the higher military officers I have known, none had a clearer intuitive conception of this than General Sherman. In the opinion of many competent persons, he was the ablest commander of them all. I remember a remarkable utterance of his when we were speaking of Grant's campaign. "There was a difference," Sherman said, "between Grant's and my way of looking at things. Grant never cared a damn about what was going on behind the enemy's lines, but it often scared me like the devil." He admitted, and justly so, that some of Grant's successes were owing to this very fact, but also some of his most conspicuous failures. Grant believed in hammering—Sherman in maneuvering. It had been the habit of the generals commanding the Army of the Potomac to cross the Rappahannock, to get their drubbing from Lee, and then promptly to retreat and recross the Rappahannock again. Grant crossed the Rappahannock, got his drubbing from Lee, but did not recross the Rappahannock again in retreat. He sturdily went on, hammering and hammering, and, with his vastly superior resources, finally hammered Lee's army to pieces, but with a most dreadful sacrifice of life on his own part. Now, comparing Grant's campaign for the taking of Richmond with Sherman's campaign for the taking of Atlanta—without losing sight of any of the differences of their respective situations—we may well arrive at the conclusion that Sherman was the superior strategist and the greater general.

Later on, when a presidential election was approaching, Republican newspapers suggested General Sherman's nomination as the Republican candidate. One day about this time I happened to meet the General on a ferry-boat between Jersey City and New York, and in the course of our conversation I referred to the Republican papers so using his name. Sherman at once burst out in his characteristic fashion: "What?" said he, "do they think I am a damned fool? They know that I don't know anything about politics, and am not fit for the presidency. At least, I know it. No, I am not a damned fool. I am a happy man now. Look at

Grant! Look at Grant! What wouldn't he give now if he had never meddled with politics! No, they must let me alone. They can't bedevil me!" There was a treasure of the rare wisdom of self-knowledge in this rough speech, and it was thoroughly sincere.

When he called himself a "happy man," there was a tone of just exulation in his words. He was, indeed, a happy man. He had won great renown as a soldier, and an immense popularity all over the Northern country. This he knew, and he thoroughly relished it. All sorts of so-cieties and public organizations had made him their honorary member, and he appeared among them as often as he could. Whenever he entered a theater, which he did very often, the orchestra would strike up "Marching through Georgia," and the whole audience would rise and clap their hands, sometimes even sing the tune, and his rugged face fairly glowed and beamed with pleasure. Every social circle greeted him as a most welcome guest, and at receptions, and evening parties, and other gatherings, the "pretty girls" would come up and kiss him —and how he did enjoy all this!

As he grew older his mind lost little if anything of its original vi-vacity. His conversation bubbled with quaint conceits, and odd ex-pressions poured forth in the utmost abundance with great freedom. There could be no more entertaining dinner companion. While he lived in New York he sometimes dined with me and I with him; but he was most interesting when he came uninvited and unexpected, "just to make a call," which he did now and then in the evening after dinner. Then he usually seemed to have something on his mind that he wanted to talk about. So I remember him one evening after nine o'clock suddenly bursting into my drawing-room, when, after having saluted my family, he at once precipitated himself upon the subject then uppermost in his thoughts. "Do you know," he said, "that ancient myth of Jason and the 'golden fleece' is no mere myth at all. It is history. You know those old Greeks were great pirates and filibusters. They heard somehow that in a foreign country not very far away there were rivers or creeks carry-ing gold sand, and that the natives managed to get that gold sand by putting sheepskins with the wool on into the rivers or creeks, in which the gold sand floating down stream would stick fast. Those sheepskins with the wool full of gold were the 'golden fleece,' don't you see? Then the Greek pirates sailed for those countries and stole the golden fleeces, and occasionally took some native girls along home with them. That was the origin of the myth of Jason and Medea, but the whole thing is substantially as true as anything in history." Thus he would go on for a while, in the liveliest style, elucidating his story with all the joyousness of new discovery. This theme exhausted, he would jump up, thank us for the pleasant evening he had had, and leave us as abruptly as he had come. He was indeed a happy man, largely owing to his wise abstinence from affairs for which he did not feel himself fitted; and when he died, everybody that knew him regretted he was not permitted to enjoy his happiness some years longer.

CHAPTER XVIII

My Meeting with Bismarck

In the autumn of 1867 my family went to Wiesbaden, where my wife was to spend some time on account of her health, and I purposed to join them there about Christmas time for a few weeks. Great changes had taken place in Germany since that dark December night in 1861 when I rushed through the country from the Belgian frontier to Hamburg on my way from Spain to America. The period of stupid reaction after the collapse of the revolutionary movements of 1848 was over. King Frederick William IV. of Prussia, who had been so deeply convinced and arduous an upholder of the divine right of kings, had died a helpless lunatic. King William I., his brother and successor, also a believer in that divine right, but not to the extent of believing as well in the divine inspiration of kings—in other words, a man of good sense and capable of recognizing the superior ability of others,—had found in Bismarck a minister of commanding genius. The sweeping victory of Prussia over Austria in 1866 had resulted in the establishment of the North-German Confederacy under Prussian hegemony, which was considered as a stepping-stone to the unification of all Germany as a constitutional empire. Several revolutionists of 1848 now sat in the Reichstag of the North-German Confederacy, and one of the ablest of them, Lothar Bucher, was Bismarck's confidential counsellor. The nation was elated with hope and there was a liberal wind blowing even in the sphere of the government. I did not doubt that under these circumstances I might venture into Germany without danger of being seriously molested, yet as my personal case was technically not covered by any of the several amnesties which had been proclaimed in Prussia from time to time, I thought that some subordinate officer, either construing his duty with the strictness of a thorough Prussian, or wishing to distinguish himself by a conspicuous display of official watchfulness, might give me annoyance. I did not, indeed, entertain the slightest apprehension as to my safety, but I might have become involved in sensational proceedings which would have been extremely distasteful to me, as well as unwelcome to the government. I therefore wrote to Mr. George Bancroft, the American Minister at Berlin, requesting him, if possible, to inform himself privately whether the Prussian government had any objection to my visiting Germany for a few weeks, and to let me have his answer at Bremerhaven upon the arrival there of the steamer on which I had taken passage. My intention was, in case the answer were unfavorable, to sail at once over from Bremen to England and to meet my family there. Mr. Bancroft very kindly complied with my request and assured me in his letter, which I found at Bremerhaven, that the Prussian government not only had no objection to my visiting Germany, but that I should be welcome.

I had hardly been twenty-four hours at Wiesbaden when I was called upon by the president of the police department (Polizei-Praesident) of the province, a high dignitary, who introduced himself as an old university acquaintance and in the most affable manner bade me welcome, assuring me also that it would give him the sincerest pleasure to be of service to me during my stay. He added that he hoped I would visit Berlin before my return to the United States, for I would see many things there which would probably please me as an old Forty-eighter.

After having spent Christmas with my family in Wiesbaden I went to Berlin. I wrote a note to Lothar Bucher, whom I had last seen sixteen years before as a fellow refugee in London, and whom I wished very much to meet again. Bucher answered promptly that he would indeed be glad to see me again, but would I not like to make the acquaintance of "the Minister" (Bismarck), who had expressed a wish to have a talk with me? I replied, of course, that I should be happy, etc., whereupon I received within an hour an invitation from Count Bismarck himself (he was then only a count) to visit him at eight o'clock that same evening at the Chancellor's palace on the Wilhelmstrasse. Promptly at the appointed hour I was announced to him and he received me at the door of a room of moderate size, the table and some of the furniture of which were covered with books and papers, evidently his working cabinet. There I beheld the great man whose name was filling the world—tall, erect and broad-shouldered, and on those Atlas shoulders that massive head which everybody knows from pictures—the whole figure making the impression of something colossal—then at the age of 53 in the fullness of physical and mental vigor. He was dressed in a general's undress uniform, unbuttoned. His features, which evidently could look very stern when he wished, were lighted up with a friendly smile. He stretched out his hand, which gave mine a vigorous grasp. "Glad you have come," he said in a voice which appeared rather high-keyed, issuing from so huge a form, but of pleasing timbre. "I think I must have seen you before," was his first remark while we were still standing up facing one another. "It was sometime in the early fifties on a railway train from Frankfurt to Berlin. There was a young man sitting opposite to me who, from some picture of you which I had seen in a pictorial paper, I thought might be you." I replied that this could not be, as at that period I was not in Germany. "Besides," I added,—a little impudently per- haps,—"would you not have had me arrested as a malefactor?" "Oh," he exclaimed with a good-natured laugh, "you mistake me. I would not have done such a thing. You mean on account of that Kinkel af- fair. Oh, no! I rather liked that. And if it were not highly improper for His Majesty's Minister and the Chancellor of the North-German Confederacy, I should like to go with you to Spandau and have you tell me the whole story on the spot. Now let us sit down." He pointed out to me an easy-chair close to his own and then uncorked a bottle which stood with two glasses on a tray at his elbow. "You are a Rhinelander," he said, "and I know you will relish this." We touched glasses, and I found the wine indeed very excellent. "You smoke, of course," he continued, "and here are some good Havanas. I used to be very fond of them, but I have a sort of superstitious belief that every person is permitted to smoke only a certain number of cigars in his life, and no more. I am afraid I have exhausted my allowance, and now I take to the pipe." With a burning strip of paper, called in German "Fidibus," he lighted the tobacco in the porcelain bowl of his long German student pipe and presently blew forth huge clouds of smoke.

This done, he comfortably leaned back in his chair and said: "Now tell me, as an American Republican and a Forty-eighter of the revolu- tionary kind, how the present condition of Germany strikes you. I would not ask you that question," he added, "if you were a privy- counsellor (a Geheimrath), for I know what he would answer. But you will tell me that you really think." I replied that I had been in the country only a few weeks and had received only superficial impres- sions, but I had become sensible of a general atmosphere of newly in- spired national ambition and a confident hope for the development of more liberal political institutions. I had found only a few old fogies in Nassau, and a banker in Frankfurt, who seemed to be in a disappointed and depressed state of mind. Bismarck laughed heartily. The disgruntled Nassauers, he said, had probably been some sort of purveyors to the late ducal court, and he would wager that the Frankfurt banker was either a member of one of the old patrician families, who thought they were the highest nobility in all the land, or a money maker complaining that Frankfurt was no longer, as it had been, the financial center of Southern Germany. Here Bismarck gave full rein to his sarcastic humor. He had spent years in Frankfurt as the representative of the defunct "Bundestag," and had no end of funny anecdotes about the aristocratic pretensions of the patrician burghers of that ancient free city, and about their lofty wrath at the incorporation of that commonwealth in the Prussian monarchy.

Then he began to tell me about the great difficulties he had been obliged to overcome in bringing about the decisive struggle with Austria, one of the most serious of which difficulties, as he said, consisted in the scrupulous hesitancy of old King William to consent to anything that seemed to be in any sense unconstitutional or not in harmony with the strictest notion of good faith. In our conversation Bismarck constantly called the King "der alte Herr"—"the old gentleman"—or as it might also have been translated, "the old master." One moment he would speak of the old gentleman with something like sentimental tenderness, and then again in a tone of familar freedom which smacked of anything but reverential respect. He told me anecdotes about him which made me stare, for at the moment I could not help remembering that I was listening to the Prime Minister of the Crown to whom I was an entire stranger and who knew nothing of my discretion and sense of responsibility. As if we had been confidential chums all our lives, he gave me, with apparently the completest abandon and exuberant vivacity, inside views of the famous "conflict" period between the Crown and the Prussian Parliament when, seeing the war with Austria inevitably coming, he had, without legislative authorization, spent millions upon millions of the public funds upon the army in preparation for the great crisis; how the liberal majority of the chambers and an indignant public opinion, not recognizing the great object of national unification in view, had fiercely risen up against that arbitrary stretch of power; how the King himself had recoiled from such a breach of the constitution; how the King had apprehended a new revolution which might cost each of them his head—which might have become true if they had failed in the Austrian war—how then he had "desperately used his spurs to make the noble old horse clear the ditch and take the risk," and how, the victory having been won, they were, on their return from the war, received by the people with the most jubilant acclamations instead of having their heads cut off, which had pleased the old gentleman immensely and taught him a lesson as to his reckless Prime Minister.

It was not the cautious and conservative spirit of the King alone that he had occasionally to overcome. Still more was he clogged and not seldom exasperated by what he called the stupid old bureaucracy which he had to get out of its accustomed ruts whenever anything new and bold was to be done. He fairly bubbled over with humorous anecdotes, evidently relishing himself his droll descriptions of the antiquated "Geheimrath" (privy-counsellor) as he stared with his bleared eyes wide open, whenever anything unusual was proposed, seeing nothing but insuperable difficulties before him and then exhausting his whole ingenuity in finding the best sort of red tape with which to strangle the project. His patience tried to the utmost, he, the minister, would then go to the King and tell him that such and such a rusty official could no longer be got along with and must necessarily give place to a more efficient person—whereupon the "old gentleman," melting with pity, would say, "Oh, he has so long been a faithful servant of the state, would it not be cruel to cast him aside like a squeezed-out orange?—no, I cannot do it." "And there," said Bismarck, "there we are." I ventured to suggest that an offer to resign on his part, if he could not have his way, might make the King less tender of his inefficient friends in high places. "Oh," said Bismarck, with a laugh, "I have tried that so often, too often, perhaps, to make it impressive. What do you think happens when I offer my resignation? My old gentleman begins to sob and cry—he actually sheds tears, and says, 'Now you want to leave me, too?' Now, when I see him shed tears—what in the world can I do then?" So he went on for a while from one funny anecdote and from one satirical description to another, while I grew more and more amazed at the apparently reckless freedom of his talk with a person unknown to him. My amazement would have been less had I then known what I afterward learned, that this style of conversation was not unusual with him and that the old King only smiled when he heard of it.

He then came back to the Austrian war and he told me much about the diplomatic fencing which led up to it. With evident gusto he told me story after story showing how his diplomatic adversaries at that critical period had been like puppets in his hands, and how he had managed the German princes as they grouped themselves on one side or the other. Then he came to speak of the battle of Koeniggraetz and especially of that "anxious moment" in it before the arrival of the Crown Prince in the rear of the Austrians, when some Prussian attacks had failed and there were signs of disorder among the repulsed troops. "It was an anxious moment," said Bismarck, "a moment on the decision of which the fate of empire depended. What would have become of us if we had lost that battle? Squadrons of cavalry, all mixed up, Hussars, Dragoons, Uhlans, were streaming by the spot where the King, Moltke, and myself stood, and although we had calculated that the Crown Prince might long have appeared behind the Austrian rear, no sign of the Crown Prince! Things began to look ominous; I confess I felt not a little nervous. I looked at Moltke, who sat quietly on his horse and did not seem to be disturbed by what was going on around us. I thought I would test whether he was really as calm as he appeared. I rode up to him and asked him whether I might offer him a cigar, as I noticed Moltke was not smoking. He replied that he would be glad if I had one to spare. I presented to him my open case in which there were only two cigars, one very good Havana, and the other of rather poor quality. Moltke looked at them, and even handled them with great attention, in order to ascertain their relative value, and then with slow deliberation chose the Havana. 'Very good,' he said composedly. This reassured me very much. I thought if Moltke can bestow so much time and attention upon the choice between two cigars, things cannot be very bad. Indeed, a few minutes later we heard the Crown Prince's guns, we observed unsteady and confused movements in the Austrian positions, and the battle was won."

I said that we in America who had followed the course of events with intense interest, were rather surprised at the time that the conclusion of peace followed the battle of Koeniggraetz so quickly and that Prussia did not take greater advantage of her victory. Bismarck replied that the speedy conclusion of peace had been a great surprise to many people, but that he thought it was the best thing he had ever done, and that he had accomplished it against the desire of the King and of the military party who were greatly elated by that splendid triumph of the Prussian arms and thought that so great and so successful an effort should have a greater reward. Sound statesmanship required that the Austrian Empire, the existence of which was necessary for Europe, should not be reduced to a mere wreck; that it should be made a friend, and, as a friend, not too powerless; that what Prussia had gone to war for, was the leadership in Germany, and that this leadership in Germany would not have been fortified, but rather weakened, by the acquisition from Austria of populations which would not have fitted into the Prussian scheme. Besides, the Chancellor thought that, the success of the Prussians having been so decisive, it was wise to avoid further sacrifices and risks. The cholera had made its appearance among the troops, and, that so long as the war lasted, there would have been danger of French intervention. He had successfully fought off that French intervention, he said, by all sorts of diplomatic maneuvers, some of which he narrated to me in detail. But Louis Napoleon had become very restless at the growth of Prussian power and prestige, and he would, probably, not have hesitated so much to put in his hand, had not the French army been weakened so much by his foolish Mexican adventure. But now when the main Prussian army was marching farther and farther away from the Rhine, and had suffered serious losses, and was threatened by malignant disease, he might have felt encouraged by these circumstances to do what he would have liked to do all the time.

"That would have created a new situation. But to meet that situation, I would have had a shot in my locker which, perhaps, will surprise you when I mention it."

I was indeed curious. "What would have been the effect," said Bismarck, "if under those circumstances I had appealed to the national feeling of the whole people by proclaiming the constitution of the German Empire made at Frankfurt in 1848 and 1849?"

"I think it would have electrified the whole country and created a German nation," I replied. "But would you really have adopted that great orphan left by the revolution of 1848?"

"Why not!" said the Chancellor. "True, that constitution contained some features very objectionable to me. But after all it was not so very far from what I am aiming at now. But whether the old gentleman would have adopted it, is doubtful. Still, with Napoleon at the gates, he might have taken that jump too. But," he added, "we shall have that war with France anyhow."

I expressed my surprise at this prediction—a prediction all the more surprising to me as I again thought of the great statesman carrying on his shoulders such tremendous responsibilities, talking to an entire stranger,—and his tone grew quite serious, grave, almost solemn, when he said: "Do not believe that I love war. I have seen enough of war to abhor it profoundly. The terrible scenes I have witnessed, will never cease to haunt my mind. I shall never consent to a war that is avoidable, much less seek it. But this war with France will surely come. It will be forced upon us by the French Emperor. I see that clearly."

Then he went on to explain how the situation of an "adventurer on a throne," such as Louis Napoleon, was different from that of a legitimate sovereign, like the King of Prussia. "I know," said he with a smile, "you do not believe in such a thing as the divine right of kings. But many people do, especially in Prussia—perhaps not as many as did before 1848, but even now more than you may think. People are attached to the dynasty by traditional loyalty. A King of Prussia may make mistakes, or suffer misfortunes, or even humiliations, but that traditional loyalty will not give way. It may be somewhat disturbed in spots, without on the whole being dangerously shaken. But the adventurer on the throne has no such traditional sentiment behind him. He has constantly to play to the galleries. His security depends upon personal prestige, and that prestige upon sensational effects which must follow one another in rather rapid succession to remain fresh and satisfactory to the ambition, or to the pride, or, if you will, to the vanity of the people—especially to such a people as the French. Now, Louis Napoleon has lost much of his prestige by two things— the Mexican adventure, which was an astounding blunder, a fantastic folly on his part—and then by permitting Prussia to become so great without his obtaining some sort of 'compensation' in the way of an acquisition of territory that might have been made to appear to the French people as a brilliant achievement of his diplomacy. It was well known that he wanted such a compensation, and tried for it, and was maneuvered out of it by me without his knowing what happened to him. He is well aware that thus he has lost much of his prestige, more than he can afford, and that such a loss, unless soon repaired, may become dangerous to his tenure as emperor. He will, therefore, as soon as he thinks that his army is in good fighting condition again, make an effort to recover that prestige which is so vital to him, by using some pretext for picking a quarrel with us. I do not think he is personally eager for war, and would rather avoid it, but the precariousness of his situation will drive him to it. My calculation is that the crisis will come in about two years. We have to be ready, of course, and we are. We shall win, and the result will be just the contrary of what Napoleon aims at—the total unification of Germany outside of Austria, and probably Napoleon's downfall."

This was said in January, 1868. The war between France and Prussia and her allies broke out in July, 1870, and the foundation of the German Empire and the downfall of Napoleon were the results. No prediction was ever more shrewdly made and more accurately and amply fulfilled.

I have here introduced Bismarck as speaking in the first person. I did this to present the substance of what he said to me in a succinct form. But this does not pretend to portray the manner in which he said it —the bubbling vivacity of his talk, now and then interspersed with French or English phrases; the lightning flashes of his wit scintillating around the subjects of his remarks and sometimes illuminating as with a searchlight a public character, or an event, or a situation; his laugh now contagiously genial, and then grimly sarcastic; the rapid transitions from jovial, sportive humor to touching pathos; the evident pleasure taken by the narrator in his tale; the dashing, rattling rapidity with which that tale would at times rush on, and behind all that this tremendous personality—the picturesque embodiment of a power greater than any king's—a veritable Atlas carrying upon his shoulders the destinies of a great nation. There was a strange fascination in the presence of the giant who appeared so peculiarly grand, and yet so human.

While he was still speaking with unabated animation I looked at the clock opposite me and was astounded when I found that midnight was long behind us. I rose in alarm and begged the Chancellor's pardon for having intruded so long upon his time. "Oh," said the Chancellor, "I am used to late hours, and we have not talked yet about America. However, you have a right to be tired. But you must come again. You must dine with me. Can you do so to-morrow? I have invited a commission on the Penal Code—mostly dull old jurists, I suppose, but I may find some one among them fit to be your neighbor at the table and to entertain you." I gladly accepted the invitation and found myself the next evening in a large company of serious and learned-looking gentlemen, each one of whom was adorned with one or more decorations. I was the only person in the room who had none, and several of the guests seemed to eye me with some curiosity, when Bismarck in a loud voice presented me to the Countess as "General Carl Schurz from the United States of America." Some of the gentlemen looked somewhat surprised, but I at once became a person of interest and many introductions followed. At the table I had a judge from Cologne for my neighbor who had enough of the Rhenish temperament to be cheerful company. The dinner was a very rapid affair—lasting hardly three-quarters of an hour—certainly not more. My judge from Cologne confidentially remarked to me that his appetite outlived the feast. Coffee and cigars were served in a rather plain looking salon. The guests divided into groups among which the Chancellor went to and fro amusing them with humorous remarks. But before the smokers could have got half through with their cigars, the Minister of Justice, who seemed to act as mentor and guide to the gentlemen of the Penal Code Commission, took leave of the host, which was taken by the whole company as a signal to depart. I followed their example, but the Chancellor said: "Wait a moment. Why should you stand in that crowd struggling for your overcoat? Let us sit down and have a glass of Apollinaris." We sat down by a small round table, a bottle of Apollinaris water was brought and he began at once to ply me with questions about America.

He was greatly interested in the struggle then going on between President Johnson and the Republican majority in Congress, which was then approaching its final crisis. He said that he looked upon that struggle as a test of the strength of the conservative element in our political fabric. Would the impeachment of the President and, if he were found guilty, his deposition from office, lead to any further conflicts dangerous to the public peace and order? I replied that I was convinced it would not; the executive power would simply pass from the hands of one man to the hands of another according to the constitution and the laws of the country without any resistance on the part of anybody; and on the other hand, if President Johnson were acquitted, there would be general submission to the verdict as a matter of course, although popular excitement stirred up by the matter ran very high throughout the country.

The Chancellor was too polite to tell me point blank that he had grave doubts as to all this, but he would at least not let me believe that he thought as I did. He smilingly asked me whether I was still as firmly convinced a republican as I had been before I went to America and studied republicanism from the inside; and when I assured him that I was, and that, although I had in personal experience found the republic not as lovely as my youthful enthusiasm had pictured it to my imagination, but much more practical in its general beneficence to the great masses of the people, and much more conservative in its tendencies than I had imagined, he said that he supposed our impressions or views with regard to such things were largely owing to temperament, or education, or traditional ways of thinking. "I am not a democrat," he went on, "and cannot be. I was born an aristocrat and brought up an aristocrat. To tell you the truth, there was something in me that made me instinctively sympathize with the slaveholders as the aristocratic party in your civil war. But," he added with earnest emphasis, "this vague sympathy did not in the least affect my views as to the policy to be followed by our government with regard to the

United States. Prussia is and will steadily be by tradition as well as by well-understood interest, the firm friend of your republic, notwithstanding her monarchical and aristocratic sympathies. You may always count upon that."

He asked me a great many questions concerning the political and social conditions in the United States, the questions themselves, in the order in which they were put, showing that he had thought much on those things and that he already knew much about them—in fact more than any European I had met, who had never been in this country. What new information I could give him he seemed to receive with great pleasure. But again and again he wondered how society could be kept in tolerable order where the powers of the government were so narrowly restricted and where there was so little reverence for the constituted or "ordained" authorities. With a hearty laugh in which there seemed to be a suggestion of assent, he received my remark that the American people would hardly have become the self-reliant, energetic, progressive people they were, had there been a privy-counsellor or a police captain standing at every mud-puddle in America to keep people from stepping into it. And he seemed to be much struck when I brought out the apparent paradox that in a democracy with little government things might go badly in detail but well on the whole, while in a monarchy with much and omnipresent government, things might go very pleasingly in detail but poorly on the whole. He saw that with such views I was an incurable democrat; but would not, he asked, the real test of our democratic institutions come when after the disappearance of the exceptional opportunities springing from our wonderful natural resources which were in a certain sense common property, our political struggles became—which they surely would become—struggles between the poor and the rich, between the few who have, and the many who want? Here we entered upon a wide field of conjecture.

The Chancellor was much interested in hearing from me whether the singular stories he had been told about the state of discipline existing in our armies during our Civil War were true. I had to admit that that state of discipline would in many respects have shocked a thoroughbred Prussian Officer, and I told him some anecdotes of outbreaks of the spirit of equality which the American is apt to carry into all relations of life, and of the occasional familiarities between the soldier and the officer which would spring from that spirit. Such anecdotes amused him immensely, but I suppose his Prussian pride inwardly revolted when I expressed the opinion that in spite of all this the American soldier would not only fight well, but would, in a prolonged conflict with any European army, although at first put at a disadvantage by more thorough drill and discipline, after some experience prove superior to all of them.

The conversation then turned to international relations, and especially public opinion in America concerning Germany. Did the Americans sympathize with German endeavors towards national unity? I thought that so far as any feeling with regard to German unity existed in America at all, it was sympathetic; among the German-Americans it was warmly so. Did Louis Napoleon, the emperor of the French, enjoy any popularity in America? He did not enjoy the respect of the people at large and was rather unpopular except with a comparatively small number of snobs who would feel themselves exalted by an introduction at his court. There would, then, in case of a war between Germany and France, be no likelihood of American symapthy running in favor of Louis Napoleon? There would not, unless Germany forced war on France for decidedly unjust cause.

Throughout our conversation Bismarck repeatedly expressed his pleasure at the friendly relations existing between him and the German Liberals, some of whom had been prominent in the revolutionary troubles of 1848. He mentioned several of my old friends, Bucher, Kapp and others, who, having returned to Germany, felt themselves quite at home under the new conditions, and had found the way open to public positions and activities of distinction and influence, in harmony with their principles. As he repeated this, or something like it, in a manner apt to command my attention, I might have taken it as a suggestion inviting me to do likewise. But I thought it best not to say anything in response. I simply dropped a casual remark in some proper connection that my activities in the United States were highly congenial to me and that, moreover, I was attached to the American Republic by a sense of gratitude for the distinctions which it had so generously bestowed upon me.

Our conversation had throughout been so animated that time had slipped by unawares, and it was again long past midnight when I left. My old friends of 1848 whom I met in Berlin were of course very curious to know what the great man of the time might have had to say to me, and I thought I could, without being indiscreet, communicate to them how highly pleased he had expressed himself with the harmonious coöperation between him and them for common ends. Some of them thought that Bismarck's conversion to liberal principles was really sincere, that he was charmed with his popularity, and that he would thenceforth endeavor to keep it by being in the true sense a constitutional minister. Others were less sanguine, believing as they did, that he was indeed sincere and earnest in his endeavor to create a united German Empire under Prussian leadership; that he would carry on a gay flirtation with the Liberals so long as he thought that he could thus best further his object, but that his true autocratic nature would assert itself again and he would throw his temporarily assumed Liberalism unceremoniously overboard as soon as he felt that he did not need its support any longer, and especially as he found it to stand in the way of his will.

Twenty years later Carl Schurz again met Bismarck. But the author did not live to record his final impression of the Chancellor.

INDEX OF PERSONS